1/02

UNDERSTANDING
THE CONTEMPORARY
MIDDLE EAST

UNDERSTANDING ——————————————————————————
Introductions to the States and Regions of the Contemporary World
Donald L. Gordon, series editor

Understanding Contemporary Africa, second edition
edited by April A. Gordon & Donald L. Gordon

Understanding Contemporary China
edited by Robert E. Gamer

Understanding Contemporary Latin America
edited by Richard S. Hillman

Understanding the Contemporary Middle East
edited by Deborah J. Gerner

UNDERSTANDING THE CONTEMPORARY MIDDLE EAST

edited by
Deborah J. Gerner

LYNNE
RIENNER
PUBLISHERS

BOULDER
LONDON

Cover photos: Syrian woman, Palestinian boy playing in snow, and Egyptian father and son by Deborah J. Gerner. Israeli man with violin by Jennifer A. Smith.

Published in the United States of America in 2000 by
Lynne Rienner Publishers, Inc.
1800 30th Street, Boulder, Colorado 80301
www.rienner.com

and in the United Kingdom by
Lynne Rienner Publishers, Inc.
3 Henrietta Street, Covent Garden, London WC2E 8LU

Library of Congress Cataloging-in-Publication Data
Understanding the contemporary Middle East / edited by Deborah J.
    Gerner
    p.   cm. — (Understanding)
    Includes bibliographical references (p. –) and index.
    ISBN 1-55587-706-0 (hc. : alk. paper).
    ISBN 1-55587-725-7 (pbk. : alk. paper)
    1. Middle East. 2. Africa, North. I. Gerner, Deborah J.
II. Series: Understanding (Boulder, Colo.)
DS44U473   2000
956—dc21   99-37486
                                                              CIP

British Cataloguing in Publication Data
A Cataloguing in Publication record for this book
is available from the British Library.

Printed and bound in the United States of America

      The paper used in this publication meets the requirements
  ∞   of the American National Standard for Permanence of
      Paper for Printed Library Materials Z39.48-1984.

    5 4 3

▪ Contents ▪

▪ Maps, Tables, and Figures ▪

■ MAPS

■ TABLES

■ FIGURE

▪ Photographs ▪

▪ Preface ▪

Understanding the Contemporary Middle East draws on the expertise of more than a dozen scholars to create a truly interdisciplinary text that is up-to-date and student friendly. Individual chapters introduce the key themes, controversies, and research within geography, history, economics, demography, politics, international relations, sociology, anthropology, gender studies, conflict resolution, religion, and literature. Although each chapter is intended to stand on its own, the various authors have consciously attempted to integrate their discussion with material across chapters so that the book functions as a unified entity.

The Introduction confronts directly the stereotypes that students often have about the Middle East and also introduces one of the themes that is woven throughout this volume: the interaction between the ancient and the modern that is so much a part of the region. In Chapter 2, Ian R. Manners and Barbara McKean Parmenter describe the great diversity that exists within the Middle East. They suggest that, rather than imposing on the region a single, static "geography," it is more appropriate to think about *multiple* geographies reflecting various types of shifting landscapes: political boundaries, physical attributes such as the presence or absence of water, and cityscapes. This approach allows for a fuller exploration of the interplay of humans and their environments and illustrates the ways that borderlessness is at least as important as borders in interpreting the Middle East.

Arthur Goldschmidt Jr. describes, in Chapter 3, the lengthy history of the region, beginning with the ancient empires of Egypt and Sumer more than 5,000 years ago. Here a central motif is the continual transformation that occurs as invaders conquer or are turned back and as the indigenous peoples resist or accommodate these outsiders. Goldschmidt gives particular attention to the creation of the Islamic Middle East as an autonomous political and social system and the challenges to that system that came from its interactions with the West in the eighteenth, nineteenth, and twentieth centuries.

Deborah J. Gerner and Philip A. Schrodt pick up where Goldschmidt ends, discussing the domestic politics of Middle Eastern countries. In Chapter 4, they highlight several factors that have influenced the evolution of these states, such as their colonial legacy and patterns of economic development, before turning to a description of the various political ideologies and forms of governmental organization that characterize the Middle East today. Gerner and Schrodt also elucidate a key distinction between attributes of Middle Eastern political systems that are unusual or even unique to the region and those characteristics that are more widespread globally.

These themes are also present in Chapter 5, in which Mary Ann Tétreault examines the international relations of the region. The chapter illustrates how involvement with the Great Powers has frequently undercut the ability of Middle Eastern countries to act autonomously in the global arena. Tétreault analyzes, as well, the functioning of the Middle East as a regional subsystem, with attention given to several recent conflicts, including the Arab-Israeli dispute, the Kurdish issue, the war between Iran and Iraq, and Iraq's invasion of Kuwait.

Chapter 6, by Simona Sharoni and Mohammed Abu-Nimer, is unusual in two respects: it deals entirely with a single conflict and it is jointly written by an Israeli Jew and a Palestinian with Israeli citizenship. This scholarly collaboration allows for a carefully nuanced discussion of the often controversial Israeli-Palestinian conflict. Sharoni and Abu-Nimer present the historical evolution of this antagonistic relationship and explain its international dimensions, then turn to a consideration of the central issues that divide many Israelis and many Palestinians. Finally, they summarize past and current attempts to resolve the conflict and challenge the common belief that such a resolution can only occur with the involvement of the United States and other third parties.

In Chapter 7, by Elias H. Tuma, we turn to a study of the varied patterns of economic development that Middle Eastern countries have experienced. Tuma's argument is that virtually all these countries began with a problematic developmental context (e.g., poor infrastructure, lack of a stable government, low level of technical and scientific knowledge), further complicated by the domination of foreign forces (as discussed in earlier chapters). Even today, Tuma writes, most Middle Eastern economies are characterized by low labor productivity, external debt, and dependent patterns of trade and investment.

Chapter 8, by Valentine M. Moghadam, provides additional detail about Middle Eastern economies, with a focus on the connections among population growth, urbanization, (un)employment, poverty, and income inequality. Moghadam portrays the current labor situation with a particular sensitivity to differences between women and men in various parts of the Middle East. Her discussion is augmented by brief case studies of social and demographic trends in Morocco, Tunisia, Egypt, and among Palestinians.

Laurie King-Irani's analysis of kinship, class, and ethnicity in Chapter 9 adds additional texture to the complex representation of the Middle East that this book's authors create. Drawing on the anthropological literature, King-Irani illustrates how different social realities connect to each other and to other aspects of Middle Eastern life. She also provides insights into the gender and family relationships that are often a source of confusion to outsiders, stressing that many aspects of kinship, ethnicity, and class are highly adaptive in their Middle Eastern context.

This idea is continued in Chapter 10, in which Lisa Taraki delves in greater detail into the status of women. Taraki situates Middle Eastern women with respect to the modern nation-state and investigates the impact of traditional norms and values on opportunities for women. In addition, she provides an extensive typology of modes of women's political participation and illustrates the diversity of experience that is a constant refrain throughout this book.

Chapter 11, by John L. Esposito and Mohammed A. Muqtedar Khan, returns to two subjects addressed by several earlier chapters: the interface between religion and politics and the existence of both modern and traditional social structures within the Middle East. Esposito and Khan summarize the historical role of Judaism, Christianity, and Islam in the region, then consider the myriad ways that religion, particularly in its more fundamentalist forms, continues to influence Middle Eastern politics and society.

In Chapter 12, miriam cooke describes beautifully the historical and cultural underpinnings of Middle Eastern literature: poetry, short stories, novels, and plays. As cooke makes clear, literature does not exist in a vacuum but instead reflects and influences its environment—the cultural ferment, the impact of colonization and struggles for independence, the experience of exile and emigration—in profound ways.

Finally, Chapter 13 presents several crucial challenges facing the region in the twenty-first century: determination of the appropriate role of religion and culture in state-society relations, the need for increased economic development, the historical legacy of colonialism and the conflicts that have arisen in its aftermath, and the widespread grassroots demand for increased political accountability.

* * *

This book could not have come into existence without the assistance of numerous individuals. I was truly fortunate in my collaborators, a diverse group of dedicated educators from North America and the Middle East, all of whom have spent significant time in the region. Although a few were friends before this project (and still are—I *think*), many were known to me only by reputation and through their work. The opportunity to work with these top-notch scholar-teachers—to get to know them and to learn more about their disciplines—has been an honor and a privilege. That such a group of well-regarded and busy researchers care enough about education to participate in the creation of this text should provide reassurance to those who would claim that scholarship and teaching are somehow incompatible.

Special thanks to Thomas Hartwell, a professional photographer based in the Middle East, many of whose evocative images grace these pages. I am indebted to Barbara Parmenter and Ian Manners for the financial support they obtained from the University of Texas, Austin, to help cover the cost of preparing the photographs, and to Tom for his generosity in sharing his work. Jeffrey W. Neff created hand-drawn maps for the book that, unfortunately, disappeared when I moved both my home and office in the midst of final preparations. Thanks to the publisher's production staff for creating new maps to include in the book.

Two anonymous reviewers, as well as series editor Donald L. Gordon, provided excellent suggestions for making this book as student friendly as possible. I also appreciate the level of editorial support we received from Lynne Rienner, Sally Glover, Lesli Brooks Athanasoulis, and Beth Partin. In particular, Lynne's wise counsel throughout this project strengthened the book immeasurably. I could not have asked for a better publisher to oversee my first editing experience.

At the University of Kansas, Philip Huxtable shared his editorial expertise and advice; Rajaa Abu-Jabr cheerfully joined me at the end to track down those pesky last minute citations and added her excellent proofreading skills. My colleague and husband Philip A. Schrodt has been my partner over the years exploring the Middle East in all its amazing complexity; perhaps I could have done this work without him, but it wouldn't have been nearly as much fun! Finally, a special thanks must go to Carol J. Fabian, L. Elaine Kennedy, Marilee K. McGinness, and Rita Stucky, without whom my involvement in this project would quite literally not have been possible.

This volume is dedicated to all our former professors of the Middle East, those women and men who first opened our eyes to the possibilities for research on this fascinating part of the world. *Thank you.*

—*Deborah J. Gerner*

▪ 1 ▪

Introduction

Deborah J. Gerner

The most frequent response I receive when I tell someone I study and teach about the Middle East is: "Are you crazy? Isn't it dangerous? Don't all Muslims hate Christians and Jews? How can you be a feminist and still respect the culture 'over there'?" The mental picture of the Middle East held by most North Americans is of an area full of violent conflict, a region crawling with religious fanatics, where terrorism is endemic and women are little more than chattel.

I'm never quite sure how to respond to this reaction, for the Middle East I have come to know bears little resemblance to these stereotyped representations. *Understanding the Contemporary Middle East* challenges these popular images and presents a more nuanced portrayal of the Arabs who constitute a majority of the region's population, as well as of the Turks, Persians, Israelis, Berbers, and Kurds who live in this diverse and fascinating region.

As used in this book, the term *Middle East* refers to several distinct groups of countries covering more than 6 million square miles of deserts, mountains, and rich agricultural lands (roughly twice the area of the lower forty-eight U.S. states). There are the oil-producing countries of the Arabian Peninsula: Bahrain, Kuwait, Oman, Qatar, Saudi Arabia, the United Arab Emirates, and Yemen. These states, along with those of the Fertile Crescent region (Israel, Jordan, Lebanon, Syria, and the Palestinian autonomous areas within the West Bank and the Gaza Strip), are frequently viewed as the "core" Middle East. The North African countries of Algeria, Egypt, Libya, Morocco, and Tunisia are included in this region, as are the sub-Saharan states of the Comoros Islands, Djibouti, Mauritania, Somalia, and Sudan (primarily by virtue of their membership in the League of Arab States). In addition to Israel, the non-Arab states of Turkey and Iran are also important. In its earlier incarnation as the Ottoman Empire, Turkey ruled virtually all of the lands of the Middle East; today the vastly

1

smaller Turkish state straddles central Asia, Europe, and the Middle East. Iran, too, looks in more than one direction: toward the east are Afghanistan and central Asia, whereas to the west lies Iraq and the rest of the Arab world.

All three of the major monotheistic religions—Judaism, Christianity, and Islam—have their roots in the Middle East, and each still has significant communities of believers in the region. The imagery and lessons of the Hebrew scriptures, the New Testament, and the Quran—the ethical teachings, the stories, and the people—are an integral part of how people in the West understand the world, whether or not one is a member of any of these faith communities.

Many people use the words *Muslim, Middle Eastern,* and *Arab* interchangeably. This is quite incorrect and misleading. To begin with, not everyone who is a Muslim is an Arab. Islam is a major world religion, second in number only to Christianity, with nearly a billion adherents. Well over half of the worldwide Islamic community is African or Asian (including Persians, Turks, Indians, Pakistanis, Indonesians, and Chinese). Only about 20 percent of Muslims are Arab, with the remainder spread throughout the former Soviet Union, Europe, and North America. It *is* true that within the Arab world, where Islam originated, more than 90 percent of the population is Muslim. But there are also Arabs who are Christian or Druze or Bahai or Jewish. In particular, there are a large number of Palestinian, Lebanese, and Egyptian Christians.

The interplay of the ancient and the modern affects both the world's perception of the Middle East and how the Middle East views itself. The shopkeeper standing on the stone streets within the walls of the Old City of Jerusalem—or the ancient souks (markets) of Damascus, Baghdad, or Cairo—has a more intense awareness of history than the proprietor of a Baskin-Robbins ice cream store in a Toronto strip mall. Conflict with and competition over the Middle East has figured in European history since before the time of the Roman Empire, expressing itself variously in military, religious, economic, and colonial contention. Even the early United States, seemingly isolated across a wide Atlantic Ocean, found itself engaged militarily and diplomatically in this region in the early nineteenth century as it contested the power of the "Barbary pirates" of North Africa.

Yet the contacts between the West and the Middle East have not been entirely antagonistic. European and North American cultures have been continually influenced by the Middle East, often in profound ways. During the Middle Ages, much of the Middle East was substantially more advanced than Europe in the fields of science, medicine, mathematics, architecture, literature, the visual arts, and education. Works of Greek philosophy that were lost to Western Europe survived in the Arab-Islamic world and were first reintroduced to the West through Arab intermediaries.

Some of these influences lie buried and forgotten in our everyday language. For instance, *algebra* and *alcohol* both come from Arabic originally; they became part of the English language by way of the Arab mathematical and scientific writings that helped fuel the rebirth of scientific knowledge in Europe at the end of the Middle Ages. The archaic English verb *cipher*—the act of numerical calculation—comes directly from the Arabic word for *zero;* it was through the Arabs that Europeans first learned the technique of flexibly calculating with the decimal system rather than using the awkward and limiting system of Roman numerals.

The influence of Middle Eastern culture is not limited to science and religion alone but also can be found in literature. Over the past century, various Middle Eastern poets and philosophers have risen to great literary popularity in the West. The medieval Arabic and Persian language fables and stories collected as *A Thousand and One Nights* were first translated into French in the early eighteenth century. By the late twentieth century—courtesy of the Disney corporation—modern renditions of the tales of Aladdin, Ali Baba, and Sinbad the Sailor were staples in every day-care center and preschool in the industrial world. *The Rubaiyat of Omar Khayyam* enthralled Western readers after its translation by Edward FitzGerald in the nineteenth century. In the 1960s, the "flower children" hitchhiked across the United States carrying the works of the Lebanese poet Kahlil Gibran; in the late 1990s, their children have placed the poetry of the eleventh-century Persian mystic Jalal ad-Din ar-Rumi on the bestseller lists. When the Nobel Prize for Literature was awarded to Egyptian Naguib Mahfouz in 1988, millions of non-Arabs suddenly discovered the social critique of *The Cairo Trilogy* and Mahfouz's numerous other writings.

The Middle East is also significant as one of several geographical regions currently undergoing the transition from a pre-industrial to a postindustrial economy—from the world of the village to the world as a village. People throughout the Middle East, much like people in Africa, Latin America, and Asia, are facing tremendous challenges as they move from a rural to an urban economy, from a life based on tradition to a life based on innovation, and from a world of legends told by the dying embers of a fire to a world of satellite dishes, CNN, and Nintendo games. These changes can have a profound impact on the structure of the family, the roles of women and men, the status of religion in society, and the responsibilities of the individual to the state and of the state to the individual.

The diversity of the Middle East means that there are many different reactions to these socioeconomic transformations. For example, in response to the pressures of modernization and European influence, in the early 1920s Kemal Atatürk and the "Young Turks" transformed Turkish society by eliminating the Islamic norms of the old Ottoman Empire and establishing a secular Turkish state. Yet just across the border from Turkey, the Iranian revolution of 1978–1979, led by the Ayatollah Ruhollah Khomeini, responded to the pressures of modernization by overthrowing a secular, Western-oriented state and reestablishing an Islamic republic based on classical Islamic norms.

As you explore various dimensions of the Middle East through this volume, you will find a world that you knew existed but about which you perhaps knew very little. These chapters will confirm some of your perceptions—but challenge many others. It is a world of immense diversity but of shared traditions; a world of extremes of wealth and poverty but of many common ideals and aspirations. This is the world of the Middle East. Enjoy.

■ 2 ■

The Middle East:
A Geographic Preface
Ian R. Manners and
Barbara McKean Parmenter

A camel caravan crossing desert dunes, oil derricks pumping thick black crude, rows of men kneeling in prayer, bearded protesters shouting slogans—more than likely these are some of the images conjured up when the outside world thinks of the Middle East. Each of us carries our own "geography" of the world and its places in our heads, our own way of visualizing and interpreting the earth on which we live. Professional geographers attempt to correct preconceived notions and present a broader perspective. Typically, a geographical description of the Middle East, like that of any other region, would begin with an overview of the physical environment— geology, geomorphology, climate, flora, and fauna—as a backdrop for a discussion of human activities in the region, land use, resource development, population distribution, urbanization, and political organization. Yet even the best of these descriptions often fail to convey what the Middle East is "really" like.

The Middle East cannot be easily compartmentalized into book chapters or neatly divided by border lines on a map. Sharp boundaries are blurred, discontinuities appear unexpectedly, the familiarity of everyday life surprises us in our anticipation of the exotic and dangerous. Timothy Mitchell (1988) has described how European travelers to Egypt in the nineteenth century were frequently confused by what they saw when they reached Egypt: They had seen the ancient Egyptian artifacts that had been collected and displayed in Europe's capitals, even visited the Egyptian Hall at the Exposition Universelle held in Paris; some had read the *Description de l'Egypte*, the twenty-two-volume work prepared by the French artists and scholars who had accompanied Napoleon to Egypt, but nothing

5

they saw or experienced quite matched up to what they had been expecting to see. There was often a palpable sense of disappointment. Where was the "real Egypt"? In a similar way, contemporary visitors to the Middle East are likely to find that their geographical knowledge has to be reformulated as they encounter a world that challenges many of their expectations.

The difficult path to understanding the Middle East in all its complexity is not traveled only by outsiders. In the Iranian film *Bashu,* director Bahram Bayza'i tells the story of a boy from the deserts of Khuzistan in southwestern Iran whose village is caught in a bombardment. Bashu understands little of the reasons for the conflict between his government and its neighbor, Iraq; he knows only that he is now both homeless and orphaned. Seeking refuge in the back of a truck, he falls asleep. When he awakes, he is bewildered to find himself in a quiet world of cool, deep-green forests, a paradise he never dreamed existed. The truck has brought him to Gilan province in northwestern Iran, where he is taken in by a peasant woman despite the disapproval of her neighbors. Bashu is of Arab descent and speaks a mixture of Arabic and Persian common to the borderlands of Khuzistan; the woman speaks Gilaki, a dialect of Persian. Unable to communicate with either his caregiver or her neighbors, Bashu struggles against their prejudices. But he is not alone in being different. The woman who has taken him in is struggling to manage the farm on her own while her husband is away fighting in the war. When her husband returns and demands that the boy be sent away, she refuses to comply. In a very real sense, the film is a small reflection of much larger issues in Middle Eastern society, exploring the ways in which people deal with differences and face changes related to environment, culture, government, religion, and gender.

Thus, although the term *Middle East* may appear to suggest a degree of homogeneity, the region is extraordinarily diverse in its physical, cultural, and social landscapes. For many, the desert seems the central physical metaphor for the Middle East, an image frequently repeated in films and novels. The sand seas of the Rub'al-Khali (the Empty Quarter) in Arabia perhaps best fit this image. Yet the landscapes of the Middle East also encompass the coral reefs that draw scuba divers to the Red Sea, permanent snowfields and cirque glaciers on the slopes of the great volcanic peaks of Mount Ararat (5,165 meters) in eastern Anatolia and Mount Damavand (more than 5,600 meters) in the Elburz Mountains of Iran, the salt-crusted flats and evaporation pans of the Dasht-e Kavir in central Iran, and the coastal marshes and wetlands of the Nile Delta. Most emphatically, and despite the vast expanses of desert and steppe, the Middle East is also very much an urban society, with more than half the population living in cities that face much the same environmental, infrastructural, and social problems of cities around the world.

© Deborah J. Gerner

Photo 2.1 *The area around the ancient West Bank town of Jericho/Ariha, located 250 meters below sea level, is a mixture of hill, desert, and lush oasis.*

© Thomas Hartwell

Photo 2.2 *Full of modern concrete, steel, and glass buildings, Riyadh is the capital of Saudi Arabia and its largest city, recently surpassing Jeddah.*

There is likewise great cultural diversity in the Middle East. Much of the area came under Arab Muslim influence during and after the seventh century. At various times, Persian and central Asian peoples and influences flowed westward into the lands around the eastern Mediterranean. Most people in the region are Muslims, but there are significant communities of Christians and Jews. The three major languages are Arabic, Turkish, and Persian, all of which are quite distinct linguistically (Arabic is a Semitic language, Persian is Indo-European, and Turkish is Ural-Altaic). Nonetheless, they have been heavily influenced by each other. Persian is written in Arabic script, as was Ottoman Turkish; only since 1928 has Turkish used a modified Latin alphabet. All three languages contain numerous words from the others, and each has a subset of distinct dialects. In addition, other peoples with their own languages are found throughout the region. There are, for example, Berber speakers in Morocco and Algeria and Baluchi speakers in southeastern Iran. Kurdish-speaking people probably constitute the fourth-largest linguistic group in the region, and the revived Hebrew language has been a central integrating force among Jews in Israel.

How, then, to describe the geography of the Middle East? In this chapter we choose to present multiple geographies of the Middle East, different ways of seeing and depicting the region. In this way, we hope to present a richer description of the area than would normally be possible in a few pages, although one that is far from comprehensive.

■ BOUNDARIES

A geography of the Middle East must first come to grips with how to define *the Middle East*. Compared to the area portrayed in any Western atlas published in the late nineteenth century, the political landscape of the region we know today as the Middle East is virtually unrecognizable. The atlas published by the *Times of London* in 1895, for example, provides a series of maps entitled "The Balkan Peninsula," "The Caucasus," "Asia Minor and Persia," and "Palestine." Nor would these places, as depicted in the atlas, have been any more familiar to those living in the region, who would have recognized no unified geographical entity but rather a mosaic of regions. Al-Iraq referred to the area around the Shatt al-Arab waterway, and al-Jazira identified the lands between the Tigris and Euphrates Rivers, including Baghdad. Sham indicated the area immediately around Damascus and Bilad al-Sham (or country of Sham) the larger region now comprising Syria, Lebanon, Jordan, and Palestine. Egyptians still call their country *Misr*, but originally the term referred only to the Nile Delta and its narrow valley, not to the vast territory contained within its present-day boundaries. Today's map reveals a very different geography. Almost without exception, the present sovereign states are new creations, in large measure the products of European intervention and the dismemberment of the Ottoman Empire.

The term *Middle East* is itself an unabashedly Eurocentric term. It seems to have been used first in 1902 in reference to British naval strategy in the Gulf at a time of increased Russian influence around the Caspian Sea and German plans for a Berlin-to-Baghdad railway. Largely through the columns of the *Times*, the term achieved wider circulation and came to denote an area of strategic concern to Britain lying between the Near East (another Eurocentric designation, essentially synonymous with the area remaining under the control of the Ottoman Empire), the expanding Russian empire in central Asia, and the Indian Raj (Chirol, 1903). During World War I, the British expeditionary force to Mesopotamia was generally referred to as "Middle East Forces," as distinct from Britain's "Near East Forces," which operated from bases in Egypt. After the war, these two military commands were integrated as an economy measure, but the "Middle East" designation was retained.

With the passage of time, the name became both familiar and institutionalized, first in the military commands of World War II and later in the specialist agencies of the United Nations (Smith, 1968). Yet there remain ambiguities and uncertainties in terms of its more precise delimitation. Does the Middle East include Afghanistan to the east? With the demise of the Soviet Union, should the region be reconstituted to include the new sovereign states of Armenia and Azerbaijan? Frequently, the Maghreb states of Morocco, Tunisia, and Algeria are included in discussions of the Middle East based on the fact that they share so much of its culture and history. For similar reasons, Sudan is sometimes included despite the presence of a large non-Muslim, non-Arabic-speaking population in the southern part of the country (Blake, Dewdney, and Mitchell, 1987). In this book, we have opted for a broad interpretation by including in its discussion Turkey, Iran, and Israel, together with all the states that belong to the Arab League.

What is surprising is that the term *Middle East* is also used by people within the region. The literal Arabic translation, *al-sharq al-awsat,* and the Turkish, *orta docu,* can be found in books, journals, and newspapers. Interestingly, the term is most widely used in discussions of geopolitical strategies in the region. Arab commentators, for example, might discuss "American policy in the Middle East" or "Israel's relationship to the Middle East." Thus, it is perhaps more a reference to how others, either outside the region or outside the predominant culture, view the region and less a self-describing term.

The "map view" of a region is the most skeletal of possible geographies but is both formative and informative. Looking at a contemporary political map of the Middle East, the predominance of long, straight boundary lines stretching across hundreds of miles of desert is striking (see Map 2.1). Another revealing feature of today's map, as Bernard Lewis points out, is that the names of countries are, for the most part, restorations or reconstructions of ancient names (Lewis, 1989:21–22). *Syria,* for instance, is a term that first appears in Greek histories and geographies and was subsequently adopted by the Romans as the name for an administrative province. But from the time of the Arab-Islamic conquest of the seventh century, the name virtually disappears from local use. Its reappearance dates from the nineteenth century, largely through the writing and influence of Western scholars. Similarly, although Europeans have been referring to the lands of Anatolia and Asia Minor as Turkey since the time of the Crusades, the inhabitants of this region did not use this name until the establishment of the Republic of Turkey in 1923.

To understand the changes that have occurred in the political map of the Middle East, it is helpful to recall that at the end of the sixteenth century the authority of the Ottoman Empire extended from the borders of Morocco in the west to the borders of Iran in the east, and from the Red Sea in the south to the northern and eastern shores of the Black Sea (see Map 2.2). In Europe the Ottomans twice laid siege to Vienna. But the eighteenth and nineteenth centuries saw a gradual retreat from these high-water marks. In the Tartar and Turkish principalities from the Crimea to the Caucasus, Ottoman sovereignty was replaced by Russian domination; in the Balkans, the Ottomans confronted growing nationalist aspirations and a concerted assault by Austria and its allies; in North Africa, the Ottomans had to deal with the expansion and imposition of colonial authority involving the French in Algeria (1830) and Tunisia (1881) and the Italians in Libya (1911).

In other areas, Ottoman power was greatly weakened by the emergence of strong local rulers. In the aftermath of Napoleon's unsuccessful invasion of Egypt, for example, an Ottoman military officer named Mehmet (Muhammad) Ali established a dynasty that made Egypt virtually independent of Ottoman rule. The bankruptcy of the Egyptian administration after efforts to modernize the country's economy and infrastructure in turn opened the way to more direct European intervention in the country's affairs through a French-British Debt Commission and British occupation in 1882, although the country still remained nominally under Ottoman sovereignty. In Lebanon, following a massacre of Maronite Christians by Druze in 1860 and the landing of French troops in Beirut, Britain and France forced the Ottoman sultan to establish the semiautonomous province of Mount Lebanon with a Christian governor to be appointed in consultation with European powers (Drysdale and Blake, 1985:196).

Thus, even where European powers did not control territory outright, by the end of the nineteenth century they had become deeply involved in

Map 2.1 Political Map of the Middle East

Map 2.2 Extent of the Ottoman Empire

Legend:
- Ottoman Turks, 1300
- Acquisitions, 1359–1451
- Acquisitions, 1451–1481 (Mehmed II)
- Acquisitions, 1512–1520 (Selim I)
- Acquisitions, 1520–1566 (Suleiman the Magnificent)
- Acquisitions, 1566–1683
- Boundary of the Ottoman Empire at its greatest extent, 1683–1699

the region's commerce and governance. The defeat of Ottoman Turkey in World War I helped create the current map of the Middle East (Fromkin, 1991). In the final dissolution of the Ottoman Empire, the remaining Arab provinces were reconstituted into the territories of Iraq, Syria, Lebanon, Transjordan, and Palestine and subjected for a brief period to direct British and French administration, albeit under the guise of a League of Nations mandate.

The map of the Middle East, then, is both very recent and frequently a cause of conflict. From a resource perspective, the lack of correspondence between political and hydrological boundaries has complicated the development of scarce water resources. From a cultural perspective, the Kurds, a non-Arab, predominantly Muslim people numbering several million, are spread across Turkey, Syria, Iraq, and Iran. Their quest for autonomy has at one time or another involved them in clashes with all four of these states. The distribution of Sunni and Shi'a Muslims, the two major subgroups of Islam, likewise does not adhere to national boundaries. The fault lines of this division cross the oil fields of southern Iraq and northern Arabia.

From a political perspective, the appearance, disappearance, and tentative reappearance of Palestine demonstrates that borders are still in flux. Assigned the mandate for Palestine in 1921, Britain sought to fulfill its 1917 promise to facilitate the establishment of a national home for the Jewish people while simultaneously ensuring that, as stated in the Balfour Declaration, the civil and religious rights of non-Jewish communities in Palestine were safeguarded. The establishment of Israel in 1948 realized the Zionist vision of an independent homeland in which the Jewish people could live free of persecution, a return to the land from which they had been physically separated during nearly 2,000 years of exile. A consequence of these events has been the departure, through emigration to Israel, of large numbers of Jews whose families had lived for centuries in cities and towns throughout the Middle East and the displacement of another people, the Palestinian Arabs, who fled or were forced from their homes and lands during the fighting and sought refuge in Egypt, Jordan, Syria, Lebanon, and elsewhere in the region.

In such ways have the cartographies of the region been reimagined and refashioned in the course of the twentieth century. As the century has progressed, a complex body of interests has grown up around the new states of the Middle East. Lewis (1989:38) sees a hardening of the boundaries created by colonial administrators and the emergence of new identities based on a sense of loyalty and attachment to country. Yet the revived vitality of Islam, expressed differently in different parts of the region, is an eloquent reminder that the issue of identity is still being worked out.

Likewise, the movement of people across borders should remind us that these states are not disconnected spaces. Labor migration, for instance, has played and continues to play a major role in shaping social and economic structures throughout the area, through the remittance of foreign earnings and through the direct experience of living and working overseas. Both inter- and intraregional migrations occur: there are Turkish *gastarbeiter* (guest workers) in Germany and laborers from the Maghreb in France, and (prior to the 1990–1991 Gulf War) Egyptians, Yemenis, and Jordanians made up the majority of the labor force in Saudi Arabia and the Gulf states. Finally, some individuals cross borders more or less permanently as refugees and exiles. It is often those who are forced to leave who write most eloquently about the attachments that exist between people and places (Parmenter, 1994). In such ways, migration, whether forced or voluntary, touches on the experience of many of us and raises questions that are central to much writing in contemporary cultural geography about the nature of place and identity in the midst of globalization (Massey and Jess, 1995).

■ **ARIDITY AND WATER**

Imagine now that we move from our map view of the region to a closer scale. Other geographical phenomena come into focus, perhaps none so important as the presence or absence of water. Aridity is a pervasive element in land and livelihood throughout the Middle East. This is perhaps most evident during the long, hot summer drought when only the lush greenery of irrigated fields interrupts the hazy brown landscape of bare hillsides and steppes, roads and dusty towns. Palestinian writer Laila Abou-Saif describes Cairo as

> sand-colored, and the people's faces are of the same color, as if they had been sculpted and layered out of the surrounding intertwining desert. . . . Even the trees are dusty and layered with the golden sand. Cairo is always beige. (Abou-Saif, 1990:6)

Yet the degree of aridity varies enormously within the region. The winter months bring rainfall to many areas, particularly the higher elevations of Asia Minor, the Zagros and Elburz Mountains of Iran, and the hills of Lebanon, Israel, and the West Bank. Heavy snowfalls can occur even as far south as Amman and Jerusalem, and the melting of winter snows has historically contributed to heavy spring flooding in the Tigris and Euphrates River basins. In these areas, the rainfall associated with mid-latitude depressions moving through the Mediterranean basin during the winter months is prolonged, abundant, and reliable. It is sufficient for successful long-term cereal cultivation relying exclusively on dryland farming, or rain-fed methods. In the more mountainous areas, poorer soils and steeper slopes may restrict the opportunities for farming, but elsewhere villages are clustered closely together, and the onset of the winter rains marks the beginning of the agricultural cycle of plowing, sowing, and harvesting.

As one moves southward across the region, however, the winter storms occur less frequently. Alexandria receives an average of less than 200 millimeters of rainfall a year, only a fifth of that recorded at Antalya, 200 miles to the north on the Turkish coastline. Rain-fed agriculture becomes an increasingly precarious and risky proposition. In southern Jordan and in the northern desert of Saudi Arabia, rainfall is likely to be in the form of intense and highly localized storms when it does occur. Here the steppe merges imperceptibly into desert, traditionally the domain of nomadic pastoralists. In this zone, any form of agricultural activity other than herding is possible only where major rivers transport water from better-watered regions, as in the Nile and the Tigris-Euphrates basins, or where springs and groundwater provide a supplementary water supply for irrigation.

In a very immediate sense, water has been and remains the critical "life-sustaining resource." The Quran states that every living thing is made from water, and everyone from the nomadic pastoralist to the sophisticated city dweller shares an interest in its availability and distribution. Over the centuries, Middle Eastern societies developed a range of techniques for dealing with water scarcity, many of which revealed a close adjustment to the conditions of supply (Manners, 1990). Along the Nile, for instance, traditional basin irrigation permitted effective use of the river's floodwaters for millennia. Each year farmers constructed mud embankments in the river's floodplain, dividing the land into a series of basins. Drawings and paintings from Pharaonic Egypt suggest that similar methods of water management were in use as early as the fourth millennium B.C.E.[1] As the Nile rose in summer, the silt-laden floodwaters were diverted into the basins and retained there for several weeks. Once the level of the Nile dropped, surplus water could be drained back into the river and a winter crop—wheat, barley, lentils, beans, berseem (Egyptian clover)—cultivated in the saturated alluvial soils. Harvesting took place in March or April, after which the land lay fallow until the next flood season. By ensuring a reliable and controlled flow of water and by contributing to the maintenance of soil fertility, basin irrigation allowed for the development of a highly productive agricultural system. Equally critical from the point of view of long-term stability, the flushing action of the annual flood prevented the buildup of salts harmful to crop growth. Basin irrigation remained the dominant method of irrigation in the Nile Valley until the end of the nineteenth century, by which time the modern phase of water development had begun to take shape through the construction of barrages, annual storage reservoirs, and summer canals intended to allow for year-round irrigation and multiple cropping.

Like the basin irrigation system developed in the Nile Valley, other traditional water management devices such as the *qanats* of Iran, the

© Deborah J. Gerner

Photo 2.3 In the mountainous Dhofar region of Oman, watering troughs have been built to help the bedouin maintain strong camel herds.

shadufs of Egypt, and the *norias* of the Orontes River in Syria had a common purpose: to make effective use of a critical resource and thereby enable societies to survive and flourish under conditions of scarcity and uncertainty. The *qanat,* a sophisticated technique for developing, collecting, and distributing groundwater through a network of underground tunnels, may well have been in use in Iran as early as the first millennium B.C.E.: that it represented an extremely successful adaptation to a variety of local conditions is evident in the diffusion of this technique to other parts of the Middle East and North Africa, particularly during the early Arab caliphates, and from North Africa to Spain and later the "New World."

As the demand for water has grown, however, newer technologies of water development intended to make more productive use of both surface water and groundwater have frequently disrupted and displaced traditional systems. The construction of the Aswan High Dam in the 1960s, for example, enabled all of Egypt to be irrigated on a perennial basis, made possible two, and in some cases even three, crops per year, and generated power for countrywide electrification projects. These benefits came with environmental side effects, however, including serious problems of soil salinization (White, 1988).

Herein lies one of the major challenges facing the region today. The burgeoning demand for water to meet agricultural, industrial, transportation, and urban needs would be difficult enough to satisfy even if water supplies were more abundant. In the Middle East the problem is greatly complicated by the uneven distribution of water resources and by the lack of correspondence between political and hydrological boundaries. As a result, those countries where irrigated agriculture is of paramount importance (Egypt, Iraq, and, to a lesser extent, Israel, Jordan, and Syria) are unable to control the sources of water on which their populations and their economies depend. Roughly two-thirds of the water supply available to Arab countries has its source in non-Arab countries (Gleick, 1994). In Israel, by some estimates, between one-half and two-thirds of the water currently used for irrigation and domestic and industrial purposes actually originates outside the country's pre-1967 boundaries. In particular, the major aquifers that supply groundwater to municipalities and farms in Israel's coastal plains are actually recharged through rainfall occurring over the West Bank. In such circumstances, it is hardly surprising that water rights and allocations have been a key issue in the peace negotiations between Israelis and Palestinians over the future status of the West Bank.

The extent to which control over water resources empowers some countries at the expense of others is well illustrated in the case of the Euphrates River. The Euphrates rises in eastern Turkey, punches its way through the edge of the Anatolian Plateau in a series of dramatic gorges, then flows across the increasingly arid steppes of Syria and Iraq to a confluence with the Tigris River (which also originates in Turkey) just above Basra, Iraq. From here the two rivers flow together as the Shatt al-Arab to the Gulf. Although most of the Euphrates' huge drainage basin is actually in Iraq, nearly 90 percent of the annual flow of the river is generated within Turkey. This means that the downstream users, Syria and Iraq, are vulnerable to Turkey's future development plans for the Euphrates River.

Iraq has long-established claims to the Euphrates; indeed, Mesopotamian power and culture was linked to effective control over the waters of these rivers (Jacobsen and Adams, 1958). The later Sassanian and Abbasid periods (fourth to twelfth centuries) were marked by a considerable expansion of the irrigation system. In the twentieth century, first during the British mandate and later after independence, the irrigation systems were rehabilitated and new control structures erected. In the 1970s Iraq began planning a major storage reservoir that, like the Aswan High Dam, was intended to provide long-term storage. Despite setbacks caused by war, Iraq's long-term plans still envision greater use of Euphrates water. Syria, like Iraq, is steadily making greater use of Euphrates water for irrigation development and power generation and in 1973 completed the huge al-Thawra Dam.

But it is Turkey that holds the real key to what happens in the future, and Turkey is currently in the process of implementing a truly massive water development project in southeastern Anatolia (the Güneydocu Anadolu Projesi, or GAP) that involves both the Tigris and the Euphrates Rivers. If fully implemented, the GAP would involve as many as twelve dams and storage reservoirs on the Euphrates and ten on the Tigris, plus additional power-generating facilities. This immense undertaking is intended to pump new life into Turkey's hardscrabble, semiarid southeast provinces where living standards are far below the national average, but it is clearly more than just another water development project. These provinces are home to the majority of Turkey's Kurdish population. By providing people with a more secure and comfortable livelihood, the government hopes to undercut support for the Kurdish separatist movement and bring an end to a costly and bloody conflict.

In 1990 Turkey began filling the reservoir behind the Atatürk Dam, triggering protests from both Syria and Iraq. By some estimates, the Atatürk Dam and other proposed storage and diversion projects on the Euphrates could reduce downstream flows to Syria by 40 percent and to Iraq by as much as 80 percent, especially during the dry years. Clearly, if all the proposed water projects are carried out, the total water demand will be well in excess of the normal flow of the river. Moreover, water quality is likely to be an issue for downstream users since an increasing proportion of the available flow will consist of return irrigation flows containing high concentrations of agricultural chemicals and salts.

Some see in this situation of growing competition for limited water supplies the potential for future conflict. Unfortunately, in none of the major river basins do there exist formal agreements among all riparian states (those bordering on rivers) over water rights; there is no such agreement for the Jordan River or for the Tigris and Euphrates Rivers, and legal agreements for the Nile River involve only Egypt and the Sudan, to the exclusion of the seven other upstream riparian states. Boutros Boutros-Ghali's comment when he was still Egypt's foreign minister to the effect that "the next war in our region will be over the waters of the Nile, not politics," has been widely repeated. An alternative, more hopeful view, is that water could be a vehicle for regional cooperation. Sharing of knowledge and experience with regard to using water less wastefully, for instance through drip and subsurface irrigation systems and the recycling and reuse of wastewater, or the transfer of water from water surplus to water deficit states, as in the case of the proposed peace pipeline from Turkey through Syria to Jordan, the West Bank, Israel, and Gaza, are examples of cooperation that could transform regional geographies.

As Will D. Swearingen has described in *Moroccan Mirages,* for many hydraulic engineers and government administrators, the ideal vision of water development has been "not a drop of water to the sea" (Swearingen, 1987:39). Likewise, the region's marshes and wetlands have often been targets for major hydraulic engineering projects because they are perceived as empty spaces that "waste" potentially valuable land and water resources. But water is more than just a commodity with economic value to society, a resource to be developed, its flow regulated on a liter by liter basis: water has other values and meanings to those living in the region.

People are increasingly recognizing that water sustains a range of ecological processes, which in turn support communities of fishers, hunters, reed gatherers, salt producers, and the like. The coastal lagoons of the Nile Delta, the marshes of the Shatt al-Arab, Lake Hula in Israel and Jordan's Azraq oasis, Lake Ishkeul in Tunisia, and other wetlands scattered throughout the region are highly productive ecosystems that provide habitat and sustenance for diverse communities of plants and animals. Those living around wetlands have traditionally exploited these resources, maintaining a diverse and relatively sustainable livelihood. Other nonconventional values of wetlands include absorbing and treating human sewage and other organic wastes, recharging groundwater aquifers, and acting as vital resting and feeding sites for waterfowl and shorebirds migrating between breeding grounds in northern Eurasia and wintering grounds in Africa. In many cases, these wetlands have been drained, severely polluted, or dried out as a result of groundwater withdrawals, with devastating impacts on local communities. Fishing villages around Lake Maryut near Alexandria, Egypt, have seen livelihoods destroyed due to dumping of industrial wastes. In Iraq, the government has drained portions of the Shatt al-Arab marshes at least in part for political reasons: to exercise greater control over the Marsh Arabs, a largely Shi'ite people opposed to Saddam Hussein's rule.

A framework for conserving the region's remaining wetlands is the Convention on Wetlands of International Importance (commonly known as the Ramsar Convention) signed in 1971. To date, ten of the countries covered in this book are contracting parties to the convention, protecting forty-two wetland areas totaling 1.8 million hectares, and are committed to following the convention's guidelines of wise use in the management of these sites (Ramsar Convention Bureau, 1998). These guidelines include setting up the legal framework for protection and participatory processes to involve local communities (Parmenter, 1996). What these initiatives will achieve in practice remains to be seen, but their very existence testifies to a growing awareness of the complexity of water issues.

There are connections here between water and life that are crucial to any understanding of environment and culture in the Middle East. The Quran holds out to all believers the promise of a paradise that is filled with fountains and cool, shaded watercourses, "gardens beneath which rivers flow" (Schimmel, 1985). Images of gardens and water, inspired by descriptions of paradise in the Quran, have had a profound influence on Islamic art and poetry (MacDougall and Ettinghausen, 1976). Nor was this promise limited to literary and artistic representations; it also found expression in a love of gardens that were imagined and conceived as a reflection of the beauty and serenity of paradise on earth.

This linking of the sacred and the secular, of water and life, is eloquently conveyed in a story Annemarie Schimmel relates about the puzzling question she "was first asked in Anatolia by an old woman, *'Ankara' da rahmet var mi?'* [Is there mercy in Ankara?]." I wondered what the question might mean in a casual conversation with some unknown person. But it meant "Is there rain in Ankara?" In Turkish, *rahmet* means both God's mercy and the blessing of rain, for it is through the blessing of rain that everything that is seemingly dead is made alive again (Schimmel, 1985:6).

■ CITYSCAPES

Closing in on our scale still further, we move from regional phenomena like water to local environments, particularly the city. In the film *Raiders of the Lost Ark,* Indiana Jones stands on a rooftop overlooking an assemblage of small white-domed houses. His Egyptian host gestures toward the scene. "Cairo," he says. "City of the living. A paradise on earth." The scene that they are looking at is more likely a small village in Tunisia. Cairo, even in the 1930s when the story takes place, was a large sprawling metropolis filled with apartment buildings, factories, government offices, theaters, museums, and all the other accouterments of modern urban life. The film is confirming our imaginative expectations and our own assumed position vis-à-vis this Arab city. It is exotic, alluring, and inscrutable—we gaze comfortably at this fantasy place from a high vantage point and leave it to the intrepid Indy to plunge into the labyrinthine alleyways and bazaars of Cairo itself.

The Cairo that the film did not show would have perhaps seemed rather mundane: a vibrant, bustling city, home to just over 1 million people carrying on their daily lives in ways that were far from mysterious. But vision and imagination are powerful weapons, and Middle Eastern cities have been the object of intense imaginings over the course of their history. Nowhere in the Middle East is this more evident than in Jerusalem, a city sacred to three religions. Jews, Christians, and Muslims have struggled for centuries to make Jerusalem "their" city. "The chronicles of Jerusalem," Meron Benvenisti writes, "are a gigantic quarry from which each side has mined stones for the construction of myths—and for throwing at each other" (Benvenisti, 1996:4).

Cities have always been important in the history of the region, frequently developing as nodes connecting the well-traveled routes of armies and traders. To rulers, cities were constituted as centers of power and authority. In the eyes of travelers and traders, cities were almost literally oases of security, walled and protected, centers of commerce, learning, and entertainment. Al-Hariri, in a famous twelfth-century adventure story, *al-Maqamat* (The Assemblies), wrote admiringly of Basra in present-day Iraq: "Thy heart's desire of holy things and worldly thou findest there" (al-Hariri, 1898:164). Today the old walled cities of the region are in most cases small fractions of the larger urban fabric that changes with each passing day. As Janet Abu-Lughod has observed, "A city at any one point in time is a still photograph of a complex system of building and destroying, of organizing and reorganizing" (Abu-Lughod, 1987:162). This system includes both the formal visions imposed by governors, conquerors, and administrators and the vernacular forces of ordinary citizens working to establish their own territories and routines.

Istanbul is a prime example of this dialectic between formal and vernacular. In the fourth century, the Emperor Constantine moved the seat of the Roman Empire from Rome to the site of a former Greek settlement, Byzantium, located on a promontory bordered on one side by the Golden Horn and on the other by the Sea of Marmara. Although the city's official name was always Konstantinoupolis Nea Rome, "the city of Constantine that is the new Rome," it quickly became known as Constantinople, a name that retained currency even among Turks, whose documents and coins frequently referred to the city as *Konstaniniye* until the end of the Ottoman Empire (Çelik, 1986:12). Christianity enjoyed a special status in this new Rome, which was seen as a sacred city, its churches and monasteries housing a unique collection of holy relics and shrines that symbolized God's special favor. Justinian's great church of Haghia Sophia, its domed basilica rising above the city, epitomized the close relationship between the Byzantine state and the Christian church. But other buildings and monuments—palaces, walls, columns, churches, and aqueducts—remain embedded within today's urban fabric to recall more than 1,000 years of Roman-Byzantine rule.

When the Ottomans finally captured the city in 1453 after an eight-week siege, Sultan Mehmet II inherited a prized imperial city but one in a sad state of dilapidation. The sultan initiated a massive program of repopulation and reconstruction intended to restore the city to its past grandeur

© Jennifer A. Smith

Photo 2.4 Located along the Bosporus Strait, Istanbul, Turkey, symbolically links Europe and the Middle East in a single dynamic city of 8 million people.

and prosperity. Thousands of people were relocated to the city, since 1930 known popularly as Istanbul, from all quarters of the empire. These included skilled artisans and craftspeople to assist in the immense task of reconstruction. New palaces, great mosques with their schools, libraries, and charitable institutions, extensive bazaars and markets, and improved systems of water supply transformed the appearance of the city. These were the symbols of power and prosperity befitting the capital of a great empire.

In the twentieth century, with the final collapse of the Ottoman Empire, Turkish nationalists desiring to establish a secular republic along European lines made their own statement through urban planning and design. Turning their backs on Istanbul, they decided to construct a new capital in central Anatolia, hundreds of miles to the east of Istanbul, adjacent to the small town of Ankara. The design of the new Ankara was carefully planned to create an entirely different way of public life, one divorced from the Ottoman and Islamic past (Keleş and Payne, 1984). A German urban planner and architect, Hermann Jansen, was engaged to lay out a master plan for the city along the lines of a Garden City, a scheme popular in Europe at the time and considered to embody the "rational" approach to urban planning. The plan specified separate zones for residences, businesses, and industry, separated by wide boulevards and interspersed with parks and public squares. The government encouraged new styles of architecture that were intended to give public expression to the nation's modern image (Bozdocan, 1994). These styles applied even to the design of ordinary residences, symbolizing the desire to shape not only the structure of the city but also the fundamentals of private life.

Istanbul and Ankara are only two examples of how visions backed up by political power organize and reorganize urban landscapes. Cairo was originally laid out by the Fatimid ruler Mu'izz al-Din in the tenth century to serve as a formal, ordered imperial capital next to the bustling commercial town of Fustat. Fustat itself had grown from the encampment of the Arab army that laid siege to the fortified Byzantine settlement of Babylon during the Arab conquest of Egypt in 640 C.E.[2] In her study of Cairo, Abu-Lughod relates that by one account the conquering Fatimid general "carried with him precise plans for the construction of a new princely city which Mu'izz envisaged as the seat of a Mediterranean Empire" (Abu-Lughod, 1971:18). The new city was named "al-Qahira," the victorious city, and its monumental architecture was to become a favorite subject of European artists.

As in other cities in the Middle East, the nineteenth and twentieth centuries have seen many attempts to "modernize" and "improve" Cairo. In 1867, the ruler of Egypt, Isma'il Pasha, who already had a keen interest in urban development, attended the Exposition Universelle in Paris. There he reportedly met with Baron Georges-Eugène Haussman, the urban planner who had remade Paris into the city of broad boulevards and gardens we know today. Eager to create a modern capital before the deluge of foreign visitors who would follow completion of the Suez Canal began to arrive, Isma'il quickly translated Haussman's principles into a new plan for Cairo. With no time to waste, Isma'il chose to leave the medieval city essentially as it was, without gas, water, sanitation, or paved streets. Instead, he concentrated on building a new European-style city to the west, complete with Haussman-style boulevards and parks, powered by steam and lit by gaslight. This was the city foreigners would see, and their only forays into the old Cairo would be as tourists viewing the scattered monuments of a distant past (Abu-Lughod, 1971:98–111).

On the other side of this dialectic between formal and vernacular is the sheer persistence and energy of ordinary citizens. Life grows up and around, through and between, formal plans like vines on a trellis.

Abu-Lughod (1987:163) has noted how residential neighborhoods formed a crucial building block of cities in the Islamic world during medieval and even later times. These neighborhoods, which often housed people related to each other or with common ethnic or religious backgrounds, enjoyed a large measure of autonomy. The state was concerned primarily with regulating the commerce and ensuring the defense of the city. Thus meeting the needs and protecting the interests of the neighborhood was primarily a local community responsibility. This involved such things as cleaning and maintaining the streets, providing lighting, and supervising and sanctioning behavior. A wealthier neighborhood might have its own charitable institutions, organize its own water supply with public fountains, or appoint night watchmen for internal security, often paid for through endowments to religious foundations.

When Europeans tried to penetrate these neighborhoods, they were confused and threatened by what they saw as a chaotic warren of streets that frequently ended in cul-de-sacs. Yet the intent in the layout and structure of neighborhoods and even individual buildings was to minimize physical contact and protect visual separation. Thus Islamic building laws regulated the placement of windows, the heights of adjacent buildings, and the mutual responsibilities of neighbors toward one another so as to guard and protect privacy (Abu-Lughod, 1987:167). Of course, the majority of the urban population lived in modest circumstances that bore little resemblance to the luxurious lifestyles of the rich and powerful, and this reality was reflected in the shabby construction and cramped quarters of many neighborhoods.

Nor was urban life free of hazards. The common use of wood construction in Istanbul, for example, made the city particularly vulnerable to fires. Between 1633 and 1839 the city suffered as many as 109 major conflagrations, many of which wiped out entire neighborhoods; between 1853 and 1906, this number reached 229 as fires increasingly came to play a major role in reshaping and redesigning urban architecture (Çelik, 1986: 52–53). Diseases were another harsh aspect of city life, particularly bubonic plague, which until the nineteenth century periodically reappeared to carry off large numbers of the city's population.

As in many other parts of the world, the experience in Middle Eastern cities in recent years has been one of rapid urbanization, largely as a result of the influx of rural migrants in search of employment and better living conditions. These demographic shifts have dramatically transformed not only the physical appearance of cities but also the daily lives and routines of millions of people. In 1900 perhaps 10 percent of the region's population lived in urban settlements; by 1990, an estimated 57 percent resided in urban communities (United Nations, 1992). The dominant impression of urban life in the region today is one of incessant construction and a struggle to deal with the consequences of unrestrained growth. Everywhere one looks there are sprawling housing projects and lines of apartment blocks alongside new ring roads: in older neighborhoods, residents add more floors to buildings, squeezing space out of places where there seems to be none available.

The most explosive phase of urban growth has occurred within the last forty years as a result of migration, but many cities in the region began to experience an increase in growth in the late nineteenth century as improvements in sanitation and hygiene were reflected in declining mortality rates. By the beginning of the twentieth century, for instance, Istanbul had already begun to spread beyond the land walls that delimited the Byzantine-Ottoman city at the head of the Golden Horn. Today, the city's boundaries extend for miles along the Bosporus and along the European and Asian shores of the Sea of Marmara. Villages that in the 1950s still retained a distinctive identity now remain only as names on a map, submerged beneath a tidal wave of immigrants. The construction during the 1980s of two bridges across the Bosporus, linking Europe and Asia, symbolized the emergence of this new "greater" metropolitan Istanbul.

Cairo, which at the beginning of the nineteenth century had a population of around 250,000, had grown to a city of 1 million people by the mid-1930s. By 1960 the city's population had reached 3.5 million and by 1970 more than 5 million. Today, there are by more conservative estimates 12 million residents and by less conservative estimates 16 million residents of Greater Cairo. Put slightly differently, in the past thirty years, Cairo has added to its population three cities comparable to the one that existed in 1960. The boundaries of today's city extend far into the desert, and the government has constructed new "satellite" cities in a desperate attempt to keep pace with the housing and employment needs of recent immigrants. Within the city, planners have elected to build elevated highways

Photo 2.5 *The Cairo-Giza metropolis is home to some*
12 million people and continues to expand rapidly.

through neighborhoods, facilitating movement between the new, upscale residential suburbs on the city's periphery and the banks, offices, and ministries in the center (Denis, 1997:9). Older neighborhoods near the center have been cleared away to make room for modern luxury apartments, conference centers, and five-star hotels, and the former residents relocated in public housing projects. Despite the dislocation and disruption that this entails in daily living and working arrangements, the government's efforts to transform and "improve" the appearance of the city are matched by the practices and resolve of those who have been relocated, who reconstruct the housing the state has built for them by illegally erecting partitions, adding balconies, and creating new public and private spaces to suit their needs (Ghannam, 1997:17–20).

Clearly, the pace of urbanization has overwhelmed planners. Traffic congestion, lack of services, loss of amenities and open space, air pollution, inadequate water supply, and overloaded sewage treatment systems have become an all-too-familiar experience in many cities. Perhaps only in Saudi Arabia and the Gulf states, where preexisting urban populations were smaller and where infrastructure costs and housing subsidies could be more easily absorbed, have planners been successful in imposing order on the pattern of urban growth. Elsewhere, most attempts at long-range planning have foundered as planners and politicians have tried to cope with the immediate needs of a rapidly growing population.

Even short-term government efforts to keep pace have frequently fallen short, most conspicuously in the lack of adequate low-income housing for urban migrants. Many newcomers to the cities live in "temporary" housing, often referred to as squatter settlements. By one estimate there are more than 100 *ashwa'iyyat* (spontaneous communities) housing more than 6 million people in Greater Cairo (Bayat and el-Gawhary, 1997:5–6). In Turkey such spontaneous settlements are called *gecekondus*—literally, "placed there at night"—reflecting the speed with which houses are illegally erected on vacant land. By some estimates, more than 50 percent of Istanbul's population lived in such areas in the 1980s. For those of us who see such settlements only from the outside, Latife Tekin's compelling novel, *Berji Kristin: Tales from the Garbage Hills* (1996), conveys some sense of what life must be like in a squatter settlement on the edge of Istanbul, the experiences, the fears, the rumors, the wind, and the dust.

Although governments have on occasions attempted to demolish illegal settlements, a more popular approach has been periodically to offer construction pardons and provide title to land. Over time, therefore, many of these squatter settlements have acquired legal status and have become functionally and administratively integrated into the urban fabric. Makeshift houses have been replaced by more permanent residences and modest apartment blocks. Thus, temporary housing has been transformed into a more permanent feature of most large Middle Eastern cities, with numerous local variations such as Cairo's City of the Dead, where families have taken over the aboveground tombs for housing. In these new neighborhoods, where public services remain inadequate, residents often organize themselves or seek assistance from nongovernmental or religious organizations to pave streets, install water lines, organize garbage collection, establish a health clinic, or start a bus service. Neighborhood self-help and improvement associations play an important, albeit often unacknowledged role in transforming neighborhoods and nurturing a sense of community and identity among recent migrants to the city. Thus for many urban residents, the neighborhood still constitutes the most important element, both spatially and socially, in their conception of the city.

■ CONCLUSION

In his essay "Geography Is Everywhere," Denis Cosgrove writes about what he sees as "the real magic of geography—the sense of wonderment at the human world, the joy of seeing and reflecting upon the richly variegated mosaic of human life and of understanding the elegance of its expression in the human landscape" (Cosgrove, 1985:120). We hope that this chapter reflects that rich mosaic and conveys a sense of interconnectedness: the ways in which water links politics, economy, and religion; the ways in which cities are shaped both by global (trading connections, colonial experiences, labor migration, flows of capital) and local practices and imaginings; and the ways in which species, water, people, goods, capital, and ideas move across political boundaries. We would also like to emphasize the connections that places have with their pasts (Massey, 1995). By this we mean not simply the ways in which the past is present materially in the present-day landscape of the Middle East, but the ways in which the past may be present in the memories of people and in the conscious and unconscious constructions of the histories of places (Massey, 1995:187).

All of this suggests that we need to think about borderlessness as much as we do about borders in terms of understanding people's knowledge and experience of place. Connections between past and present and the absence of boundaries are brilliantly evoked in Amitav Ghosh's *In an Antique Land: History in the Guise of a Traveler's Tale* (1994), in which the writer, a Hindu researcher from India, reconstructs the journey and experience of a former Indian slave who, early in the twelfth century, had traveled to Cairo on behalf of Abraham Ben Yiju, a Jewish trader from Tunisia living in Mangalore. At one level, the writer parallels the slave's journey, traveling to Tunisia and Egypt, living with a Muslim family in a small village outside Cairo, and learning a form of spoken Arabic that later proved helpful in reading medieval documents. At another level, the research, based on the "Geniza Documents" (letters and other items found in the *geniza,* or storeroom, of a Cairo synagogue), "bears witness to a pattern of movement so fluent and far-reaching that they make the journeys of later medieval travelers, such as Marco Polo and Ibn Battuta seem unremarkable in comparison" (Ghosh, 1994:157).

As the letters between Ben Yiju and other merchants indicate, travel between Morocco, Egypt, Syria, Yemen, and India, although not free of risk (one letter describes how a merchant had been captured by pirates off the coast of Gujarat), was frequent and regular. Here is a very different construction of the geography of the region. Looking at today's political map and the divided world of the Middle East, it is very hard for us to step back and imagine the possibility of a world in which frontiers were not clearly or precisely defined, a place where Muslims and Jews and Christians traveled freely and crossed paths frequently in the course of everyday life and commerce. S. D. Goitein describes this period, roughly from the tenth through the thirteenth centuries, as the High Middle Ages when the Mediterranean area "resembled a free-trade community [in which] the treatment of foreigners, as a rule, was remarkably liberal" (Goitein, 1967: 66). Goitein notes that, with few exceptions, the hundreds of documents

and letters in the Geniza archive describing travels to or in foreign countries "have nothing to say about obstacles put in the way of the traveler for
political reasons" (Goitein, 1967:59).

Not only merchants and traders but also artisans, scholars, and craftspeople were involved in this "continuous coming and going." Add to this
the many Muslims making the hajj (pilgrimage to Mecca). Until the advent
of the steamship in the nineteenth century, most hajjis traveled to Mecca
with one of the great overland caravans that set out each year from Cairo,
Damascus, or Baghdad. But even in the fifteenth and sixteenth centuries,
caravans could consist of several thousand camels, hundreds of horses, and
30,000 to 40,000 people (Peters, 1994), giving some sense of the large
numbers of people involved. In earlier centuries, the round-trip journey
could take several years for people from North and West Africa, China,
and Southeast Asia. From India, the seventeenth-century pilgrim Safi ibn
Wali Qazvini spent a year getting to and from Mecca (Pearson, 1994:45–
46). Like other literate pilgrims, Qazvini wrote an account of his travels
that was intended at least in part as a guide for others, providing a wealth
of details about the pilgrimage route and practical information about rest
stations, watering points, and the costs of purchasing supplies.

The hajj is still an extraordinary undertaking for many Muslims in
terms of both logistics and financing. But for the 2 million who now make
the hajj each year, the same sort of information contained in Qazvini's narrative, together with visa application forms, is to be found on the Internet.
And once again, through such experiences as the hajj, local places and
communities are linked to and become part of the world beyond. Tourists
traveling along the Nile may be surprised to see paintings of jumbo jets
adorning the mud brick walls of humble houses. Here is a poignant and el-
egant reminder of the significance of the hajj in the lives of these villagers,
conveyed in a tradition that has evolved over the past century whereby the
experience of a lifetime, circling the Ka'bah, praying at Ararat, and making a joyful homecoming, is graphically captured and portrayed in folk art
and architecture (Parker and Neal, 1995).

In contemporary atlases, the Middle East is usually divided up into a
familiar mosaic of nation-states, each nation with its distinctive color like
detachable pieces of a jigsaw puzzle. Benedict Anderson (1991:6–7) sees
nations as "imagined political communities" in the sense that members of
the nation do not know most of their fellow members yet imagine themselves part of a broader community sharing a deep sense of fraternity and
comradeship. For Anderson, the "map-as-logo" contributes to this imaginative process, not least because as "this 'jig-saw' effect became normal,
each 'piece' could be wholly detached from its geographic context" (Anderson, 1991:175). Our desire is that this chapter will encourage people to
explore what lies beneath the surface of the map, to reconnect the map

© Thomas Hartwell

Photo 2.6 Paintings on the outside wall of this house in Luxor, Upper Egypt, indicate the owner has made the hajj (pilgrimage) to Mecca, Saudi Arabia.

with its geographic context, to ask critical questions about how our maps and knowledge of the region have been constituted, and to imagine alternative geographies.

■ NOTES

We would like to express particular thanks to Kay Ebel and Zjaleh Hajibashi for their helpful comments on an early version of this chapter.

1. B.C.E., Before the Common Era, is viewed by non-Christians as a more neutral term for marking history than B.C., Before Christ.

2. C.E., or Common Era, is a neutral term for A.D. (Anno Domini, or Year of our Lord).

■ BIBLIOGRAPHY

Abou-Saif, Laila. 1990. *Middle East Journal: A Woman's Journey into the Heart of the Arab World*. New York: Charles Scribner and Sons.

Abu-Lughod, Janet. 1971. *Cairo: 1001 Years of the City Victorious.* Princeton: Princeton University Press.
————. 1987. "The Islamic City—Historic Myth, Islamic Essence, and Contemporary Relevance." *International Journal of Middle Eastern Studies* 19:155–176.
Al-e Ahmad, Jalal. 1985. *Lost in the Crowd.* Trans. by John Green. Washington, D.C.: Three Continents Press.
Anderson, Benedict. 1991. *Imagined Communities.* London and New York: Verso Books.
Bayat, Asef, and Karim el-Gawhary (eds.). 1997. "Cairo: Power, Poverty and Urban Sprawl." *Middle East Report* 202:2–30.
Benvenisti, Meron. 1996. *City of Stone: The Hidden History of Jerusalem.* Trans. by Maxine Kauffman Nunn. Berkeley: University of California Press.
Blake, Gerald, John Dewdney, and Jonathan Mitchell. 1987. *The Cambridge Atlas of the Middle East and North Africa.* Cambridge and New York: Cambridge University Press.
Bozdocan, Sibel. 1994. "Architecture, Modernism and Nation-Building in Kemalist Turkey." *New Perspectives on Turkey* 10:37–55.
Çelik, Zeynep. 1986. *The Remaking of Istanbul.* Seattle and New York: University of Washington Press.
Chirol, V. 1903. *The Middle East Question, or Some Political Problems of Indian Defence.* London: John Murray.
Cosgrove, Denis. 1985. "Geography Is Everywhere: Culture and Symbolism in Human Landscapes." Pp. 118–135 in Derek R. Gregory and Rex Walford (eds.), *Horizons in Human Geography.* London: Macmillan.
Denis, Eric. 1997. "Urban Planning and Growth in Cairo." *Middle East Report* 202:8–12.
Drysdale, Alasdair, and Gerald Blake. 1985. *The Middle East and North Africa: A Political Geography.* New York and Oxford: Oxford University Press.
Fromkin, David. 1991. "How the Modern Middle East Map Came to Be Drawn." *Smithsonian* 22, no. 2:132–148.
Ghannam, Fara. 1997. "Relocation and the Use of Urban Space in Cairo." *Middle East Report* 202:17–20.
Ghosh, Amitav. 1994. *In an Antique Land: History in the Guise of a Traveler's Tale.* New York: Vintage Books.
Gleick, Peter H. 1994. "Water, War and Peace in the Middle East." *Environment* 36, no. 3:6–15, 35–42.
Goitein, S. D. 1967. *A Mediterranean Society: Economic Foundations.* Berkeley: University of California Press.
al-Hariri. 1898. *The Assemblies of al Hariri: Translated from the Arabic, with an Introduction and Notes Historical and Grammatical, by Thomas Chenery.* London: Williams and Norgate.
Jacobsen, Thorkild, and Robert M. Adams. 1958. "Salt and Silt in Ancient Mesopotamian Agriculture." *Science* 128, no. 3334:1251–1258.
Keleş, Ruşen, and Geoffrey Payne. 1984. "Turkey." Pp. 165–197 in Martin Wynn (ed.), *Planning and Urban Growth in Southern Europe.* London and New York: Mansell.
Lewis, Bernard. 1989. "The Map of the Middle East: A Guide for the Perplexed." *American Scientist* 58, no. 1:19–38.
MacDougall, Elisabeth B., and Richard Ettinghausen (eds.). 1976. *The Islamic Garden.* Washington, D.C.: Dumbarton Oaks Trustees for Harvard University.
Manners, Ian R. 1990. "The Middle East." Pp. 39–66 in Gary A. Klee (ed.), *World Systems of Traditional Resource Management.* New York: Halstead Press.

Massey, Doreen. 1995. "Places and Their Pasts." *History Workshop Journal* 39: 182–192.

Massey, Doreen, and Pat Jess (eds.). 1995. *A Place in the World? Places, Cultures, and Globalization.* Oxford: Oxford University Press for the Open University.

Mitchell, Timothy. 1988. *Colonising Egypt.* Cambridge and New York: Cambridge University Press.

Parker, Ann, and Avon Neal. 1995. *Hajj Paintings: Folk Art of the Great Pilgrimage.* Washington and London: Smithsonian Institution Press.

Parmenter, Barbara. 1994. *Giving Voice to Stones: Place and Identity in Palestinian Literature.* Austin: University of Texas Press.

———. 1996. "Endangered Wetlands and Environmental Management in North Africa." Pp. 155–174 in Will D. Swearingen and Abdellatif Bencherifa (eds.), *The North African Environment at Risk.* Boulder, Colo.: Westview Press.

Pearson, M. N. 1994. *Pious Passengers: The Hajj in Earlier Times.* London: C. Hurst.

Peters, F. E. 1994. *The Hajj: The Muslim Pilgrimage to Mecca and the Holy Places.* Princeton: Princeton University Press.

Ramsar Convention Bureau. 1988. *Contracting Parties to Ramsar Convention on Wetlands, as of 30 October 1998. Key Documents of the Ramsar Convention.* Online: http://www.ramsar.org/key_cp_e.html. December 10, 1998.

Schimmel, Annemarie. 1985. "The Water of Life." *Environmental Design* 2:6–9.

Smith, Gordon C. 1968. "The Emergence of the Middle East." *Journal of Contemporary History* 3, no. 3:3–17.

Swearingen, Will D. 1987. *Moroccan Mirages: Agrarian Dreams and Deceptions, 1912–1986.* Princeton: Princeton University Press.

Tekin, Latife. 1996. *Berji Kristin: Tales from the Garbage Hills.* Trans. by Ruth Christie and Saliha Parker. London and New York: Marion Boyars.

United Nations. 1992. *Demographic Yearbook.* New York: United Nations.

White, Gilbert. 1988. "The Environmental Effects of the High Dam at Aswan." *Environment* 30, no. 7:4–11, 34–40.

■ 3 ■

The Historical Context

Arthur Goldschmidt Jr.

History is the study of humanity's recorded past; that of the Middle East is the world's longest. In this area many staple crops were first cultivated, most farm animals were first domesticated, and the earliest agricultural villages were founded. There, too, were the world's oldest cities, the first governments and law codes, and the earliest ethical monotheistic systems. A crossroads for people and ideas, the Middle East has undergone many fundamental changes, yet some aspects stay the same. At times the area has contained a single political or cultural system; at others it has split into competing fragments. During eras of internal cohesion and power, Middle Easterners ruled over remote parts of Europe, Asia, and Africa. At times of dissension and weakness, however, they were invaded and ruled by outsiders. When they could not drive out the interlopers, they adjusted to them and subtly made their rulers adapt to their own ways. The interplay between invasion and accommodation is characteristic of the region. In this chapter we briefly summarize Middle Eastern history: the ancient empires, the rise of Islam and its civilization, the area's subordination to European control, and its struggle for political independence.

■ THE ANCIENT MIDDLE EAST

Environment has shaped much of the region's history. As the polar ice caps retreated, rainfall declined, and hunters and food gatherers had to learn how to control their sources of sustenance. Hunting and gathering as a way of life died out in North Africa and Southwest Asia some 5,000 years ago, giving way to pastoral nomadism and settled agriculture. As Ian R. Manners and Barbara McKean Parmenter discussed in Chapter 2, there is insufficient rainfall in many parts of the Middle East to support settled agriculture. Yet the world's oldest farming villages have been discovered

33

in northeastern Africa and in the highlands of Asia Minor. Many men and women migrated into the valleys of the Nile, the Euphrates, and the Tigris Rivers, where they learned how to tame the annual river floods to water their fields.

As grain cultivation spread, peasants gradually improved their implements and pottery. They needed governments to organize the building of dams, dikes, and canals for large-scale irrigation, to regulate the distribution of river waters, and often to protect cultivators from invading herders. Although the nomads at times served the settled people as merchants and soldiers, they also pillaged their cities and farms. Despite the tension between the sedentary peasants and the nomadic herders, they needed each other. Without both groups, no cities, states, or civilizations would ever have come into being.

The earliest known governments arose in the oldest agrarian societies, Egypt and Sumer, more than 5,000 years ago. Starting in the third millennium Before the Common Era (B.C.E.), ancient Middle Eastern peoples underwent a series of invasions from outsiders, succumbed to their rule, acquired new ideas and institutions, and eventually absorbed or expelled their conquerors. The result was a succession of ecumenical states that blended the cultures of the rulers and their subjects, culminating in the Roman Empire.

The first states based on settled agriculture were the kingdoms of the Upper and Lower Nile, which combined around 3000 B.C.E. to form Egypt; and the kingdom of Sumer, which had arisen a bit earlier in Mesopotamia, the land between the Euphrates and the Tigris Rivers. Both developed strong monarchies supported by elaborate bureaucracies, codes of conduct, and religious doctrines that integrated the political system into a cosmological order. Their governments marshaled large workforces to protect the lands from floods and invaders. A complex division of labor facilitated the development of writing, calculation, architecture, metallurgy, and hydraulic engineering.

☐ Semitic and Indo–Iranian Invasions

The river states were disrupted and partially transformed by outside infiltrators and invaders. Sumer was conquered by peoples who spoke Semitic languages, producing Babylonia, which reached its height during the reign of the lawgiver Hammurabi (r. 1792–1750 B.C.E.). Meanwhile, Indo-European invaders from the north mixed with local peoples in Anatolia and Iran and introduced the horse into Mesopotamia. By using the horse-drawn chariot, another Semitic people were able to occupy the Nile Delta from 1720 to 1570 B.C.E. Whereas the Babylonians absorbed their invaders, the Egyptians drove theirs out and extended their empire into Syria.

© Deborah J. Gerner

Photo 3.1 The Great Sun Temple of Abu Simbel was constructed along the banks of the Upper Nile, 50 miles north of the border with Sudan, during the reign of Egyptian pharaoh Ramses II (thirteenth century B.C.E.).

Internal dissension and external pressures finally weakened Egypt and Assyria, leading around 1000 B.C.E. to a bewildering succession of invasions and emerging states. As the Middle East's climate grew drier, Semitic peoples, including the Phoenicians and the Hebrews, migrated from the Arabian desert into the better-watered lands of Syria and Mesopotamia. The Phoenicians of the Syrian coast became the great traders, seafarers, and colonizers of the ancient world. They also invented the phonetic alphabet. Under King David, who ruled in the early tenth century B.C.E., the Hebrews set up a kingdom in Palestine (which they called "the land of Israel") with its capital at Jerusalem; this state later split and succumbed to powerful conquerors. The Hebrews developed a faith in one God who, according to the Bible, appeared to Moses on Sinai and later to the prophets. Elements of this ethical monotheism had existed in earlier Middle Eastern religions, but the Hebrews' ideas, crystallized in Judaism, profoundly influenced the intellectual history of both the Middle East and the West.

The introduction of cheap means of making iron tools and weapons led to larger and longer-lasting empires. About 1350 B.C.E., Babylonia gave way to Assyria, centered in northern Mesopotamia. This first Iron Age empire underwent several cycles of rise and decline; at its height (around 700 B.C.E.), Assyria ruled all of Mesopotamia, Syria, and even Egypt. Its Semitic rival and successor, Chaldea, upheld Babylon's glory for another century. Then Mesopotamia, and indeed the whole Middle East, was taken by Persia's King Cyrus (r. 550–529 B.C.E.).

From Cyrus's reign to modern times, the political history of the Middle East has centered on the rise and fall of successive multinational empires: Persia, Greece, Rome, the Arabs, the Seljuk Turks, the Mongols, and the Ottomans. Like Babylon, most of these empires were formed by outside invasions. The rule of these invaders unleashed forces of local resistance that eventually sapped the rulers' strength, leading to political fragmentation and new invasions. Often the conquerors adopted the institutions and beliefs of their Middle Eastern subjects; rarely could they impose their own uniformly.

The Persian empire of Cyrus and his successors, the Achaemenians, was the prototype of this multinational system. Sprawling from the Indus Valley to the Nile, the empire could not make its subjects think and act alike. Instead, it tolerated their beliefs and practices so long as they obeyed its laws, paid their taxes, and sent men to the Persian army. The provincial governors were given broad civil, judicial, and fiscal powers by the Persian emperor. A feudal system of landownership kept the local aristocrats loyal, and a postal system and road network—along with a uniform coinage, calendar, and administrative language—helped further unite the empire.

The state religion, Zoroastrianism, originated in Persia. It stressed the dualism of good and evil, people's responsibility to choose between them in this life, and their duty to bear the consequences after they died. Zoroastrianism and its offshoot, Mithraism, were widely practiced in ancient times and left their imprint on Christianity and Islam. Achaemenian Persia survived two centuries before it succumbed to Alexander the Great in the fourth century B.C.E.

☐ Greek and Roman Rule

Alexander's whirlwind conquest of the Middle East between 332 and 323 B.C.E. marks a critical juncture in the area's history. For the next millennium, the Middle East was part of the Hellenistic world. Alexander wanted to fuse Greek culture with that of the Middle East, taking ideas, institutions, and administrators from the Egyptians, Mesopotamians, and Persians. This fusion did not occur in his lifetime, nor was it ever complete, but from Alexander to Muhammad the Mediterranean world and the Middle East shared a common civilization. The coastal cities, the greatest of which was Alexandria (named for its founder), were the centers of this cultural blending. Alexander's successors in Egypt, the Ptolemies, ruled the country for three centuries. They erected monumental public buildings, such as the Alexandria Lighthouse, one of the seven wonders of the world, and the Museum, or academy of scholars, which housed the largest library in antiquity.

Southern Anatolia, Syria, and Mesopotamia were ruled for two centuries by the Seleucids, who were the descendants of one of Alexander's generals. In the third century B.C.E., the Seleucids lost control of their eastern lands to another dynasty descended from some of Alexander's soldiers, and they lost Persia to a Hellenized Indo-European family, the Parthians.

Meanwhile, a new state was rising farther west: Rome. Having taken Carthage, Macedonia, and Greece by 100 B.C.E., the Roman legions marched eastward, conquering Asia Minor, Syria, and Egypt. Once again most of the Middle East was united under an ecumenical empire; only Persia and part of Mesopotamia were ruled by the Parthians. Like earlier empires, Rome absorbed much from its Middle Eastern subjects, including several religions, two of which, Mithraism and Christianity, vied for popular favor throughout the Roman Empire. Christianity finally won. After his conversion, the Emperor Constantine (r. 306–337 C.E.) moved the capital—and Rome's economic and cultural center—to Byzantium, renamed Constantinople. But the city gave its old name to Rome's successor state,

© Deborah J. Gerner

Photo 3.2 Located just south of Amman, Jordan, the town of Madaba is home to beautiful mosaics dating from the Byzantine era.

the Byzantine Empire. Even now, Arabs, Turks, and Persians say *Rum* to mean the Byzantine Empire, its lands, and also Greek Orthodox Christianity and its adherents.

Under Roman rule, commercial cities flourished. Syrian and Egyptian merchants grew rich from the trade between Europe, Asia, and eastern Africa. Arab camel nomads, or bedouin, prospered as carriers of cloth and spices. Other Middle Easterners navigated the Red Sea, the Gulf, and the Indian Ocean. But Roman rule was enforced by a large occupying army, and grain-producing Syria and Egypt were taxed heavily. Rome's leaders did not always tolerate their subjects' beliefs. Roman soldiers destroyed the Jewish temple in Jerusalem, and many of Jesus' early followers were martyred. Christian Rome proved even less tolerant. Many Christians in North Africa and Egypt espoused heterodox beliefs that the emperors viewed as treasonous. Their efforts to suppress heresy alienated many of their Middle Eastern subjects in the fifth and sixth centuries of the Common Era.

Rome (and later, Byzantium) had one major rival: Persia. There the Parthians gave way in the third century to the Sassanid dynasty. Bolstered by a powerful military aristocracy and the resources of many Hellenized religious refugees from Byzantium, Sassanid Persia threatened Byzantine rule in the Middle East. Early in the seventh century, the Sassanids briefly

© Deborah J. Gerner

*Photo 3.3 One of the most impressive Roman ruins
in the Middle East is at Baalbek, in the northern Bekaa Valley of Lebanon.
This temple was completed around 150 C.E.*

overran Syria, Palestine, and Egypt. The Hellenistic era of Middle Eastern history was coming to an end.

■ THE ISLAMIC MIDDLE EAST AS AN AUTONOMOUS SYSTEM

The revelation of Islam to an unlettered Meccan merchant in the early seventh century, the unification of hitherto feuding Arab tribes under this new religion, the rapid conquest of the Middle East and North Africa, the conversion of millions of Asians and Africans to Islam, and the development of Arab-Islamic civilization under a succession of empires marked a new epoch. Egyptians, Syrians, and Persians influenced the beliefs of their Arab conquerors just as they had transformed and absorbed earlier invaders. Yet the rise of Islam created new ideas and institutions, monuments and memories, which continue to affect Middle Eastern peoples profoundly.

□ The Arabs Before Islam

Once the camel had been domesticated, roughly 3000–2000 B.C.E., bands of people began roaming the Arabian Peninsula in search of water and forage for their flocks. Milk and dates—rarely meat and bread—constituted their diet. They augmented their income by raiding or guarding the commercial caravans that plied between Syria and the Indian Ocean and by fighting as auxiliaries in the Persian and Roman armies. Sometimes these Arabs moved into fertile lands, built cities, and established states in what are now Syria, Jordan, and Yemen.

Unable as nomads to develop architecture, sculpture, or painting, these early Arabs composed poems that embodied their code of values: bravery in battle, patience in misfortune, persistence in revenge, protection of the weak, defiance of the strong, loyalty to the tribe, hospitality to the guest, generosity to the needy, and fidelity in carrying out promises. These were the virtues needed to survive in the desert. Their poems, recited from memory, expressed the joys and sorrows of nomadic life, hailed the bravery of their heroes, lauded their own tribes, and lampooned their rivals. Even now Arabs recite these poems and often repeat their precepts.

In Roman times the southern Arabs played a larger role in the world; they developed Yemen, colonized Ethiopia, and crossed the Indian Ocean. The northern Arabs were relatively isolated. Some adopted Judaism or Christianity, but most practiced ancestor worship or animism (the belief that every object, whether animate or inanimate, has a spirit). One of the northern tribes, the Quraysh, built a shrine, the Ka'bah, at a small desert city called Mecca on the main trade route between Syria and Yemen. Once a year, the pagan tribes of northwestern Arabia suspended their quarrels to make pilgrimages to the Ka'bah, which housed 360 idols representing tribal gods or goddesses. Some Meccans grew rich on the proceeds of the caravan trade and the annual pilgrimage.

□ Muhammad

In Mecca, around 570, was born one of the world's greatest religious leaders, Muhammad, to a minor branch of the Quraysh. Orphaned at an early age, Muhammad was reared by an uncle as a caravan trader. When he reached manhood, he became the agent for a rich merchant widow, Khadijah, whom he married. Until he was forty, Muhammad was simply an honest Meccan trader. But he was troubled by the widening gulf between the accepted Arab virtues of bravery and generosity and the blatantly acquisitive practices of Mecca's commercial leaders. Often he went to one of the hills near Mecca to meditate.

One day in the Arab month of Ramadan, Muhammad heard a voice exhorting him to recite. In awe and terror he cried, "I can't recite." The voice replied:

> Recite in the name of thy Lord, the Creator
> who created man of a blood-clot.
> Recite, for thy lord most generous
> who taught by the pen,
> taught man what he knew not.

Fearing that he had gone mad, Muhammad rushed home and asked Khadijah to wrap him in a cloak. Again the voice sounded:

> O thou enshrouded in thy mantle,
> rise and warn!
> Thy lord magnify
> thy raiment purify
> and from evil flee!

Reassured by his wife, Muhammad came to accept the voice as the Angel Gabriel's command to proclaim God's existence to the Arabs and to warn them of an imminent judgment day when all people would be called to account for what they had done. He received more revelations and began to share them in the community. Those who accepted Muhammad's divine message called themselves *Muslims* and their religion *Islam,* meaning submission to the will of God, the creator and sustainer.

Muhammad's public recitation of his revelations disturbed the Meccan leaders. Did their wealth and power not matter? If the Arabs accepted Islam, would they stop their annual pilgrimages to the Ka'bah, so lucrative to local merchants? Why did God reveal His message to Muhammad, rather than to one of the Quraysh leaders? The pagan Meccans reviled the Muslims. After Muhammad's uncle and protector died, life in Mecca became intolerable for Muslims. Finally the Arabs of Medina, a city north of Mecca, asked Muhammad to arbitrate their tribal disputes and accepted Islam as the condition for his coming there.

The *hijrah* (emigration) of Muhammad and his followers from Mecca is for Muslims the most important event in history. The Muslim calendar begins in the year it occurred, 622 C.E., for it was in Medina that Muhammad founded the Islamic *ummah,* a community ruled by a divine plan that was revealed to him gradually. Politics and religion are united in Islam; God, speaking to humanity through Muhammad, is the supreme lawgiver. Thus the Prophet became a political leader, and when the Meccans tried to destroy the *ummah,* a military commander as well. Buttressed by their faith, the Muslims of Medina vanquished Meccan armies larger and stronger than their own, converted most of the pagan Arab tribes, and finally converted Mecca to Islam. In 630 Muhammad made a triumphal pilgrimage to the Ka'bah, smashed its pagan idols, and declared it a Muslim shrine. Two years later, having united much of Arabia under the banner of Islam, he died.

□ Islamic Beliefs and Institutions

Muslims believe there is one God, all-powerful and all-knowing, having no partner and no offspring. God has spoken to a succession of human messengers, of whom the last was Muhammad. To the Jewish prophets God imparted the Torah and to Jesus and his disciples the Gospels. Muslims believe that Jews and Christians corrupted their scriptures, so God sent a perfected revelation, the Quran (recitation), to Muhammad. Although Muslims view the Quran as truer than the Bible in its present form, they may not deny any of God's prophets, including Abraham, Moses, and Jesus. Muslims also believe in a day of judgment, when God will assess all people and consign them to Heaven or to Hell.

Muslim duties are often summed up as the "five pillars of Islam": statement of belief in God and in Muhammad as God's Prophet; ritual prayer five times daily; fasting in the daylight hours of the month of Ramadan; payment of part of one's property or income to provide for the needy; and the pilgrimage to Mecca. Muslims also abstain from drinking alcoholic beverages, eating pork, gambling, and all forms of licentious and

dishonest behavior. Standards of sexual morality are strict, limiting contacts between unmarried men and women. Marriages in most Muslim societies are arranged by parents or other family members. Muslims ascribe
human misdeeds to ignorance or forgetfulness and believe that God for-
gives those who repent.

Islam is a way of life: It prescribes how people relate to one another
as well as their duties to God. Muhammad's *ummah* aspired to serve as the
ideal earthly setting in which believers could prepare for the judgment day.
In the centuries following Muhammad's death, Muslim scholars (*ulama*)
developed an elaborate legal code, the Shari'ah, to regulate all aspects of
human behavior. The Shari'ah was derived from the Quran, the words and
deeds of the Prophet (or those actions of Muhammad's followers that he
sanctioned), the consensus of the *ummah*, analogical reasoning, and judicial opinion. Dynastic and doctrinal schisms soon divided the *ummah;*
however, the Shari'ah, upheld by the *ulama,* brought together Muslims of
diverse races, cultures, regions, and political allegiances.

□ The Arab Conquests and the Islamic Empire

When Muhammad died, his followers hastened to name a successor.
No one could succeed Muhammad as the Prophet, but someone had to lead
the *ummah*, and Abu Bakr was chosen as the first caliph (successor). During his caliphate the Muslims won back the rebellious tribal Arabs and deflected their energies outward against Byzantium and Persia. Under Umar
ibn al-Khattab, the second caliph, these rebellious Arabs routed armies
mightier than their own, wresting Syria and Egypt from Byzantine control
and absorbing Sassanid Persia. The Arabs conquered most of the Middle
East in a generation and much of the Old World in a century. Many Syrians, Egyptians, and Persians welcomed Arab rule as a respite from Byzantine intolerance and Sassanid exploitation. They were forced neither to
speak Arabic nor to become Muslims, although gradually some chose to do
one or both.

The new Arab rulers retained local administrative customs and languages and even the bureaucrats themselves; the Arabs lacked the numbers
and the experience to govern their new empire unaided. They asked every
non-Muslim to pay a head tax in return for exemption from military service. Several centuries passed before most people living in lands under Islamic rule actually were Muslims, for some early caliphs even discouraged
conversions to Islam lest they reduce tax revenues. Jerusalem under Arab
rule remained a religious center and pilgrimage site for Jews and Christians, but it became a holy city for Muslims as well.

Although Arab toleration of local customs sustained stability, the conquests strained the *ummah* itself. The caliphs set aside some of the captured

booty for charitable or communal use and put the troops on a payroll, but the sudden influx of wealth led to unrest. In 656 the third caliph, Uthman, was murdered, and his friends suspected his successor, Ali, of taking part in his assassination. Demanding revenge, Uthman's supporters fought Ali's backers in a battle that led to a mediation favoring Uthman's cousin, Mu'awiyah, the governor of Syria. He named himself caliph, moved the capital to Damascus, pacified the dissident Muslims, and made the caliphate hereditary in his own family, the Umayyad branch of the Quraysh tribe, replacing the earlier elective system.

The Umayyad caliphs were more political than pious. They crushed their opponents and spread Arab rule to North Africa and Spain, central Asia, and what is now Pakistan (see Map 3.1). The Umayyad era (661–750) was resented by many Muslims. One of these dissidents was the Prophet's grandson, Husayn, who died during a revolt at Karbala (Iraq) in 680. Husayn's martyrdom led to a political and religious opposition movement known as Shi'ism. Even now a split remains between the Shi'ites, who accept only Ali and his descendants as rightful leaders of the *ummah,* and the Sunnis, who recognize the caliphs who actually ruled. Today Sunnis outnumber Shi'ites in most parts of the Muslim world, but Shi'ism is the state religion of Iran and differentiates the Persians from other Middle Eastern peoples.

□ The Arab Empire

The Umayyads' power depended on their main fighting force, the Arab tribes, which the caliphs favored even after many non-Arabs converted to Islam. Some non-Arab Muslims turned to revolutionary movements, often pro-Shi'ite, against Umayyad rule. One such rebellion was led by the Abbasid family, who toppled the Umayyads in 750 and set up their own caliphate in Baghdad. At this point, the formal unity of the *ummah* ended, for the Umayyads kept control over Spain. The North African Berbers, tribal peoples whose conversion from Christianity and Judaism to Islam did not mean their acceptance of Arab political dominance, soon cast off Abbasid rule. Elsewhere, ambitious governors, warlords, and religious leaders carved out their own states. Two sons of the renowned caliph Harun al-Rashid (r. 786–809) fought each other in a civil war that symbolized the Arab-Persian struggle. The Persian-backed candidate won. The Arabs either reverted to nomadism or intermarried with their conquered peoples, many of whom were now Arabized in language and culture.

Despite its turbulent politics, the Abbasid era (which lasted in weakened form until 1258) was one of agricultural and commercial prosperity. As industry and trade flourished, so did science and letters. Rulers competed with one another in patronizing the translation of scientific and

Map 3.1 Extent of the Islamic Empire

WESTERN TURKS

Aral Sea

Samarkand

Kabul

Caspian Sea

Shiraz

Arabian Sea

Persian Gulf

Sanaa

Euphrates

Medina

Dnieper

Black Sea

Mecca

Red Sea

Tarsus

Damascus

Jerusalem

Constantinople

Danube

BYZANTINE EMPIRE

Mediterranean Sea

Alexandria

Nile

Dongola

FRANKISH KINGDOM

Venice

Rome

Naples

Oea (Tripoli)

Tunis

ISLAMIC CALIPHATE

Barcelona

Lisbon

Tangier

Expansion under the Prophet Mohammad, 622–632

Additions during the Patriarchal Caliphate, 632–661

Additions during the Umayyad Caliphate, 661–750

philosophical works from Greek into Arabic, supporting court poets and historians, building mosques and palaces, and sponsoring astronomical and medical research. Thus Muslims preserved and improved their classical patrimony, which they passed on to medieval Europe, helping to spark the Renaissance.

□ Invasions from East and West

The influx of Turks from eastern Asia began in the tenth century. Many had already been imported as slave soldiers and bureaucrats for the Abbasid caliphs; others served the Abbasids or local Muslim rulers as frontier guards against non-Muslims farther east. Schooled in the arts of government and war, the Turkish *ghazi*s (border raiders) were more reliable than the caliphs' other Muslim subjects and often rose to positions of power.

One Turkish family serving a Persian dynasty received an *iqta‘*—some land granted for military or administrative service to the government—in Ghazna (in what is now Afghanistan) around 960. This family, the Ghaznavids, built up an empire spanning eastern Persia, central Asia, and parts of northern India. The Ghaznavids in turn gave *iqta‘* to Turkish clans from central Asia. One of these, the Seljuks, proceeded to conquer lands westward across Persia and Mesopotamia and into Anatolia, where they defeated the Byzantines in 1071. The military gains of these families attracted other Turks to serve as *ghazi*s, opening the way for large-scale immigration of Turkish tribes with their horses, two-humped camels, sheep, and goats. Soon Azerbaijan (northwestern Persia), northern Iraq, and much of Anatolia, highland areas never taken by the Arabs, became mainly Turkish.

The Turks were devout Sunni Muslims who built new cities and refurbished old ones. They rescued the Abbasid caliph, who had been taken hostage by Shi‘ite bureaucrats, and restored his authority, although not his power. For several generations the caliph ruled in Baghdad beside a Seljuk sultan (holder of power). The Turks strengthened Sunni educational institutions, promoted Sufism (organized Islamic mysticism), and discouraged reinterpreting the Shari‘ah. Sufism gave Muslims more involvement in their faith but caused some to withdraw from worldly pursuits. Once the Sunni Muslims could not revise the Shari‘ah, changing social needs made rulers and subjects bypass it, and practices diverged ever farther from Islamic precepts.

As Turkish nomads poured in from the East, a different group of invaders came from the West. In 1096 the pope proclaimed a Crusade to regain the Holy Land for Christianity. Muslims had ruled Jerusalem for more than four centuries without harming Christian interests, but the Seljuk invasion of

Anatolia had weakened the Byzantine Empire and threatened the Christian pilgrimage routes to the Holy City. The Crusaders helped the Byzantines to stem the Seljuk advance and then went on to take western Syria and Palestine from divided and weak Muslim rulers. For almost a century, Jerusalem, purged of its Muslim and Jewish inhabitants, was the capital of a European Christian kingdom.

Both Christians and Muslims tend to overemphasize the Crusades. Outside Jerusalem, the Crusaders rarely uprooted the local population, and they never took the Muslim power centers: Cairo, Damascus, Aleppo, and Mosul. Once Egypt and Syria were united under a strong Sunni Muslim ruler, Saladin, the Crusaders could no longer threaten their cities, and the Muslims retook Jerusalem in 1187. The Crusaders held part of coastal Syria for another century and twice invaded the Nile Delta, but Saladin's descendants, the Ayyubids, kept them in check.

Far more damaging to the Middle East were the thirteenth-century invasions by the Mongols, who came from the lands north of China. Mongol armies led by Genghis Khan (r. 1206–1227) defeated weak Muslim rulers and conquered central Asia and eastern Persia. His grandson, Hülegü, pressed farther into Persia and Mesopotamia and in 1258 took Baghdad and wiped out the Abbasid caliphate. The Mongols were not Muslims. Horse nomads accustomed to grassy steppes, they saw no need for cities or the peasants who supported them, so they destroyed irrigation works in Persia, Mesopotamia, and Syria, impoverishing the land and its people. Many Muslim rulers, even the surviving Seljuks in Anatolia, became Mongol vassals. But in 1260 the Mongols failed to take Palestine and Egypt, where the Ayyubids had recently been overthrown by their Turkish slave soldiers, the Mamluks. The Mamluk rulers went on to build a prosperous empire in Egypt and Syria, the bulwark of Muslim power until their conquest by the Ottoman Turks in 1516–1517. Meanwhile, Persia's Mongol rulers soon adopted Islam, accepted Persian culture, and rebuilt much of what they had earlier destroyed.

Europe's harnessing of gunpowder in the fourteenth century would alter the West's relationship with the rest of the world. The invention was used initially to destroy fortifications and only later to kill animals and people. Firearms and long-distance sailing ships soon enabled Europeans to explore and conquer distant lands and finally to encircle the Muslim world. States using gunpowder as their main weapon require large, disciplined infantries rather than the feudal cavalries of medieval times. Europe's adoption of firearms sparked the growth of strong monarchies, a commercial middle class, and eventually the Industrial Revolution. In the Middle East, some Muslim states learned how to use firearms on land and sea; others never did. The gunpowder revolution weakened the land-owning

horse soldiers there, too, but failed to stimulate modernization on the European pattern.

□ The Ottoman Empire

The Ottoman Empire was the archetypal Muslim state built on the use of firearms. From their humble beginnings in the late thirteenth century as Turkish *ghazis* for the Seljuks, the Ottomans expanded their landholdings into an empire that stretched—at its height in the late sixteenth century—from central Europe to the Gulf and from Algeria to Azerbaijan. Like most *ghazis*, the early Ottomans raided peasant lands on horseback. During the fourteenth and fifteen centuries, however, they developed a disciplined corps of professional foot soldiers, the famous janissaries, who used siege cannon and lighter firearms against the Europeans or their Muslim neighbors. The Ottoman state took boys from their Christian subjects as a form of tribute. Converted to Islam, they were taught Turkish and Arabic and trained as soldiers or, less often, as administrators. As slaves of the Ottoman sultan, the janissaries were forbidden to marry or to own land and had to live in barracks in order to be ready to fight whenever they were needed. This system of recruitment and training was called *devshirme,* as were, collectively, the Ottoman soldiers and bureaucrats it produced.

Backed by well-equipped armies and loyal, competent administrators, the Ottoman sultans conquered the Christian peoples of the Balkans and surrounded Constantinople. In 1453 they took the city and ended the 1,000-year-old Byzantine Empire. Once the world's greatest Christian city, Constantinople (now Istanbul) became a Muslim center. During the following century, the Ottomans subjugated most of their Muslim neighbors, including the Mamluks of Egypt and Syria. Only the Persians, ruled after 1501 by the Safavids, remained independent, in part due to their conversion to Shi'ism, but also because they, too, learned to use firearms.

Ottoman power rested on two basic practices: (1) the power of the ruling class was balanced between the traditional aristocracy and the *devshirme* soldiers and administrators; and (2) the subject peoples were organized into religious communities, called *millets*, that had autonomous control over their laws, schools, and general welfare. These internal divisions strengthened the sultan. So long as the sultan could play the aristocracy off against the *devshirme* class, both ruling groups performed their tasks as defenders and managers of the Ottoman Empire. The subject peoples, divided into Jewish and various Christian and Muslim communities, were self-sufficient but geographically scattered, unable to combine against their Ottoman overlords. These subjects looked to their communal leaders—rabbis, priests, and *ulama*—whose most prominent members

were named by and responsible to the sultan, to mediate between them and the government. For centuries, this approach to social and political organization endured in the region. Even now, many Middle Easterners appear to identify themselves by their religion more than by their nationality.

Of all the factors that weakened the Ottoman Empire, the greatest was the triumph of the *devshirme* bureaucrats and janissaries over the aristocracy. This occurred during the reign of the greatest sultan, Suleiman the Magnificent (r. 1520–1566), when he appointed a series of chief ministers who had risen from *devshirme* origins. Unchecked by neither the less competent succeeding sultans nor by the declining aristocracy, these one-time slaves corrupted the Ottoman government to serve their own interests. Janissaries married, bought property, and enrolled their sons in the corps, which stopped training and degenerated into a hereditary, privileged caste. Military ineptitude and corrupt government ensued. Taxes rose, especially for peasants, who were least able to avoid paying them. Agricultural and commercial prosperity declined, partly because the trade routes between Asia and Europe shifted away from the Middle East. Many once-loyal subjects rebelled against Ottoman misrule. By the late seventeenth century, the Ottoman Empire was no longer the scourge of Christian Europe.

■ THE SUBORDINATION OF
THE MIDDLE EAST TO THE WEST

During the eighteenth and nineteenth centuries the West gained military, political, and economic superiority over Middle Eastern peoples, who had until then looked down on Europe. Whereas Arabs and Turks had once controlled the routes between Europe and Asia and traded with both on their own terms, by 1800 Europe sold its manufactures to the Middle East in exchange for raw materials and agricultural products. Europeans in Muslim lands were exempted from local taxes and legal jurisdiction; in the Ottoman Empire this exemption was guaranteed by treaties called Capitulations. Whereas once the Mediterranean Sea and the Indian Ocean were controlled by Muslim navies, now European sailing ships dominated the high seas. Whereas once the Ottoman sultan could choose the time and place for an attack on Europe and could then dictate the peace terms, now his armies feared the stronger forces of Hapsburg Austria and czarist Russia. The greatest shock came when Napoleon occupied Egypt in 1798, for France had been an Ottoman ally.

□ Westernizing Reforms

As early as the seventeenth century, some Ottoman sultans and their ministers saw the need for internal change. At first they regarded reform as the restoration of the institutions and practices that had made their empire strong in the past. But being defeated by Western armies taught them that conditions had altered, necessitating more drastic modifications. The first Westernizing reforms took place within the military. Sultan Selim III (r. 1789–1807) tried to establish a new army corps trained and equipped in the European fashion. The janissaries, afraid that these interlopers would take away their power, rebelled, destroyed the new corps, and deposed Selim. The conservatism of the *ulama* and trade guilds blocked reform in other aspects of Ottoman life. Even the introduction of printing was long opposed by the *ulama* and scribes, one group condemning an innovation contrary to Islam and the other fearing the loss of their jobs.

Rulers saw that reform could not be confined to the military and divorced from the rest of society. In addition, the failure of early reform efforts taught the Muslim rulers that defense against European expansion meant concentrating power in the state. Westernizing reform meant autocracy, not democracy. Three Middle Eastern reformers serve as examples: Mehmet (Muhammad) Ali (r. 1805–1849) of Egypt, Sultan Mahmud II (r. 1808–1839) of the Ottoman Empire, and Nasir al-Din Shah (r. 1848–1896) of Persia. Each tried to concentrate power in his own hands; each found himself hamstrung by European actions serving imperialist interests.

The ablest was Mehmet Ali, an Ottoman officer leading an Albanian regiment sent to Egypt. He gained control of that Ottoman province after Napoleon's forces pulled out in 1801 and proceeded to eliminate every rival contender for Egyptian power. He massacred the Mamluks and curbed the *ulama,* who had enjoyed special power and prestige in Egypt, by exploiting their rivalries and seizing the endowments that supported them. Using French advisers and equipment, he developed the region's strongest army and navy. He subordinated the rural aristocracy to the state by taking control of all agricultural land. Not only did he become Egypt's main landowner, but also he decided what crops the peasants might grow. He supplied their seeds, fertilizer, and tools; purchased their harvests; and sold the crops, often abroad, for as high a profit as possible.

Under Mehmet Ali's rule, Egypt became the first Middle Eastern country to make the transition from subsistence to market agriculture. Tobacco, sugar, indigo, and cotton became Egypt's cash crops, earning revenues to fund Mehmet Ali's ambitious projects for industrial development and military expansion. The first non-Western ruler to accept the Industrial Revolution, he set up textile mills and weapons factories with the aid of European advisers. He sent hundreds of his subjects to Europe for technical and military training and imported European instructors to staff military academies and schools in Egypt. He even conscripted Egyptian peasants as soldiers. Officered by Turks, they became such a potent force that Mehmet Ali's son, Ibrahim, conquered Syria in 1832 and would have taken over the whole Ottoman Empire in 1839 if Britain had not intervened. Although the

Ottoman Empire recognized Egypt's autonomy in 1841, Mehmet Ali felt that his ambitions had been thwarted and let his reforms lapse. However, his heirs ruled Egypt, with only nominal Ottoman control, up to the British occupation in 1882, and the monarchy remained part of Egypt's political structure until King Farouk was overthrown in 1952.

Mehmet Ali's Ottoman contemporary, Sultan Mahmud II, also tried to reform his state by a centralizing policy but had less immediate success. Having learned the lesson of Selim III, he waited until he was able to wipe out the janissary corps, the main obstacle to change. Then he reorganized the army, ended the *iqta'* system of military land grants, and began to reform finance, education, and provincial government. But Mahmud's efforts were hampered by the diversity and extent of his domains, various local rebellions, the lack of a loyal and trained bureaucracy, the Greek war for independence (backed by Britain, France, and Russia), and the growing need of industrialized states to buy Ottoman raw materials and sell their own manufactures.

After Mahmud died in 1839, his son issued a reform decree that began the *tanzimat* (reorganization) era, marked by more intense centralization and Westernization of the Ottoman Empire. The *tanzimat* reforms worked better than those of Mahmud, but they did not protect the Ottomans against Russian expansion in the Balkans, so Britain and France helped them defeat Russia in the Crimean War (1853–1856). The victors then made their Ottoman ally issue another decree that gave Christians and Jews legal equality with Muslims within the empire.

Persia was the only core Middle Eastern state never to fall under Ottoman rule. From the fifteenth century, various Turkish-speaking dynasties ruled over that sprawling and heterogeneous country, either in uneasy alliance or open contention with the nomadic tribes, rural landlords, urban merchants, and *ulama*. The rulers' revival of ancient Persian customs preserved a national identity that was reinforced by their adherence to Shi'ism, in contrast with the Sunni Islam prevalent in the Ottoman Empire. In the sixteenth and seventeenth centuries, Persia flourished under the Safavid shahs, who adorned their capital at Esfahan and formed commercial and diplomatic ties with the European countries needing allies against the Ottoman Empire.

After Safavid rule fell apart, a military adventurer named Nader Shah (r. 1736–1747) conquered much of India and drove the Ottomans out of Azerbaijan. But Persia, too, declined. The Qajar dynasty (1794–1925) weakly resisted dissolution from within and Russian and British encroachments from without. During the first three years of Nasir al-Din Shah's reign, his energetic chief minister began a series of military, financial, and educational reforms. But in 1851 the shah executed his minister, and the country became embroiled in tribal and religious uprisings. Later in his reign, Nasir al-Din began selling concessions to British investors and hiring Russian officers to train his army. Instead of using reform to protect Persia from foreigners, the shah encouraged them to take over. His subjects repudiated his policies; a nationwide tobacco boycott made him cancel one of his most lucrative concessions in 1892, and he was finally assassinated. Subsequent Qajar shahs were even less reform-minded than Nasir al-Din and even more submissive to Anglo-Russian interference.

□ European Policies and Imperialism in the Nineteenth Century

If European power inspired Middle Eastern reform, European policies and actions kept it from succeeding. From 1815 to 1914, European governments preserved peace among themselves by maintaining a balance of power. For the Middle East, this meant that neither Britain nor Russia could let the other become supreme. Fearing that breaking up the Ottoman Empire would give Russia control of the Balkans and of the straits linking the Black Sea to the Aegean, Britain usually tried to preserve its territorial integrity. Thus the British led European opposition to Mehmet Ali's threat in Ottoman Syria in 1839, Russia's occupation of the Romanian principalities in 1853 that led to the Crimean War, and Russia's frequent efforts to exploit rising nationalism in the Balkans.

The British government backed reforms that would enable the Ottoman Empire to resist Russia, especially those during the *tanzimat* era that promised equality to non-Muslims. But Britain also made sure to open Middle Eastern markets to its own manufactures, using a tariff treaty that stopped the Ottoman government from protecting local industries from European competition. In addition, Russia's expansionist aims, its claim to protect the sultan's Orthodox Christian subjects, and its support of Balkan nationalist movements thwarted Ottoman reform efforts.

While guarding its routes to India, Britain vied with France for power in the eastern Mediterranean; it fought to expel Napoleon from Egypt and later to remove Mehmet Ali from Syria. Britain signed treaties with tribal leaders in the Gulf and occupied Aden in order to outflank Mehmet Ali and his French allies. A British company started steamship navigation on the Euphrates River in the 1830s; another built the first railroad from Alexandria to Cairo in 1851. But it was a French diplomat, Ferdinand-Marie de Lesseps, who won a concession from the Egyptian government to cut a canal across the Isthmus of Suez, joining the Red Sea to the Mediterranean and slashing the time it took to go from Europe to South Asia. Britain tried at first to block this mainly French project, but it became the principal user of the Suez Canal soon after it was opened in 1869. France also expanded its empire across North Africa, capturing Algeria between 1830 and 1847 and establishing protectorates over Tunisia in 1881 and Morocco in 1912.

□ The Middle Eastern Reaction to the West

By the 1860s a number of Middle Easterners were wondering whether Westernization had gone too far. In the Ottoman Empire, many Muslims espoused pan-Islam, the idea that all Muslims should unite behind the sultan, to counter outside threats and the divisive nationalist movements of non-Muslim Balkan subjects. Pan-Islam reaffirmed the tradition of Muslims uniting to defend the *ummah,* but this doctrine took on a new meaning: the Ottoman sultan claimed for himself the caliphate, hence the political allegiance of all Muslims, regardless of who actually ruled them. Because Britain, France, and Russia all had Muslim subjects within their empires, Europeans soon saw the fearsome potential of pan-Islam.

Pan-Islam was one manifestation of the intellectual changes occurring in the Middle East. The Ottoman and Egyptian reforms were creating new elites versed in Western techniques. As Middle Easterners attending Western universities, mission schools, or Ottoman and Egyptian state academies learned to work like Europeans, they also began to think like them. They found out that bad governments could be altered or overthrown; that individuals had rights and freedoms; and that they belonged to political communities called "nations" based on race, language, culture, and shared historical experience. In the late nineteenth century, these liberal and nationalist ideas gave birth to new movements: the National Party in Egypt, the New Ottomans and later the Young Turks in the Ottoman Empire, the Arab secret societies in Beirut and Damascus, the Constitutionalists in Persia, and the Young Tunisians. Each of these groups rebelled against its rulers' monopoly on power and tried to set up a more constitutional government. None wholly succeeded.

□ The Beginnings of Egyptian Nationalism

Mehmet Ali's grandson, Isma'il (r. 1863–1879), resumed Westernizing reforms and secured Egypt's fiscal and administrative autonomy from the Ottoman Empire. He sent explorers to find the sources of the Nile River and army expeditions to conquer southern Sudan. Sections of Cairo and Alexandria were transformed by broad boulevards, public gardens, and huge mansions. Factories and public works built up the economy, as a cotton boom caused by a drop in U.S. production during the Civil War, the growing availability of European capital, and the construction of the Suez Canal made Egypt an attractive field for investment.

Egypt's economy skyrocketed, but so did Isma'il's problems. In 1866 he set up a representative assembly to advise his government and raise revenue. Timid at first but later incited by a burgeoning press, this new body began calling for constitutional government. Isma'il borrowed vast sums from foreign banks to cover his expenditures. Unable to repay his debts, he sold his government's Suez Canal shares to Britain, accepted British and French control over Egypt's finances, and finally admitted representatives of these two creditor states into his cabinet. Egyptians resented these changes. The assembly demanded a cabinet that would be responsible to the assembly and devoid of European members, a say in the government's budget, and a reversal of budget cuts that were harming many Egyptians. In 1879 Isma'il dismissed his "European cabinet" and named one that heeded the assembly's call for constitutional government, whereupon the European powers pressured the Ottoman sultan to replace Isma'il with his son, Tawfiq.

Obeying his European advisers, Tawfiq Pasha purged the dissidents from his regime and tried to retire some of his father's debts. But many Egyptians, harmed by European interference, called for independence. Their main backers were some Egyptian army officers led by Colonel Urabi Pasha, who wanted Egypt freed from both Turks and Europeans. In 1881 Urabi's troops surrounded the palace and called for a new cabinet responsible to an elected parliament. Tawfiq gave in, and soon Egypt had a constitution. Nationalism's triumph was brief; its leaders were split, the Europeans threatened to intervene, and Tawfiq turned against the nationalists in 1882. The British landed in Alexandria, invaded the Suez Canal, and marched on Cairo. Urabi yielded, ending Egypt's first constitutional era.

When Britain occupied Egypt, it promised to withdraw its troops as soon as order was restored to the country. It was easy to defeat the nationalists and prop up Tawfiq on his throne, but it was harder to remedy the causes of Egypt's disorder: huge debts, a peasantry burdened by high taxes, and a revolt in Sudan. The longer Britain stayed on to tackle Egypt's problems, the harder it was to leave. A talented administrator, Sir Evelyn Baring, Lord Cromer, became Britain's diplomatic representative in Cairo. Backed by British troops, he reformed Egypt's finances and administration and gradually emerged as its ruler in all but name.

Although the country prospered, British advisers sapped the authority and initiative of the Egyptian ministers. The British claimed to be preparing the Egyptians for self-rule, but in fact Egypt became a training ground for British colonial administrators. They often forgot that Egypt was not a British colony but rather an autonomous Ottoman province temporarily occupied by British troops. For example, the extension of irrigation under British rule was not paralleled by expanded education or industrial development. Cromer became autocratic and spiteful in undercutting Tawfiq's

son, Abbas II. When Abbas succeeded Tawfiq in 1892, he assembled a
cabal of young Egyptians to help him thwart Cromer's power. Their
spokesman, an articulate lawyer named Mustafa Kamil, founded the National Party. The Nationalists urged Britain to withdraw its forces from
Egypt and later demanded a new constitution. Cromer ignored them, but
his successor promised to hasten Egypt's progress toward self-rule. Unfortunately for the Nationalists, Mustafa Kamil died prematurely in 1908, and
his followers split, some turning to terrorism or to pan-Islam. A more repressive British policy forced the leading Nationalists into exile. At the
outbreak of World War I, the British declared Egypt a protectorate, deposed Abbas, and severed its last ties with the Ottoman Empire.

□ Turkish Liberalism and Arab Nationalism Within the Ottoman Empire

As the *tanzimat* reforms waned, a group of Westernized intellectuals
and army officers known as the New Ottomans agitated for a more liberal
regime. In 1876, amid Balkan revolts, growing state indebtedness to Europe, and threats of a Russian invasion, a military coup placed a liberal
sultan on the throne. He was soon replaced by Abdülhamid II, who issued
a constitution in December of that year to forestall possible partition of his
empire by the Russians. For about a year, the Ottoman Empire had a popularly elected parliament, but as Russia attacked anyway and advanced on
Istanbul, Abdülhamid shut it down and suspended the constitution. For
thirty years the sultan further centralized state control and suppressed nationalist and liberal movements. A group of Westernized students and army
officers, convinced that the empire could be saved only by restoring the
1876 Constitution, formed the Committee of Union and Progress, or the
Young Turks. In 1908 they forced the sultan to restore the constitution and
hold free elections; in 1909, after an abortive countercoup, they deposed
him. But the Young Turk regime soon became a military junta. As Balkan
revolts and Western imperialism took one Ottoman province after another,
the leaders increasingly adopted Turkish nationalism, offending those subjects who did not identify with Turkish culture.

Among the Ottoman subjects who resisted Turkish nationalism were
those who spoke Arabic. Long divided by local, sectarian, or family rivalries, the people of Syria, Mesopotamia, and Arabia began to view themselves as one Arab nation. Arabic-speaking lawyers, teachers, students,
and army officers formed nationalist societies in the main Ottoman cities.
Some wanted internal autonomy and equality of status with the Turks as
Ottoman subjects; others demanded Arab independence from Turkish rule.
Some called for restoring the caliphate to an Arab ruler. Although Arab

nationalism initially had few adherents, its ideas helped spark the Arab Revolt during World War I.

☐ Persian Constitutionalism

Liberalism spread in Persia because the Qajar shahs were autocratic and weak. They could not protect the peasants and city dwellers from nomadic tribes, nor could they stop Russian military incursions or the commercial ascendancy of the British and other Europeans. The Constitutionalists included three groups: merchants, Shi'ite *ulama,* and liberal intellectuals. The merchants resented the shahs' concessions to foreign companies, which threatened their livelihood; the *ulama* feared that Westernization would undermine Islam generally and their own influence in particular; and the intellectuals, influenced by Western liberal and nationalist ideas, viewed the shah, backed by foreign advisers and money, as an obstacle to Persian reforms.

Clearly, these groups had disparate ends, yet united by nationalist and anti-imperialist feelings, they engineered a tobacco boycott in 1892 and a national revolution in 1906. In response, the shah granted a constitution that provided for a popularly elected parliament (*majlis*), but in 1907 his successor called in Russian troops to suppress the *majlis* and its revolutionary backers. Outside the capital, however, the Constitutionalists continued their struggle. A prominent tribal leader helped them retake Tehran, and they replaced the shah with a more docile relative.

Once in power, the Constitutionalists failed to implement their program for national reform. Their political revolution did not transform social and economic conditions, they were split into factions, and outsiders exacerbated their problems. Western liberals hailed the Constitutionalists for bringing liberty to a country long blighted by corrupt and autocratic rulers, but they did not understand the revolution. The British government mainly sought to protect commerce and defend India. Meanwhile, a British firm got a concession to explore southern Persia for oil. The first major discovery came in 1908, and the Anglo-Persian Oil Company was formed the next year. Soon it built a refinery at Abadan, and when Britain's fleet switched from coal to oil in 1912, Persia's new role as an oil producer made it central to British imperial strategy.

Britain and Russia had agreed in 1907 to define spheres of influence within Persia. Russia's sphere covered the country's northern third, including Tehran. Britain, whose area bordered on northwestern India, acquiesced in Russian efforts to tighten its grip on Persia's government before and during World War I. Even the 1917 Bolshevik Revolution and the consequent withdrawal of Russian troops only briefly interrupted their efforts to control Persia.

☐ World War I, the Ottoman Jihad, and the Arab Revolt

World War I completed the continuing subordination of Middle Eastern peoples to Western political control. Since the eighteenth century, Russia had won control over the lands north and west of the Black Sea, the Caucasus Mountains, most of the Caspian Sea coast, and vast stretches of Muslim central Asia. Persia was virtually a Russian protectorate, and the czarist regime expected to gain Istanbul and the Bosporus and Dardanelles Straits in the war. Britain held Egypt, the strategic Mediterranean island of Cyprus, and Aden at the southern entrance to the Red Sea; it also had treaties requiring it to protect most of the Gulf rulers. British and French capitalists had immense investments in Middle Eastern land, buildings, factories, railroads, and utilities. In 1914 Germany seemed likely to become protector of the remnants of the Ottoman Empire; a German military mission was reorganizing its army, and German capital was financing construction of a rail line from Istanbul to Baghdad, raising its influence in the Ottoman interior.

Istanbul's decision to enter World War I as Germany's ally sealed the fate of the Ottoman Empire. The Ottoman proclamation of jihad (struggle for Islam) failed to rally the Muslims under Allied rule to rise in rebellion. As Britain repulsed Turkish attacks on the Suez Canal and sent expeditionary forces into Mesopotamia and Palestine, the Arabs' loyalty to the Ottoman sultan waned. Husayn ibn Ali, the emir (prince) of Mecca and sharif (leading descendant of Muhammad) of the prestigious Hashemite family, negotiated secretly with Sir Henry McMahon, Britain's high commissioner in Egypt, who pledged his government's support for Arab independence if Husayn rebelled against the Turks. However, the British reserved Baghdad and Basra for separate administration and excluded Mersin, Alexandretta, and "portions of Syria lying to the west of the districts of Damascus, Homs, Hama, and Aleppo." These terms fell short of the nationalists' dream of independence for all Arabic-speaking Ottoman lands. Although Husayn was disappointed, the Ottoman government's repression of the Arabs in Syria enraged him and led him to proclaim the Arab Revolt in 1916. Together, the Arabs and the British drove the Turks from Palestine and Syria, while Anglo-Indian troops took Mesopotamia (Iraq). The Ottoman Empire formally surrendered in October 1918.

Because the Arabs predominated in Palestine, Syria, and Iraq, their leaders expected Britain to grant them independence in return for their support during the Arab Revolt. U.S. president Woodrow Wilson urged autonomy for these former Ottoman lands in the twelfth of his Fourteen Points, which Britain and France accepted as the basis for making peace. According to the Husayn-McMahon correspondence, confirmed in 1918 by new British and French assurances to the Arabs, the Fertile Crescent and the Hejaz were to be ruled by Sharif Husayn's family, the Hashemites.

But this was not to be. During the war Britain had made conflicting commitments to other interested parties. In a series of secret pacts, the Allies had agreed that the Bosporus and Dardanelles Straits, Istanbul, and eastern Anatolia were to go to czarist Russia, portions of western Anatolia to the Greeks and the Italians, and most of the Arab lands to Britain and France. The 1916 Sykes-Picot Agreement designated part of the Syrian coast for direct French control and a larger zone of French influence in the Syrian hinterland as far east as Mosul. Britain was to govern lower Iraq and to have a sphere of influence covering the rest of Iraq and Palestine, except that the Christian holy places would be under an international administration. Only in the desert were the Arabs to be free from Western rule.

Meanwhile, there was another group, the Jewish nationalists, or Zionists, who were pressing the Western powers to recognize their claim to Palestine, or *eretz Israel*. Beginning in the 1880s (in part due to the Russian pogroms against Jews), some European Jews settled in Palestine, which was still under Ottoman rule and inhabited mainly by Arabs. During World War I, Chaim Weizmann, a distinguished chemist and Zionist leader living in England, made his views known to the cabinet, which authorized Foreign Secretary Sir Arthur Balfour to declare the British government's support for the establishment in Palestine of a national home for the Jewish people. He cautioned that nothing would be done to prejudice the civil and religious rights of Palestine's "existing non-Jewish inhabitants," then over nine-tenths of its population. The 1917 Balfour Declaration was a major victory for the nascent Zionist movement.

☐ The Postwar Peace Settlement

All of these contradictory commitments were aired at the 1919 Paris Peace Conference. Sharif Husayn's son, Faisal, spoke for the Arab provisional government that the Hashemites had set up in Damascus. Seeking to learn what Arabs in Syria and Palestine wanted, Wilson sent out the King-Crane Commission, which found that the Arabs opposed French rule and Zionist colonization and preferred independence. Its report was ignored. The British let the French troops enter Beirut and later acceded to French control over Syria, including Lebanon but not Palestine. Arab nationalists in Damascus declared Syria's independence in March 1920 and vowed to resist, but the French defeated their forces in July and toppled the Arab provisional government.

By this time, the Allies had agreed on how to divide and administer the conquered Ottoman provinces. Respecting Wilson's principle of self-determination, Britain and France did not annex these territories to their empires, as earlier conquerors had done. Under the League of Nations Covenant, Ottoman lands captured during the war were designated as countries that had developed enough so that their independence could be provisionally recognized, subject to a brief period of foreign tutelage under League supervision. Accordingly, France became the mandatory power in Syria and Lebanon and Britain in Iraq and Palestine. In principle, the mandatory powers were to administer their mandates for the benefit of the inhabitants and to prepare them to rule themselves. In practice, the mandates benefited mainly Britain and France, not their new and resentful subjects.

France split Syria into smaller administrative units to ensure its control, thus embittering the nationalists. Faisal, ousted from Damascus, was crowned in Baghdad in 1921 as the British tried to suppress a general revolt in the new state of Iraq, a hastily cobbled combination of the old Ottoman provinces of Mosul, Baghdad, and Basra, minus the emirate (principality) of Kuwait. For Faisal's brother Abdullah, who had been promised the throne in Iraq, the British created the emirate of Transjordan, a desert land inhabited by bedouin tribes. Britain helped Abdullah weld his new state into a cohesive unit by forming the Arab Legion, a camel corps made up of men from most of the tribes and led by British officers. The Zionists protested that Abdullah's kingdom was not open to Jewish colonization, and Arab nationalists decried the fragmentation of what they felt should have been a unified Syria. Abdullah himself hoped that, once the French left Syria, he could move from dusty Amman to historic Damascus.

Britain's mandate west of the Jordan River required it to enforce the Balfour Declaration by letting Jewish immigrants settle in Palestine. Its Arab leaders, fearful lest their majority be submerged in the Jewish state that the Zionists hoped to form, led rebellions in protest. Thus were sown the seeds of enmity between Arabs and Jews and between Muslims and the West in the aftermath of World War I. Future generations would reap a bitter harvest.

■ THE MIDDLE EAST SINCE WORLD WAR I

When Europe's armies laid down their weapons at the end of World War I, Britain seemed to dominate the whole Middle East. Its troops patrolled western Arabia, Palestine, Syria, Iraq, some of Persia, parts of the Caucasus long under the czars, and the Turkish straits. But the rise of nationalism limited Britain's ability to rule the Middle East. Egypt and Iraq were soon convulsed by nationwide revolutions against the British occupying forces. The Arabs rioted in Palestine against the Jewish immigrants and in Syria against the French colonists, for they viewed both groups as serving British imperial interests.

Abandoned by its Young Turk leaders, the defeated Ottoman government let the British and French occupy the straits, but Ottoman attempts to demobilize the Turkish army as Greek forces invaded western Anatolia set off a national mutiny led by its ablest general, Mustafa Kemal (later named Atatürk, "Father of the Turks"). Soon Kemal's followers set up a nationalist government in Ankara that replaced and then abolished the Ottoman sultanate. The new Turkish Republic rejected the 1920 Treaty of Sèvres that the Allies had imposed on the sultan, a pact filled with clauses hated by the Turks, and negotiated with the Allies at Lausanne to gain a more acceptable treaty, signed in 1923.

In Persia, Britain drafted a treaty with the Qajar rulers that would have turned their country into a British protectorate, but the *majlis* rejected the pact, and revolts broke out in various parts of the country. In 1921 an officer in the shah's guard, Reza Khan, took control and set up a military dictatorship, reducing Britain's role to the protection of its oilfields in southwestern Persia.

□ Western Imperialism in the Arab Lands

After the war, the British did what they could to keep their communication links across the region to India. Egypt's revolutionaries did not win the independence they had sought in 1919, but the British promised in

Photo 3.4 A huge Turkish flag and a flag honoring Mustafa Kemal Atatürk commemorate Republic Day in Istanbul, Turkey.

1922 to end the protectorate and let the Egyptians draw up a formal constitution, creating a parliament that would vie with the king for power.
British troops remained to guard Cairo, Alexandria, the Suez Canal, and
such vital infrastructure as airports and radio transmitters. Sudan remained
under a formal Anglo-Egyptian condominium, but the British held almost
all the power. London also reserved the right to defend Egypt against outside aggression and to protect foreigners and minorities from nationalists
or Muslim extremists. Under the new constitution, the Egyptians held parliamentary elections in 1923, and their former delegation (in Arabic, Wafd)
to the Paris Peace Conference turned into the overwhelmingly popular
Wafd Party.

Palestine came directly under the control of Britain's Colonial Office,
with a high commissioner governing in Jerusalem. The Jewish community
had a Jewish Agency and an elected assembly to manage its internal affairs. The Muslim and Christian Arabs had no such organizations, and their
leaders rejected a proposed legislature in which they would not have been
given majority control. Jews and Arabs spoke different languages, lived in
distinct villages or separate neighborhoods, and related as little as possible
to each other as communities, although some got along well on the individual or family level. Jewish immigrants from war-torn revolutionary
Russia or central Europe viewed local Arabs as threatening brigands or
greedy landlords, whereas the Palestinian Arabs feared that the Zionist
movement would dispossess them of their lands and their homes. Jews and
Arabs, both with long memories of powerlessness, showed scant sympathy
for each other as they began their contest for Palestine.

The French accepted control over Syria but resented having to forgo
Palestine and oil-rich western Iraq. France was determined to parlay its
League of Nations mandate over Syria into a colony. Soon after French
troops had driven out the Arab nationalists, France divided the country into
districts: Damascus, Aleppo, the north Mediterranean coast for the Alawis
(a breakaway Shi'ite sect), the highlands south of Damascus for the Druze
(also a past offshoot of Shi'ism), and a special Republic of Lebanon.

This last-named state, the only one of these fragments to outlive the
French mandate, was the enlarged version of the Ottoman province of
Mount Lebanon, which had enjoyed some autonomy under European protection between 1860 and 1914. Mount Lebanon's inhabitants had been
mostly Maronite Christian (originally a breakaway sect from Greek Orthodox Christianity that later entered into communion with Roman Catho-
licism). The French hoped that by enlarging Lebanon, they could preserve
a Maronite plurality large enough to give them effective control over its
other inhabitants, be they Druze, Sunni or Shi'a Muslim, Greek Orthodox,
or adherents of other Christian sects. The Republic of Lebanon, which in
the 1920s had a slight Christian majority, soon won substantial autonomy

under Maronite leadership. French rule in Syria did benefit farmers and merchants, as the mandatory government invested in roads and other public works, but this failed to allay the rancor of the nationalists who had craved Arab independence.

In North Africa, the French treated Algeria as an integral part of France. European settlers held most of the cultivable land, dominated political life, and controlled Algiers and the other major cities. The Algerian Muslims, mainly Berber but including many Arabs, had no political rights and only belatedly formed a secular nationalist party. A Muslim bey (governor) reigned in Tunisia and had Muslim ministers, but real power was held by the French governor-general and his advisers. The presence of European settlers was less visible than in Algeria, however, and there was opposition from an emerging professional class, which formed the Destour (Constitution) Party.

Morocco, which unlike the rest of North Africa never experienced Ottoman control, was now divided between a Spanish area in the north, the international city of Tangier, and a French protectorate over most of the country. The sultan and his ministers submitted to advice from a French governor-general. A large-scale rural rebellion was suppressed in 1925 only with great difficulty, and urban nationalists formed the Istiqlal Party, but the French invested heavily in agriculture and mining, expecting to remain in Morocco. Italy, which had seized Tripolitania from the Ottoman Empire in 1911, slowly managed to capture Cyrenaica and the Fezzan as well, creating what is now Libya. Its administration was especially brutal, and efforts to colonize Libya with Italians displaced many Arabs but attracted only a few settlers.

□ Independence in Turkey, Iran, and the Arabian Peninsula

It is one of the great ironies of Middle Eastern history that the Arabs, who had thrown in their lot with the Allies during World War I, did not achieve their political goals after 1918, whereas the Turks, who had joined the Central Powers and shared in their defeat, managed to retain their independence once the war was over. The Turkish-speaking lands of Thrace and Anatolia could have been divided among Britain, France, Greece, Italy, and possibly even the United States, and some eastern areas might have been turned over to Armenians and Kurds. Instead, Kemal led a nationwide revolt that gradually won the support of the Union of Soviet Socialist Republics (USSR), France, and Italy, expelled the Greek invaders who had occupied much of western Anatolia, and persuaded the British to withdraw their troops from the Dardanelles and the Bosporus Straits. The new treaty signed at Lausanne in 1923 freed Thrace and Anatolia (with no special enclaves for the Armenians or the Kurds) from foreign rule and accepted Turkey's abolition of the Capitulations that had exempted European expatriates from Ottoman control.

Kemal also abolished the sultanate and the other political institutions of the moribund Ottoman Empire in 1923. Ankara became the capital of Turkey, the first republic in the modern Middle East. More drastic reforms soon followed, as Kemal ended the Islamic caliphate and dismantled Turkey's Muslim institutions, including its Shari'ah courts and schools, its dervish and Sufi orders, and even its holidays. The Arabic alphabet, in which Turkish had been written for a thousand years, was replaced by the Roman one. The Gregorian calendar and Western clocks became standard, as did the metric system of weights and measures. Kemal discouraged women from veiling their faces and ordered men to wear hats with brims in place of the fezzes that had become the customary head covering for Muslim officers and officials. The *ulama* lost most of their power as judges and educators. Kemal wanted to wrest Turkey out of the Middle East and make it a part of Europe. Because he had saved his country from Allied occupation, most Turks adored him and obeyed his orders.

Kemal had an imitator in Persia, the country we now know as Iran. Reza Khan, an army colonel, had seized control in 1921. But when Persia's politicians proved too quarrelsome and the shah incompetent, Reza decided to monopolize power in his own hands. Crowning himself as the new shah, he founded the Pahlavi dynasty and declared that Persia should be called Iran (meaning land of the Aryans). Like Kemal, Reza Shah weakened the *ulama* and secularized their courts, schools, and welfare institutions; in addition, he outlawed the veiling of women and required both sexes to wear European-style clothing. The new shah also curbed the nomadic tribes that had dominated most of rural Persia by forcing them to settle down as farmers. In an effort to strengthen state control over the countryside, he extended the telegraph lines and road network and decreed the construction of the Trans-Iranian Railway. The presence of the Anglo-Iranian (formerly Anglo-Persian) Oil Company, owned and managed by the British, limited Iran's economic sovereignty, but Reza Shah did manage to renegotiate the terms of its concession in the host country's favor. As oil output expanded, however, a growing proportion of the Iranian people went to work for the company, and as nationalist feelings spread throughout Iran, many wondered why such a vital resource should be controlled by foreigners.

Petroleum exploration began in other countries as well. British companies found new deposits in Iraq and Kuwait, as did U.S. companies operating in Bahrain. A coalition of U.S. firms that became the Arabian American Oil Company (ARAMCO) prospected for oil in the deserts of Arabia. This peninsula had long been dominated by fractious Arab tribes, but during the early twentieth century a remarkable military leader named

Abdul Aziz ibn Saud took over much of Arabia. Having subdued most of the tribes in central and eastern Arabia, Ibn Saud managed to reclaim Mecca and Medina from the Hashemites in 1925. After rounding off his conquests with Asir, Ibn Saud proclaimed the Kingdom of Saudi Arabia in 1932. His country remained poor until ARAMCO struck oil, and it was only after World War II that Saudi Arabia evolved into an economic giant.

Yemen remained a separate state under a hereditary dynasty of Zaydi Shi'ite imams (religious leaders), mountainous and colorful but dominated by nomads and lacking schools, health care, industry, and oil. To the south of Yemen, where the Red and Arabian Seas meet, lay the British colony of Aden. Many of the tribal shaikhs near the coasts of the Arabian Sea and the Gulf had treaties that placed them under British protection. Oman, which in previous centuries had been an autonomous actor in regional affairs, also became a British protectorate, although British control was minimal. Oil was found in some of these areas, too, but no significant amounts were extracted or sold until the 1960s.

□ The Retreat of Western Imperialism

With the spread of education and communications, nationalism grew among the Arabic-speaking peoples under British and French control. This feeling was expressed either as Arab nationalism, the idea that all people who speak Arabic should be united in one nation-state, or as a more localized patriotism. As more Arabs attended schools and colleges and as a growing number of newspapers fueled their desire for independence and self-rule, they openly attacked the British and French mandates in the Fertile Crescent and the prolonged British domination over Egypt and Sudan. Indeed, the British themselves wanted to prepare Iraqis, Transjordanians and Palestinians, Syrians and Lebanese, Egyptians and Sudanese for self-rule and eventual independence, but as separate countries.

Leading the Arabs' march to independence was the Kingdom of Iraq. Although its people were less well-educated than the Syrians or Egyptians, the British were prepared to certify that Iraq was ready for sovereign statehood. In 1932 Iraq achieved formal independence and was admitted to the League of Nations. The next year King Faisal I died suddenly and was succeeded by his minor son. A rebellion by the Assyrians (Nestorian Christians) was suppressed by Iraqi troops, who massacred many Christian villagers. Other ethnic minorities (mainly non-Arab Kurds and Turcomans living in the north, who made up one-fifth of Iraq's population, but also Jews in Baghdad) were barred from power. Although most of Iraq's Arab Muslims were Shi'ites, they too suffered from discrimination.

Iraq's parliament was dominated by landowning tribal leaders, and certain aristocratic families monopolized cabinet posts. A series of military coups brought various army officers to power, culminating in an Arab nationalist government that was toppled by a British military intervention in 1941, leaving a legacy of anti-Western hostility that would resurface under such Iraqi leaders as Abdel Karim Qasem in 1958–1963 and Saddam Hussein since 1979.

The brother of Iraq's King Faisal I, Abdullah, managed to unite Transjordan, which became formally independent in 1946. Its most viable institution, the Arab Legion, helped the British suppress riots in Palestine west of the Jordan River, the area afflicted by the Jewish-Arab struggle for the "twice-promised land."

The Zionist movement had hoped to persuade enough Jews to immigrate to Palestine to form a Jewish state. During the 1920s, however, few came, and the Arab majority relaxed. But in 1929 a quarrel at the Western Wall sparked large-scale rioting in which many Arabs and Jews were killed or injured. The British government sent out an investigating commission, which reported that sales of Arab-owned lands to Jewish settlers were causing many Palestinian Arab peasants to lose their tenancy rights and hence their livelihoods. The Jewish settlers blamed Arab violence for the riots and claimed they had brought prosperity to Palestine.

The Nazi takeover in Germany speeded up Jewish immigration in the 1930s, fueling Arab fears that they would soon become a minority. In 1936 the Arab political parties, hitherto divided on family and religious lines, united as the Arab Higher Committee, which organized a general strike against the mandate. A three-year civil war ensued. A British commission of inquiry visited Palestine in 1937 and recommended the establishment of a separate enclave in part of Palestine for Jewish immigration and settlement. Small though the proposed enclave was, Palestine's Arabs, backed by newly independent Iraq and Egypt, opposed the partition, as did a meeting of the Zionist Congress, albeit for different reasons. The British pared it down further and then, with growing fears of war with Germany, issued the May 1939 White Paper, which severely limited Jewish immigration and land purchases in Palestine. The Zionists felt betrayed, for Europe's Jews were in mortal peril and no other country would admit them. For their part, Arab nationalists did not trust British promises of Palestinian independence, even though Arabs constituted a majority in Palestine, and argued that Zionism was another manifestation of Western imperialism.

The Arabs of Syria and Lebanon hated France's mandates in Syria and Lebanon. Only the Maronites wanted the French presence; most other Christians and virtually all Muslims in Syria wanted Arab unity and independence. During an interval when a leftist government held power in Paris, the French did offer independence, only to retract it when a more conservative cabinet took over. France's sudden defeat by Nazi Germany in 1940 enabled Britain and the United States to pressure the anti-Nazi Free French to recognize the independence of Syria and Lebanon in 1943, but it was another three years before the last French troops left.

At the end of World War II, Egypt was the most populous Arab state. It had the most newspapers and magazines, the leading universities, the largest cinema and record companies, and the most influential writers. Yet it lagged behind the other Arab countries in gaining independence. While the Wafd and other political parties vied for popular support in parliamentary elections, King Fu'ad I used his influence with the *ulama,* the army, and sometimes the village leaders to increase his own power. Both contended with the continued British occupation of Egypt and Sudan. Only in 1936 did Britain and Egypt come to terms because both feared rising Italian power in Libya and Ethiopia, countries that bordered on Egypt and Sudan. The British agreed to limit their forces to the Suez Canal zone, Cairo, and Alexandria, reducing them to 10,000 men in peacetime, but Sudan remained under the Anglo-Egyptian condominium.

Egypt's King Fu'ad died in 1936 and was succeeded by his teenaged son, Farouk, who was initially adored by the Egyptian people. But he lost popular support in 1942 when the British made him appoint a cabinet that would back their presence in Egypt during World War II. Egypt was occupied by even more British imperial troops during World War II than during World War I, as Fascist Italy and Nazi Germany invaded from Libya, and the Suez Canal had to be defended at all costs. Antidemocratic movements, such as the pro-Fascist Young Egypt, the Communists, and the Muslim Brothers vied for Egyptian support. Parliamentary parties such as the Wafd seemed outdated. As soon as the war ended, Egyptians demanded that British troops leave their country, including Suez and Sudan.

☐ The Struggle Between Arab Nationalism and Political Zionism

The idea of Arab unity won growing support in the Fertile Crescent, Egypt, and the Arabian Peninsula during World War II. Arabs had decried the division of the Fertile Crescent into British and French mandates and hoped that independence would soon lead to unification. Nuri al-Said, Iraq's prime minister, proposed a union of Syria, Lebanon, Transjordan, and Palestine with his own country. But Kings Farouk of Egypt and Ibn Saud of Saudi Arabia also wanted to lead the Arabs. Egypt, therefore, called for a looser organization for all sovereign Arab states. The Arabs accepted the latter alternative, and the Arab League came into being in 1945, with its headquarters in Cairo and an Egyptian as its secretary-general. The Arab countries also joined the United Nations that same year. Although Arab leaders still advocated uniting their countries, most of whose borders had been drawn by Western imperialism, their governments went their separate ways.

The issue that seemed to unite all Arabs was Palestine. Europe's Jews, decimated by the Nazi *Shoah* (Holocaust), sought a safe haven, but Palestine's Arab majority feared a flood of refugees who would demand statehood

at their expense. As the British continued to enforce the immigration restrictions in their 1939 White Paper, some Jews resorted to terrorism. The
British government became ever more hostile to Zionism and to Jewish
settlement, and fighting intensified among Jews, Arabs, and British troops.

In 1947 Britain announced that it could no longer govern its mandate
and submitted the Palestine issue to the United Nations. The UN General
Assembly set up a special committee, which went to Palestine to look into
the problem and recommended that its lands be divided into seven parts,
three for the Jews and three for the Arabs, leaving Jerusalem and Bethlehem as a separate area under the control of the United Nations. The Arab
states opposed this plan, which awarded more than half the territory to the
Jews, who had only a third of the population and owned less than 10 percent of the land. More than two-thirds of the General Assembly voted for
the proposal, however, and UN Resolution 181 was approved.

Despite threats by Egypt, Iraq, and the other Arab states to intervene
militarily against partition, British troops prepared to pull out of Palestine,
and the UN debated how to restore order. On May 14, 1948, when the
British left Jerusalem, the Jewish Agency met in Tel Aviv to declare the independent State of Israel within the lands that they controlled. The United
States and the USSR recognized the Jewish state, even as the Arab states
sent their armies to destroy it.

Israel's creation was a revolutionary event for both Jews and Arabs. No
Jewish state had existed for millennia; now one existed as an enclave in an
overwhelmingly Arab region. The armies of Egypt, Iraq, Syria, Lebanon,
and Transjordan failed to take Palestine and often ended up working against
one another. Most Palestinian Arabs fled to the neighboring states, driven
either by the fatuous hope that the Arab armies would bring them back or
by the realistic fear that the Israelis would drive them out. The result was
the creation of more than 500,000 Arab refugees, who were placed in
camps in those areas of Palestine—the West Bank and the Gaza Strip—not
captured by the Israelis or in the neighboring countries, mainly Syria,
Lebanon, and Jordan. These Palestinian refugees refused assimilation into
the Arab countries and demanded the right to return to their homes. Israel
offered to readmit a small number of these refugees but only as part of a
general peace settlement. The Arab states signed separate armistice agreements with Israel in 1949 but refused to recognize the Jewish state. Israel
declared that all Jews had the right to come and to become citizens, took
in survivors of the *Shoah,* and gave refuge to Jews from Arab lands. The
evolution of this conflict is further explored in Chapters 4, 5, and 6.

□ Political Changes in the Arab Countries

The defeat of the Arab armies in the 1948–1949 Palestine war was one
of the causes of the army coups that afflicted some Arab countries, starting

in 1949 with three successive revolts in Syria. Arab monarchies were toppled in Egypt in 1952, Iraq in 1958, Yemen in 1962, and Libya in 1969. The demand for greater popular participation and for a fairer distribution of each country's resources probably did more to cause these revolutions than the Palestinian problem, but the general trend was toward government by an officer corps coming from middle-class (as opposed to landowning) backgrounds and committed to social reform. The presence of Palestinian refugees reminded Arabs in many countries of their old regimes' failure to defend them against Zionism and imperialism. The Palestinians themselves, although lacking the economic advantages and political rights of their Arab hosts, became increasingly educated and politicized. They often called on the Arab governments to restore their rights by fighting Israel.

Revolutionary Arab regimes espoused socialism, a neutral policy somewhere between the communism of the USSR and the capitalism of the West, and the unification of all Arabs. A leading proponent of these policies was Egyptian president Gamal Abdel Nasser. Nasser had masterminded the officers' conspiracy that overthrew the corrupt monarchy of King Farouk in 1952, but only gradually did he emerge as the Arabs' champion. He negotiated a new pact with Britain, signed in 1954, securing Britain's evacuation of the Suez Canal zone, and also renounced Egypt's claims to Sudan, allowing that Anglo-Egyptian condominium to win independence in 1956.

Nasser resisted Western efforts to draw him into an anti-Communist alliance in 1955 but agreed instead to buy $200 million worth of arms from the Soviet bloc, a move that aroused Western fears of Communist gains in the Arab world. The U.S. government, working with Britain and the World Bank, offered to lend Egypt the money to build a new dam near Aswan that would control the Nile floodwaters and greatly increase the country's farmland and hydroelectric generating capacity, but it later retracted its offer in order to punish Nasser for his pro-Communist policies. Nasser responded in July 1956 by nationalizing the Suez Canal Company. The British and French governments denounced the seizure and conspired with Israel to attack Egypt. Although the attackers retook the canal, they were opposed by nearly every UN member state. Ultimately, they had to withdraw, and Nasser emerged as a champion among the Arabs for standing up to the West.

Early in 1958, Egypt acceded to Syria's request to form an organic union of the two countries, which they called the United Arab Republic (UAR). Many nationalists hoped that other Arab states would join the new political entity. Instead, Jordan and Iraq formed their own federation, which soon foundered when a coup overthrew the Iraqi monarchy. A civil war broke out in Lebanon between Arab nationalists (mainly Muslim) who sought closer ties with the UAR and Lebanese particularists (mainly Christian) who wanted independence from the Arabs. The U.S. government occupied Lebanon in July 1958 and helped restore peace.

The general trend seemed to be toward pan-Arabism, as Yemen feder-
ated with the UAR, the army seized power in Sudan, and even Saudi Arabia replaced a weak king with a brother who was thought to favor Nasser.
Not only was Arab unity strong in the late 1950s, but many governments
followed Nasser's lead in redistributing large estates to hitherto landless
peasants, nationalizing companies owned by foreign or local capitalists,
and expanding public education and welfare institutions. The watchword
of the day was "Arab socialism." The Arabs hoped to regain their old glory
by uniting, avoiding the Cold War power blocs, modernizing, and creating
a just society.

Like the rest of the Arab world, North Africa was also becoming independent. Libya, ruled by Italy up to World War II, was the first to gain
independence in 1951. France terminated its protectorates over both
Tunisia and Morocco in 1956, but in Algeria an eight-year nationalist rebellion began in 1954. More than 1 million European settlers wanted to
keep Algeria a part of France, but the French state as a whole grew tired of
fighting rearguard colonial wars, and President Charles de Gaulle granted
independence to Algeria in 1962. Its new leaders were quick to declare
their support of Nasser and Arab socialism.

□ The Northern Tier

As stated in the Introduction, not all Middle Eastern states are Arab.
Turkey and Iran, although predominantly Muslim, are proud of their distinctive cultures and heritages. Both successfully stood up to the British and
kept their independence after World War I. Both bordered on the USSR and
had to come to terms with it. Although the Soviets helped Turkey to resist
the Greeks and the British during the rise of Mustafa Kemal Atatürk in the
1920s, the Turks resumed the Ottoman policy of opposing Russian imperialism. Ismet İnönü, who succeeded Atatürk as president in 1938, kept
Turkey out of World War II and prevented the Allies from using the straits
to supply the USSR. Stalin's postwar demand to station Soviet troops on
the Bosporus and the Dardanelles Straits led the United States to back
Turkey in the 1947 Truman Doctrine, the United States' first peacetime
commitment to aid a country in the Eastern Hemisphere.

By 1952 Turkey had joined the North Atlantic Treaty Organization
(NATO) and had committed troops to defending South Korea against the
Communists. İnönü's government even allowed a rival political party to
form and then to oust it from power in 1950. Turkey has continued to industrialize its economy and modernize its society, but its recent history has
been marked by military coups and challenges from militant Marxists,
Muslims, and Kurdish separatists. Turkey remains a bridge between the

West and the Middle East and has become a link to the former Soviet republics of Azerbaijan and central Asia.

Iran also had to develop a policy toward the USSR. Although the two countries had signed a pact in 1923 that authorized the Soviets to enter Iran whenever it was occupied by troops hostile to the USSR, Reza Shah's government sought to limit the Soviet Union's influence. In the 1930s, Iran drew close to Nazi Germany, whose doctrines of Aryan supremacy appealed to local pride and offered a means to fight Anglo-Russian control. But when the Nazis invaded the USSR in 1941, the Soviet and British governments demanded the expulsion of German advisers from Iran and seized control of the Trans-Iranian Railway to ship Western munitions to the beleaguered Soviets. Reza abdicated in favor of his son Mohammad and went into exile.

At the war's end, British troops left Iran, but the Soviets tried to set up puppet regimes in Kurdistan and Azerbaijan. It took a general UN condemnation, U.S. threats, and clever Iranian diplomacy to make the Soviet army withdraw. Britain still controlled Iran's oil, however, and in 1951 a nationalist government headed by Mohammad Mosaddeq took over the Anglo-Iranian Oil Company. Iran's nationalists were elated, but the Western countries supported Britain by refusing to buy any oil from Iran. In 1953 an army coup, engineered in part by British and U.S. intelligence agencies, overthrew Mosaddeq's government. The shah, who had fled the country during the turmoil, was restored to power by the army. He began a policy of concentrating control in his own hands at the expense of Iran's landowners, merchants, and *ulama*. He also signed an anti-Communist alliance with Turkey, Pakistan, Britain, and Iraq. Britain and the United States saw Iran, Turkey, and Pakistan as a bulwark against a possible Soviet drive toward the oil-rich Gulf. The West sold vast quantities of weapons to these countries, but skeptics wondered whether those arms would just be used to keep their regimes in power.

□ The Intensification of the Arab–Israeli Conflict

In the late 1950s and early 1960s, Israel's conflict with its Arab neighbors seemed to die down as Arab states tried to unite and leaders struggled for power. The United Arab Republic collapsed when Syria broke away in 1961. A popular nationalist movement, the Ba'th Party, committed to both Arab unification and socialism, seized power successively in Iraq and Syria early in 1963. The Ba'th tried to form a new Arab union with Egypt, but the talks quickly failed. Soon Iraq and Syria were arguing with each other. An army coup had ousted the Yemeni monarchy in 1962, but the new republican regime needed Egyptian military aid and troops to stay in power. Saudi Arabia began backing tribes loyal to the ousted imam, leading to a draining civil war in Yemen.

What brought the Arabs back together was Israel's completion of a large-scale development scheme that took quantities of water from the Jordan River to irrigate new agricultural lands within the Jewish state. Early in 1964, Nasser invited the other Arab heads of state to Cairo to discuss ways of countering the Israeli scheme, which would deprive Jordan and other Arab states of fresh water needed for their irrigation projects. The Arabs agreed to prepare for future action against Israel and formed the Palestine Liberation Organization (PLO) to unite the Palestinian Arabs politically. Meanwhile, Fatah, led by a Palestinian engineer named Yasser Arafat, launched commando raids inside Israel. Although abetted by Syria, these attacks tended to come from the West Bank, which was controlled by Jordan. Israel's army, hoping to deter these raids, counterattacked against West Bank villages late in 1966, although many Israelis wanted to punish Syria.

An aerial dogfight broke out between Israel and Syria in April 1967. The USSR convinced Egypt that Israeli troops were massing for an attack on Syria. Nasser, anxious to prove that Egypt remained the champion of Arab nationalism, ordered the UN to withdraw its peacekeeping forces, which had been patrolling the Sinai and the Egyptian-Israeli border since the 1956 war. As Israel mobilized its reserves, Egypt declared a blockade against Israeli shipping in the Gulf of Aqaba. The Arab governments, their press and radio stations, and their people all threatened to destroy Israel and restore the Palestinians to their homes.

Although many in the United States and Western Europe supported Israel, their governments hoped to avoid a war by taking the issue to the UN. The Israelis, fearing an Arab offensive, decided to launch a preemptive strike. On June 5, 1967, Israeli fighter planes attacked Egypt's military airfields and wiped out most of the Egyptian air force. Before the Arabs could strike back, the Israelis bombed the other Arab air forces. They invaded the Egyptian Sinai, the Jordanian-ruled sector of Jerusalem and the West Bank, and finally Syria's Golan Heights. In six days, using its superior technology, organization, and mastery of the air, Israel defeated Egypt, Syria, and Jordan, tripling the area under its control.

Although the Arab states agreed to UN-mediated cease-fires, they refused to make peace. At a summit held in Khartoum, Sudan, the Arab leaders agreed not to negotiate with Israel, but to rearm and regain their lost lands by force. The PLO tried unsuccessfully to mobilize the Palestinians of the Gaza Strip and the West Bank, numbering more than 1 million people under Israeli military rule, to rebel. After five months of debate, the UN Security Council unanimously passed Resolution 242, which called on Israel to withdraw from lands occupied in the recent war but also ordered all countries to recognize the right of "every state in the area" to exist "within secure and recognized boundaries." Israel, Egypt, Jordan, and Syria, as UN members, were all bound under the UN Charter to accept Security Council resolutions, but each made its own interpretation of this one, to which all countries have paid lip service since 1967. Resolution 242 made no mention of the Palestinians, who felt that neither the major powers nor the Arab governments really cared about their interests.

After 1967, the PLO under Arafat's leadership became the umbrella organization for the Palestinians. Many became guerrillas and resorted to acts of violence against not only Israel but also any Arab government that worked closely with the West, notably Jordan and Lebanon. Palestinian guerrilla groups seemed to stand up to Israel more effectively than had the armies of Egypt, Syria, and Jordan in 1967. Israeli-inspired propaganda attacks against Arab terrorism caused Arab public opinion to back the PLO.

It was partly to counter Palestinian claims to military leadership that Nasser launched his 1969 War of Attrition against Israel's troops in the Sinai. Israel's counterattacks obliged Egypt to turn to the USSR for more military aid, and soon there were aerial dogfights over the Suez Canal. U.S. secretary of state William Rogers proposed a peace plan that would halt the War of Attrition and set up indirect talks to bring Egypt and Israel to a peace settlement based on Resolution 242. Nasser accepted the Rogers Peace Plan but indirectly sabotaged it by moving Soviet missiles up to positions near the Suez Canal. Meanwhile, Palestinian guerrillas threatened to take over Jordan, but the Jordanian army, loyal to King Hussein, crushed them. Nasser's efforts to restore peace among the Arabs contributed to his fatal heart attack on September 28, 1970. His funeral in Cairo led to demonstrations of grief all over the Arab world because of his heroic stand against Western imperialism. Nasser's successor, Anwar al-Sadat, vowed to continue the fallen leader's policies of Arab unification, opposition to Israel, nonalignment, purchases of Communist arms, and socialism. Soon, however, Sadat began liberalizing Egypt's economy and society and ordered most Soviet advisers to leave in 1972.

The Rogers Peace Plan collapsed in 1971 as both Israel and the Arabs refused to make the needed concessions. Sadat often threatened to renew the war against Israel if it did not withdraw from the Sinai and recognize Palestinian political rights. He also tried to cement a union with Syria, Libya, and Sudan. Neither his threats nor his union scheme worked. Palestinian commando groups carried out terrorist actions against civilian Israelis and foreigners, hoping to convince Israel and its backers that the Arab lands captured in 1967 were not worth keeping. But Israel believed that it had to retain the territories until the Arabs were willing to negotiate for peace. As the Arabs quarreled among themselves and Egypt distanced itself from its erstwhile Soviet backers, Israel and its backers became complacent.

Israel's complacency was shaken on October 6, 1973, when Egyptian and Syrian forces attacked Israeli positions in the Sinai and the Golan Heights. Although the Israelis were ill-prepared, they called up their reserve soldiers and brought them to the two fronts. By the second week, Israel was driving back the Syrians and Egyptians. The USSR and the United States rushed to rearm their Middle Eastern clients on a massive scale. Then the Arabs decided to unsheathe an economic weapon. In 1960 the leading nonindustrialized oil producers had created the Organization of Petroleum Exporting Countries (OPEC), which tried to limit oil supplies and set common prices. OPEC had begun to affect the world oil market in 1971, and the October 1973 war gave it a pretext to drive up prices 400 percent. The Arab members of OPEC announced that they would sell no oil to the United States and the Netherlands and would cut supplies to other oil importers until Israel withdrew from all occupied territories and recognized the Palestinians' political rights. So vital had Arab oil become to Europe and Japan that many countries promised to support the Palestinian cause to ensure winter supplies. The UN Security Council adopted Resolutions 338 and 340, calling for a cease-fire and for immediate negotiations between Israel and its Arab neighbors.

The Israelis won militarily, but as other governments turned against them, they felt that they had lost politically. U.S. secretary of state Henry Kissinger worked to disentangle the Egyptian and Israeli armies and to set up a general peace conference that met briefly in Geneva in December 1973. Kissinger began flying between Jerusalem and Cairo, dealing with Egypt's and Israel's leaders separately. Finally they agreed to separate the Israeli and Egyptian armies by creating demilitarized zones between them, and after that tensions lessened and the oil embargo ended. Kissinger engineered a similar agreement between Israel and Syria. One characteristic of both agreements was that the Arab states regained some of the lands that Israel had taken in 1967 or 1973, but both sides took steps that, it was hoped, would lead toward future peace talks.

A second agreement between Egypt and Israel in 1975, also brokered by Kissinger, led to a further Israeli pullback and to an Egyptian renunciation of force to settle the Arab-Israeli conflict. Both sides feared political deals: the Israelis might jeopardize their security by conceding too much to the Arabs; Egypt and Syria did not want other Arabs, especially the Palestinians, to view them as traitors. In 1974 the Arabs had agreed that only the PLO could speak for the Palestinians, but Israel refused to talk to what it viewed as a terrorist group. When an ultranationalist coalition, led by former terrorist Menachem Begin (who played an active role in the underground paramilitary group Irgun Zvai Leumi), won Israel's 1977 election, the country seemed to be on a collision course with the Arabs. U.S.

president Jimmy Carter wanted to join the USSR in reconvening the Geneva Conference and including Palestinian representatives in the new talks, much to Israel's dismay.

Then Egyptian president Sadat surprised the world by announcing that he would go to Jerusalem to talk peace directly with Israel's government. Although startled, Begin agreed to receive him, and a new peace process began, leading to U.S. mediation and finally to an extraordinary summit held at Camp David, with Carter as host and Sadat and Begin as chief negotiators. A tentative agreement was reached for peace between Egypt and Israel, and the three leaders signed the pact in September 1978. Diplomats ironed out the details, and the final Egyptian-Israeli peace treaty was signed in March 1979. The treaty provided for a phased Israeli withdrawal from the Sinai, full diplomatic relations between Cairo and Jerusalem, and ongoing negotiations about the status of Palestinians under Israeli occupation. The other Arab states, as well as the PLO, denounced Sadat's policy, broke diplomatic ties with Egypt, and vowed to oppose Israel.

□ The Islamic Revolution in Iran

While the West watched the Egyptian-Israeli peace talks, a revolution was brewing against the government of Mohammad Reza Shah Pahlavi, who had ruled Iran for almost thirty-seven years. The United States and most European countries had long backed the shah as a bulwark against Soviet expansionism and Arab nationalism, selling Iran billions of dollars worth of Western arms. Iran's surging income caused by the oil price hikes in 1973 drew U.S. and European investors to Tehran, where the shah proclaimed grandiose projects to develop the country. These plans, run from the top down, gave little attention to what the Iranian people wanted or needed. They stressed showcase projects instead of making basic changes in the villages where most Iranians lived or in the factories or on the farms where most Iranians worked. The shah brooked no opposition to his policies; a large intelligence bureau known by the acronym SAVAK spied on dissidents and jailed or tortured his critics.

Opposition to the shah came from nationalists who had backed Mosaddeq in 1951–1953, labor union leaders, Marxists, intellectuals, and students. None of these groups was strong enough to withstand threats of imprisonment, torture, or even death at the hands of SAVAK agents. The best-organized and most popular opposition came from Muslim leaders, in part because Iran is a Shi'ite country, and Shi'ism empowers its *ulama* to reinterpret Islamic law. One such inspiring leader was the Ayatollah Ruhollah Khomeini, who inveighed in his sermons and writings against the shah's tyranny and U.S. interference in Iranian affairs. Exiled from

Iran in 1964, Khomeini continued to stir up opposition from Iraq and later from Paris. His sermons were smuggled into Iran and passed from hand to hand; some were even read aloud in the mosques.

An attack on Khomeini in the Iranian press sparked popular demonstrations early in 1978, and government efforts to suppress them led instead to larger protests. Growing numbers of Iranians turned against the shah's government and demanded the civil liberties and human rights advocated by President Carter. Even many in the United States doubted that the regime could survive and argued for a nationalist government that would unite the Iranian people. The shah, stricken with cancer and cut off from the people, appointed a nationalist premier and left Iran in January 1979, expecting the same level of U.S. support for his troubled regime as he had received in 1953. This did not occur.

The Iranian people, elated at the shah's departure, staged demonstrations to bring back the ayatollah. In February the government let Khomeini return, the shah's army defected to the ayatollah's side, and the government turned over its power to the revolutionaries. A cabinet whose members held opinions ranging from nationalist to Marxist to ultra-Islamic temporarily took charge of Iran, and revolutionary *komiteh*s (committees) rounded up SAVAK agents and the shah's supporters, trying many and jailing and executing some of them. A popular plebiscite backed Khomeini's proposal that Iran become an Islamic republic.

The Iranian revolution was one of the turning points in modern Middle Eastern history. A government committed to rapid Westernization was toppled by a popular regime dedicated to making Islam the basis of its policies and the guide for its economy, society, and culture. The new regime promised to export its revolution throughout the Muslim world. The emirates and shaikhdoms of the Gulf, with their vast oil revenues and wide disparities between rich and poor, were vulnerable. Some had large and oppressed Shi'a populations. Iran's seizure of the U.S. Embassy and the taking of fifty-two hostages outraged Westerners, but it also empowered Muslims to criticize Washington and other Western governments viewed as hostile to Islam.

U.S. diplomatic and military efforts to secure the release of the hostages failed. Soviet troops, mindful of U.S. weakness after the Iranian revolution, occupied Afghanistan in December 1979. Military aggression seemed to be in fashion, as Iraqi president Saddam Hussein renounced a treaty he had signed with the shah's government in 1975 letting Iran share control with Iraq over the confluence of the Euphrates and Tigris Rivers, the Shatt al-Arab waterway, and proceeded to invade Iran in 1980. The Shatt al-Arab dispute was a pretext for deeper antagonisms: Iraq wanted to replace Egypt as the Arabs' leader; Iran called on Muslims everywhere, especially Shi'ites, to replace their secularized governments with Islamic republics. Iraq attacked Iran in its southwestern province, which contains most of Iran's oil and has Arab inhabitants who might have rallied to Hussein's Arab nationalism.

Iraq made huge inroads into Iran at first, but the Iranians fought back and eventually regained the captured lands and even managed to take some strategic islands near Iraq's second largest city, Basra. Neither the Shi'ite majority in Iraq nor the Arab minority in Iran rebelled against its government, but each country spent huge sums on weapons and suffered heavy losses of personnel and equipment, as well as destruction of oil refineries, homes, shops, and factories. Both sides drafted what males they could find, even foreign workers and young boys, into their armies to replenish their fallen soldiers. Both, but especially Iraq, resorted to missile attacks against the enemy's cities and the use of poison gas against their foes.

Iran soon realized that it would have to release the U.S. hostages to gain international support for its war effort. Algerian diplomats mediated the dispute and secured the release of all fifty-two hostages after 444 days in captivity. President Ronald Reagan's administration seemed to favor Iraq but sold U.S. missiles and spare parts to Iran in exchange for secret funds that could later be used to finance anti-Communist insurgents in Nicaragua. When Iran and Iraq attacked each other's oil tankers in the Gulf and then started firing on the ships of other countries, the U.S. government took to reflagging Kuwaiti tankers and using its warships to escort them. In 1988 the United States and Iran almost went to war with each other when a U.S. naval officer accidentally shot down an Iranian passenger airplane over the Gulf, but Tehran found that almost no country would support it. The UN Security Council passed a resolution calling for a cease-fire between the warring states. Iraq accepted the resolution, and in July 1988 Iran also did so.

But the Iranian revolution had many repercussions beyond the war with Iraq. Between 1979 and 1987, Tehran undertook to foment uprisings throughout the Muslim world, using its Islamic Republican Party to export revolutionary ideas. Iranian guerrillas set up training camps for revolutionary groups as far-ranging as the Moros of the Philippines and the Polisario rebels fighting against Moroccan control of the Western Sahara. Especially important, however, was Iran's aid to Lebanon's Shi'ites, once poor and unheeded but emerging in the 1980s as a major player in that country's civil war.

□ Lebanon: Cockpit of Middle Eastern Rivalry

Ever since independence, Lebanon had presented one face to the West: that of a democratic, highly urbane society, the "Switzerland of the Middle

East." To many of its own inhabitants, and certainly to other Arabs, however, it showed another face: one of unfair privileges enjoyed by the Christians at the expense of the Muslims (both Sunni and Shi'a) and the Druze. As more Lebanese moved to the cities, where disparities of wealth and power were obvious, and as the Muslim percentage of Lebanon's population rose relative to that of the Christians, discontent grew. Economic and social conditions improved after the 1958 civil war, but Lebanese Muslims and Palestinian refugees still resented their inferior status. Skirmishes sometimes broke out between Muslims and Christians or between Palestinians and Lebanese. Usually they were settled quietly, but in 1975 Sunni Muslim and Maronite Christian militias started fighting in earnest, the PLO soon joined in, and a major civil war began. In 1976 the Lebanese government invited Syria into the country to help suppress Muslim and Palestinian militias. Syrian troops did indeed buttress the Maronite-dominated government in 1976, but they remained in Lebanon and soon shifted to the Muslim side. Early in 1978 Israel invaded southern Lebanon, partly to keep the Syrian army away from their northern border, but withdrew after the UN stationed a buffer force in southern Lebanon.

Low-intensity conflict dragged on into the 1980s. Palestinian commandos sometimes raided northern Israel; Israeli troops bombed suspected PLO bases in Lebanese villages and even Beirut neighborhoods. In 1982 Israel launched a massive invasion of southern Lebanon, repulsed the Syrian army and PLO militias, bypassed the UN force, and even besieged Beirut. Lebanon's parliament elected a Maronite president aligned with Israel against the Palestinians and their Arab backers. When he was killed in an explosion, Israel's troops invaded Beirut. While they were there, Maronite militias broke into mainly Palestinian neighborhoods, where they killed hundreds of men, women, and children. Aghast at the massacre (which many blamed on Israel), the Western powers sent in a multinational force.

Washington hoped to persuade Syria and Israel to leave Lebanon and the various militias to hand over their arms and their powers to a reconstituted Lebanese government. Instead, the Israelis and the multinational force angered not just the Sunni Muslims and Palestinians but also Lebanon's formerly quiet Shi'ite population. Soon Lebanese Shi'ites, trained by Iranian revolutionaries, were driving trucks loaded with explosives into Western embassies, the barracks of the foreign armies, and Maronite strongholds, killing or injuring hundreds. These Shi'ite suicide squads wrought such havoc among the European, U.S., and Israeli forces that they withdrew, although Israel retained a military presence in southern Lebanon. Their success in ousting at least some foreign troops from Lebanon raised the prestige of the Iran-inspired Muslim militancy.

Photo 3.5 *In the late 1990s, a significant number of buildings in central Beirut, Lebanon, remained in a state of total disrepair, a visual reminder of the intermittent war that engulfed the country for more than two decades.*

☐ The Iraq–Kuwait Crisis and Israeli–Arab Negotiations

Iraq has long suffered from always being the number two Arab state, whether subordinate to Egypt as the Arabic cultural center or second to Saudi Arabia as the area's largest oil producer. Iraq's own potential has gone unrealized, and its war against Iran in the 1980s left it heavily indebted to the Saudis and other Arab Gulf states. Iraqis also believe that Kuwait is a creation of British imperialism, an anachronism in the modern world, a dynastic enclave that serves the interests of Western oil importers. At times Iraq has tried to annex Kuwait, hoping to enlarge its coastline and become the leading power on the Gulf. In July 1990 Iraq claimed that Kuwait was "slant-drilling" for oil beneath Iraqi territory and was demanding repayment of loans it had made to Iraq during the war against Iran. When other Arab governments failed to satisfy Iraq's claims, Saddam Hussein ordered his troops to occupy Kuwait on August 2, 1990, beginning the Gulf War.

Iraq failed to foresee that U.S. president George Bush would fiercely oppose its annexation of Kuwait. Once Arab pressure had failed to make the Iraqis withdraw, the Bush administration began an intense campaign to liberate Kuwait, initially by diplomacy, later by sending troops and matériel to Saudi Arabia in what came to be called "Operation Desert Shield."

Some in the United States feared that military involvement in the Middle East would be costly, resented by most other countries, and likely to undermine U.S. interests in the region. Economic sanctions backed by increasingly strident UN Security Council resolutions were meant to warn Iraq to remove its troops from Kuwait. Kuwaitis who escaped to other Arab lands called for military measures instead of economic sanctions. Saudi Arabia, hitherto opposed to any concentration of foreign troops in its territory, which includes the two holiest Muslim cities, became a base for a coalition of Arab and foreign forces opposed to Iraq's action, which could have menaced the Saudis.

Far from being intimidated, Hussein warned that any attempt to dislodge the Iraqis from their new province would lead to the torching of Kuwait's oilfields. Nevertheless, the U.S.-led coalition went to war against Iraq on January 16, 1991, launching "Operation Desert Storm." When six weeks of intense allied bombing did not lead to Iraq's retreat from Kuwait, the coalition forces began a ground war that succeeded, within 100 hours, in driving Iraq's forces from Kuwait. Bush then stopped the hostilities, even as the allied coalition was entering southern Iraq.

Shi'ites in the south and Kurds in the north rose in rebellion against Iraq's central government, but the help that they needed from the United States and its allies never came, and both uprisings were suppressed. Any dissident officers in the Iraqi army who might have wanted to topple their leader were killed, jailed, or driven from Iraq. The UN sanctions remained in effect, keeping Iraq from importing food or medicine for its people, but Saddam Hussein stymied the UN inspectors who could have certified destruction of his nuclear, chemical, and biological weapons. It was a hollow victory for the allied coalition.

The Bush administration did convene a peace conference, initially in Madrid and later in Washington, D.C., and Moscow, in which delegations from Israel and most of the Arab states met to talk peace. Although Israel shunned talks with the PLO, representatives from the Occupied Territories were admitted into a joint Jordanian-Palestinian delegation. While public talks dragged on, representatives of Israel and the PLO met secretly in Norway and hammered out an agreement that surprised the whole world when it was first publicized in August 1993. The public signing of a "Declaration of Principles" by Israel and the PLO in the presence of President Bill Clinton marked the start of intense negotiations, focused initially on the withdrawal of Israeli troops from Gaza and Jericho.

After many delays, Israel reached an agreement in May 1994 with Palestine's "self-governing authority" enabling Arafat to return to Gaza. Israel still controlled the supposedly autonomous Palestinians by retaining troops in Gaza and the West Bank and by barring Palestinian workers from entering Israel during times of crisis, although few jobs were available within the autonomous areas. Some frustrated Palestinians forsook the

PLO for more radical movements such as Hamas. Jordan and Israel signed a peace treaty in October 1994, and several North African and Gulf states showed readiness to enter into diplomatic or commercial relations with the Jewish state. Israel reached a further agreement with the PLO in September 1995, providing for Israeli troop withdrawals from major West Bank population centers, but Jerusalem's status was left for future negotiations, and most Palestinian lands remained under Israel's control. Prime Minister Yitzhak Rabin was assassinated by an Israeli who believed that his government had already given up too much to the Arabs. A new government, headed by Benjamin Netanyahu, was elected in May 1996 and stepped up Jewish settlements and repressive policies against Palestinians. Only intense U.S. pressure made Netanyahu give up part of Hebron in 1997 and turn over other occupied lands in 1998. Netanyahu's coalition was fragile and eventually collapsed, forcing him to call for early elections. On May 17, 1999, Netanyahu lost his bid for reelection to Labor leader Ehud Barak.

■ CONCLUSION

The peoples and the countries of the Middle East are not at peace, either with one another or, indeed, with themselves. Secular nationalism competes with Islam as the leading ideology for many Middle Eastern Arabs, Iranians, and Turks. The breakup of the Soviet Union has drawn some Middle Eastern countries into competition over the new republics of the Caucasus and central Asia. The Cold War may have ended, but Washington cannot articulate its policy goals for the Middle East. Boundaries between countries, often created by Western imperialists for their own interests, rarely reflect natural borders and are often violated by the armies of strong states preying upon their weaker neighbors. Many Middle Eastern peoples have moved into burgeoning cities, acquired years of schooling, and been exposed to radio and television propaganda, swelling their ambitions beyond what their societies actually have to offer. Young adults feel especially frustrated, a feeling often enhanced by their migration from countries of high population and little oil (such as Egypt) to others that are poor in labor but rich in oil (such as Saudi Arabia), separating them from their parents, spouses, children, and friends. Other chapters in this book will show that no other area poses so great a danger to world peace as the volatile Middle East.

■ BIBLIOGRAPHY

Abun-Nasr, Jamil M. 1987. *A History of the Maghrib in the Islamic Period.* New York: Cambridge University Press.
Cleveland, William L. 1994. *A History of the Modern Middle East.* Boulder, Colo.: Westview Press.

Fisher, Sydney Nettleton, and William Ochsenwald. 1997. *The Middle East: A History.* 5th ed. 2 vols. New York: McGraw-Hill.

Goldschmidt, Arthur, Jr. 1999. *A Concise History of the Middle East.* 6th ed. Boulder, Colo.: Westview Press.

Hodgson, Marshall G. S. 1974. *The Venture of Islam.* 3 vols. Chicago and London: Chicago University Press.

Hourani, Albert. 1991. *A History of the Arab Peoples.* Cambridge: Harvard University Press.

Issawi, Charles. 1982. *An Economic History of the Middle East and North Africa.* New York: Columbia University Press.

Julien, Charles-André. 1970. *History of North Africa from the Arab Conquest to 1830.* Trans. John Petrie, ed. C. C. Stewart. New York: Praeger.

Keddie, Nikki. 1981. *Roots of Revolution: An Interpretive History of Modern Iran.* New Haven and London: Yale University Press.

Lapidus, Ira M. 1988. *A History of Islamic Societies.* New York: Cambridge University Press.

Lewis, Bernard. 1995. *The Middle East: A Brief History of the Last 2,000 Years.* London: Weidenfeld and Nicolson.

Mansfield, Peter. 1991. *A History of the Middle East.* New York: Viking.

Perry, Glenn E. 1997. *The Middle East: Fourteen Islamic Centuries.* 3d ed. Upper Saddle River, N.J.: Prentice-Hall.

Saunders, J. J. 1965. *A History of Medieval Islam.* New York: Barnes and Noble.

Zürcher, Erik J. 1993. *Turkey: A Modern History.* London and New York: Tauris.

■ 4 ■

Middle Eastern Politics
Deborah J. Gerner and Philip A. Schrodt

Saudis Warmly Greet Iranian Leader . . . U.N. to Keep Force in Western
Sahara . . . Gunmen Kill Palestinian Official . . . Kuwait Women Get Vote
for 2003 . . . Five Algerian Soldiers Killed in Attack . . . Iraqi Dissidents
to Seek U.S. Help . . . Former Dictator Returns to Sudan . . . Hezbollah
Fire Rockets on N. Israel . . . New Leader Transforming Qatar . . . Coalition Talks Fall Apart in Turkey
—Associated Press, May 1999

Viewed from the perspective of daily headlines, politics in the Middle East
appear confused, chaotic, and often violent. When asked why they are interested in taking a course in Middle Eastern politics, students often say
they want to be able to understand the news stories they listen to or read
but don't know where to begin. This chapter focuses on the current political situation of the Arab world, Iran, Israel, and Turkey. It first describes
several general factors that influence contemporary Middle Eastern politics, such as the colonial legacy, the changing international context, and
the impact of economic development, and then reviews a variety of political institutions and ideologies that function in the region. Particular attention is given to clarifying those characteristics of Middle Eastern domestic
politics that are relatively unusual—for example, the prevalence of ruling
monarchies—from those attributes that are more common, such as close
relations between the state and the military establishment. The critically
important issue of gender, on which we will touch only briefly here, is
treated more comprehensively in Chapters 8, 9, and 10.

■ THE COLONIAL LEGACY

Domestic politics in the Middle East are influenced by a paradox: this
ancient region, with a history that dates back to the earliest years of human

settlements, has only recently been organized politically into modern states, that is, centralized political units with sovereignty over a fixed territory and population. In Chapter 3, Arthur Goldschmidt Jr. described the paths these countries took to reach the end of the twentieth century. This section briefly summarizes one of the most significant aspects of that history for understanding contemporary politics: the impact of European imperialism in the region.

The term *imperialism* refers to the establishment of political and economic control by one state or empire over a foreign territory. In the context of the Middle East, the involvement of European powers, particularly Britain and France, was highly interventionist and, from the perspective of regional history, often arbitrary. At the same time, there was considerable variation in the extent and nature of European control, both between subregions (e.g., North Africa versus the Arabian Peninsula) and also between adjacent areas within a single region (e.g., Syria versus Jordan). Finally, decisions made during the colonial era had a number of effects that persisted to this day and continued to influence the Middle East's political development well after the formal colonial systems themselves had disappeared.

In contrast to the Americas, sub-Saharan Africa, and Asia, which were subjected to colonial exploitation only after being "discovered" by Europeans, the geographical extent and the resources of the Middle East had always been known to the political powers of Europe. However, prior to the middle of the nineteenth century, widespread colonial activity by Europe was blocked by the military power of the Ottoman Empire. Consequently, when Europeans finally began to assert their authority, which occurred opportunistically as Ottoman control weakened, this was done in the context of existing European imperial systems. The pattern of a single colonizer exercising control over a large contiguous region—as the British did in North America and South Asia, or as the Spanish did in Latin America—did not occur, and so the colonial experience of states in the Middle East varied substantially across time and region.

The case of Egypt provides a good example of the political complexity of colonialism. At the beginning of the nineteenth century, Egypt was occupied by Napoleonic France. French forces were defeated by the British, who restored Ottoman control of Egypt; however, Ottoman rule was soon challenged by Mehmet (Muhammad) Ali—a soldier originally appointed by the Ottomans to administer Egypt—who began to develop Egypt as a powerful and independent state. Although they attempted to rule as monarchs, Ali's successors were unable to continue this independence, and in conjunction with construction of the Suez Canal, the country fell into deep debt to European financiers. These financial problems provided the pretext for a British invasion in 1882 and the consolidation of forty years of direct British control. In 1923, Britain granted nominal independence to Egypt but maintained the pro-British monarchy and re-served the right to station troops in the country. Egypt became a battle-ground in World War II as Germany sought to gain control of the Suez Canal; and even after the British-imposed monarchy was overthrown in 1952, Egypt was briefly invaded by Britain and France in 1956 in a final attempt to reassert their authority over the canal.

Although the details vary, the intensity and complexity of colonial in-volvement can be found in most of the major countries of the region. Al-geria was actually made an administrative part of France and won inde-pendence only through a long and costly war. British and French colonial interests competed throughout the region. Sometimes this nearly caused war between the European states, as with the Fashoda dispute in Sudan in 1898; at other times Britain and France agreed to sweeping divisions of authority, as with the Sykes-Picot Agreement in 1916 that divided up for-mer Ottoman territories into areas that became modern-day Syria, Lebanon, Iraq, Jordan, Israel, and the Palestinian territories. The Gulf re-gion was considered peripheral during most of the period—allowing Abdul Aziz ibn Saud to assemble an independent state on the Arabian Peninsula without external interference—but it became important in the 1930s with the discovery of oil, leading Britain to establish a number of small, de-pendent protectorates on the shores of the Gulf. Britain and France were responsible for most of the colonial activity in the region, but other Euro-pean states—notably Italy in Libya and Russia in Iran—also exercised substantial influence.

The complexity of these colonial interactions has left a patchwork of widely differing political circumstances. Probably the most extreme ex-ample can be found by comparing the experiences of Israel, Jordan, and Lebanon. The heavily populated parts of these countries occupy a small geographical area that, in the absence of borders, could be easily driven around by car in a day. But in the second half of the twentieth century, the experiences of the three countries could not be more different. Lebanon—in the French sphere of influence under the Sykes-Picot division—devel-oped as a confessional parliamentary democracy that attempted to balance Muslim and Christian interests while maintaining the dominant position of the latter. Modern Israel developed out of a League of Nations mandate for Palestine—itself a relic of the Ottoman Empire—that under British control was promised to the Zionist movement in the 1917 Balfour Declaration. Jordan was forged from another area under British control but politically constituted as an Arab monarchy. As the twentieth century draws to a close, still another political entity—some form of Palestinian state or au-tonomous region—is emerging between Israel and Jordan. Three or four very different states have come out of an area that for most of its history had been quite similar in culture and resources.

As this example shows, the colonial experience, although relatively short-lived in the context of the whole of the history of the Middle East, has been critically important in determining the political circumstances of today. The current distinctions between the North African states of Morocco, Algeria, Libya, and Egypt reflect the fact they were, respectively, under Arab, French, Italian, and British control during the early twentieth century. When British prestige in the Gulf waned, it was smoothly replaced with U.S. influence, whereas the Algerian political system was strongly influenced by the bloody war for independence from France. A few states in the region—Morocco, Turkey, Saudi Arabia, and Oman—escaped direct European control almost entirely (although they were still profoundly affected by the threat of this control), whereas others—Djibouti, for instance, or the Western Sahara, which will hold a referendum on independence in 2000—were among the last areas in the world to achieve political sovereignty. In many cases the boundaries imposed by European powers had little correspondence to the distribution of ethnic groups on the ground—most notably in the division of the Kurdish region between Turkey, Iraq, and Iran—or created states whose legitimacy could be called into question, as with Iraq's claims on Kuwait or Syria's claims on Lebanon. The colonial empires are gone, yet their effects not only linger but have substantial influence.

■ A CHANGING INTERNATIONAL CONTEXT

Following European decolonization during the 1940s, 1950s, and 1960s, the foreign affairs of the Middle East have been dominated by two major conflicts: the Cold War and the Arab-Israeli dispute. At the beginning of a new century, the first of these has disappeared, and the second may be approaching some form of resolution. Both conflicts and their termination have implications for the region's domestic politics.

The end of the Cold War and the dissolution of the Soviet Union has had profound effects on Soviet clients such as Syria, Iraq, Libya, and the former People's Democratic Republic of Yemen (PDR Yemen). Foreign military aid is no longer available (although Russia will still gladly *sell* arms for hard cash), nor is Russia interested in providing the preferential trade arrangements that were often used by the Soviet Union to secure alliances.

Allies of the United States face an even more difficult choice. Opposing communism was not a difficult agenda to sell to a Muslim population, although the Reagan administration's attempt to convince the Arab states that their main enemy was the Soviet Union rather than Israel was a dismal failure. In the absence of the "Communist threat," the new enemies the United States seeks to deter may be Arab, Islamic, or both. Governments that are seen as too dependent on U.S. support may find that this policy generates significant domestic opposition, as both Egypt and Saudi Arabia have learned.

One of the most dramatic consequences of this global shift can be observed in Somalia, which has been in the midst of civil war since the early 1990s. A centralized revolutionary state existed in Somalia from 1960 to 1991, but this government was almost entirely the result of outside support from colonial and later Cold War patrons. With the end of the Cold War, Somalia lost its importance to outsiders. The previously extensive military and economic assistance declined significantly, and political control devolved almost immediately to traditional clan allegiances. An attempt by the United States and the United Nations in 1992–1993 to restore a single unified government failed miserably. The violence in Somalia did subsequently subside, but it remains unclear how this highly decentralized system of governance will function in an international political and economic system that presupposes strong, sovereign governments.

In contrast to the Cold War, the Arab-Israeli conflict still simmers, but at a much lower level than in earlier years. Egypt and Jordan have officially normalized relations with Israel, and visitors can now pass freely, if not easily, among these three countries. At the time of this writing, Israel appears poised to withdraw completely from Lebanon, ending two decades of partial occupation. Syria, economically disadvantaged and deprived of Soviet support, can refuse negotiations on the Israeli-occupied Golan Heights, but it cannot force the issue militarily. With the election of Israeli prime minister Ehud Barak in May 1999 and the resumption of Israeli-Palestinian talks in August, there is now a brief history of negotiations and the beginnings of a Palestinian state. (Mary Ann Tétreault, in Chapter 5, and Simona Sharoni and Mohammed Abu-Nimer, in Chapter 6, explore this issue more fully.)

The implications of these changes for the Arab-Israeli political landscape are likely to be most profound in Israel. A common saying in Israel is that once its number one problem—survival—is solved, then it will have to confront its number two problem—the nature of the Jewish state. Thus Israelis feel serious concern about violent Jewish fundamentalist movements, the rise of ethnically defined political parties, and heated debates on the extent to which the government should legislate religious practices (Kyle and Peters, 1993; Sprinzak and Diamond, 1993; Evron, 1995). Ironically, at the time Israel is being reluctantly accepted in the Arab world, its political problems are also coming to resemble those of its neighbors.

Jordan and Egypt, and perhaps someday Lebanon and Syria, must also accommodate the transformation of Israeli-Arab relations. With the Israeli threat removed, it becomes more difficult for these states to justify politically the large militaries that absorb unemployed young males and provide patronage for political allies. At the same time, there has been little in the way of an economic "peace dividend": Israel markets its products globally, not locally, and joint economic ventures have been largely confined to tourism and a few conspicuous demonstration projects. Although the end of the Arab-Israeli conflict may bring peace to the region, it seems less likely to bring prosperity, at least initially.

In the long run—perhaps another fifty years—the situation could prove more promising. A U.S. expatriate who spent most of his life in Ramallah, a town located just north of Jerusalem in the West Bank, told us stories of the years before 1967, when he could go to Beirut for the weekend, and friends who lived in Jerusalem commuted daily to work in Amman. Those of us who have only lived in the era of a politically divided Middle East forget that the great cities of the Levant—Beirut, Damascus, Amman, Jerusalem, and Jaffa–Tel Aviv—are all within about a 50-mile circle centered on the Sea of Galilee. If appropriate roads were in place and border controls removed, each could be reached from the others in a morning's drive, much as Europeans can now move among Paris, Brussels, Bonn, and Amsterdam.

■ ECONOMIC DEVELOPMENT

Like all decolonized areas, the states of the Middle East confront the problem of economic development. This issue will be covered in detail in Chapters 7 and 8; here we point out several aspects that are most salient to domestic politics (see Richards and Waterbury, 1996, for an extensive and excellent treatment of the Middle East's political economy).

Any discussion of economics must deal separately with states that have significant oil revenues and those that do not. The oil wealth of the Organization of Petroleum Exporting Countries (OPEC) era made possible policies of almost unimaginable extravagance—such as growing wheat in the desert using desalinated water—and the subsequent decline in the price of oil to pre-1973 levels (when adjusted for inflation) leaves a series of new political problems for the petroleum-based economies. In contrast, states that have little or no oil face a fairly conventional set of development issues, similar to those of any newly industrializing country.

The drop in oil revenues has created several possible sources of domestic instability. The most obvious issue is that governments have fewer funds available to deal with potential opponents of the regime, either by co-opting them or paying for the coercive power required to suppress them. (This is further complicated in the monarchies because the line between state and private ownership is blurred and individual economic problems can have political implications.) These constraints occur when many states have had to reduce social services and subsidy programs, potentially decreasing support for the ruling elites. In a number of countries, economic restructuring programs mandated by the International Monetary Fund in the 1980s and 1990s led to "bread riots" and civil unrest.

A more subtle political change could also be under way: When oil revenues were abundantly available, most oil-rich states relied heavily on expatriate workers not only for menial labor but also for professional services such as banking, engineering, and education. Because they were foreigners, these individuals had no say in the politics of the country. As these expatriate professionals are replaced by citizens, a growing indigenous middle class will be created. If the Middle East follows the pattern of numerous other countries, this will lead to pressures for greater democratic openness. This has not yet occurred to a significant degree, but the potential is clearly present.

Outside the oil-rich states, the political problems of development differ little from those found elsewhere in the world. On average, the Middle East is neither unusually wealthy nor unusually poor, although there are extremes on either end: Turkey and Israel have achieved economic growth comparable to that of the successful Asian newly industrializing countries, whereas resource-poor Djibouti, Mauritania, Sudan, and Somalia have very limited prospects for development. International war has disrupted economic expansion in Iran, Iraq, and Kuwait; civil war has had the same effect in Lebanon and Algeria.

Arab intellectuals wonder why there aren't any "Arab tigers," rapidly growing economies on the model of Taiwan or South Korea. One explanation is that in past decades skilled businesspeople from states without oil (e.g., Egyptians, Lebanese, Palestinians) could make plenty of money as expatriate workers in the Gulf but had neither the incentive nor the power to improve these economies or those of their home countries. An excessive government focus on regional conflicts and military expenditures has also hindered the development of internationally competitive economies.

As these political issues retreat into the background and as the region confronts the joint problems of rising population and declining oil revenues, economic development is likely to become increasingly salient as a political issue.

■ INFORMAL STRUCTURES OF POWER

To fully understand the processes of Middle Eastern politics, one must look beyond the formal structures of governance—kings, parliaments, and prime ministers—that are discussed below. Of particular importance are the informal structures of family and social networks: the average citizen in the Middle East, whether Arab, Israeli, Turk, or Persian, finds these far more important in influencing political loyalties than would typically be the case for a citizen of North America or Western Europe.

The word that many Western analysts have attached to these networks is *tribes*, but this term is not particularly accurate since Middle Eastern political networks frequently do not differ in language, religion, or cultural traditions, attributes that are distinguishing characteristics of a *tribe* as the word is commonly used. (When such distinctions do exist, however—for instance, with the complex religious differences within Lebanon or the linguistically distinct Kurds—they usually translate into politically important alignments.) Instead, as Laurie King-Irani discusses in Chapter 9, the networks are usually based on extended families and geographical connections to a region or village.

Within these networks, linkages are first and foremost social or economic and only then political. However, as politics becomes more local, the strength of the existing social networks increases. As a consequence, political control can change at the top of the system with relatively little change at the bottom: Egypt was under foreign political control for 2,284 years—from the defeat of the last Pharaonic dynasty by Alexander the Great in 332 B.C.E. to the overthrow of British-supported King Farouk in 1952—yet in the villages of the Nile Delta or the neighborhoods of Cairo, a distinctly Egyptian style of local politics persisted. The Ottoman Empire recognized this aspect of Middle Eastern life and guaranteed local control of local issues through its *millet* system (which placed each religious community under the jurisdiction of its own religious authorities for most legal, social, and cultural affairs). In contrast, the efforts by European colonial powers to develop centralized and uniform governance were frequently the cause of chaos.

At the same time, the old systems of social networks are less pronounced today than a century ago. Within the Middle East, rapid urbanization has disrupted and weakened centuries-old alliances based in isolated villages. Although immigrants to major cities such as Cairo, Istanbul, and Tehran are still influenced by family and village, the bonds are challenged by new loyalties and affiliations. These traditional loyalties are further eroded by the migration of many expatriate workers—often the best and brightest young people of a generation—to jobs in the Gulf, Europe, or North America, where the old ties are difficult to maintain, particularly for an immigrant's sons and daughters born in a distant land.

Consequently, the contemporary Middle East sees a mix of traditional and modern political structures. Hafez al-Assad of Syria, Saddam Hussein of Iraq, King Fahd of Saudi Arabia, and King Abdullah of Jordan still base much of their power—particularly in the military and security services—on traditional systems of loyalty based on family and village. Most of Saddam Hussein's inner circle of advisers and administrators come from his home village of Tikrit; the Jordanian monarchy's security services are dominated by desert bedouins, not the Palestinians who form the majority of the population.

In contrast, the economic elites of Beirut and Istanbul are more likely to follow a European model of social relationships, and some may, in fact, feel more comfortable in European circles than in Arab or Turkish social groups. This spills over into politics: these countries have large, European style bureaucracies, flexible political patronage systems, and substantial (if interrupted) periods of parliamentary government.

However, the two systems can coexist. Within Israel, the Labor Party, which tends to attract individuals whose parents or grandparents immigrated to Israel from Europe, has a European-style system of flexible loyalties based on ideology. In contrast, the Shas Party, which emerged in the 1990s as a major player in Israeli politics, attracts voters from the ethnically Arab Jewish communities who immigrated from Morocco, Yemen, and Iraq. Shas places far greater importance on traditional relationships and political guidance from conservative rabbinical leaders. This tension between various styles of political organization is likely to be a pervasive factor in Middle Eastern politics for the foreseeable future.

■ THE MYTH OF POLITICAL INSTABILITY

Early on, any discussion of the domestic politics of the Middle East that is directed to a Western audience must confront one of the most pervasive—but at the same time most conspicuously untrue—myths about the region: that governments in the Middle East are precarious and extremely changeable. Nothing could be further from the truth. In the past several decades, many have been extraordinarily stable. Indeed, a meeting of Arab leaders held today would feature a number of the same men who were in power in 1970: Muammar Qaddafi of Libya, Syria's Hafez al-Assad, Oman's Sultan Qaboos, Shaikh Zayed of the United Arab Emirates (UAE), and Palestinian leader Yasser Arafat. Until his death from cancer in 1999, King Hussein of Jordan was the longest-ruling leader in the region, having served as king for nearly five decades. King Hassan II, who also died in 1999, had governed Morocco since 1961. Djibouti has had only two leaders since gaining independence in 1977: Hassan Gouled Aptidon, president until April 1999, and his nephew Isma'il Omar Guelleh, who was elected to succeed him. Saudi Arabia's King Fahd, Jabir al-Sabah of Kuwait, and Iraq's Saddam Hussein have each been in power for more than twenty years. A meeting of today's European leaders, in contrast, would have no individuals in common with a similar gathering held in 1970.

In addition, both Egypt and Saudi Arabia have handled transfers of power smoothly under the difficult conditions of assassination; Jordan, Oman, and Tunisia have replaced, more or less gracefully, leaders whose mental or physical condition had deteriorated. The political system established in Turkey in the 1920s has survived to the present day and has been far more stable than the governments of European Mediterranean states such as Spain, Italy, Yugoslavia, and Greece during the same seventy-year period, notwithstanding three coups by the Turkish military. Significant revolutionary transformations have occurred—conspicuously, in Iraq (1958), Libya (1969), and Iran (1979) with the overthrow of Western-imposed monarchies—but even these changes were arguably no more dramatic than those that occurred in Eastern Europe and the Soviet Union in the late 1980s and early 1990s. Furthermore, the resulting governments have been substantially more stable than those in most of the successor states of the former Soviet Union.

To be sure, there are military interventions, irregular transfers of power, and internal political intrigues in the Middle East, but no more so than in Latin America or Southeast Asia and less so than in much of Africa. The Middle East probably did experience an unusual number of political upheavals in the years immediately following decolonization (as did almost every other newly independent region), but the norm since the mid-1960s has been continuity.

Although the political systems in the Middle East have generally been very stable since the early 1970s, the region is currently facing a series of challenges brought on by political and economic changes in the global system. These occur at the same time that a number of the leaders in the region are growing old and facing health problems, most notably King Fahd of Saudi Arabia, al-Assad of Syria, and Palestinian leader Yasser Arafat. This natural aging of the postcolonial leadership—combined with a very large population of adolescents who have been exposed to the economic, political, and cultural currents of the global political economy—could lead to substantial changes in the coming decades (a prospect welcomed by some and feared by others). Indeed, this has already begun to occur: Jordan's new king, Abdullah, Bahrain's Emir Hamad ibn Isa al-Khalifah, and King Mohammed VI of Morocco are significantly younger than their fellow monarchs, and Israel's political leadership is also shifting to a younger generation.

■ PROSPECTS FOR DEMOCRATIZATION

With the virtual demise of Marxist-Leninist governments around the world, liberal democracy, characterized by the regular, open, honest electoral competition of political parties and protection of rights to organize politically, has become the dominant ideological basis for legitimizing political power. (The one possible competitor, the "Confucian capitalist" model of Asia, has no intrinsic appeal or cultural support in the Middle East.) The term *liberal democracy* reflects the union of two related processes: political liberalization and political democratization. Rex Brynen, Bahgat Korany, and Paul Noble explain:

> *Political liberalization* involves the expansion of public space through the recognition and protection of civil and political liberties, particularly those bearing upon the ability of citizens to engage in free political discourse and to freely organize in pursuit of common interests. *Political democratization* entails an expansion of political participation in such a way as to provide citizens with a degree of real and meaningful collective control over public policy.
>
> The distinction is an important one, since it is possible to have elements of one without the other. Political repression can be relaxed without expanding political participation. . . . Conversely, some political systems may claim widespread popular participation (for example, revolutionary regimes that empower previously marginalized groups) while restricting political freedoms (for example, repressing those deemed counterrevolutionary). (Brynen, Korany, and Noble, 1995:3–4)

In contrast to many areas of the world that have successfully adapted Western liberal democratic structures and norms to local conditions (Japan, India, and Latin America, for instance), democratization poses several problems in the Middle East. Perhaps the most fundamental challenge lies in the preexistence of many democratic—but not *liberal* democratic—institutions in the region. The successful monarchies have maintained and expanded extensive traditional consultative structures and in Jordan, Kuwait, and Morocco have even established liberal democratic institutions, albeit with highly constrained powers. The revolutionary regimes base their legitimacy on mass political party structures, even though these have deteriorated into mere shells. Consequently the Middle East, although not liberal democratic, is not totally devoid of structures for political participation either (in contrast, for instance, to the military regimes of Latin America in the 1970s). The claim of a regionally constructed "Arab democracy" has some credibility.

Second, the existing Middle Eastern models for liberal democracy all have significant flaws. The extreme secularism of Atatürk's constitution for Turkey is not acceptable in the current environment of Islamic revivalism. Lebanon's initial attempts at confessional democracy—a system that assumes religious affiliation is the primary factor in how society is organized politically and constitutionally ensures the power of various groups—led to a devastating civil war. As a non-Islamic state, and in the eyes of much of the region an illegitimate one, Israel does not appeal as a model (although ironically, long exposure to Israeli democracy may have an impact on the Palestinian development of democratic institutions).

Finally, the major liberal democratic powers have done little to encourage democracy in the region. Britain left absolute monarchies in place as it retreated. The United States has consistently tolerated undemocratic policies in its allies, including the monarchy of Saudi Arabia, the police-state of Reza Pahlavi (the shah of Iran), and the single-party rule of Egypt. France's experiment in Lebanon failed, and France has been accused of complicity in the cancellation of elections in Algeria in 1992.

Given this set of circumstances, why should one expect that democratization will even be an issue in the Middle East? At least three factors suggest that it will be. First, the creation of a literate, urbanized middle class has consistently, in a variety of cultures, led to pro-democratic political movements. Second, the most dynamic economies of the region—Turkey, Israel, and pre–civil war Lebanon—have been democratic, a fact that has not gone unnoticed. Third, many of the conditions that supported and legitimized nondemocratic regimes—including postcolonial politics, the Cold War competition, and oil wealth—are declining in importance.

The democratic transition will not be easy, however. Clearly any liberal democratic movement will need to accommodate Islam explicitly in some form. According to Arab democratic theorists, this presents few problems: many interpretations of Islamic theology are at least as sympathetic to democratic ideals as is Protestant Christianity (and are more so than the Hinduism of India, where nonetheless a thriving liberal democracy has been established). But many of the most politically powerful trends in contemporary Islam are highly conservative, appealing to traditional institutions and seeking to impose antidemocratic cultural norms (for example, regarding the role of women).

Second, most contemporary democratic theory (notably Putnam, 1993) emphasizes the importance of the institutions of "civil society" in buttressing liberal democracy. As Egyptian sociologist Saad Eddin Ibrahim explains:

> While there are a variety of ways of defining [the concept of civil society], they all revolve around *maximizing volitional, organized, collective participation in the public space between individuals and the state*. In its institutional form, "civil society" is composed of non-state actors or non-governmental organizations (NGOs), including political parties, trade unions, professional associations, community development associations, and other interest groups. Normatively, "civil society" implies values and behavioral codes of tolerating—if not accepting—others and a tacit or explicit commitment to the peaceful management of differences among

individuals and collectivities sharing the same "public space"—that is, the polity. (Ibrahim, 1995:29)

Traditional Middle Eastern society has a rich set of institutions and nonstate actors that mediate between public and private space, but they generally exist in the nondemocratic context of the mosque, family, or clan. A farmer does not need to form a cooperative when his village has been sharing in the task of the olive harvest for generations; a mother has less interest in forming a Parent-Teacher Association when her child's instructor is a cousin she has known since birth. Transplanting Western institutions of civil society into the Middle East—an objective of many North American and European development projects—is like trying to pour coffee into a cup that is already full: very little new coffee will remain in the cup, and in the meantime one has created a mess.

Finally, any democratic movement must deal with the issue of ethnic minorities, an unresolved issue in Turkey, Iran, Iraq, Lebanon, Israel, and elsewhere. In addition to indigenous religious-ethnic groups such as the Copts of Egypt and the Kurds of Turkey, Iraq, and Iran, many of the smaller states have very large populations of "foreign" workers, some of whom have been resident for generations. Establishing the rights and roles of minorities is a problem even for established democracies, as the experience of the United States, France, or Germany illustrates; it is more difficult still in states for which political independence is relatively new and liberal democracy is an experiment some already regard with skepticism.

■ THE ROLE OF THE MILITARY

Throughout the Middle East, the military has played (and continues to hold) a critical role in both the construction and the implementation of domestic policy, much more so than in the European or North American contexts; furthermore, the region is the most highly militarized in the world. Several factors, some specific to the area, others more generally applicable to newly independent states, explain why "the balance between governmental institutions of administration and coercion, on the one hand, and political structures, on the other" is tipped so strongly in favor of the former (Bill and Springborg, 1994:228).

First, neither the period of European colonization and occupation nor the political situation immediately after independence was conducive to the establishment of popular civic groups. Colonial powers, intent solely on exploiting the resources of the region, discouraged or suppressed indigenous institutions for fear that these would be used as centers of opposition to colonial rule. Many of these policies continued after independence, particularly when rulers had been installed by the departing European power or were supported through the anti-Communist agenda of the United States. When states were allied with the Soviet Union, the opposite problem occurred: most civic activity was channeled into officially recognized, state-controlled institutions, leaving little room for independent activity.

Instead of the creation of institutions of civil society, the focus of social organization was on rapid modernization and the creation of a military capable of addressing internal and external threats to the fragile regimes. In both Turkey under Mustafa Kemal Atatürk and in the Iran of the Pahlavis, authoritarian rule was justified as necessary to the economic development of the country. Elsewhere, civil and international conflicts—the Iran-Iraq War, the invasion of Kuwait, long-standing Arab-Israeli tensions, civil war in Sudan, Kurdish autonomy movements, and so on—provided a justification (some would argue an excuse) for a massive buildup of military forces throughout the region.

At present, the Middle East, with less than 4 percent of the world's population, accounts for about 10 percent of the world's armed forces, or 2.3 million soldiers in 1995 (U.S. ACDA, 1996:7). Through the 1980s and 1990s, the area accounted for an astonishing 40 percent of global arms imports ($13.8 billion in 1995), although most of these purchases are concentrated in a small number of countries: Saudi Arabia, Egypt, Israel, Kuwait, Iran, and the UAE. Saudi Arabia alone accounted for 27 percent of world arms imports in 1995 (U.S. ACDA, 1996:13). Table 4.1 illustrates the overall military expenditures of Middle Eastern countries. The budgetary priority granted to defense spending has given greater political influence to the military, even in the domestic arena, than in countries in which the military establishment accounts for a much smaller portion of central government spending.

Second, military power frequently played a key role in the origins of the ruling regimes, resulting in a significant intertwining of the political and military elites. For instance, the unification of the central Arabian territory into the state of Saudi Arabia during the first three decades of this century can be attributed almost entirely to the military prowess of Abdul Aziz ibn Saud (although Ibn Saud also deserves credit for the political consolidation of the areas he conquered). In Algeria, the eight-year war of independence left the country virtually demolished, with the National Liberation Front (FLN) the one political-military institution that was intact and able to rule. Muammar Qaddafi came to power in Libya in 1969 through a military coup, and the military remains an important source of power for the Libyan leader.

During Israel's early years, the military was clearly associated with the Mapai (which later evolved into the Labor Party); thus the political and the military were inextricably associated. In recent years, the military has become more autonomous (especially with the decline in Labor's political

Table 4.1   Military Expenditures of Middle Eastern States, 1996

Country	Total Expenditures (U.S.$ millions)	As % of GDP	Per Capita (U.S.$)	Armed Forces (thousands)
Algeria	1,764	4.0	62	123.7
Bahrain	279	5.5	476	11.0
Djibouti	20	5.2	31	8.4
Egypt	2,629	4.5	43	440.0
Iran	3,301	5.0	49	513.0
Iraq	1,224	8.3	56	382.5
Israel	9,359	12.1	1,624	175.0
Jordan	390	5.6	85	98.7
Kuwait	3,505	12.9	2,218	15.3
Lebanon	474	4.4	116	48.9
Libya	1,272	5.1	227	65.0
Mauritania	31	2.9	13	15.7
Morocco	1,539	4.3	54	194.0
Oman	1,876	15.6	955	43.5
Qatar	740	10.2	1,334	11.8
Saudi Arabia	16,999	12.8	1,030	162.5
Sudan	397	4.3	13	89.0
Syria	1,553	4.8	105	421.0
Tunisia	390	2.0	42	35.0
Turkey	6,856	3.9	110	525.0
United Arab Emirates	2,028	5.2	830	64.5
Yemen	354	3.7	24	42.0
United States	265,823	3.6	1,001	1,484.0

Source: UNDP (1998:170–171, 197).

dominance), but it is still quite powerful. The common military experience of virtually all Jewish Israeli citizens has left an indelible mark on that country's politics: high rank, preferably in a selective army unit, and combat experience in one or more of Israel's many wars are important attributes for success in the political arena.

Finally, in a number of countries, elite military units, combined with effective secret intelligence forces (in Arabic, *mukhabarat*), are essential in securing the regime against political opposition. This is certainly the case in Iraq, which has sixteen divisions of military intelligence, with varying degrees of power, each of which is responsible for a specific type of crime (Makiya, 1993:339). Admittance into the military academies requires membership in the Iraqi Ba'th Party; once accepted, military personnel are expected to show absolute commitment to Iraq and to the dictates of Saddam Hussein. In the aftermath of the Gulf War that followed Iraq's invasion of Kuwait in 1990, there have been reports of mutinies and high-level defections from the elite Republican Guard. However, the *mukhabarat* and other security services still function efficiently, which minimizes the possibility of organized opposition to the regime.

Photo 4.1   Female soldiers participate in a military parade in Algiers, Algeria.

   Often, a leader will assign relatives or long-term allies to handle crit
ical security functions. Within the Saudi military establishment, close family members hold all the significant positions: the minister of defense is
King Fahd's full brother Sultan; Sultan's deputy is his brother Turki; the
minister of the interior is another full brother; and the National Guard is
headed by Crown Prince Abdullah. Similarly, in Jordan an overwhelming
majority of the military officers are from East Bank bedouin families with
links to the royal family that go back to the earliest days of the state and
before.
   The implications of extensive military involvement in the governance
of Middle Eastern countries are profound. When a regime must rely on the
military to protect it from opposition movements, terrorism, or civil unrest,
that regime becomes vulnerable to praetorianism, a situation in which "the
civil authorities face constant threats from powerful military forces who
try to shape all kinds of political decisions while remaining formally out of
government" (Wilson, 1996:135). The repeated ultimatums given by the
Turkish military in 1997 to force the resignation of Prime Minister
Necmettin Erbakan, head of the Islamic Refah Party, illustrate how these
pressures operate. Furthermore, "once they begin to perform the functions
typically associated with parties, legislatures, and interest groups, . . . militaries render those political institutions irrelevant" (Bill and Springborg,
1994:235), which makes political liberalization all the more difficult.

■ POLITICAL IDEOLOGIES, INSTITUTIONS, AND LEADERSHIP

As is true for most newly independent countries, the basic political challenge for the Middle East in the post–World War II era has been the task of state building: the creation of governments that are legitimate, stable, and capable of acting autonomously both regionally and globally (Hudson, 1977). For a variety of reasons, this has not been easy. First, the current political structures of many Middle Eastern countries were imposed by outside powers, rather than resulting from a gradual, internally driven process. Thus the governments of these newly independent countries often lacked the political, economic, and social institutions and the widespread legitimacy that would have existed had the state-building activity begun at the grassroots level. In many countries, the presence of powerful multinational corporations (notably international petroleum companies) meant that the new states were immediately drawn into the global political economy without having the opportunity to determine the type of relationship that would be of greatest benefit to their own economy. This, too, has made the tasks of governance more difficult.

A further complication has been "the blurred boundaries between [the] state and [the] collective, supra-state identity inspired by common Arab-Islamic culture, history, and vision" (Sela, 1998:4). As a result, there is a significant tension between the utopian dream of a united pan-Arab nation with a shared history, culture, and sense of common identity stretching from the Strait of Hormuz to the Atlantic and the practical dictates of more than twenty politically sovereign Arab states. In a different world, a single Arab nation-state might have emerged. The region is at least as ethnically cohesive as India, Russia, or Indonesia and is comparable in size. However, European colonial involvement and the competing interests of both indigenous and international elites prevented this outcome. Nonetheless, some Arabs view the existing political divisions as illegitimate and problematic and reject, for instance, the separation of Lebanon from Syria. In this context, they believe it is perfectly appropriate for one state to intervene in the internal affairs of another, since all are part of the greater Arab nation. From the Arab perspective, the contemporary nation-state model may always be a shoe that doesn't fit quite right, creating a blister or sore in one place or another.

□ Sources of Governmental Legitimation

Throughout the 1950s and 1960s, Arab leaders attempted to gain legitimacy in a variety of ways and with considerable ideological innovation (e.g., Ba'thism), balancing state-based claims with the aspirations of the Arab nation as a whole. By the early 1970s, two forms of governance—

conservative monarchies and military or single-party revolutionary republics—dominated the political landscape. The traditional monarchies,
such as those of the Arabian Peninsula, were strongly patriarchal, with the
king or emir taking on the role of domineering yet benevolent father doing
what he believes is best for his family. Constitutional monarchies like
those of Jordan, Morocco, and Iran under the shah maintained the monarch
as the ultimate political authority but also established elected legislatures
with modest amounts of authority and developed significant governmental bureaucracies.

In contrast, some of the revolutionary states functioned under authoritarian personalistic leadership (most notably Libya, Syria, and Iraq),
whereas others (e.g., Algeria, Egypt, Mauritania, Tunisia, and PDR
Yemen) relied on the strength of a dominant political ideology, as expressed through a single political party, to provide support and legitimacy
for the state leadership. The distinctions between these models should not
be overstated, however; in the Middle Eastern context there are a variety
of ways in which they overlap (see Anderson, 1991). Lebanon stands out
as the one Arab country that had neither a king nor revolutionary leadership in the twentieth century. Its creation as an explicitly Christian-dominated Arab state, codified in the 1943 National Pact, made it unique.

Turkey, Iran, and Israel do not fit neatly into either a monarchical or
a revolutionary model. Yet they reflect the same pressures of political development and the struggles for governmental legitimacy that have influenced the entire region. The governments of both Turkey and Israel are
products of late-nineteenth-century and early-twentieth-century liberal
European ideologies such as nationalism that were superimposed onto a
background of more traditional societies. In the creation of their political

structures, both countries were inspired by Western-style political
modernization approaches (in the
case of Turkey, due to its proximity to Europe; in Israel, as a consequence of its initial origins as a diaspora nationalist movement) rather
than by the family-oriented, personalistic style of rule present in
much of the region. Consequently,
the Israeli and Turkish regimes are
based on secular and formally democratic norms—although without

*Photo 4.2 Female guards hold back the
crowds at a state rally in Tripoli, Libya.
The large posters picture Qaddafi.*

© Thomas Hartwell

Photo 4.3 Posters of Saddam Hussein are ubiquitous throughout Baghdad, Iraq. The woman is carrying loaves of bread on her head.

the political integration of ethnic or religious minorities—and accept the principle of public accountability for the political leadership. By the late 1990s, however, both countries were dealing with substantial challenges from religious fundamentalists seeking to radically redefine the role of religion within these states, as well as to challenge their liberal democratic nature.

□ Political Islam

The political patterns established in the initial years of independence continue to exist today, although with some modifications in response to pressures for increased political liberalization (Norton, 1995). At the same time, in recent decades a new model—the Islamic republic—has mounted an increasingly significant challenge to the secular, nationalist ideologies used to legitimize both existing regimes and opposition movements in the revolutionary states. This should not surprise us, for it mirrors two more globally general patterns. First, it is common for people who see their world changing, feel that the values they hold dear are threatened, and believe the government is not responsive to their concerns to turn to religion as a source of tradition and stability. Religious expression thus becomes a way to articulate frustration with the existing political structures. For instance, the twentieth-century founder of the Muslim Brotherhood, Hassan al-Banna (1906–1948), argued that the colonial domination of the region in the nineteenth and twentieth centuries was a direct result of the declining importance of Islam in the lives of ordinary people; a return to Islam would allow for an improved political situation. Second, individuals often focus on the political dimensions of religion when they perceive themselves as oppressed by the existing secular government. In the Middle East, there are a number of countries with "brutal and all-pervasive internal security structures" that create an atmosphere conducive to Islamic opposition movements (Bulliet, 1999:192).

Both elements were present in Iran under the rule of the Pahlavi leader Mohammed Reza Shah. The shah combined extreme repression of opponents and claims of a historical right to rule with strongly Western-oriented modernization moves such as the White Revolution. A few years before the

Iranian revolution that led to the establishment of the Islamic Republic, the shah held an incredibly expensive celebration linking his rule to that of the ancient Persian empire. This was regarded with great skepticism by the majority of the Iranian population and, in retrospect, illustrated the fragility of the shah's position. Unlike the Turkish and Israeli systems, the Iranian model ultimately proved unstable.

Although the first and most successful contemporary implementation of political Islam occurred at the edge of the Arab world, in Iran, the Islamic model has subsequently been applied in Sudan and Mauritania; presents a major challenge in Algeria; and has influenced political dynamics across the entire region, including Egypt and previously Christian-dominated Lebanon. Islam's grounding in the impressive history of the region; its emphasis on the socioeconomic equity and justice promised but not achieved by the nationalist revolutionary ideologies; its comprehensive belief system, which gives guidance on virtually all aspects of life; and its extensive critique of Western goals and values are all crucial to understanding Islam's success as an instrument of political action.

□ A Framework for Grouping Middle Eastern Countries

As suggested above, governments in the Middle East can be roughly classified into one of four groups: nationalist revolutionary republics, monarchies, Islamic states, and democracies. Nationalist revolutionary republics such as Algeria, Libya, Egypt, Syria, and Iraq are generally characterized by single-party rule with a strongly institutionalized state structure. Monarchies, whether traditional or parliamentary, include Jordan, Morocco, Saudi Arabia, and a number of small Gulf states. Iran, Mauritania, and Sudan are among the countries that have labeled themselves Islamic republics, whereas Turkey, Israel, and Lebanon are generally classified as democratic states, although each has elements that may call this into question.

Of course, any such effort at classification is a static, imperfect reflection of reality; most countries' political institutions have elements of several different systems. For instance, the Islamic Republic of Iran holds regular and contested elections, and Islam plays a significant role in several of the revolutionary republics. This categorization does, however, provide a convenient way to discuss the diversity of forms that Middle Eastern governments take (Table 4.2).

■ NATIONALIST REVOLUTIONARY REPUBLICS

For much of the twentieth century, the nationalist revolutionary state has been one of the most important political models for the Middle East.

Table 4.2 Formal Political Participation in the Middle East, 1999

Country (year of independence)	Executive and Legislative System	Political Parties Legal?	Date of Female Political Suffrage	Dates Females First Represented in Parliament
Algeria (1962)	President, National People's Assembly	yes	1962	1962
Bahrain (1971)	Absolute monarchy, appointed Consultative Council	no	a	a
Comoros (1975)	Military coup, May 1999	n.a.	1956	1993
Djibouti (1977)	President	n.a.	1946	—
Egypt (1922)	President, prime minister, National Assembly	yes	1956	1957
Iran (1925)	Supreme religious leader, president, Islamic Consultative Assembly	no	1963	1963
Iraq (1932)	President, National Assembly	yes	1980	1980
Israel (1948)	President, prime minister, National Assembly	yes	1948	1949
Jordan (1946)	King, prime minister, National Assembly	yes	1974	1989
Kuwait (1961)	Emir, National Assembly	no	b	b
Lebanon (1943)	President, prime minister, Chamber of Deputies	yes	1952	1991
Libya (1951)	General, General People's Assembly	no	1964	n/a
Mauritania (1960)	President, prime minister, Parliament	yes	1961	1975
Morocco (1956)	King, prime minister, National Assembly	yes	1963	1993
Oman (1951)	Absolute monarchy, partially elected Consultative Council	no	a	c
Palestinian Territories[d]	President, Legislative Council	yes	1996	1996
Qatar (1971)	Emir, elected advisory Municipal Council	no	1999	—
Saudi Arabia (1932)	Absolute monarchy, appointed Consultative Council	no	a	a
Somalia (1960)	No functioning government	n.a.	n.a.	n.a.
Sudan (1956)	President, National Assembly	no	1964	1964
Syria (1946)	President, People's Council	yes	1953	1973
Tunisia (1956)	President, prime minister, Chamber of Deputies	yes	1959	1959
Turkey (1923)	President, prime minister, Grand National Assembly	yes	1934	1935
UAE (1971)	Federation of emirates	no	a	a
Yemen (1990)[e]	President, National Assembly	yes	1967[f]	1990

Source: UNDP (1998:168–169, 194); data on executive and legislative systems—except for Comoros, Djibouti, Qatar, Somalia, and the United Arab Emirates—from Levine (1998:16).

Notes: a. Neither women nor men have suffrage or the right to stand for election.

b. Women do not have suffrage or the right to stand for election. In 1999, the emir of Kuwait issued a decree giving women full political rights, but it has not yet been ratified by parliament.

c. Women have been appointed to a nonelected consultative council.

d. Not yet recognized as independent.

e. Date refers to unification of the Yemen Arab Republic and PDR Yemen.

f. Refers to the former PDR Yemen.

n.a. Information not available.

Although the region suffered from its proximity to Europe by experiencing two centuries of colonial intervention and interference in the development of regional politics, this proximity provided at least one possible compensating advantage: intense exposure to the intellectual currents that accompanied the consolidation of the modern industrialized state in Europe, notably nationalism, political liberalism, and socialism.

As a result, as Arthur Goldschmidt Jr. outlined in Chapter 3, the "Arab awakening" (Antonius, 1946) began in the early to mid-1800s and culminated in a series of independence and self-determination movements in the twentieth century. Due to the constraints of colonialism, few of these ideas could be implemented prior to the 1950s, but the intellectual groundwork had been provided, at least some of the relevant political writings were in Arabic, and this literature spoke to regional history (Khalidi, 1991; Tibi, 1997). In this respect the Middle East was in a quite different situation than Asia or sub-Saharan Africa, which were relatively isolated from European political developments by the sheer impact of physical distance in the days before telecommunications.

The first successful twentieth-century nationalist movement in the Middle East, that of Atatürk following the end of World War I, shows the effects of these influences. Atatürk's single most dramatic innovation—the secularization of Turkey—was completely consistent with liberal revolutionary movements from the times of the American and French Revolutions forward. Although Atatürk was reluctant to share power, he did support the adoption of European political forms, such as a parliamentary system with a prime minister and cabinet chosen from the unicameral Grand National Assembly. This meant that the necessary structures for participatory government were in place after Atatürk's death.

In contrast, early efforts by the intelligentsia and the middle classes in Iran to limit the power of the Qajar monarchy and give control to an elected assembly failed. By the mid-1920s, the Qajar ruler had been replaced by Reza Khan, who founded the relatively short-lived Pahlavi dynasty. Reza Khan and his son Mohammad Reza Pahlavi combined social, economic, and military modernization with repression and authoritarian rule. Little was done to nurture the nascent parliament or develop other democratic institutions (Halliday, 1979).

Due to colonialism and global wars, another three decades would pass before the process of state building could begin in the Arab Middle East, but when decolonization began in earnest in the 1950s, significant ideological movements were ready and waiting to challenge the immediate postcolonial political structures imposed by Britain, France, and the United States. Thus the 1950s and 1960s saw a proliferation of alternative political approaches, often incorporating Islamic political values and histories into a formally secular framework. Much to the distress of the United States, Britain, and France, most of these new ideologies drew as much upon the theories of Karl Marx and V. I. Lenin as on those of Thomas Jefferson and John Locke. As a consequence, they emphasized a strong, centralized (and bureaucratized) state, a characteristic that persists to this day even in countries that have in other ways moved away from this approach.

When viewed in the context of the 1950s and 1960s, there are several reasons for the appeal of "leftist" approaches to politics, none of which have anything to do with "Arab exceptionalism" or a distinctly Middle Eastern respect for centralized power and authority. First, the consolidation of state power was consistent with the prevailing Western political trends in government. During the previous two decades, the liberal democracies of Western Europe and North America had increasingly centralized authority, initially to counter the effects of the Depression and then to mobilize their economies for World War II. Both Marxists and progressive political theorists argued that such an expansion in central governmental authority was necessary to counter the economic power of industrialized capitalism.

Second, from the perspective of the 1950s—not the 2000s—elements of the Soviet Union's Communist model were quite attractive. In a mere twenty-five years, the Soviet Union had gone from a quasi-feudal society to an industrialized power capable of withstanding the military assault of one of the most advanced economies of Europe during World War II. It had survived the Great Depression that had devastated most of the capitalist world, and in the 1950s, the toll that Stalin's brutal policies had extracted from the Soviet people was not widely known or understood. Thus, varieties of socialism were attractive not just in the Arab world but in every area undergoing decolonization (e.g., China, Vietnam, Cuba, parts of Africa). It is likely that socialism would have been implemented even more widely than it actually was if not for the efforts of the U.S. Central Intelligence Agency (CIA) and other Cold War agents of containment.

Finally, it was the political left rather than the right that had consistently opposed colonialism. As discussed below, the monarchies, without exception, allied themselves with the colonial powers or their successor, the United States. Even in the era of colonialism, progressive and socialist groups had provided greater assistance in the anticolonial cause than had the liberal democracies. Two of the most conspicuous of the European liberal democracies—Britain and France—had been the two most conspicuous meddlers in Arab affairs. Although the United States might have been able to exploit its anticolonial policies to promote a liberal democratic agenda (as it did during the 1956 Suez crisis), it consistently subordinated such a goal to the pursuit of a simple anti-Communist agenda. The CIA overthrow of Mohammad Mossadeq in 1952, anti-Nasserist policies following the

Suez crisis, the 1958 military intervention in Lebanon, and by the mid-1960s, the deepening U.S. military activity in Indochina ended any anti-colonial credibility the United States might once have had.

A full discussion of the diverse intellectual currents in Arab political thought during this period would fill several dozen books (and has). Here we will summarize the tenets of two ideological approaches that had a significant impact in the Middle Eastern political arena—Ba'thism and Nasserism—before turning to a brief discussion of the contemporary situation of three of the nationalist revolutionary republics: Egypt, Tunisia, and Syria.

□ Ba'thism

The Ba'th Party is one of the only political movements that is truly indigenous to the Arab world. In the 1940s, the Arab Ba'th Party was founded by two Syrians, Greek Orthodox Michael Aflaq (who was the group's intellectual leader) and Sunni Muslim Salah al-Din al-Bitar (who served as the political strategist). This group merged in 1953 with a second group, the Arab Socialist Party, to create the Arab Socialist Resurrection Party, also known as the Ba'th Socialist Party. The first members of the Ba'th Party came primarily from the intellectual elite, but the Ba'th quickly gained support among disadvantaged groups and established itself as a mass movement.

The basic Ba'thist ideology combined a set of principles that drew on many traditional sources of legitimacy in the Arab world: history, religion, nationalism, modernity, freedom, and socialism. Most important, Ba'thism called for social reform and economic justice, to be achieved through Arab socialism. Aflaq resisted the temptation to rely exclusively on European socialist thinkers, with their emphasis on class struggle. Instead, he emphasized that the Ba'thist economic model was neither capitalist nor Communist: it was a middle way that was the product of the Arab world's unique history. A second key element of Ba'thism was its emphasis on pan-Arab unity, which was understood to involve the unification of existing Arab states into a single political entity as a replacement for patriotism centered on a specific state. Third, Ba'thism was anti-imperialist and anti-Zionist; it stressed the achievement of true Arab independence from all forms of colonialism.

Finally, Ba'thism called for a toleration of religious minorities within an overall Arab-Islamic political framework that included representative government and civil rights. Aflaq maintained that Islam was a "historically formative force but one with no specific contemporary ideological or political role" (Bill and Springborg, 1994:73). As a result, Ba'thism could appeal both to the majority Muslim population and to Christians who would be left out of a more explicitly Islamic formulation of nationalism. The Ba'th is the dominant political actor in both Syria and Iraq and plays a more minor role in Jordan, Lebanon, and elsewhere.

□ Nasserism

Gamal Abdel Nasser was part of the Free Officers group who engineered the 1952 coup in Egypt that overthrew King Farouk. By the end of 1954, Nasser had begun to consolidate his position as president, prime minister, and head of the Revolutionary Command Council that controlled Egyptian political life. To maintain power, the charismatic Nasser created a strong state bureaucracy and a variety of nationalist institutions, such as the Arab Socialist Union (ASU), that he could dominate. Nasser's pan-Arab ideals and increasing interest in leftist ideologies evolved into a political and socioeconomic doctrine that came to be known as Nasserism.

Nasser maintained that socialism had to be adapted to the specific needs of Egypt rather than following the Marxist model of the European states, with its rejection of religion. Instead, in part as a way of responding to the Muslim Brotherhood, Nasser attempted to root his economic approach in the Islamic ideal of equitable economic distribution:

> The Islamic ideal meant a society without injustice, which meant freedom from hunger, want and exploitation, which in turn implied common ownership of the means of production and a planned society. Within the framework of national unity all would be encouraged to co-operate for the national good. (Hopwood, 1985:100)

Unlike Ba'thism, however, "Nasserism was not a well-conceived thesis by one or more ideologues, but emerged as an ideology out of a series of practical responses to the problems, domestic and foreign, that Egypt . . . faced as it tried to consolidate its newly won political and economic independence" (Hiro, 1996:217). Thus its impact as a political movement declined after Nasser's death, and many of the Nasserist parties that had been established outside of Egypt collapsed.

□ Single–Party States

Very few countries in the Middle East have genuine multiparty political systems. Instead, there is often a single "government" party that dominates the political landscape and a set of ineffectual, often restricted, opposition parties that have little ability to influence the political direction of the country.

In this sense, Egypt is the quintessential model of a single-party bu-reaucratized state. Egypt's 1971 Constitution, as amended in 1990, identi-fies Egypt as a democratic, socialist Arab republic. It calls for a strong pres-ident, supported by a National Assembly of at least 350 people. (Currently, there are 444 elected and ten appointed representatives.) The Egyptian Na-tional Assembly nominates the president; that name is then put to the gen-eral population in a national referendum. The person is declared president if the nomination is approved by a simple majority of those voting. Origi-nally the constitution stipulated that the president could hold only two six-year terms, but President Anwar Sadat had this article amended to state that the president could be reelected for an unspecified number of terms. In 1999, Mubarak was "elected" for a fourth six-year term.

During the period between Egypt's independence in 1922 and the Free Officers' coup in 1952, a limited multiparty system was put in place. For the next twenty-five years, the ASU was the only legal political party. When it was dissolved in 1977, shortly after Anwar Sadat announced Egypt would return to a multiparty system, it was replaced by the Na-tional Democratic Party (NDP), which has continued to dominate Egyp-tian politics (see Korany, 1998). In 1984, multiparty elections were held for the first time, and there are now more than ten recognized groups in addition to the ruling NDP. However, opposition representation in the as-sembly is trivial; all the opposition parties together won only fourteen seats in the November 1995 national elections, which were marred by boycotts and widespread accusations of fraud and intimidation. Further-more, efforts at founding an Islamic political party are consistently re-pressed. Given this, it is not surprising that most of the opposition groups boycotted the April 1997 local council elections.

The Egyptian political system has survived two crises that might well have led to its demise: the death of the charismatic Nasser three years after Egypt's disastrous military defeat by Israel in 1967 and the assassination of Sadat in 1981. The highly bureaucratized nature of the state, the combination of co-optation and control of opposition parties, extremely limited moves oward political liberalization, and

Photo 4.4   Egyptian president Hosni Mubarak has been in power since 1981.

© Thomas Hartwell

economic liberalization (the relaxation of state controls on the economy so that markets can play a greater role) have kept the governmental system established by Nasser essentially intact. The question is whether Egypt is in the midst of a democratic transition, or if, as Eberhard Kienle (1998) argues, it is in the process of deliberalization and has actually become less democratic than it was in the 1980s.

Tunisia provides another good example of a formally multiparty state in which a single party completely dominates politics. As in Egypt, Tunisia's first leader after independence and the abolition of the monarchy was a strong, authoritarian figure who was able to set the direction for the country. President Habib Bourguiba claimed he "invented" Tunisia, and, indeed, his impact over three decades was enormous. According to the 1959 Constitution, Tunisia is a "presidential republic" in which the president has much more power than the elected National Assembly. Under Bourguiba, Tunisia implemented a secular, Western-style legal system and, until the 1970s, pursued socialist-style economic development. Grassroots political participation was channeled through what was for many years Tunisia's only legal political party: the Neo-Destour Party and its successor, the Destour Socialist Party.

In the 1980s, serious economic difficulties brought on by economic liberalization led to riots and instability in Tunisia. Advisers urged Bourguiba to open up the political process, but he refused and instead became highly repressive, directing particular attention to leaders of the opposition Islamic Tendency Movement (MTI). Eventually, the situation became so serious that Bourguiba was overthrown by Prime Minister Zine Abidine Ben Ali in a bloodless coup that took advantage of a part of the Tunisian Constitution that says if the head of state is incapacitated, the job should be performed by the prime minister.

> Ben Ali's November 7, 1987, coup inaugurated the heady period of political reform that swept across the Middle East and North Africa in the 1980s. The new president promised to establish the rule of law, to respect human rights, and to implement the kind of democratic political reforms that Habib Bourguiba had steadfastly refused. Along with Algeria, Jordan and Yemen, Tunisia rode the leading edge of what many hoped would be a wave of democratic transitions in the region. (Alexander, 1997:34)

President Ben Ali, who was elected to a five-year term in 1989 and re-elected in 1994 and 1999, publicly committed himself to introducing genuine political pluralism in Tunisia. However, this has not occurred. On the positive side, Tunisia now has a multiparty political system, with at least five opposition political parties that have been approved to compete for limited representation in the National Assembly. However, significant repression of Islamic political groups remains. The Hizb al-Nahdha (Party of

the Renaissance), the successor to the MTI, is widely described as reformist rather than revolutionary and has indicated its willingness to work
within the rules of a competitive, representative democracy; however, it
continues to be excluded from the electoral process. Furthermore, opposition groups have boycotted national elections, arguing that the electoral
system is heavily biased in favor of the government, and results tend to
support this contention. Thus, Tunisia, like Egypt, remains de facto a single-party state, despite its formal multiparty label.

☐ Personalistic Systems

The distinction between single-party and personalistic states is not
sharp, as James A. Bill and Robert Springborg make clear in their description of personalism:

> Middle Eastern societies and political systems grew out of tribal constella-
> tions, and the personalism that prevailed in the family and the clan has had
> a pervasive and protracted influence. The Middle Eastern leader has led by
> virtue of his personal relations with his followers. Formal organizations
> and institutions have seldom effectively intervened. Even when institutions
> such as formal bureaucracies have developed, the real business of ruling
> and political decision making has resided in personal networks. (1994:160)

Current examples of this approach include Syria, Libya, and Iraq, all with
strong leaders who govern as dictators despite the formal presence of legislative bodies.

Syria's political system combines Ba'thism and a cult of personality
around President Hafez al-Assad. Syria gained independence as a republic
in 1946 after twenty-six years under a mandate granted to France by the
League of Nations. With little experience as a modern autonomous entity,
Syria initially experienced tremendous political instability: between 1949
and 1954, there were four military coups. After Syria's short-lived and disastrous merger with Egypt between 1958 and 1961, the Ba'thists achieved
a dominant position within the Syrian government as a result of the March
1963 military coup. The party has remained in control ever since.

Hafez al-Assad assumed power in 1970 in a bloodless coup and became president in 1971. He has been reelected every seven years since
then, which is not difficult because he is the only candidate on the ballot.
According to the 1973 Constitution, Syria is a socialist and democratic republic with a strong president and legislation based on Islamic law. There
is some involvement of the population in governance of the country
through a 250-person People's Assembly that approves the national budget
and responds to laws issued by the Ba'th Central Committee. In recent
years, several minor political parties have served as a token "loyal opposition" to the dominant Ba'th Party and are represented in the assembly.

Syria has been relatively stable under al-Assad, especially when compared with its early years of independence. This stability can be attributed to a number of factors, including "the fact that Syria was dominated by only one all-powerful political faction with a highly reliable and effective security apparatus" (Van Dam, 1996:137). In addition, the severe economic crisis of the 1980s, with its potential for political repercussions, has been alleviated somewhat by the transition away from a statist economy and toward economic liberalism (Melhem, 1997; see also Kienle, 1994).

There are, however, serious potential challenges to the legitimacy of the regime, particularly from the Muslim Brotherhood, which has attempted to overthrow the regime on several occasions (most dramatically in an uprising in the city of Hama in 1982). Furthermore, the same continuity of leadership that has lent stability to the regime could create difficulties in the future since few of the political and military elite are young. There is also the issue of who can successfully replace the ailing al-Assad after his demise. His eldest son, Basil, was considered a likely contender until his death in a car accident in January 1994. Now political analysts speculate that Basil's younger brother, Bashar, is being groomed as the successor. (One indication of this is that the ubiquitous posters with Hafez al-Assad's smiling face that once filled shop windows throughout Syria have been replaced by equally ubiquitous posters featuring Hafez and Bashar together.) At one time, Hafez al-Assad's brother Rifaat seemed another option, but he is now formally out of the power structure, having been removed as one of Syria's three vice presidents on February 8, 1998.

■ TRADITIONAL AND PARLIAMENTARY MONARCHIES

The Middle East is the only area of the world where traditional monarchies (as distinct from constitutional monarchies, which exist in parts of Europe) have persisted in a number of states. At times, this has been used to label the domestic politics of the region "medieval" or even "primitive." A closer look suggests that the monarchical regimes might better be characterized as an adaptation of established forms of patrimonial leadership (see Weber, 1947) to the contemporary nation-state system. Drawing on a variety of traditional sources of legitimacy such as custom, a history of family governance, ancestral ties to the Prophet Muhammad, a leader's personal attributes, and the royal family's role as a symbol of nationalism, the current Arab monarchies have proved remarkably resilient.

This persistence is particularly striking when we recall that in the 1950s and 1960s six monarchies were unable to survive the critical postcolonial period and were removed from power: Egypt, 1952; Tunisia, 1956; Iraq, 1958; Yemen, 1962; South Arabia (which became PDR Yemen),

1967; and Libya, 1969. Yet since 1969 only a single additional monarchy has been overthrown (in Iran), suggesting that the remaining royal rulers have found ways to repress democratic sentiment, co-opt opposition movements, or otherwise adapt their rule to address, at least minimally, popular pressures for political reform. The challenge for the Arab monarchies today is less one of validating the legitimacy of their political control through tradition and more one of "establishing a linkage with modernity," as Michael C. Hudson argued more than twenty years ago (1977:230). Sociopolitical structures such as the *diwan* (informal gatherings in the homes of elites at which there is wide-ranging discussion regarding contemporary issues), along with the Islamic concept of *shura* (consultation), have allowed for a fair amount of grassroots input without moving to a liberal-democratic model. Furthermore, significant economic resources have made it possible in some instances to buy off the opposition (Gause, 1994). In addition, all of these states have chosen to align themselves politically with the West. In the name of anticommunism (originally) or anti–Islamic revivalism (currently), the United States in particular has been willing to supply the Arab ruling elites with whatever weapons and expertise they require to maintain internal security.

In four countries—Bahrain, Kuwait, Morocco, and Oman—the same extended family has held political power for more than 200 years. The current ruling family in Oman has governed the coast of the country (although not the interior) since 1749; Sultan Qaboos became the leader in 1970 when he overthrew his father in a bloodless coup that was supported by the British. The Kuwaiti al-Sabahs trace their rule back to the early 1700s, when a group of formerly nomadic clans settled along the northeastern Arabian coast; the related al-Khalifah family established its authority in Bahrain in 1782 after defeating the Iranians who had previously controlled the islands.

The most enduring Arab regime is in the kingdom of Morocco. Monarchical government in that country dates back twelve centuries. The Alawi family, which traces its roots to the Prophet Muhammad, came to power in the 1660s and consolidated its control over virtually all of modern-day Morocco in the early 1700s. Unlike most of the Arab world, Morocco escaped both European and Ottoman colonialism. After a brief period of European control in the early twentieth century, Morocco regained its independence in 1956 and is now governed by King Mohammed VI, who succeeded his father, King Hassan II, in July 1999. The Moroccan regime consequently fits into a small set of states in which a long-standing monarchy was able to resist the inroads of colonialism and emerge intact in the postcolonial period. (Ethiopia, prior to the overthrow of Haile Salassie, and Siam/Thailand are two other examples of this unusual pattern.)

The other Arab monarchies are either the result of twentieth-century consolidations of power, as in the case of Saudi Arabia, or are relatively recent "dynasties" that gained their political position either in part (Qatar, the UAE) or entirely (Jordan) from the assistance of the retreating colonial powers. In the 1800s, the British signed treaties with a variety of local leaders in the Gulf, adopting a policy of indirect rule and support for the specific families with whom they signed agreements. This served to reinforce the position of the Gulf's ruling families and convert them into "royalty" that then took over full control of the newly independent countries when the British withdrew from the Gulf.

Some of these artificially created dynasties failed due to incompetence, as in Iraq, where neither of the two successors to King Faisal I were able to hold the country's diverse population together. Others, such as the Idris regime in Libya, were never accepted by the population on whom they were imposed and could not survive in power once European support was withdrawn. In non-Arab Iran, the Pahlavi dynasty that replaced the Qajar dynasty in a bloodless coup in the 1920s maintained control only with the support of the CIA and was eventually overthrown.

☐ Unique Aspects of Arab Kingship

It is important to note that the Arab concept of kingship differs significantly from the European model. Hudson notes that "the ideal Arab monarchy, perfectly legitimized, . . . would be an Islamic theocracy governed by the ablest leaders of a tribe tracing its lineage to the Prophet." Legitimacy in general must be earned by capable leadership, and "there are no strongly legitimized succession procedures—neither inheritance nor election—in Arab culture" (Hudson, 1977:167).

These criteria lead to two significant differences between the European and Arab institutions of monarchy. First, the conflict between the monarchy and the political power of the church that characterized so much of the European feudal system has no counterpart in the Arab world. The authority of an Arab monarch still can be challenged on religious grounds—as occurred with the revolt in Arabia of the religiously fundamentalist Ikhwan (brethren) against Abdul Aziz ibn Saud in the late 1920s. But there is no Islamic "pope" (or Confucian bureaucracy) to whom a monarch can appeal for legitimacy independent of his own religious authority, or, conversely, who can threaten a monarch by withholding approval.

Second, the absence of a widely recognized succession procedure limits the development of the extended family dynasties such as the Hapsburgs in Austria (r. 1282–1918) and the German-English House of Hanover. The status of *sharif*—a descendant of the Prophet—enhances the legitimacy of a ruler, but at any given point there are hundreds or thousands of potential leaders with this designation. Consequently, being a sharif does not carry the same power as being the eldest son of a king would in Europe, and marriage into such a family does not, by itself, guarantee that someone can claim political control.

The advantage of the Arab system is that it tends to result in relatively effective rulers. Arab monarchies do not show the pattern—common in Europe—of a weak or decadent leader (for example, George III of Great Britain or Louis XVI of France) being kept in power in order to preserve the traditions that also legitimize the power of organized religion and the lower nobility. A weak or otherwise problematic ruler can be overthrown by a family member—as happened in modern times in Oman and Qatar—without threatening the legitimacy of the entire regime.

Furthermore, because the ruler must demonstrate leadership and piety, he must be accessible to the population through a wide range of traditional institutions. For instance, shortly after he became king in 1999, Abdullah II of Jordan disguised himself as a taxi driver, left behind his bodyguards, and drove around Amman listening to ordinary citizens complain about the government. This unusual action, reminiscent of Abdullah's father King Hussein in the early years of his reign, was widely acclaimed and echoed the legends of great Arab monarchs in classical times who would leave their palaces disguised as beggars and roam the streets and marketplaces to assess public opinion. The "absolute" power of the Bourbons of France or the Romanovs of Russia—who ruled in nearly complete isolation from the populations of their territories—has no counterpart in Arab tradition. (This is of particular note because "Orientalist" images often ascribe to the Arab monarch greater unfettered power than that found in European monarchies.)

One disadvantage of this system is that Arab monarchies are potentially more vulnerable than European monarchies to leadership crises upon the death of a ruler because the line of succession may be less well established. Furthermore, because the system is entirely patrilineal, half the population is excluded from direct power. Although the Arab system has avoided weak kings such as George III of England and Nicholas II of Russia, it has also never produced strong queens such as Elizabeth I and Victoria of England or Catherine the Great of Russia.

□ Saudi Arabia

Among the Gulf states, Saudi Arabia is clearly the most powerful; it is "also the most inscrutable" to non-Saudi "researchers and reporters [who are] all but barred from the country while American soldiers and oil company staff live inside fenced compounds" (Carapico, 1997:1). Widespread restrictions on civil rights and political freedoms further limit knowledge about the kingdom. Officially, Saudi Arabia is ruled by King Fahd, the fourth son of the country's founder Abdul Aziz ibn Saud to serve as monarch. Due to Fahd's extensive health problems, however, his half-brother, Crown Prince Abdullah, has taken on increasing responsibilities in recent years.

Drawing on its considerable political and economic resources, the Saudi leadership has consistently argued that it has pursued domestic policies in support of modernization and development with an emphasis on cooperation, negotiation, and compromise that is consistent with the Quran. Nonetheless, the royal family has not been immune to criticism and threats to its political legitimacy. Opponents of the regime—whether secular or religious—maintain that the oil wealth has been used to enrich the Saudi family more than the country as a whole, that the government is corrupt, and that the refusal of the House of Saud to share power is non-Islamic. There is also dissatisfaction among some with the close ties between Saudi Arabia and the United States.

Shortly after the Gulf War, a group of Western-educated intellectuals tried to persuade the king to introduce democratic reforms in Saudi Arabia: the creation of a constitutional monarchy, greater respect for human rights, and the opportunity for political parties and universal suffrage. In response, a number of religious leaders urged Fahd instead to transform Saudi Arabia into a fully Islamic state along the lines of Iran. In an attempt to quell this nascent dissent, in February 1992 King Fahd announced the establishment of a sixty-man *Majlis al-Shura* (consultative council) whose appointed members were drawn from the professional, academic, religious, business, and retired military elites of the country. In July 1997, the king appointed a new *majlis* and expanded its membership from sixty to ninety persons. In the current *majlis,* 37 percent are academics (from both religious and secular institutions), 43 percent are bureaucrats and professionals, and 20 percent are businessmen, police, diplomats, and military personnel (Dekmejian, 1998:209). The council can propose legislation, but its actions have no binding force; however, "whenever the opinions of the Majlis and the Council of Ministers are concordant on a specific matter, a law will be issued following the king's consent" (Dekmejian, 1998:207).

At the same time the initial Consultative Council was created, Fahd also reorganized the provincial system of government and proclaimed a new Basic Law that, among other changes, provided a new procedure that makes the grandsons as well as the sons of Abdul Aziz eligible for royal succession. The latter was extremely important, given that there are no clear rules for how power is passed within any of the Gulf's ruling families. Crown Prince Abdullah is only two years younger than King Fahd, and it is not at all clear who will be named crown prince when Abdullah becomes king.

☐ States of the Arabian Peninsula

The remaining monarchies of the Arabian Peninsula have several attributes in common: They are all relatively small in terms of both land and population, with little arable land; each has a significant expatriate population that is responsible for much of the economic activity; and all rely on petroleum and natural gas for a significant portion of their export revenue. The rulers of each country face internal pressures for political liberalization; most have chosen to respond cautiously by lifting restrictions on speech and the media, decentralizing the government and giving greater power to individual ministries, establishing consultative councils, and introducing constitutions. At present, however, none of the Gulf states permits political parties.

Qatar, Oman, and the UAE. Similar to Saudi Arabia in some ways, Qatar is a religiously conservative, traditional emirate, ruled by Hamid ibn Khalifah ibn Hamad al-Thani, who ousted his father Khalifah in a nonviolent coup on June 27, 1995. In this wealthy emirate, the decisions of the monarch are binding, and members of the al-Thani family hold many of the significant political positions: the prime minister is Hamid's brother Abdullah, the deputy prime minister is another of Hamid's brothers, and the foreign minister is his cousin and brother-in-law. Hamid, who is significantly younger than the other Gulf leaders (except for Bahrain's Hamad ibn Isa al-Khalifah), sees himself as a modernizing ruler. He has allowed for increased political debate in the public arena and has begun to enfranchise the population: on March 8, 1999, some 23,000 Qatari women and men voted in the first-ever elections for a twenty-nine-member advisory Municipal Council. (The number of voters is small because individuals who are in the military or police and those who have been Qatari citizens for less than fifteen years were ineligible to participate, as was the more than 75 percent of the population that is expatriate.) Six women were among the more than 200 candidates, although none of the women were elected. The Municipal Council has a term of four years, after which Qatar is expected to establish an elected parliament that will have genuine, although limited, legislative authority.

Oman, too, has begun to move slowly toward constitutional rule and limited popular political participation. An eighty-member Consultative Council advises the government, reviews legislation, and provides a formal means for community leaders to provide input to the government. Membership in the council is determined by Sultan Qaboos, who chooses among candidates selected from each of Oman's fifty-nine districts. Two members of the council are female, as are four members of the forty-five-person state council appointed by the sultan. A new Basic Law, implemented in November 1996, addressed the critical question of leadership continuity in Oman (given that Sultan Qaboos has no heir). Article 5 of the Basic Law indicates that Qaboos's successor must be "a Muslim, judicious, of sound mind and [a] legitimate son of Omani Muslim parents" (quoted in O'Reilly, 1998:83); he must also be a descendent of Sayyid Turki ibn Said ibn Sultan (Sultan Qaboos's great-great-grandfather who ruled Oman between 1871 and 1888).

The third of the small, traditional Gulf states is the UAE, union of seven shaikdoms formed when Britain withdrew from the Gulf in the early 1970s. Independence was to be followed by the creation of a permanent constitution and elections, but this never occurred. Thus, although the UAE is technically a republic, in reality it is a federation of emirates with no suffrage and no political parties. Governance of the 3 million residents (only about 20 percent of whom are indigenous to the area) is by the Supreme Council, composed of the leader of each emirate and headed by Shaikh Zayed of Abu Dhabi. There is also a forty-person Federal National Assembly, whose membership reflects the power distribution of the UAE: Abu Dhabi and Dubai have eight representatives each; Sharjah and Ras al-Khaimah have six each; and Umm al-Quaiwan, Fujairah, and Ajman have only four each. Periodically, tensions erupt among the emirates over the dominance of Abu Dhabi and Dubai; however, because these are the largest and wealthiest regions, the federation could not easily exist without their involvement, and criticism is constrained.

Bahrain and Kuwait. The constitutions of both Bahrain and Kuwait call for a legislative body; however, in the multi-island country of Bahrain, parliamentary rule is a legal fiction. The thirty-person National Assembly, partially elected by a small number of male Bahraini citizens in 1973, was suspended in 1975 after it "balked at endorsing a broadly-written decree that would enable the government to detain critics and opponents at will for 'statements' or 'activities' deemed to threaten the country's 'internal or external security'" (Stork, 1997:34). Emir Isa ibn Salmon al-Khalifah (who ruled Bahrain from independence until his death on March 6, 1999) then suspended the constitution and dismissed the parliament. In place of the parliament, the emir created an appointed Consultative Council in December 1992; however, this "largely cosmetic emblem of democratic reform" (Fakhro, 1997:175) did little to quell popular desires for greater political participation.

More than two-thirds of the Bahraini population is Shi'a, and over the years there have been allegations of Iranian-supported plots to overthrow the Sunni-controlled government. In December 1994, opposition groups incited a popular uprising that has continued off and on ever since. Demands of the opposition members include political rights for women, the restoration of the constitution and parliament, and more economic opportunities.

The response of the government was to increase political repression: detaining dissidents without charge, using torture, and increasing restrictions on freedom of expression (Human Rights Watch, 1997). Opposition leaders expressed cautious optimism that the new emir, Hamad ibn Isa al-Khalifah, would be more open to limited power sharing, at least with the country's elites, if not with the general citizenry.

Of all the Gulf states, Kuwait has arguably been the most successful in preempting revolutionary pressures. This is due in large part to

> the massive and successful program of the al-Sabah dynasty . . . to preserve its power by building the region's first modern welfare state. . . . For decades, the Kuwaiti government has lavishly subsidized everything from electricity to housing, has underwritten travel abroad for those seeking education or medical treatment, and has created comfortable, well-paying, white collar jobs for 96 percent of its working citizens. (Sadowski 1997:7)

Between the dramatic decline in worldwide oil prices and the cost of reconstructing Kuwait after the Iraqi invasion, however, Kuwait's ability to buy off dissent has declined, creating a potentially unstable situation.

At present, Kuwait is the only Middle Eastern country in which men but not women are permitted to vote. Until 1996, suffrage was granted only to adult males who were residents of Kuwait prior to 1920 and their male descendants; now male descendants of the (very few) naturalized citizens can also vote, but the electorate is still tiny compared with the total population. The fifty-person National Assembly has a checkered history: it was dissolved in 1975, reconstituted in 1981, and suspended again in July 1986. At the time, the al-Sabah family argued that Kuwait could not afford the divisiveness that democracy encouraged. Under popular pressure to revive the legislature, the royal family created an Advisory National Council in June 1990. The council was suspended during the war with Iraq but was restored in July 1991 and remained in place until the National Assembly began operation again in 1992.

The 1992 election was heavily contested, and its results were a shock to the Kuwaiti royal family: opposition candidates won thirty-one seats, defeating many pro-government candidates. Sixteen of these were associated with various Islamic factions; the remainder were liberal or leftist figures, many of whom were quite critical of the al-Sabah family. Islamists are also well represented in the current assembly, which was elected in 1996; however, secular opposition figures were less successful than they had been in 1992, reflecting popular dissatisfaction with the 1992 assembly. In May 1999, Shaikh Jabir al-Sabah dissolved the parliament and called for early elections after legislators strongly criticized a cabinet member. A few weeks later, the emir announced his desire that women be permitted to vote and run for office beginning in 2003.

Jordan and Morocco. These two states, although monarchies, are arguably moving toward a form of constitutional monarch more similar to that found in contemporary Europe. The role of their parliaments is more substantial than in the other Middle Eastern monarchies: they are popularly elected, and political parties are permitted to function, although in Morocco the fundamentalist "Justice and Charity" movement is not recognized.

Jordan, the only royal kingdom remaining in the Levant, has been a constitutional monarchy since the 1928 Constitution established an elected legislative council (although ultimate responsibility still rested with the Hashemites). A new constitution promulgated in February 1947 called for a bicameral national assembly, with an eighty-person lower house elected by popular vote and a smaller upper house appointed by the king. From 1953 to 1999, the country was ruled by King Hussein, the grandson of King Abdullah and the great-grandson of Sharif Husayn ibn Ali of Mecca. Upon Hussein's death, the throne passed to his son Abdullah II.

The October 1956 elections brought to power a leftist government that challenged the young King Hussein, whose response was to declare martial law and ban all political parties. After the Six Day War with Israel and the Israeli occupation of the West Bank, which Jordan still claimed, the feeling was that no parliamentary elections could be held. Eventually, in 1984, an amendment to the constitution allowed for a reconvening of the ninth parliament (in place in 1967) with by-elections to replace the deceased deputies; however, this was widely viewed as unsatisfactory. Four years later, Hussein formally gave up administrative responsibility for the West Bank, thus opening the way for nonpartisan parliamentary elections in November 1989—the first in more than two decades.

In reopening the political process slightly, Hussein was attempting "to pre-empt a crisis . . . [and] to find a political balance—one which gives his people the reformed political system . . . that they want, and which guarantees the future of Hashemite rule" (Yorke, 1989:18). Faced with a strong Islamic movement, the king chose to integrate Islamists into the government rather than banning them, as occurred in Algeria, Egypt, and Tunisia. One result was an increase in laws restricting activities such as the consumption of alcohol or requiring gender separation in public swimming pools and sports facilities. At the same time, participation in the government required the Islamists to compromise and forge alliances with other political entities (Ahmad, 1997).

Subsequent multiparty elections were held in 1993 and 1997. In 1993, some two dozen parties reflecting a diversity of views contended for representation. By the November 1997 elections, however, there was a serious reversal in Jordan's moves toward democratization. Prior to the elections, Human Rights Watch reported with dismay that there was "a clear intent to discourage Jordanians from organising and participating in public discussion of political issues that segments of the civil society deem to be of national importance" and questioned whether, under these circumstances, any elections could be considered free and fair (cited in Andoni, 1997:19). In addition, changes in the election law clearly strengthened the position of tribal leaders at the expense of opposition groups. As a result, nine opposition parties, including the large Islamic Action Front, boycotted the election, leaving the field wide open for pro-government candidates to gain a substantial majority in the lower house.

As is true of a number of states, the kingdom of Morocco has attempted to address political dissent through a new, slightly more liberal constitution. However, just as in Kuwait and Jordan, the king can dissolve the parliament at will and indeed did so for more than a decade beginning in 1965. Under the 1996 Constitution, the king maintains significant political control: he must approve all members of the cabinet and can override the parliament at will.

At present, Morocco has a two-tiered legislative body: a 325-member Chamber of Representatives that is directly elected for a five-year term and a Chamber of Councilors that is indirectly elected by local councils, professional organizations, and labor groups for staggered nine-year terms. Both women and men have suffrage. In the November 1997 elections, the opposition (which is dominated by the Istiqlal Party and the Socialist Union of Popular Forces [USFP]) gained a plurality of seats in the lower

Photo 4.5   King Hassan II receives an honor guard in Casablanca, Morocco. Notice his hat, which is unlike the head covering worn by other Arab leaders.

© Thomas Hartwell

chamber. The new coalition government included twenty-two members of the opposition out of a total of forty-one ministers; USFP leader Abderrahmane Youssoufi became Morocco's prime minister.

■ ISLAMIC STATES

In February 1979, following months of increasingly widespread civil unrest, the staunchly pro-Western, authoritarian Pahlavi regime in Iran was overthrown. Much to the surprise of Western observers—although not to many observers in the region—the victorious new government came not from a palace coup by Iranian elites, nor from leftist movements that the shah had brutally suppressed, but from a conservative Islamic movement led by Ayatollah Ruhollah Khomeini, a prominent Shi'a cleric who returned from exile in Paris. With the success of the Iranian revolution, a new era of political Islam was born.

Khomeini's new "Islamic Republic" was a radical departure from the earlier revolutionary movements in the Middle East. In contrast to Nasserism and Ba'thism, which combined a variety of anticolonial, Western, and Arab ideas, Khomeini and his followers implemented a conservative political agenda that derived entirely from traditional Islamic thought and practice. Although the details of the nature of "Islamic" governance are complex and hotly debated (including—in fact, particularly—within the Islamic Republic itself), three characteristics distinguish it.

The first is the use of Islamic law—the Shari'ah—in place of various systems of civil law. This went directly against the twentieth-century tendency in the Middle East and other postcolonial regions to replace traditional legal systems based on religion and custom with uniform secular legal codes, often derived from the legal systems of former colonial powers. In practice, the implementation of Shari'ah also involves the imposition of additional conservative social norms that are not actually addressed in the Quran, most conspicuously regarding restrictions on the behavior of women.

Second, the Islamic Republic of Iran placed the supreme authority of the state in the hands of religious councils. These councils also chose a supreme religious leader, a post held by Khomeini until his death in 1989. However, the remaining familiar structures of a modern state—a president, parliament, court system, and so forth—remained intact. The decisions of these secular structures can be overturned by the religious authorities, but such decisions must be made on the basis of Islamic law and tradition rather than personal whim. Candidates for election to the secular government require approval from the religious authorities, and during his lifetime Khomeini retained absolute authority on issues regarding war and other foreign policy matters, although he often chose not to exercise his power.

Finally, Khomeini followed an approach to Islam that placed a high priority on missionary efforts. Consequently, the Islamic Republic saw itself in the vanguard of an international revolution and immediately sought to export its model of conservative political Islam to other states. (In this regard, the agenda of Iranian fundamentalism appeared to the West to be very similar to that of international communism, despite some notable differences, and was treated similarly.) Iran has had only limited success in its effort to promote political Islam, but the concept of a conservative Islamic state following Shari'ah has had tremendous influence throughout the Middle East during the past two decades.

Twenty years after Khomeini's triumphant return to Iran, the experiment of the Islamic Republic can be regarded as a mixed success. Contrary to the predictions of many skeptics who expected an early end to a "medieval" governing structure imposed on an industrializing, urbanizing state, the Islamic Republic has survived, has been generally stable, and has thus far successfully coped with several major difficulties, including a devastating war

© Thomas Hartwell

Photo 4.6   Nearly 2 million people have been killed by fighting and famine during the civil war that has engulfed eastern and southern Sudan since the early 1980s. Millions more have lost their homes and must live in makeshift shelters like this one.

with Iraq, the collapse of the price of oil, and substantial refugee inflows from Iraq and Afghanistan. However, the power of the religious authorities has weakened since the death of Khomeini, and the Iranian model has not been adopted by any other major state in the region.

Two factors account for this. First, in contrast to many depictions in the West, the Iranian model is not one of a totalitarian religious state. A functioning secular government remained in place, both for theological reasons (Islam emphasizes the importance of the *ummah,* the Muslim community as a whole, and not merely the *ulama,* the religious elites) and presumably because the Shi'a clerics had little interest in taking on the responsibility for filling potholes and collecting garbage. These secular political institutions provide a natural source of opposition to the power of the religious authorities, particularly in urban areas. Furthermore, the religious authorities themselves derive their power from the approval and respect of their followers, not from any intrinsic "divine right." Khomeini had very broad support within Iran and therefore could mobilize millions of people, but no leader of Khomeini's stature has emerged since his death, and competition for leadership within the religious councils has weakened their control.

Second, the fact that Iran's Islamic Republic is based on Shi'a theology limits the direct appeal that the Iranian model can have elsewhere in the Islamic world. A small number of other areas—notably in southern Iraq, southern Lebanon, and Bahrain—have sufficiently large Shi'a populations that attempts could be made to apply the model directly (although in Lebanon, Syrian and Israeli military control have made even this impossible; elsewhere, Shi'a political movements have been suppressed by domestic security forces). In the predominantly Sunni populations elsewhere in the Middle East, many of the *general* principles of the Islamic Republic may be attractive, but the specifics of the Shi'a implementation are not.

As a consequence, groups seeking the establishment of a conservative "Islamic" state have become important as sources of opposition throughout the Middle East but have come to power in only three states: Sudan, Mauritania, and, to the east of Iran, Afghanistan. These countries are all very poor, geographically marginal, and, in the cases of Sudan and Afghanistan, weakened by decades of civil war. Islamic movements have mounted significant challenges in Egypt, Syria, Turkey, Gaza and the West Bank, and Algeria; in both Syria and Algeria, these escalated to the point of civil war. But as of November 1999, all these states remain formally secular.

■ DEMOCRATIC POLITIES

As discussed above, a few states in the Middle East—Israel, Lebanon, and Turkey—can be considered at least nominally democratic. These countries developed political arrangements along the lines of the European powers, with parliamentary (rather than presidential) systems of governance. Yet even these countries are not fully "liberal." Instead, due to the emphasis on religion and ethnicity that is inherent in their political structures, all three might better be labeled "conditional" democracies. To a certain extent, these countries used the liberal democratic model—adopting European norms and appealing for European assistance—to make the best of a bad situation (Turkey to recover what it could from the remains of the Ottoman Empire; Lebanon because it was small and divided; and Israel because it was considered illegitimate by its Arab neighbors). But because of the institutional distinctions based on religion or ethnicity that exist between groups of citizens, there are important differences between the democracy found in these three states and the liberal democratic tradition of Europe and North America.

□ Turkey

In Turkey, power rests with members of the assembly, whose terms run for five years. (Earlier elections may be called by the president, who is elected by the assembly for a seven-year term.) Political parties are permitted; however, the government consistently denies the right of Kurds to organize an ethnically based political party and attempts to limit their power as a distinct ethnic group. The government's position is that Kurds may have full civil rights as Turks but cannot express these in the context of Kurdish self-determination. Turkey has also moved to restrict political expression by Islamic movements, most recently (as discussed earlier) by forcing the Refah Party out of the National Assembly. The repeated (although short-lived) interventions by the military to preserve the Atatürk model, as well as long-term suppression of the civil liberties of the Kurds, weaken Turkey's democratic credentials.

□ Israel

For its Jewish citizens, Israel is the most open political system in the Middle East. Its founding principle of maintaining the Jewish character of the state and its failures in dealing with the political rights of the Palestinians, both within Israel and (particularly) in the Occupied Territories, limit the extent to which it can be called fully "liberal," however; furthermore, in the 1990s, a substantial challenge to democratic norms by "Jewish revivalism" has emerged.

Israel's political system is based directly on democratic norms. Most of the leaders of the Zionist movement that led to the founding of Israel were advocates of democratic socialism, and Israel has had liberal democratic institutions from the very beginning. Although military service is important in advancing a political career, the Israeli military has never intervened to overthrow a government, and non-Jewish citizens—notably the sizable Palestinian minority within Israel—are permitted to vote and stand for election, although non-Jewish members of the Israeli parliament (Knesset) were not included in governing coalitions until quite recently.

The structure of power in Israeli politics has gone through three distinct phases. In the early years of the state, politics were dominated by a single party, Labor, whose leadership consisted almost entirely of individuals of European descent. The Labor Party exercised control not only through the legislative mechanisms of the Knesset but also through interlocking control of the labor unions and state enterprises, which provided ample opportunities for patronage.

In 1977, the Labor Party dominance was challenged by a group of conservative parties that coalesced under the name Likud. In addition to providing alternatives to Labor policies—for example, Likud was more interested in expanding settlements in the territory Israel occupied in 1967 and in restraining the Labor-dominated state enterprises—Likud appealed to a number of Jewish voters who had emigrated from places such as Morocco, Yemen, and Iraq. Likud broke the Labor monopoly on political control of Israel and held power for a number of years, either alone or in "national unity" coalitions with Labor.

The third phase began with a change in electoral laws—effective in 1996—that provided for the direct election of a prime minister. Prior to this, the leader whose party gained a plurality of votes in an election was given the first opportunity to negotiate with other party leaders to create a ruling coalition. If successful, that person became the prime minister; if not, the president would turn to the party with the second-highest number of votes and give that leader the same chance to form a government.

Although intended to make the prime minister less dependent on the unstable parliamentary coalitions within the Knesset, the direct election of the prime minister had the unexpected effect of encouraging the growth of a number of small, single-interest parties in the elections of 1996 and 1999. Both Labor and Likud lost substantial numbers of seats to new, ethnically oriented parties, notably Israeli B'Aliyah, which primarily represents recent Russian emigrants, and Shas, which now has the third-largest number of seats in the Knesset.

In addition to the potential parliamentary instability caused by the proliferation of small parties, the liberal character of Israeli democracy is also openly questioned by some of the religious parties, who wish to see much more power granted to religious authorities. For example, the relative domains of secular and religious courts are being sharply contested, despite the fact that religious councils already have considerably greater power in Israel than they have in most other liberal democracies. Consequently, Israel is confronting many of the same issues of balancing secular and religious power facing Muslim states in the region.

□ Lebanon

The situation in Lebanon is complicated. Constitutionally, Lebanon is a parliamentary republic with an elected 128-member Chamber of Deputies reflecting a convoluted confessional division with at least eighteen separate entities. The 1989 Taif Accords attempted to modify the balance of political power to reflect more accurately the various groups; however, it did not fundamentally modify the notion of defining people by their political-religious affiliation.

The return to democracy after fifteen years of civil and international conflict has not been easy. In September and October 1992, Lebanon held its first general elections in twenty years. Many Lebanese, especially Christians, boycotted because they said the electoral framework was unfair; others, however, argued that the real issue was that Lebanese Christians were no longer given the drastically disproportionate representation they had held in the past.

Due in part to the boycott but also reflecting both Lebanese preferences and Lebanese pragmatism, pro-Syrian candidates and Islamic groups aligned with Iran won a number of the seats. The new prime minister, who also served as the finance minister, was Rafiq Hariri, a Sunni and Lebanese-Saudi national born in Lebanon. Hariri, a billionaire who made his money in the construction industry, had the support of both Syria and Saudi Arabia (which was essential). The parliament chose Christian Elias Hrawi to be the new president. Top cabinet leadership reflected the continuing use of family ties and confessional distinctions in the allocation of positions of power. Nabih Berri, head of the Syrian-backed Shi'a party Amal (Hope), became the speaker of the parliament. President Hrawi's son-in-law, Fares Buwayz, was named foreign minister, and the minister of defense was Mohsen Dalloul, a Shi'a who had ties to Syria.

The second post–Taif Accords parliamentary elections were held in August and September 1996, under a new election law passed the previous July. Opponents maintained that the revised law violated the Taif Accords in ways that benefited government supporters; however, they were unable to stop the law's passage. During the campaign season, an informal alliance of the Lebanese government, represented by Hariri, Nabih Berri of Amal, and the Druze leader Walid Jumblatt, joined together to minimize the electoral success of Hezbollah, a position consistent with Syria's desire to support the more secular Amal over Hezbollah. When the votes were tallied, Hariri's cross-confessional coalition had won a bloc of twenty seats, as had Amal's cross-confessional coalition. Ten seats went to the Druze and their Christian allies; Hezbollah and its allies received nine seats.

Under the new election law, there was supposed to have been a presidential election in fall 1995 to replace Elias Hrawi since a president is only permitted to serve a single six-year term. However, the parliament ignored this requirement and on October 19, 1995, voted to extend Hrawi's term for an additional three years, angering many Lebanese who saw it as a blatant attempt to curry favor with the Syrians. Three years later, in October 1998, Emile Lahoud was elected president.

■ CONCLUSION

At the dawn of a new millennium in the Christian calendar, the states of the Middle East are confronting three major political challenges. First, the region is undergoing a generational change in both its leaders and political issues: the faces and agendas that dominated the last three decades of the twentieth century seem unlikely to be as critical in the first decades of the twenty-first century. Second, virtually every state in the region is experiencing tensions from competing political perspectives advocating either increased democracy or greater religious influence in government. Finally, there are growing pressures on governments to implement policies that will improve economic performance and respond to a global economy that does not place a premium on oil. In this concluding section, we will look briefly at each of these issues.

As we noted earlier, most governments in the Middle East have been remarkably stable, with individual leaders remaining in power for decades. However, many pivotal figures in the region are elderly and ailing and are likely either to die or become incapacitated in the near future. Even when successors have been clearly designated—as in Iraq and in the recent transfer of power in Jordan and Morocco—the new leaders will not have the experience or outlook of their predecessors. When succession is unclear—as in Egypt, Libya, or the Palestinian Authority—substantial periods of instability are possible.

As the leaders of the elder generation are fading, so are many of the older issues. The Cold War—during which the superpowers both used and were used by many states in the region—ended at the beginning of the 1990s. The last elements of Arab-Israeli dispute—Lebanon, the Golan Heights, and the Palestinians—appear closer to resolution than at any time in the past. The revolutionary secular ideologies of the postcolonial period—Nasserism and Ba'thism—have faded and no longer inspire serious intellectual debate. The future agenda appears unlikely to mirror the past.

In place of these concerns, a new issue clearly dominates: the often competing pressures for either democratic or religious governance. Most of the states in the region are experiencing demands for greater popular involvement in government, and several have made significant progress to accommodate this. Such moves toward greater democratization are consistent with trends in most of the world.

The Middle East, however, is almost unique in the strength of politicized religion—usually in a very conservative form—as an alternative to secular democracy. This has affected the full range of states, including countries such as Turkey and Israel that have strong parliamentary traditions. This resurgence of the political power of religion has come as a surprise to many analysts, and its future is difficult to predict.

Finally, as the regional and military conflicts of the region fade and the high oil prices of the OPEC decade become a distant memory, the issue of economic development is becoming more important in politics. With the decline in oil revenues, there will be greater pressure on Middle Eastern regimes to industrialize and diversify their economies. The professional class of accountants, engineers, and doctors who once lived as politically powerless expatriates are likely to demand a greater share of political power. The Middle East will also need to reassess its role in the global economy to decide, for instance, whether or not to pursue regional integration, link with the more developed economies of Europe, or join with the less developed economies of Africa and southern and central Asia. These will be difficult questions for the new generation of Arabs, Iranians, Israelis, and Turks as they enter the twenty-first century.

■ NOTE

This chapter benefited enormously from the comments of Donald L. Gordon and Gwenn Okrulick, neither of whom should be held responsible for whatever errors of fact or interpretation remain despite their wise counsel.

■ BIBLIOGRAPHY

Ahmad, Mumtaz. 1997. "Political Islam: Can It Become a Loyal Opposition?" *Middle East Policy* 5, no. 1:68–74.
Alexander, Christopher. 1997. "Authoritarianism and Civil Society in Tunisia." *Middle East Report* 27, no. 4:34–38.
Al-Haj, Abdullah Juma. 1996. "The Politics of Participation in the Gulf Cooperation Council States: The Omani Consultative Council." *Middle East Journal* 50, no. 4:559–571.
Anderson, Lisa. 1991. "Absolutism and the Resilience of the Monarchy." *Political Science Quarterly* 106, no. 1.
Andoni, Lamis. 1997. "Jordanian Elections—Setback for Democratisation." *Middle East International* (December 5):19.
Antonius, George. 1946. *The Arab Awakening: The Story of the Arab National Movement*. New York: G. P. Putnam's Sons.
Arnold, Guy. 1997. *The Maverick State: Qaddafi and the New World Order*. Lon-

don: Cassell.

Bill, James A., and Robert Springborg. 1994. *Politics in the Middle East*. 4th ed. New York: HarperCollins.

Brynen, Rex, Bahgat Korany, and Paul Noble. 1995. "Introduction: Theoretical Perspectives on Arab Liberalization and Democratization." Pp. 3–27 in Brynen, Korany, and Noble (eds.), *Political Liberalization and Democratization in the Arab World,* Vol. 1: *Theoretical Perspectives.* Boulder: Lynne Rienner.

Bulliet, Richard. 1999. "Twenty Years of Islamic Politics." *Middle East Journal* 53, no. 2:189–200.

Carapico, Sheila. 1997. "From the Editors." *Middle East Report* 27, no. 3:1, 24.

Dekmejian, R. Hrair. 1998. "Saudi Arabia's Consultative Council." *Middle East Journal* 52, no. 2:204–218.

Evron, Boas. 1995. *Jewish State or Israeli Nation?* Bloomington: Indiana University Press.

Fakhro, Munira A. 1997. "The Uprising in Bahrain: An Assessment." Pp. 167–188 in Gary G. Sick and Lawrence G. Potter (eds.), *The Persian Gulf at the Millennium: Essays in Politics, Economy, Security, and Religion*. New York: St. Martin's Press.

Gause, F. Gregory III. 1994. *Oil Monarchies: Domestic and Security Challenges in the Arab Gulf States*. New York: Council on Foreign Relations.

Halliday, Fred. 1979. *Iran: Dictatorship and Development*. 2d ed. New York: Penguin Books.

———. 1997. *"Arabia Without Sultans* Revisited." *Middle East Report* 27, no. 3:27–29.

Hiro, Dilip. 1996. *Dictionary of the Middle East*. London: Macmillan.

Hopwood, Derek. 1985. *Egypt: Politics and Society 1945–1984*. 2d ed. London: Allen and Unwin.

Hudson, Michael C. 1977. *Arab Politics: The Search for Legitimacy*. New Haven: Yale University Press.

Human Rights Watch. 1997. *Routine Abuse, Routine Denial: Civil Rights and the Political Crisis in Bahrain*. New York: Human Rights Watch.

Husain, Mir Zohair. 1995. *Global Islamic Politics*. New York: HarperCollins College Publishers.

Ibrahim, Saad Eddin. 1995. "Liberalization and Democratization in the Arab World: An Overview." Pp. 29–57 in Rex Brynen, Bahgat Korany, and Paul Noble (eds.), *Political Liberalization and Democratization in the Arab World,* Vol. 1: *Theoretical Perspectives*. Boulder: Lynne Rienner.

Khalidi, Rashid (ed.). 1991. *The Origins of Arab Nationalism*. New York: Columbia University Press.

Kienle, Eberhard (ed.). 1994. *Contemporary Syria: Liberalization Between Cold War and Cold Peace*. New York: St. Martin's Press.

———. 1998. "More Than a Response to Islamism: The Political Deliberalization of Egypt in the 1990s." *Middle East Journal* 52, no. 2:219–235.

El-Kikhia, Mansour O. 1997. *Libya's Qaddafi: The Politics of Contradiction*. Gainesville: University of Florida Press.

Korany, Bahgat. 1998. "Restricted Democratization from Above: Egypt." Pp. 39–69 in Bahgat Korany, Rex Brynen, and Paul Noble (eds.), *Political Liberalization and Democratization in the Arab World,* Vol. 2: *Comparative Experiences*. Boulder: Lynne Rienner.

Kyle, Keith, and Joel Peters (eds.). 1993. *Whither Israel: The Domestic Challenges*. New York: I. B. Tauris.

Levine, Mark. 1998. "National Elections in the Middle East and the Arab World

Since 1980." *Middle East Report* 209:16.

Makiya, Kanan. 1993. *Cruelty and Silence: War, Tyranny, Uprising, and the Arab World*. New York: W. W. Norton.

Melhem, Hisham. 1997. "Syria Between Two Transitions." *Middle East Report* 27, no. 2:2–7.

Norton, Augustus Richard (ed.). 1995. *Civil Society in the Middle East*. Vol. 1. Leiden: E. J. Brill.

Omaar, Rageh. 1997. "Jordan: A Changed Landscape." *Middle East International* (December 5).

O'Reilly, Marc J. 1998. "Omanibalancing: Oman Confronts an Uncertain Future." *Middle East Journal* 52, no. 1:70–84.

Penrose, Edith. 1993. "From Economic Liberalization to International Integration: The Role of the State." Pp. 3–25 in Tim Niblock and Emma Murphy (eds.), *Economic and Political Liberalization in the Middle East*. London: British Academic Press.

Putnam, Robert D. 1993. *Making Democracy Work: Civic Traditions in Modern Italy*. Princeton: Princeton University Press.

Richards, Alan, and John Waterbury. 1996. *A Political Economy of the Middle East*. 2d ed. Boulder, Colo.: Westview Press.

Sadowski, Yahya. 1997. "The End of the Counterrevolution? The Politics of Economic Adjustment in Kuwait." *Middle East Report* 27, no. 3:7–11.

Sela, Avraham. 1988. *The Decline of the Arab-Israeli Conflict: Middle East Politics and the Quest for Regional Order*. Albany: State University Press of New York.

Simons, Geoff. 1996. *Libya: The Struggle for Survival*. 2d ed. New York: St. Martin's Press.

Sprinzak, Ehud, and Larry Diamond. 1993. *Israeli Democracy Under Stress*. Boulder, Colo.: Lynne Rienner.

Stork, Joe. 1997. "Bahrain's Crisis Worsens." *Middle East Report* 27, no. 3:33–35.

Tibi, Bassam. 1997. *Arab Nationalism: Between Islam and the Nation-State*. 3d ed. New York: St. Martin's Press.

UNDP (United Nations Development Programme). 1998. *Human Development Report 1998*. New York: Oxford University Press.

U.S. ACDA (U.S. Arms Control and Disarmament Agency). 1997. *World Military Expenditures and Arms Transfers 1996*. Washington, D.C.: U.S. Government Printing Office.

Van Dam, Nikolaos. 1996. *The Struggle for Power in Syria: Politics and Society Under Asad and the Ba'th Party*. London: I. B. Taurus.

Weber, Max. 1947. *The Theory of Social and Economic Organization*. New York: Oxford University Press.

Wilson, Frank L. 1996. *Concepts and Issues in Comparative Politics: An Introduction to Comparative Analysis*. Upper Saddle River, N.J.: Prentice-Hall.

Yorke, Valerie. 1989. "Hussein's Bid to Legitimise Hashemite Rule." *Middle East International* (November 17).

■ 5 ■

International Relations

Mary Ann Tétreault

■ SOVEREIGNTY IN THE MIDDLE EAST

All the bounded areas on modern world maps are called *nation-states*, but their qualities as political communities are not alike. Many barely qualify as *nations*, a term usually defined as a population "sharing [a] historic territory, common myths and historical memories," a common economy, and a popular culture (Smith, 1991:14; also Connor, 1994). Some also fail the test for *states*. A state is a compulsory political organization claiming a monopoly on the legitimate use of force to execute its orders over a specific territory (Weber, 1978; Jackson, 1990). Whatever their failings when viewed from within, however, when viewed from without, nation-states today are seen as equally sovereign. As members of the United Nations (UN) General Assembly, the Organization of Petroleum Exporting Countries (OPEC), or the Arab League, every state has equal status. Sometimes called *negative sovereignty* (Jackson, 1990:27), this refers to the principle that every formally recognized state has the same rights under international law, including the right to be free from external interference in its internal affairs.

Before the twentieth century, nation-states were only one of several forms of political organization of territory. Even among nation-states, only a few were thought to have negative sovereignty. European governments and their agents—not only armies and navies but also privateers and for-profit corporations such as the British East India and West India companies—felt quite free to pursue imperial ventures of various types, almost all of them outside Europe (Doyle, 1986; Polanyi, 1944). By the late nineteenth century, the state ideal—the desire to have one's own state—had spread. Attitudes toward imperialism changed, and nationalist movements flowered. European imperialists found themselves forced to justify their continued control of foreign territories.

Adopting a common perspective toward native populations, Europeans said they were engaged in a "civilizing mission," bearing the "white man's burden" to act as custodians of nations "unfit" to govern themselves (Jackson, 1990:71; also Said, 1993). This justification wore thin during World War I. The U.S. government, under the leadership of President Woodrow Wilson, established "self-determination" as one of the goals of the war, that is, the right of a people to choose their own government. After the war, however, this principle was limited geographically to central and eastern Europe, areas where the imperialists in charge were on the losing side. The imperialists among the winners of World War I opposed the application of self-determination in Asia and the Middle East. In those regions, they were either the dominant colonial powers themselves (see, e.g., Antonius, 1946; Moynihan, 1993) or else wanted the stability of colonial rule by friendly governments to safeguard direct foreign investments by their citizens (Bromley, 1994).

The geopolitical position of the Middle East as a strategic and economic crossroads linking Europe to Asia—for example, the Suez Canal and Palestine were important waystations on the route to India—explains some of Britain's reluctance to loosen its control over much of the region (Fromkin, 1989:281–283). The French also had imperialist interests in the Middle East, including dependencies in North Africa and a long-standing connection to the Christian community on Mount Lebanon. Both Britain and France wanted privileged access to territories rumored to be rich in petroleum reserves. The U.S. government was equally committed to the continuation of colonial domination of the Middle East to protect U.S. oil investors (Bromley, 1994).

Keeping the Ottoman Empire—the "sick man" of Europe—alive had been a concern of European foreign offices for decades. European leaders feared that if the Ottoman Empire were to collapse, their countries would be forced to go to war over who would get the choicest pieces of its carcass. The picture changed as Britain and France became allies, their German rival was defeated in World War I, and the revolution and consequent preoccupation with internal consolidation that took Russia out of the "great game" (imperial competition with Britain in western Asia) altered the balance of power in Europe. The "sick man" could be allowed to die because the wartime victors were confident that they could control the "successor states" without too much conflict between themselves. But the victors did not intend to give up their imperial "burdens." Instead, they adopted the position that some states were simply too "immature" to be fully sovereign.

Consequently, colonial possessions such as Algeria remained colonies after the war. Protectorates and bonds, the "special relationships" that allowed Britain to control the foreign policies of the small Gulf states

(Anscombe, 1997), remained in effect. In addition, the League of Nations, the forerunner of today's United Nations, granted "mandates" to individual European powers, which allowed Britain and France to control nominally independent states created from territories that previously were part of the Ottoman Empire. As a result, leaders and populations throughout the Middle East felt cheated of self-determination, and achieving negative sovereignty became a cherished goal of local political regimes. At the same time, however, the persistence of "traditional ideas on the privileges and vulnerability of states and a substantial amount of confusion between the national state apparatus and those who are manipulating it . . . [resulted in] twenty-two . . . weak Arab states in a highly integrated world system" (Salamé, 1990:31).

This anomalous situation came about in part because of the way the aftermath of World War I shaped the foreign and domestic relations of Middle Eastern states. As we have seen in previous chapters, the formal boundaries defining many of these states were products of postwar Great Power politics. Rather than conforming to local interests and traditions, territories and peoples were divided and combined to satisfy the state interests of the major powers and weaken potential local challengers to their domination of the region. Large parts of Syria, the heart of the Arabs' hoped-for independent state, were sheared off by European imperialists and appropriated by ambitious local competitors. An independent Lebanon was carved from Syria to suit the French and their Maronite Christian protégés. In consequence, Syria became smaller, less viable economically, and therefore more dependent on France. Syria lost ground also to the battlefield prowess of the founder of modern Turkey. Mustafa Kemal, who was known by the name Atatürk (father of the Turks) after 1933, refused to accept the victorious powers as the sole arbiters of the boundaries defining the postwar Middle East. Instead, he extended the territory of Turkey through military conquest, adding a piece of greater Syria to the area under his new government's control.

When they redrew the map of Syria, the mapmakers neglected to give much thought to the consequences their exercise would have for Lebanon's integrity. The core of the new state, the community of Mount Lebanon, had evolved over 400 years as a politically pluralist, multicultural community under Ottoman rule (Harik, 1990:13–14). The new state of Lebanon also was multicultural, incorporating substantial populations of Muslims and Druze along with the French-favored Maronite Christians. Their minority status increased the dependence of the Maronites on their French protectors. The Maronites were able to negotiate constitutional concessions from non-Christian groups that gave Christians the lion's share of political authority in the new state. However, even as their relative proportion of the Lebanese population declined, the Maronites resisted

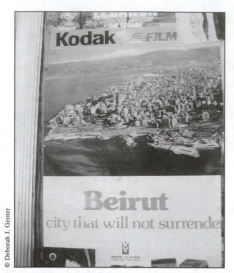

Photo 5.1 This poster, taped inside the window of a camera shop, illustrates the steadfastness of the Lebanese in the face of decades of civil war and international violence.

allowing others to enjoy the same political rights as themselves. This contributed to the delegitimation of the state and, beginning in 1958, to recurrent civil war (Maktabi, 1996).

The fate of the Hashemite dynasty is another example of actions initiated by the postwar mapmakers that, over time, corroded the sovereignty of Middle Eastern states. Partly motivated by the need to reward Abdullah ibn Husayn, a son of the Hashemite ruler of the Hejaz and a leader of the British-assisted Arab Revolt against the Turks during World War I, the British divided their Palestine mandate to create the kingdom of Transjordan. Faisal ibn Hussein, Abdullah's brother and the local leader most closely identified with the Arab Revolt, was proclaimed king of Syria in 1920. By then, Syria was far from the "Arab state" that Faisal had dreamed of leading, but as things turned out, he did not get to lead it for long. A British protégé like his brother Abdullah, Faisal was ousted from Syria by France, the mandatory power there. In 1921 Faisal became king of another British mandate, Iraq.

Iraq presents one of the clearest examples of the perversity of the mandates' boundary-drawing and state-building process. It was assembled from large segments of what used to be three Ottoman districts: Baghdad, with its majority of Sunni Muslim Arabs; Basra, where the majority of the population is Shi'a Arab; and Mosul, where oil had been discovered on the territory of primarily Sunni Muslim Kurds (Marr, 1985). Iraq's chronic problems with "state building" are rooted in its troubled history as a trinational state (Makiya, 1996). However, a number of scholars, chief among them Michael Hudson (1977), say that Iraq's problems are not unique. These writers believe that a lack of "positive sovereignty"—popular legitimacy plus the capacity to govern—is widespread throughout the Middle East.

The transition from an international system where only the most powerful enjoyed negative sovereignty to one where negative sovereignty was declared a right of every state coincided with the process of modern state formation in the Middle East. Many of the new Middle Eastern states were small, nearly all were weak, and some were dependent on external support to survive. These qualities diminished their capacity to govern independently as well as to mobilize the support and loyalty of their citizens (Salamé, 1990). Both citizen-nationalists and their governments tended to place most of the blame for their countries' problems on Western imperialism. As a result, the leaders and populations of Middle Eastern states incorporated into their national ideologies—their "state ideas"—a strong bias against external interference. Even so, where states were too weak to prevent it, external intervention by major powers persisted (Weber, 1995). Today, external intervention remains a characteristic of the international relations of many states in the Middle East.

The arbitrary nature of state boundaries in this region, coupled with high levels of cultural integration arising from common religious, historical, and linguistic roots, seems to encourage boundary violations by neighboring states. Transnational movements such as pan-Arabism, which is based on Arab nationalist ideologies, and pan-Islamism and "political Islam," movements that transcend ethnic divisions, provide ideological reasons for intervention. The ambitions of leaders of several Middle Eastern states—Egypt, Syria, Iraq, Iran, and more recently, Saudi Arabia— have long prompted them to intervene in the politics of other countries. Their leaders justify such actions as demanded by "historic missions," goals that transcend state boundaries: defeating imperialism, liberating Palestine, achieving Arab unity, or defending Islamic values (Salamé, 1994:87). However, even after the various nations of the Middle East were liberated from colonial domination, people who applied the norm of negative sovereignty against outsiders rarely used it openly to criticize the foreign policies of states within the region. This was especially true among Arab observers before the Gulf War in 1990–1991.

External intervention was not uniformly destructive to Middle Eastern states. To some, it left a legacy of oil income as a result of foreign companies, many based in Britain or the United States, discovering and developing their oil reserves. At first limited to royalties and fees, the incomes of oil-exporting governments grew at astronomical rates following the oil revolution of the early 1970s, which forced oil prices upward and transferred control of oil reserves from foreign companies to national governments (Tétreault, 1985). Oil has been a mixed blessing to its owners, however (Amuzegar, 1982). Although it did give them more choices and leverage in foreign policy than they otherwise might have had, it insulated state-building elites from domestic demands for political participation, thus retarding or reversing democratization (see, e.g., Crystal, 1990; Gasiorowski, 1991). It also fostered a strategy of economic development more responsive to external than internal needs (e.g., Luke, 1983; 1985).

Oil reserves are unevenly distributed among the states of the Middle East, but oil income affects nearly all of them. Especially before the collapse of oil prices in 1986, oil-exporting states spent large amounts on foreign aid (Hallwood and Sinclair, 1982), salaries to pay imported workers (Ibrahim, 1980), and direct foreign investments in neighboring countries (Stephens, 1976). As oil incomes rose dramatically beginning in 1970, a sizable proportion of this money was spent on arms (Dawisha, 1982–1983; Nitzan and Bichler, 1995). The ability of Middle Eastern states to distribute aid and obtain arms without depending on extraregional patrons increases their external influence. For example, Saudi aid to Sunni Islamist groups strengthens their power in Arab states like Egypt and Kuwait. In Afghanistan, Saudi money nourished the most radical Islamist factions, contributing to their capacity to dominate Afghan politics after the socialist regime was defeated. Oil revenues also make these states tempting customers for arms merchants, including foreign governments who use the strategic dependence of small oil-exporting states to extort lucrative contracts for themselves or their national armaments industries (Clawson, 1995).

■ THE MIDDLE EAST AND THE GREAT POWERS

As Deborah J. Gerner and Philip A. Schrodt discussed in Chapter 4, most areas of the Middle East began the twentieth century as clients or dependencies of one or another European power. Even modern Turkey, the core of the old Ottoman Empire, had been an economic colony of its European creditors since the establishment of the Ottoman Debt Commission in 1881 (Polanyi, 1944). The Turkish state idea incorporated elements of what Atatürk saw as the greatest strengths of the West: modernization, secularization, and state-centered nationalism. His goal was to make Turkey an equal of the Great Powers, not a dependency of any of them.

But some leaders of Middle Eastern states actually welcomed European intervention. Emir Mubarak of Kuwait (r. 1896–1915), for example, actively sought British protection toward the end of the nineteenth century, both to prevent his country from being attached to the Ottoman Empire (Rush, 1987; Al-Ebraheem, 1975) and to attract outside help in consolidating the position of himself and his descendants as the rulers of Kuwait (Anscombe, 1997). Abdul Aziz ibn Saud manipulated British officials to help him acquire more than half the territory of Kuwait in 1922 (Dickson, 1956). Until the conclusion of World War II, he relied on British and U.S. gold to help him consolidate his conquests on the Arabian Peninsula and keep the leaders of subordinate tribes firmly in his camp (Anderson, 1981; Salamé, 1990). Nearly every Middle Eastern government was eager to open its territory to oil exploration and development by foreign-owned companies. As a consequence, external intervention by the Great Powers or their agents was neither always nor uniformly condemned by Middle Eastern political leaders, though it was nearly always condemned by citizen nationalists.

Imperialism imposed grave burdens on most of the region. Along with strategic interests such as protecting the route to India, imperial powers used their colonies and dependencies primarily to make themselves rich (Wolf, 1982). Local economies were distorted by drawing national boundaries through areas and populations that were parts of larger trading and commercial markets. Colonies and economic dependencies were bled for the benefit of settlers and overseas investors. Oil companies took the lion's share of profits from the exploitation of the region's petroleum reserves (see, e.g., Rand, 1975). Local customs everywhere were violated with impunity by foreign occupiers, many of whom also belittled the religion, society, and culture of the populations they were milking (see, e.g., Ahmed, 1992; Tétreault, 1995). Continued Zionist immigration into Palestine, which had begun some years before the Balfour Declaration of 1917 pledged British support for a Jewish homeland in Palestine, threatened the communities and livelihoods of the native population. The resulting political, economic, and psychological burdens were aggravated by the imperialists' practice not only of playing social groups within countries against one another to enhance their political control (Migdal, 1988; al-Naqeeb, 1990) but also of pitting one country against others in situations such as negotiations for oil concessions, to increase the colonizers' economic returns (e.g., Chisholm, 1975).

□ Dependency

Dependency is a relationship of inequality between a developing and a developed country (Caporaso, 1978). Creating dependency is a conscious aim of colonization and imperialism. During the eighteenth century, when the American states were colonies of Britain, the British passed laws such as the Navigation Acts requiring the colonies to buy products manufactured in Britain and sell raw materials back to Britain. Britain benefited not only from this trade itself but also from being able to process raw materials purchased from the colonies. This provided additional jobs for British workers and tax revenues for the government. Even though colonial trade was a relationship of exchange, the exchange was unequal and intended to create a permanently unequal relationship between the trading partners.

During the nineteenth and twentieth centuries, imperialism enabled Europe and the United States to gain similar preferential access to natural resources located in the Middle East. Governments signed exclusive contracts with U.S. and British oil companies to develop their local industries. The companies purchased supplies and equipment from home and also

imported all but the most menial workers. Oil development took prece-
dence over the local economy. In oil-rich Hasa in Saudi Arabia, agriculture
was destroyed to accommodate pipelines and pumping stations. Most of
the oil that was produced was sold overseas as a raw material that was
both processed and consumed outside the producing countries.

Foreign oil companies no longer own Middle Eastern oil and gas reserves. However, the way these reserves were developed and the way the
domestic economies of oil-exporting countries were constructed around oil
and gas production and sales ensured the continuation of dependent economic relations between Middle Eastern states and external markets beyond their control. When oil prices fall, for example, there is little that one
or even several oil exporters can do to make them go back up and stay
there. OPEC had some success in reversing the fall in oil prices that had
occurred during the 1960s and in keeping oil prices high during the 1970s.
However, much of this success depended on ephemeral circumstances such
as the blockage of the Suez Canal by the Six Day War in 1967 and additions to oil demand from the Vietnam War. Within a few years, more permanent structural changes, such as the development of new oilfields outside OPEC countries, brought prices back down. Oil prices hit historically
low levels in the mid-1980s, leading to economic hardship and domestic
conflict in many oil-exporting countries (Hunter, 1986).

The domestic economies of many oil-exporting countries were organized to spend oil revenues rather than to produce a wide range of goods
and services to satisfy local needs and wants. The availability of cash from
oil sales, along with high demand for foreign products ranging from tanks
and machine guns to cars and TV programs, created consumption patterns
that depended on imported goods. Oil exporters were encouraged to expand production capacity to ensure that they could continue to buy what
they wanted from overseas. As capacity expanded, some oil exporters felt
compelled to produce more oil to justify their investment and to finance
other projects. Producing more oil soon glutted markets, pushing prices
down and encouraging even more production to keep total income levels
up. This vicious circle came around again in the late 1990s, when depressed oil prices once again caused hardship and domestic conflicts over
a shrinking economic pie. Despite the ups and down of the oil market over
the past thirty years, the region continues to depend on oil sales for a high
proportion of government revenues.

□ Cliency

Cliency is a strategic relationship between a major power seeking a
local base and a less powerful state controlling assets compatible with the
needs of the major power (Gasiorowski, 1991; Tétreault, 1991). Examples

of attractive strategic assets are geographic location, port and basing facilities, and a regime willing to act on behalf of the major power. In return for one or more of these assets, the major power patron transfers arms, military training and equipment, and other types of military and economic assistance to the less strategically powerful client. Both sides gain in a cliency relationship, but unlike the case in dependency relationships, often the government of the smaller state gains proportionately more than the larger partner. As the client becomes embedded in the foreign policy strategies of the patron, the dependence of the patron on maintaining its strategic assets grows while its leverage against the client government declines. Meanwhile, using extranational assets it receives from its patron, the client government can protect itself against challenges to its power by buying off foreign and domestic enemies and using military force against them.

The Cold War increased the importance of cliency in the relationships of Middle Eastern states with major outside powers, although cliency relations also were common before then. The superpowers were interested in economic gains, especially from their relations with oil-exporting states, but their primary concerns were strategic. A large portion of foreign aid from the superpowers took the form of military assistance. Nearly all of it imposed obligations in the form of services required of the Middle Eastern client state: diplomatic and military support and preferential access by the patron state and its agents to the client's domestic resources (Gasiorowski, 1991). Some of the resources provided by patron states were used by rebellious military officers against weak and unpopular client governments. One example is the 1969 overthrow of King Idris in Libya (Bill and Springborg, 1994). Some were used by client governments against their own populations, which occurred in Iran (Gasiorowski, 1991).

As international politics was reoriented around the Cold War, dependency relations also changed. The market for Middle Eastern oil concessions became more competitive, most markedly in Libya but also in the Arabian Peninsula states (Penrose, 1968). These changes contributed to shifting control of oil from foreign multinational oil companies to host governments (Tétreault, 1985). Another apparent benefit from the changed character of the external balance of power resulted from the replacement of imperialism by at least a rhetoric of external sovereignty. The accepted convention, that states were autonomous and chose their own partners, meant that the superpowers sometimes could be brought to bid for client allies, a situation that Egypt used to great advantage in financing its Aswan Dam project in the 1950s (Mosley, 1978).

Too close an alliance with either superpower risked retaliation against an overly compliant regime from disgruntled nationalists. This encouraged strong leaders to develop strategies to preserve their autonomy from Cold

War patrons. Egypt's Gamal Abdel Nasser joined other leaders of developing countries at a conference in Bandung, Indonesia, in 1955 to form the "nonaligned movement." Nonalignment promised the reality of external sovereignty to aspiring new states. Yet despite declarations of nonalignment and mutual support from other nominally nonaligned states, few countries in the Middle East were successful at finding a middle ground between the superpowers.

One of the success stories was Kuwait, a small state that had begun to orchestrate a balance of power among potential patrons as part of the state-building strategy of its first twentieth-century emir, Mubarak (Al-Ebraheem, 1975; Anscombe, 1997; Assiri, 1990; Tétreault, 1991). Kuwait's century of persistence in courting a whole panoply of external partners was rewarded after it was invaded by Iraq in 1990. Influential foreign nationals associated with Kuwaiti-owned companies were able to argue the Kuwaiti case to major world leaders immediately following news of the invasion, before they had decided how to respond, and European governments hosting major Kuwaiti investments moved rapidly to protect Kuwaiti interests (Tétreault, 1997). Due in part to a history of cordial relations between Kuwait and Moscow, including Kuwaiti foreign assistance to the Soviet Union following a major earthquake in 1989, a multinational coalition that included both the United States and the Soviet Union was rapidly assembled. Despite strong support for Iraq among the populations of nearly every state in the Middle East, the unity of their U.S. and Russian patrons, coupled with positive incentives ranging from debt forgiveness to promises of future economic assistance from Kuwait, pulled nearly all of them into the Kuwaiti camp (Tétreault, 1992).

Unlike Kuwait, most Middle Eastern states found that a nonaligned strategy was difficult to sustain in practice. Saudi Arabia proclaimed itself to be nonaligned. However, it was almost entirely oriented toward the West despite the fact that the United States and other Western governments were strong supporters of Israel (Korany, 1991; Quandt, 1981). Religious militancy and oil interests account for a large part of this anomaly. A structurally similar set of pressures upset the efforts of so-called confrontation states to remain nonaligned. To obtain military support for their wars against U.S.-supported Israel, Syria, Iraq, and Egypt drifted into the Soviet Union's orbit. As the region's total oil income increased, however, the Arab confrontation states found they could get foreign military assistance from their Arab oil-exporting neighbors (Dawisha, 1982–1983).

☐ Moving Toward Regional Autonomy

The end of the Cold War initiated a global realignment that also affected the international relations of the Middle East. During the era of the most intense East-West confrontation, "hot wars" in the Middle East were widely viewed as proxy conflicts between superpower clients. As Soviet power weakened in the late 1980s, Soviet capacity to intervene abroad also declined. Consequently, local components of regional politics became more prominent. The effects can be seen in the alignment of external powers during the Gulf War (1990–1991) and in changes in external support for the principals in the Arab-Israeli conflict.

The 1990 invasion of Kuwait by Iraq pushed the United States in a few days from rapprochement with Iraq to demands for a complete Iraqi withdrawal from Kuwait (Sciolino, 1991; Smith, 1992). Working through the UN Security Council, the United States spearheaded a series of resolutions condemning Iraq and imposing severe economic sanctions against it. The Soviet Union was a prominent part of the anti-Iraq coalition. Although it tried to promote a negotiated settlement, the Soviet government stuck with the coalition throughout the nearly six weeks of war (Melkumyan, 1992). Soviet cooperation was critical in the Security Council, the formal venue for the coordination of the coalition against Iraq. Had the Soviet Union chosen to use its Security Council veto, both the economic sanctions against Iraq imposed within days of the invasion and the multinational military operation launched in January 1991 would have been impossible to achieve. Soviet participation also muted, although it

© Thomas Hartwell

Photo 5.2 Kuwaiti troops, operating out of Saudi Arabia, prepare to liberate Kuwait in 1991. After a month-long bombing campaign, the ground war lasted just one hundred hours.

could not entirely quell, criticism of U.S. policy by those sympathetic to Iraq or opposed to unilateral military activities by the United States on the Arabian Peninsula.

Even before the end of the Cold War, the Soviet Union had softened its stance toward Israel, for example, by allowing Soviet Jews to emigrate. Consequently, the United States became the predominant extraregional power intervening in the Israeli-Palestinian conflict. However, the pro-Israeli bias of the U.S. government remained, and Palestinians were discouraged as their offers of compromise were repeatedly treated as new floors for additional rounds of negotiations (Ashrawi, 1995). The post–Cold War realignment offered an opportunity for new external participants to alter the environment of those negotiations. The Norwegian government seized the opportunity, initiating talks that allowed the Israelis and the Palestinians to engage simultaneously in public negotiations in Madrid and secret negotiations in Oslo. The agreement that they hammered out was signed in September 1993 in Washington, D.C.

The end of the Cold War initiated a period of global domination by the United States. At the same time, it also removed a lever for prying support from U.S. allies for policies they believe to be unwise, unnecessary, or contrary to their own national interests. As a result, such doctrines as "dual containment," under which the United States justifies its demands that other countries isolate both Iran and Iraq, do not have the widespread support among U.S. allies that the original containment policy against the Soviet Union did. France was the only major Western ally pursuing a notably independent foreign policy toward the Middle East during most of the Cold War (Wood, 1993). Today, however, the Oslo Accords are only one example of the growing foreign policy autonomy of countries inside and outside the Middle East under the "new world order."

■ THE MIDDLE EAST AS A FOREIGN POLICY SUBSYSTEM

When Iraq invaded Kuwait in August 1990, a common refrain was that such an event had never occurred before: Arab countries did not attack one another militarily. But this was not exactly true. Iraq had threatened and even invaded Kuwait several times previously. Although on far from the same scale as in 1990, Iraq had sent military forces to take, hold, and occupy part of northern Kuwait in the mid-1970s (Assiri, 1990). It also used "salami tactics" to acquire territory from Kuwait, periodically sending troops to the frontier to inch the border southward (Tétreault, 1995:123–124).

Other inter-Arab conflicts also are forgotten by those professing to be shocked by Iraq's 1990 invasion of Kuwait. Egypt conducted extensive military operations in Yemen in the mid-1960s in a proxy war against Saudi Arabia and has been engaged for years in recurrent border clashes with Libya. Libya and Algeria assisted the Polisario in its struggle to create a "Sahrawi nation" in formerly Spanish Morocco and part of Mauritania. Algeria also gave sanctuary to Polisario refugees fleeing Moroccan and Mauritanian troops. The government of King Hussein mounted a strong military offensive against a semisovereign Palestinian enclave in Jordan during the "black September" of 1970; the Syrians intervened militarily in Lebanon during the civil war and, like the Israelis, continue to occupy part of Lebanon today. Arabian Peninsula states have engaged in open border clashes and covert operations against their neighbors throughout most of this century. Boundary conflicts and covert operations in the Gulf in which non-Arab Iran is involved also are common.

Among the most persistent axes of conflict in the region are those involving non-Arab belligerents. Examples include the conflict between Israel and the Arab states; conflicts in which the Kurds are active participants; and the conflict between Iraq and Iran. These three conflicts intersect with and amplify one another. Like similar conflicts in other parts of the region, they often attract involvement by one or more outside powers. At the same time, the Middle East continues to foster regional governmental and nongovernmental organizations (NGOs) that reflect common economic, cultural, and policy interests. Some, such as OPEC, include both non-Arab and extraregional partners. Others, like the inclusive Arab League and the exclusive Organization of Arab Petroleum Exporting Countries (OAPEC) and the Gulf Cooperation Council (GCC), are all-Arab.

I count myself among those who are generally pessimistic about what these various attempts to promote community among Middle Eastern states have accomplished and can accomplish in the future. However, I also believe that the continuation of these efforts is useful. Eventually such efforts might institutionalize support for what now continue to be mostly ideological assertions of international "brotherhood" among various groups of states in this region.

□ The Arab–Israeli Conflict

The Arab-Israeli conflict is discussed more fully in Chapter 6, but two elements in this struggle are emphasized here: its large external dimension and the role of the Palestinians in international relations in the Middle East generally. When Zionist leaders declared Israel to be a state in 1948, both the United States and the Soviet Union rushed to recognize it. At that time, Israeli institutions such as the army and the labor movement were more socialist than liberal (Bill and Springborg, 1994:261). Even so, as Cold

War positions hardened, Israel became identified with the United States. In part, this reflected Israeli economic dependence on support from the U.S. Jewish community.

Israel's ties to the U.S. government strengthened following the Six Day War in June 1967. Then France, formerly Israel's primary foreign source of armaments, shifted toward the Arab states because of French concerns about the long-term security of oil supplies (Weisberg, 1977). Although the Israelis had bombed a U.S. intelligence vessel, the *Liberty,* to keep their war preparations from discovery, domestic politics pushed the United States to support Israel during the 1967 war. U.S. support included coordination of measures to defeat the first systematic application of the Arab "oil weapon" against Israel's allies (Sankari, 1976).

The October 1973 Arab-Israeli war was deeply embedded in Cold War politics. Following as it did the 1972 reorientation of Egypt out of the Soviet and into the U.S. orbit, this war put the Nixon administration in the difficult situation of having a foreign policy victory that threatened its domestic political position. Although U.S. officials had received a series of explicit warnings beginning in spring 1973 that war between Israel and the Arab states was imminent (Tétreault, 1985:34), Arab attacks on Israeli positions took the U.S. government by surprise. Initial Arab victories alarmed the United States, prompting a massive airlift of supplies to Israel, which reversed most of the Arab gains. The war also provided an opportunity for the Soviet Union to recoup some of its diplomatic losses in the region. When the UN-brokered cease-fire agreement made on October 22, 1973, was violated by the Israelis, the Soviet Union announced its intention to send in troops. It also approached the United States about sending a joint U.S.-Soviet peacekeeping force. U.S. president Richard Nixon, fearful of his domestic standing in the midst of the Watergate investigations, was afraid to engage in any action in the Middle East that could be construed as aiding the Arabs. Instead, he put U.S. military forces on alert, making any joint U.S.-Soviet action in the Middle Eastern war impossible (Kissinger, 1979:552–611).

The threat of global conflict was ratcheted to a high level by policymakers in several different countries attempting to juggle fundamentally incompatible domestic, regional, and global demands. National leaders could and did act in their own interests without much concern about how these actions would affect their allies. This pattern repeats the behavior of the European powers in the Middle East during and after World War I, the history of the British mandate in Palestine, and Cold War maneuvering in the region before and after the October 1973 war. The 1977 decision of Anwar Sadat to go to Jerusalem, an extraordinary gesture in pursuit of an end to the Arab-Israeli conflict, can thus be seen as a gamble whose potential benefits included the removal of a magnet for superpower confrontation, an end to the balance of terror between Arabs and Israelis, and a chance to resolve the problem of what to do about the Palestinians.

Following the victory of the Israelis in the initial 1948 war and the consequent expulsion of thousands of Palestinians from their homes (Morris, 1989), the Palestinian diaspora had fanned out all over the region, with concentrations in refugee camps and enclaves. In response to opportunities presented by oil revenues, Palestinians also formed resident communities of workers and families in oil-rich states such as Kuwait (see, e.g., Ghabra, 1987). Palestinians thus became part of the matrix forming the Arab nationalist amalgam. A reminder of the ineffectiveness of Arab armies against Israeli armies in the field, the Palestinians evoked shame, guilt, and a sense of obligation in other Arabs and their governments. Arab leaders such as Egypt's Nasser (Nasser, 1955), Libya's Muammar Qaddafi (Zartman and Kluge, 1991), Syrian president Hafez al-Assad (Seale, 1988), and Iraqi president Saddam Hussein (Ahmad, 1991) conceived regional historic missions that included the restoration of Palestinian national territory as a primary goal.

The Arab states recognized the Palestine Liberation Organization (PLO) as the legitimate government—the "state-in-exile"—of the Palestinians. For many different reasons, virtually every one of these governments was reluctant to absorb any significant number of Palestinian refugees into its own population. They supported positive sovereignty for the PLO because the PLO's lack of territory made negative sovereignty impossible to manufacture. The PLO maintained officially recognized embassies in many Arab capitals, and Arab governments in the Gulf deducted PLO taxes from Palestinian workers' paychecks. Along with regular elections to the Palestinian National Council, these tax payments, large infusions of Arab foreign aid, and the myriad informal institutions of Palestinian society encouraged the development of a distinctive Palestinian identity despite the absence of a Palestinian territorial state (see Gerner, 1994; Peretz, 1990).

The separate peace between Egypt and Israel signed in 1979 led to a loss of interest in military intervention by the remaining Arab confrontation states (that is, those states that have engaged in conflict with Israel). At the same time, the disappearance of the Soviet Union removed the status of the Arab-Israeli conflict as a cockpit of the Cold War. In consequence, the salience of the Palestinians and their plight declined. The Palestinian intifada (uprising), which began in December 1987, reflected the despair of Palestinians living under occupation at the indifference of the rest of the world. It also highlighted a fundamental change in the structure of the conflict resulting from the Egyptian-Israeli peace agreement— the "Arab"-Israeli conflict had become an Israeli-Palestinian conflict.

At first, the intifada was amazingly successful in crystallizing a coherent and disciplined resistance movement. As it went into its third year,

however, it showed signs of flagging, a result of unrelenting Israeli oppo-
sition and the exhaustion of Palestinian resources (Gerner, 1991, 1994;
Hunter, 1993). Yasser Arafat's support of the Iraqi invasion of Kuwait was
given in response to Saddam Hussein's proposal for an Arab National
Charter to coordinate efforts to liberate Palestine and his acceptance of the
PLO's positions on what that liberation would entail (Ahmad, 1991). But
Arafat's apparent endorsement of the invasion of Kuwait provided a rationale for a reorientation of other Arab governments with respect to the
Palestinians. Gulf governments, short of cash thanks first to a decade of
shrinking oil revenues and second to the need to support the war to liberate Kuwait, found Arafat's gesture a convenient pretext for halting foreign
aid to the PLO. Most Palestinians working in the Gulf countries were expelled as security risks, thus drastically reducing the external financial resources that West Bank and Gaza Palestinians had been receiving from
them. Palestinians also lost diplomatic recognition and suffered retaliation.
Even though extremist factions on both sides of the Israeli-Palestinian conflict engaged in increasingly blatant terrorist tactics to retard the peace
process, the loss of external support made accommodation an attractive
option to both sides.

☐ The Kurdish Conflict

The Kurds, like the Palestinians, are a nation without a state (Mc-
Dowell, 1996). The Kurds were promised an autonomous territory by the
European powers under the Treaty of Sèvres following World War I. However, a large slice of "Kurdistan," the Kirkuk area, was among the first oil-
producing regions in the Middle East. Because of its oil, the British
wanted Kirkuk attached to Iraq, which was one of their mandates (Marr,
1985). As a result, the Kurds, a non-Arab, non-Turkic people, were divided
among five adjoining states: Iran, Iraq, Turkey, Syria, and the former Soviet Union (now part of Azerbaijan). The persistence of Kurdish ethnic enclaves is a function of an isolating mountainous terrain, the authority of
tribal leaders over local populations, and internal Kurdish disagreements
as well as tensions between Kurds and the governments of the affected
states. The struggle is more than a set of civil wars; it also is a platform for
conflicts between contiguous states with Kurdish enclaves.

Oil and separatist politics coincide in Iraq, where one of the elements
holding the Kurds together is their long-time insistence on having an autonomous region and a share of Iraqi oil revenues. Iraqi Kurds engaged in
repeated uprisings against the central government from the earliest years
of the Iraqi state. During the 1930s and 1940s, Kurdish guerrillas led by
Mullah Mustafa Barzani fought an intermittent civil war in Iraq. Iranian
Kurds also refused to resign themselves to assimilation. During World War

II, assisted by Soviet troops, Iranian Kurds established a short-lived independent republic called Mahabad. Despite rivalry among Kurdish tribal leaders, Kurds often assist one another in civil conflicts with their various states. For example, Barzani led several thousand Iraqi Kurdish fighters into Iran to help defend Mahabad against Iranian troops.

After Mahabad fell, Barzani went into exile in the Soviet Union. Following the 1958 revolution, he was permitted to return to Iraq. The post-revolutionary Iraqi regime also released Kurdish political prisoners and appointed Kurds to important government posts. The common bond between Kurds and Iraq's new leader, Abd al-Karim Qasim, was opposition to Arab nationalism. This alliance ended when the Iraqi government began to reject Kurdish demands for autonomy as secessionist. The civil war in Iraq resumed in 1961.

Just as Kurds sometimes are willing to cooperate with one another against a state, they also form temporary alignments with one state against another state or against another Kurdish faction. Kurdish rebels in Iraq receive periodic assistance from the Iranian government, and sometimes Iraqi and Iranian troops fight one another in the Kurdish region during uprisings in one or the other state. During the early 1970s, Iraqi Kurdish rebels were aided both by Iran and, indirectly through Iran, by the United States. Ongoing negotiations between representatives of the Iraqi government and the Kurds resulted in compromises on many issues dividing the two sides. However, it was not until 1975, when the Iranian government and the United States agreed to halt military support of Iraqi Kurds in exchange for the movement of the boundary between Iraq and Iran, that this phase of the fighting ended (Ahmad, 1991).

Following the Iranian revolution in 1979, Iraqi Kurds again became a target of Iranian political manipulation. During the Iran-Iraq War, the Kurdish region was seen by Saddam Hussein as a point of strategic vulnerability. Thus, the war was conducted not only between Iraq and Iran but also between Iraqis and Kurds in both Iran and Iraq. In violation of international treaties, the Iraqi military used chemical weapons against Iraqi Kurdish villages, including Halabja, and razed hundreds more to the ground (Makiya, 1993). After the Gulf War, Iraqi Kurds rose up against the government of Saddam Hussein, but brutal repression by Iraqi troops led to a massive outflow of refugees into Iran and Turkey. Britain, France, Holland, and the United States created a "safe haven" for the Kurds, including a no-fly zone policed by aircraft deployed from bases in Turkey.

Within the safe haven, a Kurdish administration located in Erbil was established by two often-warring Kurdish factions, the Kurdistan Democratic Party (KDP) under Massoud Barzani (son of KDP founder Mullah Mustafa Barzani), and the Patriotic Union of Kurdistan (PUK) under Jalal Talabani. However, the economic isolation of the safe haven and its almost complete dependence on resources from outside bring the two factions into repeated conflict (Barkey, 1997). Their competition for scarce resources aggravates differences in the assumptions and goals of their leaders. Ignoring U.S. pleas that they try to reconcile their differences peacefully, the PUK expelled the KDP from Erbil in 1994. In turn, in 1996, the KDP faction made a deal with Saddam Hussein to unseat the PUK, and a military offensive involving close to 40,000 Iraqi troops forced the PUK to withdraw to the mountains. In the process, Iraqi forces were able to round up dissident Kurds, and Saddam Hussein could claim that he had returned to Kurdistan at the request of local leaders.

The problems that Iran and Iraq have with their Kurdish citizens are echoed in Turkey. Kurdish separatism in Turkey violates the keystone of the Turkish state idea of state-centered nationalism. Atatürk's image of Turkey as an integrated nation-state governed by a uniform civil law was linked to the end of the Ottoman *millet* system that had permitted minority communities a significant degree of self-government in matters affecting personal status. Pressure on all citizens of the new Turkey to conform to Atatürk's secular, modernist, and national norms was intense and often violent.

Atatürk also made a number of successful efforts to co-opt Kurds into supporting the state idea rather than simply repressing or killing them. As in Iraq and Iran, rebellious outbursts in Turkey's Kurdish region were entangled in national and regional political movements. During a period of severe internal conflict in Turkey in the mid-1970s, a Marxist-Leninist organization, the Kurdistan Workers Party (PKK), emerged from the leftist movement. In 1984, the PKK launched an armed insurrection that killed more than 20,000 people in about a dozen years. Continuing efforts to suppress the rebellion are estimated to cost Turkey about 3 percent of its gross domestic product (GDP) every year, and tie down about 250,000 Turkish troops and security personnel (Barkey, 1997; also McDowell, 1996).

Turkey's conflicts with its Kurdish minority have also invited intervention by neighboring states. Both Syria and Iran have supported the PKK, which established military bases in the safe haven in Iraq. Until fall 1998, Syria provided a safe haven to PKK rebels. Relations between Turkey and Syria deteriorated alarmingly, however, and under strong Turkish pressure, the Syrians expelled PKK exiles, including PKK leader Abdullah Oçalan. The following year, Oçalan was captured by Turkish agents and jailed. His 1999 trial was widely covered in the press and resulted in a sentence of death for the defendant. Non-Kurdish Turks are reported to be satisfied with the death sentence because they believe that Oçalan was responsible for terrorist acts that killed large numbers of Turkish people. However, Turkish Kurds are ambivalent, and some oppose the death sentence. The sentence currently is being appealed.

In November 1998, as UN forces were contemplating military action against Iraq for having expelled arms inspection teams, Turkey mounted operations against PKK forces that had taken refuge in Iraq. The Kurds pushed Turkey toward supporting the Iraqi government in the belief that part of the solution to Turkey's Kurdish problem was an Iraq strong enough to help it keep the PKK in check (Barkey, 1997). Reflecting Turkey's perception of mutual interests with Iraq, in late 1996 the Turkish government welcomed the resumption of Iraqi oil exports through a pipeline crossing Turkish territory. Islamist politics also shaped Turkey's stance toward Iraq, with Islamist then prime minister Necmettin Erbakan in the forefront of Turkish leaders pushing for normalization of relations with Iraq.

☐ The Conflict Between Iran and Iraq

Both the Israeli-Palestinian conflict and the Kurdish conflict intersect along several dimensions with the running conflict between Iran and Iraq. Iran is not an Arab country and never participated in the boycott against Israel mounted by Arab states opposed to its establishment and survival (Losman, 1972). In consequence, Iran was free to sell oil to Israel and also to increase oil production during Arab oil embargoes in 1967 and 1973, which undercut the effectiveness of the Arab "oil weapon" (Tétreault, 1981). Both Iran and Israel were aspiring regional military powers, and both became U.S. clients and partners during the Cold War, increasingly so after the adoption of the Nixon Doctrine advocating greater U.S. reliance on regional clients to contain Soviet power (Tétreault, 1985). It should not have been surprising that, during the Iran-Iraq War, the Reagan administration would initiate its illegal sales of weapons to Iran in exchange for money to aid the contras in Nicaragua through the agency of an Israeli intermediary (Draper, 1991).

Iraq was prominent in its defense of Palestinian demands in part because of its leaders' desires for preeminence among Arab nationalists, even before the death of Nasser. In 1967, Iraq spearheaded radical demands for an Arab oil embargo against Israel's allies in the Six Day War. The resulting drain on their economies pushed three other Arab oil-exporting countries to establish OAPEC in January 1968 to forestall similar Iraqi demands in the future (Tétreault, 1981). Iraq fought beside Syria in the October 1973 war, despite the strong political rivalry between these two Ba'thist regimes and their quarrels over economic issues ranging from Euphrates River water rights to oil pipeline transit fees. Iraq's role as a champion of the Palestinian cause remained untarnished despite its refusal to participate in the 1973–1974 oil embargo against Israel's allies (Tétreault, 1981). Before the Egyptian-Israeli peace treaty was signed in March 1979, at the Baghdad summit meeting of Arab states in November 1978, Iraq led a drive to retaliate against Egypt once it had taken that step (Ahmad, 1991).

Iraq's differences with Iran can be traced back through hundreds of years of conflicts between various Arab and Persian empires, but its modern roots are another legacy of imperialism and the cavalier attitudes of those responsible for shaping post–World War I territorial settlements. It is the territorial issue that draws the Kurds into this conflict.

> The borders between the two countries, arranged for the most part by outsiders, have never been firmly accepted by either side. . . . Iraqi fear of Persian hegemony was, in their minds, based on gradual Iranian encroachment on "Arab" land, including the Arab territory of Khuzistan (formerly al-Muhammarah) in 1925, the incorporation of the waters around Khurramshahr in 1937, and the 1975 treaty that gave Iran half of the Shatt al-Arab. (Marr, 1985:291)

Successful maneuvering by Iran in the Iraqi-Kurdish dispute in the mid-1970s moved the border between the two from the Iranian side of the Shatt al-Arab to the "thalweg line," an imaginary line down the middle of the waterway. Iran's victory reduced Iraq's access to the Gulf and increased its dependence on pipelines crossing Syria and Turkey to carry its oil to markets.

Following the successful 1978–1979 Islamist revolution in Iran, the new government's leaders challenged Iraq once again. By 1980, they had begun stirring antigovernment sentiments among Iraqi Kurds in the north and making religious appeals to Iraqi Shi'ites in the south. Saddam Hussein decided to invade Iran in September 1980 because he saw a military advantage arising from growing domestic disaffection inside Iran. He also wanted to end Iranian propaganda campaigns and border clashes challenging Iraqi sovereignty. Iraqis expected a quick victory and a postwar settlement that would reverse decades of territorial gains by Iran. They were surprised at the resistance they encountered and the lack of support from Iranian Arabs. The conflict quickly bogged down into a war of attrition similar to the trench warfare that claimed so many casualties in France during World War I.

The Iran-Iraq War had a significant oil dimension. As it ground on, Iran's superior population resources ate up the advantage Iraq had seized by its surprise attack. Each side sought to devastate not simply the soldiers on the other side but the capacity of its enemy to wage war at all. Iraq was successful in mobilizing the wealthy Arab oil exporters to support its "Arab war" against Iran despite their having banded together in the new Gulf Cooperation Council. This group included all the countries bordering the Gulf except for Iraq and Iran. Iran bombed Iraq's pipelines to cripple Iraq's capacity to buy more arms with oil revenues. However, crude production earmarked by Kuwait and Saudi Arabia to be sold "on Iraq's account" kept oil income flowing into Iraq anyway. The oil-rich Arab Gulf

Photo 5.3 Young Iraqi women train to fight in the war against Iran.

states also supported Iraq with cash and arms shipments. Kuwait imported war matériel destined for Iraq and even constructed a highway from the Shuwaikh port to the Iraqi border to transport it more efficiently. When Iran retaliated by bombing Kuwaiti oil tankers, the Kuwaitis appealed to the United States, the Soviet Union, and other naval powers for protection, resulting in the reflagging of Kuwaiti ships to discourage Iranian attacks (Assiri, 1990).

Perhaps most important as a component of the oil war, the expansion of oil production by Saudi Arabia that began in 1985 not only brought oil income to states financing the war but also depressed oil prices worldwide. For the Arab Gulf exporters with their excess production capacity, lower prices stimulated increases in production to maintain oil income, although at a lower level than before the price collapse. For Iran, already producing at full capacity and denied other sources of foreign exchange as the result of a U.S. embargo, the fall in oil prices directly reduced its capacity to rearm. The oil war was an effective counterweight to Iran's advantage in manpower, and its effects on resupply prevented an Iranian victory. However, the oil war was not sufficient to enable Iraq to win the larger war, which ended in a stalemate in 1988.

By then, conditions in the belligerent countries were far from what they had been before the war began. Despite the largesse of its Arab neighbors, Iraq had had to borrow money from Western banks. By the end of the war, Iraq owed $15 billion to nonconcessional lenders (Tétreault, 1993:96). Meanwhile, the Iraqi population, which had lived under miserable conditions throughout the war, expected the peace to live up to the promises that had been made while the war was going on (al-Khafaji, 1995). Saddam Hussein could not satisfy both the banks and his people, especially given the continuing depression in oil prices that persistent overproduction ensured.

Tim Niblock (1982) finds a link between Iraqi conflicts with Iran and Iraqi assaults on Kuwait. Iran has repeatedly challenged Iraqi sovereignty and usually has met with success. Its inability to win against Iran makes Iraq turn against Kuwait, which is much smaller and weaker but against which Iraq has very weak claims. Even so, before 1990, every time that Iraq challenged Kuwait, it received something in return—money, land, or leverage on the domestic and foreign policies of Kuwait (Assiri, 1990).

That the outcome was different in 1990 reflects changes in the external environment that made massive intervention by a coalition of extraregional states against Iraq possible though not inevitable. Not all Kuwaiti aid and investment recipients rallied to its side following the invasion. Jordan violated UN sanctions against Iraq by transporting military supplies off-loaded in the Gulf of Aqaba to the Iraqi border; Yemen supported the Iraqi position in most UN Security Council votes. Even so, the vast majority of Arab states lined up behind Kuwait. Whether, like the other GCC states, they were fighting in their own interests, or like Syria because they detested the Iraqi regime, or like Egypt because they were lured by the prospect of debt forgiveness and a new infusion of economic aid, many defied significant elements within their own populations by making that choice.

In the West, the differences between Kuwait and Iraq in the contest for allies seemed very clear. In the Middle East, this picture is not so cut and dried. Saddam Hussein's prominence as an Arab nationalist and his loud proclamations of support for the Palestinians; the vast and obvious differences in wealth between Kuwaiti tourists and impoverished populations in Egypt, Morocco, and other far less wealthy countries; and the association of the most prominent members of the coalition with past imperialism and present dependency prompted many Arabs to support Iraq rather than Kuwait. This was true not only for the common person in the "Arab street" but also for many intellectuals such as Moroccan sociologist Fatima Mernissi (1992). The diplomatic and economic isolation of Iraq following the liberation of Kuwait, despite Saddam Hussein's decision to set fire to Kuwait and repress with exemplary brutality a Shi'a intifada in the south (al-Shahristani, 1994; al-Khafaji, 1994) and a Kurdish uprising in the north (Kakai, 1994), only increased widespread sympathy for Iraq throughout the Arab world.

Since the end of the Gulf War, Saddam Hussein has engaged in cat-and-mouse games with the UN inspection teams sent to monitor the dismantling of its chemical and biological weapons. In most of these encounters, Iraq has had the support of Arab governments and populations. When the Iraqi government expelled all U.S. nationals on the UN inspection teams late in 1997, no Arab government, not even Kuwait's, supported the idea of military retaliation against Iraq. When all the UN inspectors were forbidden to undertake inspections in late 1998, six Arab governments, including Egypt and Syria, reprimanded Iraq for this action. Even so, the "rehabilitation" of Iraq has progressed among the governments and populations of the Middle East in large part because of the obvious and well-documented cost of continued economic sanctions to the Iraqi population. In view of Iranian challenges to countries on the Arab side of the Gulf, such as Iran's occupation of islands claimed by the United Arab Emirates, the hinge that connects the modern agents of clashing geopolitical ambitions and aspirations between Arabs and Iranians is unlikely to be disassembled any time soon.

□ Middle East Regionalism

Middle Eastern states were pioneers in regionalism. This post–World War II movement advocated the establishment of international organizations for particular functional purposes such as economic development and military security by countries joined by proximity, culture, and common interests. The League of Arab States (Arab League) was founded in 1945 as just such an organization, despite the refusal of the Great Powers to accept the Arab League's "strong" definition of regionalism. This definition insisted that security be a matter wholly internal to participating states rather than subject to intervention by the larger world community (MacDonald, 1965:9–11). In addition to regional organizations, functional organizations such as OPEC also were established to pursue the common interests of members (Tétreault, 1981). An important goal of both regional and functional organizations is consensus building, the development of joint positions based on consciousness of shared interests sufficiently strong to enable members to remain cohesive under pressure.

Regional and functional organizations in the Middle East offer another focal point for group identification in addition to the state and such movements as Arab nationalism and pan-Islam. Unlike the latter two, regional and functional organizations are creatures of the state. Their spread aided the practical institutionalization of negative sovereignty by legitimating agreements and structures that were both interstate and limited in membership. At the same time, regionalism theoretically restricts negative sovereignty by assigning formal responsibility for specifically delineated policies to the supranational organization. However, many such organizations, including most in the Middle East, incorporate decision rules requiring consensus. This preserves the authority of the individual member to veto policies it does not like.

The ability to mobilize a consensus on any issue wanes as the membership or the issue slate of an organization expands. Adding members may incorporate states whose core interests are marginal to those of the founders. The Arab League has been unable to progress beyond a very low level of regional integration as it has grown beyond five closely neighboring states, four of which were strongly Arab nationalist (Egypt, Syria, Iraq, and Lebanon—the fifth founding member was Jordan), to more than twenty states spread across two continents, many with vastly different histories, economies, and political cultures. The same problems afflict OPEC. Each of OPEC's five founding members (Venezuela, Iran, Iraq, Kuwait, and Saudi Arabia) had sufficient petroleum and financial resources that they could collectively exercise market power by production restraint. Adding small producers such as Gabon and Ecuador and economically desperate ones such as Nigeria to OPEC prevented effective long-term action on production restraint. Instead, OPEC's new members aggravated already endemic political conflicts within the group (Mikdashi, 1972). The founders were aware of their conflicts of interests and adopted a charter requiring OPEC decisions to be based on consensus to protect themselves. They also devised informal conventions freeing members from having to be bound by collective decisions under certain conditions (Tétreault, 1981:42). Both together allowed OPEC to pursue common interests without forcing individual members to diverge too far from their independent interests.

A decrease in common interests and purposes among the members of an international organization also can be triggered by changes in member governments and regimes. OAPEC was formed in 1968 to give its three founders, Libya, Kuwait, and Saudi Arabia, an organizational base from which to resist demands by Arab radicals that they apply the "oil weapon" regardless of their financial situations or their ability to deliver public services to their populations. But when King Idris of Libya was overthrown by a group of military officers led by Colonel Muammar Qaddafi, the new regime in Libya suddenly introduced the very militancy that OAPEC had been established to avoid into the heart of the organization.

The sensitivity of organizational cohesion to the preservation of close similarity among the structural and ideological interests of members led the founders of the Gulf Cooperation Council (Kuwait, Saudi Arabia, Qatar, Oman, Bahrain, and the United Arab Emirates) to exclude Yemen because it did not share "identical systems, identical internal and foreign policies, identical ideologies, identical aspirations and identical human, social, and political problems" [with] the Arab gulf littoral states. (Lawson, 2000)

The GCC was established in 1981 to replace bilateral security arrangements with a regional security regime and also to promote economic integration among its members. Reflecting Iraq's status as a belligerent in the Iran-Iraq War, the GCC also excluded Iraq from membership (Peterson, 1988).

Despite significant economic integration, GCC security measures have consistently fallen short. Some were conceptually defective, such as Saudi policies for centralizing police records and permitting police forces of member states to cross the border into another member state in cases of hot pursuit. Sometimes members simply failed to carry out their GCC obligations. GCC members all refused to assist Kuwait following liberation when, with a conflagration in its oilfields, it asked for a loan of up to 1 million barrels of oil per day to meet the requirements of its overseas refineries. This was a blow to GCC institutions because the group had adopted an oil-sharing agreement in 1987 to deal with production shortfalls by a member state (Tétreault, 1995:147). Thus, even where founding members perceive themselves as virtually "identical," regional organizations in the Middle East are hard-pressed to overcome the attachment of their members to negative sovereignty.

■ CONCLUSION

The international relations of the Middle East are deeply influenced by the legacies of imperialism, particularly the persistence of extraregional intervention and its perverse effects on domestic regimes. The region is noted both for its authoritarian rulers, supported if not actually installed by foreign patrons near and far, and for their ineptitude in foreign policy, domestic policy—and sometimes both. This legacy has convinced leaders and populations alike that their own efforts to change things for the better remain vulnerable to the whims of manipulative neighbors and the interests of dominant world powers.

Another imperialist legacy is a deficiency in state capacity that is reflected in the marginal legitimacy of domestic regimes. The resulting lack of positive sovereignty, joined to "a nationalist anti-imperialism nowadays degenerating into chauvinism and xenophobia" (Salamé, 1994:18), keeps many Middle Eastern countries "quasi-states" whose status depends almost entirely on norms of negative sovereignty. Repeated efforts to create strong intraregional and extraregional alliances have failed just as repeatedly. One reason is the exaggerated prominence of external sovereignty as a cherished principle. This makes national leaders unwilling to compromise until problems turn into crises that only heroic efforts can conceivably reverse. Even organizations such as OPEC, established to protect the primary mineral resource of the region, have faltered repeatedly over the refusal of members to compromise their individual differences in the general interest (see, e.g., Mikdashi, 1972; Skeet, 1988; Tétreault, 1985). Instead, national leaders conceive regional and even global historic missions with themselves in charge, creating excuses for intraregional intervention and often extraregional intervention as well.

The end of formal imperialism did not bring an end to outside interest in the Middle East or to external intervention into its affairs. Hydrocarbon resources add to the geostrategic value of the region, attracting continued economic and strategic intervention by Great Powers in their own national interests or in pursuit of their own global historic missions. One such historic mission, winning the Cold War, promoted contests between the United States and the Soviet Union for Middle Eastern clients. These contests, along with rising oil incomes, fueled a transfer of arms from all over the world to the Middle East and its many conflicts.

The interstate boundaries drawn by departing imperial powers left other legacies. Among these are festering nationalist conflicts such as in Israel-Palestine and in imaginary Kurdistan, with its far from imaginary wars and rebellions. Others include time bombs in the form of recurring outbursts such as those between Iraq and its neighbors, Iran and Kuwait. These conflicts repeatedly have attracted external intervention, as well as having led to intraregional civil and interstate wars.

The end of the Cold War inaugurated a new global strategic era that so far has been preoccupied by the simultaneous dissolution of the former Soviet empire and the consolidation of a new Chinese empire. Until now, the proliferation of local conflicts resulting from the first of these has probably deterred military intervention from abroad in Eastern Europe, central Asia, and elsewhere, such as in the Middle East. The revival of the United Nations during the second Gulf War encouraged world leaders to imagine a different kind of intervention, one in which the UN provides an alternative means for promoting conflict resolution. Where such means fail, the UN is envisioned as the agent capable of supplying highly focused intervention by temporally, geographically, and politically limited peacekeeping forces.

Another agent of intervention is the multinational corporation. Often regarded as arms of their home governments, multinationals under globalization are pursuing foreign policies to suit their own interests, sometimes in accord with and sometimes against the stated positions of political leaders. One example is pipeline politics. The rush of private investment in oil

Photo 5.4 World leaders gathered in Sharm el-Sheikh, Egypt, for an antiterrorism conference. Front row, from left to right: Yasser Arafat, Boris Yeltsin, Hosni Mubarak, Bill Clinton, Shimon Peres, and King Hussein.

and gas development in central Asia has touched off controversy regarding the number and location of pipelines required to bring these new hydrocarbon supplies to market. For mostly political reasons, the U.S. government has advocated a new pipeline through Turkey, while, for mostly economic reasons, oil companies such as Chevron and Mobil are interested in exploring the costs and benefits of a pipeline that would run through Iran. Indeed, oil company executives, along with academic observers, are among the most active advocates of reintegrating Iran into the international community. Their concern goes beyond the simple issue of where to locate a pipeline. Investors have interests in the long-term stability of the region as a whole. Few believe that stability can be achieved if Iran remains marginalized. Consequently, large corporations with interests in this region are active in attempting, by intervening in U.S. politics, to end the relative isolation of Iran imposed by the government of the United States.

Extraregional intervention in the Middle East by Great Powers, international organizations, and financial and economic actors is unlikely to end any time soon. However, intervention does not have to be either one-sided or negative. Changing investment patterns, such as Kuwait's direct and portfolio investment in Europe and the United States, can create partnerships based on mutual interests rather than relations of exploitation. Another trend that could bring positive benefits to the Middle East is globalization, with its capacity to expand the joint benefits of investment and economic development across many nations. At the same time, however, strategic issues, ranging from weapons proliferation to terrorism and the human rights violations that are endemic across this region, invite direct involvement by foreign governments and nongovernmental organizations in the domestic politics and foreign policies of particularly violent states. Indeed, some might argue that if external intervention were to end, the result would be an intensification of regional conflict because external constraints on local belligerents would disappear. But if strategic intervention also were to become "globalized," it could limit the state-to-state cliency relationships that have been so destructive to domestic and regional peace in the Middle East. Transforming dependency into interdependence gives both sides a stake in mutual prosperity, whereas transforming cliency into multilateral regimes for cooperation and monitoring is likely to reduce at least some types of violence by increasing dependence on local resources to meet strategic needs.

Complicating all of these scenarios is the persistent incapacity of so many Middle Eastern regimes to manage domestic conflicts peacefully. This problem has grown along with economic distress and the related rise in importance of religious social movements that, although they have increased domestic political competition, also have made it more abrasive. Even so, a substantial reduction in conventional forms of external intervention would be welcome. If nothing else, minimizing such relationships might allow the nations of the Middle East to move forward with the business of creating positive sovereignty and become states with the capacity to protect and support populations that, in turn, would protect and support them.

■ BIBLIOGRAPHY

Ahmad, Ahmad Yousef. 1991. "The Dialectics of Domestic Environment and Role Performance: The Foreign Policy of Iraq." Pp. 186–215 in Bahgat Korany and Ali E. Hillal Dessouki (eds.), *The Foreign Policies of Arab States: The Challenge of Change*. 2d. ed. Boulder, Colo.: Westview Press.
Ahmed, Leila. 1992. *Women and Gender in Islam*. New Haven: Yale University Press.
Amuzegar, Jahangir. 1982. "Oil Wealth: A Very Mixed Blessing." *Foreign Affairs* 60, no. 4:814–835.
Anderson, Irvine H. 1981. *Aramco, the United States, and Saudi Arabia: A Study of the Dynamics of Foreign Oil Policy, 1933–1950*. Princeton: Princeton University Press.

Anscombe, Frederick F. 1997. *The Ottoman Gulf: The Creation of Kuwait, Saudi Arabia, and Qatar.* New York: Columbia University Press.

Antonius, George. 1946. *The Arab Awakening: The Story of the Arab National Movement.* New York: G. P. Putnam's Sons.

Ashrawi, Hanan. 1995. *This Side of Peace.* New York: Simon and Schuster.

Assiri, Abdel Reda. 1990. *Kuwait's Foreign Policy: City-State in World Politics.* Boulder, Colo.: Westview Press.

Barkey, Henri J. 1997. "Kurdish Geopolitics." *Current History* 96 (January):1–5.

Bill, James A., and Robert Springborg. 1994. *Politics in the Middle East.* 4th ed. New York. HarperCollins.

Bromley, Simon. 1994. *Rethinking Middle East Politics.* Austin: University of Texas Press.

Caporaso, James A. 1978. "Dependence, Dependency, and Power in the Global System: A Structural and Behavioral Analysis." *International Organization* 32, no. 1 (winter):13–43.

Chisholm, Archibald H. T. 1975. *The First Kuwait Oil Concession Agreement: A Record of Negotiations, 1911–1934.* London: Frank Cass.

Clawson, Patrick. 1995. "U.S.-GCC Security Relations, II: Growing Domestic Economic and Political Problems." *Strategic Forum* (August).

Connor, Walker. 1994. *Ethnonationalism: The Quest for Understanding.* Princeton: Princeton University Press.

Crystal, Jill. 1990. *Oil and Politics in the Gulf: Rulers and Merchants in Kuwait and Qatar.* Cambridge: Cambridge University Press.

Daniels, John. 1971. *Kuwait Journey.* Luton, UK: White Crescent Press.

Davidson, Basil. 1992. *The Black Man's Burden: Africa and the Curse of the Nation-State.* New York: Random House.

Dawisha, Karen. 1982–1983. "The U.S.S.R. in the Middle East: Superpower in Eclipse?" *Foreign Affairs* 61, no. 4:438–452.

Dessouki, Ali E. Hillal. 1991a. "The Global System and Arab Foreign Policies: The Primacy of Constraints." Pp. 25–48 in Bahgat Korany and Ali E. Hillal Dessouki (eds.), *The Foreign Policies of Arab States: The Challenge of Change.* 2d ed. Boulder, Colo.: Westview Press.

———. 1991b. "The Primacy of Economics: The Foreign Policy of Egypt." Pp. 156–185 in Bahgat Korany and Ali E. Hillal Dessouki (eds.), *The Foreign Policies of Arab States: The Challenge of Change.* 2d ed. Boulder, Colo.: Westview Press.

Dickson, H. R. P. 1956. *Kuwait and Her Neighbours.* London: George Allen and Unwin.

Doyle, Michael W. 1986. *Empires.* Ithaca: Cornell University Press.

Draper, Theodore. 1991. *A Very Thin Line: The Iran-Contra Affairs.* New York: Touchstone Books.

al-Ebraheem, Hassan Ali. 1975. *Kuwait: A Political Study.* Kuwait: Kuwait University.

Fromkin, David. 1989. *A Peace to End All Peace: The Fall of the Ottoman Empire and the Creation of the Modern Middle East.* New York: Avon Books.

Gasiorowski, Mark J. 1991. *U.S. Foreign Policy and the Shah: Building a Client State in Iran.* Ithaca: Cornell University Press.

———. 1993. "The Qarani Affair and Iranian Politics." *International Journal of Middle East Studies* 25, no. 4:625–644.

Gause, F. Gregory III. 1994. *Oil Monarchies: Domestic and Security Challenges in the Arab Gulf States.* New York: Council on Foreign Relations.

Gerner, Deborah J. 1991. "Palestinians, Israelis, and the *Intifada:* The Third Year and Beyond." *Arab Studies Quarterly* 13, nos. 3–4:19–60.

———. 1994. *One Land, Two Peoples: The Conflict over Palestine*. 2d. ed. Boulder, Colo.: Westview Press.

Ghabra, Shafeeq N. 1987. *Palestinians in Kuwait: The Family and the Politics of Survival*. Boulder, Colo.: Westview Press.

Hallwood, Paul, and Stuart Sinclair. 1982. *Oil, Debt and Development: OPEC in the Third World*. London: George Allen and Unwin.

Harik, Iliya. 1990. "The Origins of the Arab State System." Pp. 1–28 in Giacomo Luciani (ed.), *The Arab State*. Berkeley: University of California Press.

Hopwood, Derek. 1985. *Egypt: Politics and Society, 1945–1984*. 2d ed. Boston: Unwin Hyman.

———. 1988. *Syria, 1945–1986: Politics and Society*. Boston: Unwin Hyman.

Hudson, Michael C. 1977. *Arab Politics: The Search for Legitimacy*. New Haven: Yale University Press.

Hunter, F. Robert. 1993. *The Palestinian Uprising: A War by Other Means*. Revised and updated edition. Berkeley: University of California Press.

Hunter, Shireen T. 1986. "The Gulf Economic Crisis and Its Social and Political Consequences." *Middle East Journal* 40, no. 4 (Autumn):593–613.

Ibrahim, Saad Eddin. 1980. "The Negative Effects of Difference of Income Among Arab Countries on Development in Countries with Low Per Capita Income: The Case of Egypt." In Organization of Arab Petroleum Exporting Countries, *Sources and Problems of Arab Development*. Kuwait: OAPEC.

Jackson, Robert H. 1990. *Quasi-states: Sovereignty, International Relations and the Third World*. Cambridge: Cambridge University Press.

Kakai, Falaz al-Din. 1994. "The Kurdish Parliament." Pp. 118–133 in Fran Hazelton (ed.), *Iraq Since the Gulf War: Prospects for Democracy*. London: Zed Books.

Kaufman, Burton I. 1978. *The Oil Cartel Case: A Documentary Study of Antitrust Activity in the Cold War Era*. Westport, Conn.: Greenwood Press.

al-Khafaji, Isam. 1994. "State Terror and the Degradation of Politics." Pp. 20–31 in Fran Hazelton (ed.), *Iraq Since the Gulf War: Prospects for Democracy*. London: Zed Books.

———. 1995. "War as a Vehicle for the Rise and Demise of a State-Controlled Society: The Case of Ba'thist Iraq." *Amsterdam Middle East Papers*, no. 4 (December).

Kissinger, Henry. 1979. *White House Years*. Boston: Little, Brown.

Korany, Bahgat. 1991. "Defending the Faith Amid Change: The Foreign Policy of Saudi Arabia." Pp. 310–353 in Bahgat Korany and Ali E. Hillal Dessouki (eds.), *The Foreign Policies of Arab States: The Challenge of Change*, 2d ed. Boulder, Colo.: Westview Press.

Lawson, Fred H. 2000. "Punctuated Integration and the Gulf Cooperation Council." In Kenneth P. Thomas and Mary Ann Tétreault (eds.), *Racing to Regionalize: Democrats and Capitalists Reconstructing the Post–Cold War World*. Boulder, Colo.: Lynne Rienner.

Losman, Donald L. 1972. "The Arab Boycott of Israel." *International Journal of Middle East Studies* 3 (April):99–115.

Luke, Timothy W. 1983. "Dependent Development and the Arab OPEC States." *Journal of Politics* 45, no. 4:979–1003.

———. 1985. "Dependent Development and the OPEC States: State Formation in Saudi Arabia and Iran Under the International Energy Regime." *Studies in Comparative International Development* 20, no. 1:31–54.

MacDonald, Robert W. 1965. *The League of Arab States: A Study in the Dynamics of Regional Organization*. Princeton: Princeton University Press.

Makiya, Kanan. 1993. *Cruelty and Silence: War, Tyranny, Uprising, and the Arab World*. New York: Norton.

———. 1996. "The Politics of Betrayal." *New York Review of Books* (October 17):8–12.

Maktabi, Rania. 1996. "State Formation and Citizenship in Lebanon: The Politics of Inclusion and Exclusion in a Sectarian State." Paper presented at the Conference on Citizenship and the State in the Middle East, Oslo, Norway.

Marr, Phebe. 1985. *The Modern History of Iraq*. Boulder, Colo.: Westview Press.

Maxwell, Gavin. 1983. *Lords of the Atlas*. London: Century Publishing.

McDowell, David. 1996. *A Modern History of the Kurds*. London: I. B. Tauris.

Melkumyan, Yelena. 1992. "Soviet Policy and the Gulf Crisis." Pp. 76–91 in Ibrahim Ibrahim (ed.), *The Gulf Crisis: Background and Consequences*. Washington, D.C.: Center for Contemporary Arab Studies.

Mernissi, Fatima. 1992. *Islam and Democracy: Fear of the Modern World*. Trans. Mary Jo Lakeland. Reading, Mass.: Addison Wesley.

Migdal, Joel S. 1988. *Strong Societies and Weak States: State-Society Relations and State Capabilities in the Third World*. Princeton: Princeton University Press.

Mikdashi, Zuhayr. 1972. *The Community of Oil Exporting Countries*. Ithaca: Cornell University Press.

Morris, Benny. 1989. *The Birth of the Palestinian Refugee Problem, 1947–1949*. Cambridge: Cambridge University Press.

Mosley, Leonard. 1978. *Dulles: A Biography of Eleanor, Allen, and John Foster Dulles and Their Family Network*. New York: Dial Press.

Moynihan, Daniel Patrick. 1993. *Pandemonium: Ethnicity in International Politics*. New York: Oxford University Press.

al-Naqeeb, Khaldoun Hasan. 1990. *Society and State in the Gulf and Arab Peninsula: A Different Perspective*. Trans. L. M. Kenny. London: Routledge.

Nasser, Gamal Abdel. 1955. *Egypt's Liberation: The Philosophy of the Revolution*. Washington, D.C.: Public Affairs Press.

Niblock, Tim. 1982. "Iraqi Policies Towards the Arab States of the Gulf, 1958–1981." Pp. 125–149 in Tim Niblock (ed.), *Iraq: The Contemporary State*. New York: St. Martin's Press.

Nitzan, Jonathan, and Shimshon Bichler. 1995. "Bringing Capital Accumulation Back In: The Weapondollar-Petrodollar Coalition—Military Contractors, Oil Companies, and Middle East 'Energy Conflicts.'" *Review of International Political Economy* 2, no. 3:446–515.

Penrose, Edith T. 1968. *The Large International Firm in Developing Countries: The International Petroleum Industry*. Cambridge: MIT Press.

Peretz, Don. 1990. *Intifada: The Palestinian Uprising*. Boulder, Colo.: Westview Press.

Peterson, Erik. 1988. *The Gulf Cooperation Council*. Boulder, Colo.: Westview Press.

Polanyi, Karl. 1944. *The Great Transformation*. New York: Farrar and Rinehart.

Quandt, William. 1981. *Saudi Arabia in the 1980s*. Washington, D.C.: Brookings Institution.

Rand, Christopher T. 1975. *Making Democracy Safe for Oil*. Boston: Little, Brown.

Rush, Alan. 1987. *Al-Sabah: History and Genealogy of Kuwait's Ruling Family, 1752–1987*. London: Ithaca Press.

Said, Edward W. 1993. *Culture and Imperialism*. New York: Alfred A. Knopf.

Salamé, Ghassan. 1990. "'Strong' and 'Weak' States: A Qualified Return to the Muqaddimah." Pp. 29–64 in Giacomo Luciani (ed.), *The Arab State*. Austin: University of Texas Press.

———. (ed.). 1994. *Democracy Without Democrats? The Renewal of Politics in the Muslim World*. London: I. B. Tauris.

Sampson, Anthony. 1975. *The Seven Sisters: The Great Oil Companies and the World They Shaped*. New York: Viking Press.

Sankari, Farouk. 1976. "The Character and Impact of Arab Oil Embargoes." Pp. 265–278 in Naiem A. Sherbiny and Mark A. Tessler (eds.), *Arab Oil: Impact on the Arab Countries and Global Implications*. New York: Praeger.

Sciolino, Elaine. 1991. *The Outlaw State: Saddam Hussein's Quest for Power and the Gulf Crisis*. New York: John Wiley and Sons.

Seale, Patrick. 1988. *Asad: The Struggle for the Middle East*. London: I. B. Tauris.

al-Shahristani, Hussein. 1994. "Suppression and Survival of Iraqi Shi'is." Pp. 134–140 in Fran Hazelton (eds.), *Iraq Since the Gulf War: Prospects for Democracy*. London: Zed Books.

Shwadran, Benjamin. 1955. *The Middle East, Oil and the Great Powers*. New York: Praeger.

Skeet, Ian. 1988. *OPEC: Twenty-five Years of Prices and Politics*. Cambridge: Cambridge University Press.

Smith, Anthony D. 1991. *National Identity*. Reno: University of Nevada Press.

Smith, Jean Edward. 1992. *George Bush's War*. New York: Henry Holt.

Stephens, Robert. 1976. *The Arabs' New Frontier*. London: Temple Smith.

Tétreault, Mary Ann. 1981. *The Organization of Arab Petroleum Exporting Countries: History, Policies, and Prospects*. Westport, Conn.: Greenwood Press.

———. 1985. *Revolution in the World Petroleum Market*. Westport, Conn.: Quorum Books.

———. 1991. "Autonomy, Necessity, and the Small State: Ruling Kuwait in the Twentieth Century." *International Organization* 45, no. 4:565–591.

———. 1992. "Kuwait: The Morning After." *Current History* 91:6–10.

———. 1993. "Independence, Sovereignty, and Vested Glory: Oil and Politics in the Second Gulf War." *Orient* 34, no. 1:87–103.

———. 1995. *The Kuwait Petroleum Corporation and the Economics of the New World Order*. Westport, Conn.: Quorum Books.

———. 1997. "Political Consequences of Restructuring Economic Regimes: The Kuwait Petroleum Corporation." *Millennium* 26, no. 2:379–401.

Weber, Cynthia. 1995. *Simulating Sovereignty: Intervention, the State and Symbolic Exchange*. New York: Cambridge University Press.

Weber, Max. 1978. *Economy and Society*. Ed. Guenther Roth and Claus Wittich. Berkeley: University of California Press.

Weisberg, Richard C. 1977. *The Politics of Crude Oil Pricing in the Middle East, 1970–1975*. Berkeley: University of California Press.

Wolf, Eric. 1982. *Europe and the People Without History*. Berkeley: University of California Press.

Wood, Pia Christina. 1993. "France and the Israeli-Palestinian Conflict: The Mitterrand Policies." *Middle East Journal* 47, no. 1:21–40.

Zartman, I. William, and A. G. Kluge. 1991. "Heroic Politics: The Foreign Policy of Libya." Pp. 236–259 in Bahgat Korany and Ali E. Hillal Dessouki (eds.), *The Foreign Policies of Arab States: The Challenge of Change*. Boulder, Colo.: Westview Press.

■ 6 ■

The Israeli–Palestinian Conflict

Simona Sharoni and Mohammed Abu-Nimer

It would be an understatement to say that the Arab-Israeli conflict, and especially its Israeli-Palestinian dimension, has been at the heart of Middle Eastern politics in the twentieth century. Indeed, the Israeli-Palestinian conflict provides a unique opportunity to examine a host of concepts important to the understanding of Middle Eastern politics and world politics more generally. These concepts include national identity and self-determination, security dilemmas, the role of religion, the increasing importance of non-state actors, the relative impotence of international law and international organizations such as the United Nations (UN) in dealing with complicated conflicts, Great Power involvement, globalization and economic interdependence, and forms of violent and nonviolent conflict resolution. Given the theoretical and political significance of these issues, it is not surprising that the Israeli-Palestinian conflict is among the most researched topics across academic disciplines as well as in applied settings; it also receives regular and prominent coverage in the media. Yet despite the growing body of literature and media accounts of the conflict, many people still view it either in a simplistic, one-dimensional manner or as distant and too complex to be grasped by ordinary people.

This chapter is designed to provide a framework for the understanding of the Israeli-Palestinian conflict and the prospects for its resolution. We draw extensively on the expansive body of literature on the conflict within various fields of study, and our analysis is interdisciplinary in scope, grounded primarily in our academic training in conflict resolution. Also unique about this chapter is the fact that it is coauthored by two conflict resolution scholars: a Jewish Israeli and a Palestinian who holds Israeli citizenship. Our academic expertise notwithstanding, we have both been actively involved for the past fifteen years in attempts to bring about a just and lasting solution to the conflict.

All too often, media accounts and academic scholarship on the Israeli-Palestinian conflict have fallen into a trap of false symmetry. Typically, the conflict has been presented as an intractable struggle between two national movements with competing claims over the same territory. Such an interpretation obscures the asymmetrical power relations between Israeli Jews and Palestinians, both in the past and in the present. For example, it is seldom recognized that the creation of the state of Israel in 1948, which affirmed the national aspirations of the Jews, came at the expense of Palestinians, whose desire for self-determination and territorial sovereignty remains largely unfulfilled (cf. Nakhleh and Zureik, 1980; Said, 1980; Abu-Lughod, 1982; Quigley, 1990; Aruri, 1995). We choose to stress this point from the start not to glorify one party or vilify the other. Rather, we do so because we believe that a successful resolution of this conflict depends to a great extent on the recognition of these structured inequalities and the ability to devise a framework to transform these power relations.

Toward this end, we draw both on conflict resolution literature and on our own experience and familiarity with the region to illustrate the complexity of this conflict and highlight possible venues for its resolution. As with any other conflict, a comprehensive analysis should begin with a careful examination of the parties involved and of the historical turning points that marked its escalation and de-escalation. Keeping in mind that history in general and histories of protracted conflicts in particular are never simple or objective and always reflect particular political positions, we choose to begin our analysis with a description of the parties to the conflict to provide a context for understanding their contending interpretations of history. After an overview of central turning points and crucial dynamics throughout the history of the conflict, we examine the core issues and points of contention. Finally, we offer a framework to examine past and present attempts to resolve the conflict and identify the conditions and processes that we deem essential to a just and lasting resolution.

■ THE PARTIES: TWO PEOPLES— PALESTINIANS AND ISRAELI JEWS

The Israeli-Palestinian conflict has shaped the lives of at least three generations of Israelis and Palestinians. The Arab-Israeli conflict, particularly its Israeli-Palestinian dimension, has played a central role not only in the daily lives of people throughout the Middle East but also in the lives of Palestinians and Jews living outside Israel and the Occupied Territories, many of whom see their existence as inseparable from political developments in the region (cf. Kelman, 1982; Segal, 1989; Heller and Nusseibeh, 1991; Rothman, 1992; Gerner, 1994; Tessler, 1994). Many scholarly and media accounts, however, tend to overlook this fact, presupposing the existence of two cohesive and unified parties locked into a conflict. Little or no attention is devoted to the composition of the parties themselves, that is, to differences not only between but also within the Palestinian and Israeli-Jewish collectivities.

To come to terms with the Israeli-Palestinian conflict requires a more complex analysis of the parties involved. Such an analysis ought to approach the parties as diverse and often fragmented communities and must take into account how the parties define themselves and how they are viewed by others. It is important to note, however, that the meanings assigned to particular notions of identity and community change over time. Thus, a careful examination of Palestinian and Israeli-Jewish collectivities should underscore the changes in their composition, self-image, and perceptions of and interactions with one another (Kimmerling and Migdal, 1993; Sharoni, 1995b).

Indeed, the Palestinian-Israeli conflict has played a central role in shaping the collective identities of Palestinians and Jews, for the most part in direct opposition to one another, and until recently each reflected denial of the legitimacy of the other party's identity claims (Kelman, 1982; Moses, 1990; Volkan, 1990). The terms *Palestinians* and *Israelis,* which are presently used to describe the conflict both in media and scholarly accounts, were once in themselves a topic of contention. In fact, until the mid-1970s many Jews in Israel and elsewhere as well as numerous politicians, scholars, and media analysts worldwide did not use the term *Palestinians*, thus failing to acknowledge Palestinians' rights to self-determination and territorial sovereignty (Hajjar and Beinin, 1990; Kimmerling and Migdal, 1993). Only since the 1980s has the term *Palestinians* been integrated into the mainstream discourse on the conflict, and it has been used almost exclusively (including in Israel) in both scholarly and popular references to the conflict. A similar trend has occurred in recent years, following the signing of the Oslo Accords and the establishment of the Palestinian National Authority (PNA), with the term *Palestine* gradually replacing other formulations such as *the territories* and *the West Bank and Gaza Strip* (cf. Usher, 1995a; Suleiman, 1995).

The extensive use of the term *Israelis* is relatively new as well, dating back to the establishment of the state of Israel on May 15, 1948, when the collective reference to *Jews* was replaced by the term *Israelis.* Although large segments of the international community immediately adopted the term, until the 1990s the Arab countries and a handful of sympathizers with the Palestinian cause, including several national liberation movements, avoided the use of the term *Israelis,* using instead such terms as *Jews* or *Zionists.*

The prevalent use of the terms *Palestinians* and *Israelis* underscores the view that the Israeli-Palestinian conflict is first and foremost an intractable conflict between two national movements who claim the same piece of land. In addition, the gradual acceptance and normalization of these terms signals more than a mere semantic shift; it points to a growing recognition of the legitimacy of both parties' identity claims and opens up space for a possible reformulation of these claims in ways that are not mutually exclusive (Fernea and Hocking, 1992).

□ Palestinians

The term *Palestinians* refers to the Arabs—Christian, Muslim, and Druze—who have lived in Palestine for centuries. The number of Palestinians worldwide is estimated at more than 5 million, and they are usually divided into three major subgroups: Palestinians who live in the West Bank and Gaza Strip, those who live inside Israel's pre-1967 borders and hold Israeli citizenship, and those who live in the diaspora. The Palestinian diaspora is a direct result of the creation of the state of Israel, which resulted in the destruction of Palestinian Arab society, dispersing hundreds of thousands of Palestinians to lives in exile or as refugees. Almost 70 percent of the inhabitants of the Gaza Strip and 15 percent of the inhabitants of the West Bank have lived in refugee camps since 1948 (Hajjar and Beinin, 1990; Said et al., 1990; Yahya, 1991).

The experience of displacement and the context of a national liberation struggle have contributed to a high level of politicization among all sectors of Palestinian society. The Palestine Liberation Organization (PLO) played a central role in the process of politicization and in the consolidation of a collective Palestinian identity (Cobban, 1984; Nassar, 1991; Kimmerling and Migdal, 1993). The PLO was established in 1964 by the Arab League but gradually gained considerable independence from the Arab regimes and came to serve as the umbrella organization for different political factions with varying ideological orientations and operative strategies. The major factions included Fatah, the largest group, headed by Yasser Arafat; the Popular Front for the Liberation of Palestine (PFLP); the Democratic Front for the Liberation of Palestine (DFLP); and the Palestine Communist Party (PCP). The differences between these political factions notwithstanding, most Palestinians have long regarded the PLO as their sole legitimate representative (Cobban, 1984; Nassar, 1991).

A careful analysis of Palestinian collectivity ought to pay attention to the social, economic, and religious makeup of the society as well as to political differences. For Palestinians in the West Bank and Gaza Strip and in Israel, the place of residence often reflects their socioeconomic status.

Working-class Palestinians in the West Bank and Gaza Strip—many of whom worked until recently in Israel—reside in refugee camps and in villages; the villages are also home to peasants, whereas the elites and the petit-bourgeois class, which includes merchants, traders, and professionals, can often be found in the urban centers (Hiltermann, 1990). Another crucial social sphere that is affected by social class is education. The educational experience of Palestinians varies, depending on the geographical location as well as on the historical and political context. For example, during the Palestinian uprising, known as the intifada, Palestinians' access to education in the West Bank and Gaza Strip was restricted due to the widespread closure of educational institutions by the Israeli military and the arrest, imprisonment, or expulsion of both professors and students (al-Haq, 1988:419–434). It is seldom acknowledged that despite these difficult circumstances, Palestinians have the highest per capita rate of university graduation in the Arab world and one of the highest worldwide (Said et al., 1990).

Another fact that is often overlooked is that not all Palestinians are Muslims; there are Palestinian Christians living as a minority in both the West Bank and Israel (Abu-Lughod, 1987). Nevertheless, due to specific historical and political challenges that have confronted Palestinians, religious differences within Palestinian society have by and large been set aside as Palestinians sought unity under the banner of national liberation and self-determination. In recent years, however, political Islam has come to play a more prominent role within Palestinian society and politics (Taraki, 1989; Legrain, 1990; Usher, 1995a, 1995b). The early months of the Palestinian intifada that began in December 1987 saw the emergence of the Islamic Resistance Movement (which is better known by its acronym, Hamas) in the West Bank and Gaza Strip. By the close of the 1980s, Hamas became part of the Palestinian political scene, regularly polling second only to Arafat's Fatah movement in professional and student elections across the West Bank and especially in the Gaza Strip. Since the signing of the Oslo Accords in September 1993, Hamas has established itself as the single largest political opposition group in Palestinian society (Usher, 1995b).

The redeployment of Israeli troops in some parts of the West Bank and Gaza Strip and the establishment of the PNA inevitably brought change to Palestinian society and politics. In the past two years, Palestinians have achieved limited self-rule, held general elections, and begun to establish social and political institutions such as security services, a legal system, a Palestinian supreme court, and a house of representatives called the Palestinian Council. These accomplishments notwithstanding, many Palestinians are growing impatient with the flaws and limitations of the current state-building process and with the failure of the "peace process" to improve their daily lives, let alone to lead to Palestinian self-determination and statehood (Usher, 1995a; Rabbani, 1996; Guyatt, 1998).

☐ Israelis

The term *Israelis,* which has been in use only since the establishment of the state in 1948, invokes biblical references to the people of Israel and to the ancient Israelites. Yet many scholars have pointed out numerous inconsistencies in the theses that suggest that the Jews who presently reside in Israel are the descendants of the ancient Israelites (cf. Evron, 1995; Shahak, 1995). Most scholarly and media accounts of the conflict use the term *Israelis* because they assume a natural overlap between the state and its citizens. However, this usage is highly misleading because one-sixth of Israel's population consists of Palestinians who hold Israeli citizenship (Lustick, 1980; Rekass, 1989; Rouhana, 1989; Smooha 1989, 1992). The terms *Israeli Jews* or *Jews who live in Israel,* which we use in this chapter, more accurately describe this party to the conflict.

Israeli-Jewish society identifies itself as a Zionist society, morally, politically, and technically. The moral aspect of this identification is grounded in the presupposition that Jews can never hope to achieve equality of rights as religious or cultural minorities in Gentile societies. The political aspect of this identification has been predicated upon two correlative elements: (1) the mobilization of Jews throughout the world to immigrate to Palestine; and (2) the establishment of a Jewish state in Palestine, namely the state of Israel, and the mobilization of moral and material support from Jews and non-Jews worldwide for the continued existence of Israel as a Jewish state. Finally, Israel is a Zionist society technically in that its legal structure and the routine of its everyday life are determined in every domain by the distinction between Jews and non-Jews (Davis, 1986:176–177).

Divisions do exist, however, not only between Jews and non-Jews but within the Israeli-Jewish population as well, which comprises more than 80 percent of Israel's overall population (Reich, 1985). Israeli-Jewish society is quite heterogeneous, composed of immigrants from numerous countries and reflecting a variety of ethnic and linguistic groups; religious preferences; and cultural, historical, and political backgrounds. The two main ethnic groupings are the Ashkenazi Jews, who originated mostly in Europe and North America, and the Mizrachim, whose origins can be traced mainly to North Africa and the Middle East. The term *Mizrachim* (Orientals in Hebrew) is gradually replacing other terms, such as *Sephardim,* previously used to refer to this segment of Israel's population (Shohat, 1988; Swirski, 1989). Another term that has been in use recently in reference to this group is *Arab Jews,* a term that highlights the socio-cultural similarities between Jews from the Middle East and North Africa and their fellow Arabs. The Israeli establishment sought to suppress these similarities, using the Arab-Israeli conflict as an excuse (Alcalay, 1993), and the same excuse was used to downplay the disparities in power and privilege between Ashkenazi and Mizrachi Jews. These disparities have remained largely unaddressed as the Israeli establishment utilized the salience of the Israeli-Palestinian conflict to establish unity in the face of the enemy and construct a strong sense of national identity (Sharoni, 1995a). The centrality of the conflict has also shaped the Israeli political system and the leading political parties.

At present, the Israeli political map includes fifteen parties (some of which comprise several smaller parties) with representation in the Israeli parliament, the Knesset. Historically, the two principal political parties in Israel have been Labor and Likud. The Labor Party, which is predominantly Ashkenazi and secular, controlled Israeli politics between 1948 and 1977. Its original ideology has undergone significant transformations in recent years as it attempted to reconcile the tensions between Zionism, socialism, and democratic practices (Kimmerling, 1983; Shapira, 1992). Over the years, the party's positions and policies on the Israeli-Palestinian conflict have been mixed. Officially, the party supports a "land for peace" solution, and therefore it is generally perceived to be more moderate and willing to compromise than Likud. At the same time, the Labor Party encouraged the construction of settlements in the West Bank and Gaza Strip after 1967, was tough in dealing with the intifada, and for many years opposed the establishment of an independent Palestinian state alongside Israel. More recently, however, the Labor Party and especially Shimon Peres and Yitzhak Rabin were credited with making a significant step toward peace with the signing of the Oslo Accords.

The Likud Party, which came to power for the first time in 1977, is more conservative economically and religiously than Labor and enjoys more support among Mizrachi and working-class Jews. The party has traditionally taken a more hard-line stance on the Arab-Israeli conflict in general and the Palestinian issue in particular. Its original platform claimed Jewish sovereignty over all territories occupied by Israel in 1967, with the exception of the Sinai, which was returned to Egypt following the signing of the Camp David Accords in 1979 (Lesch and Tessler, 1989; Saunders, 1985). Likud and Labor have been alternating in power since 1984, with the Likud Party headed by Benjamin Netanyahu defeating Labor in the May 1996 elections. Although Likud initially opposed the Oslo Accords and the subsequent agreements and vowed to derail their implementation, its position was somewhat modified due to both internal and international pressure. Nevertheless, the policies of the Netanyahu government led to a major stalemate in the negotiations between Israel and the Palestinians, one of many factors that resulted in early elections in May 1999, with the new Labor leader, Ehud Barak, replacing Netanyahu as prime minister.

■ THE HISTORY AND DYNAMICS OF THE CONFLICT

The conventional view among conflict resolution scholars and diplomats in the West is that dwelling on the history of conflicts in general and of the Palestinian-Israeli conflict in particular is counterproductive, mainly because the parties' interpretations of history often appear irreconcilable. At the same time, history played a central role in shaping people's collective identities, perceptions of one another, and general attitudes toward the conflict and the prospects for its resolution. According to this view, if history is ignored, it would be extremely difficult to establish the framework and conditions for a just and lasting peace. Thus, the question is not whether to deal with history, but rather how to approach history so that its examination contributes to both the analysis of the conflict and the exploration of new venues for its resolution. Toward this end, we review some of the history of the conflict presented in Chapter 3, identify a number of significant turning points in that history, and examine their contributions to the escalation or de-escalation of the conflict. In our discussion, we give particular attention to the differences and similarities in Palestinians' and Israelis' perceptions of these events.

□ Modern Zionism and the Partition of Palestine

The first turning point involves the emergence of Zionism and the beginning of Jewish immigration to and settlement in Palestine in the 1880s. The Zionist movement emerged in the late nineteenth century in Europe in response to the rise of European nationalism and anti-Semitism. During and after the Holocaust, which increased the flow of Jewish immigrants to Palestine, the Zionist movement gained significant international recognition and support.

There is no single definition for the term *Zionism*. As with many other contested terms, the meanings and practices associated with Zionism depend on the particular standpoint of the person or group defining it. Although there are different strands of Zionism (socialist or nonsocialist, religious or secular), for most Jews, Zionism is a movement for Jewish national self-determination designed to restore their right to live in the land of their ancestors (Herzberg, 1962). Palestinians and many others, however, view Zionism as an exclusive ideology that underlies the settler-colonial movement responsible for the occupation of Palestine and the dispossession and exploitation of its indigenous population (Said, 1980; Abdo, 1992; Zunes, 1994).

The divergent interpretations of this turning point by Palestinians and Jews lie not only in their differing views of Zionism both as an ideology and as a political project but also in their different perspectives regarding the origins of the conflict. According to prevalent Jewish interpretations, the conflict is centuries old, and Zionism was an attempt to ensure the return of Jews to the land of Israel, *eretz Israel,* which God promised to Abraham and his "seed" (Sachar, 1964; Parkes, 1964; Grayzel, 1968; Tessler, 1994). According to Palestinian interpretations, the Palestinian-Israeli conflict is a modern phenomenon whose origins lie not in the Bible but rather in Zionist ideology and its implementation in Palestine through policies that are reminiscent of other settler-colonial projects around the world (Khalidi, 1971; Muslih, 1992; Kimmerling and Migdal, 1993; Lustick, 1993, Finkelstein, 1995; Greenstein, 1995).

What is often overlooked in conventional accounts of the conflict is that Palestine was not "a land without people for the people without a land," as the Zionist slogan proclaimed; it had an existing indigenous population who sought independence first from the Ottoman rulers and later from the British. Thus, Jewish immigration to Palestine precipitated a century-old clash between two national movements struggling for self-determination and territorial sovereignty. Yet from the start, Palestinians were placed in a disadvantageous position. According to Palestinian historians, the root cause of the Palestinians' disadvantage lies in two political decisions made in Europe. The first decision was made in 1897 by the World Zionist Organization, which met in Basel, Switzerland, and resolved to establish a Jewish state in Palestine. The second decision, known as the Balfour Declaration, was made in 1917, undermining the rights of the indigenous Palestinian population and promising to support the establishment of a Jewish national home in Palestine (Muslih, 1992).

Given this context, the collision between Zionism and Palestinian nationalism was almost inevitable and escalated into violent confrontations in 1920 in Jerusalem, in 1921 in Tel Aviv–Jaffa and the surrounding areas, and in 1929 in Jerusalem and Hebron (Hirst, 1984). One of the most dramatic escalations of the conflict occurred during the Arab Revolt, which lasted from 1936 to 1939. This revolt was the longest-running Palestinian protest against Jewish national aspirations in Palestine prior to the establishment of the state of Israel. It was mostly a grassroots movement and involved both violent and nonviolent dimensions such as strikes, nonpayment of taxes, and other forms of civil disobedience (Khalidi, 1971; Hirst, 1984).

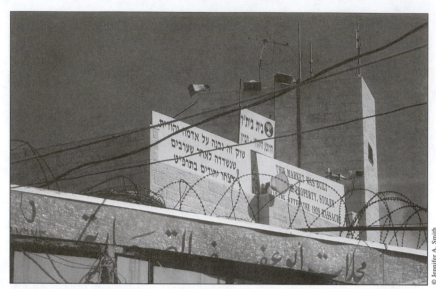

© Jennifer A. Smith

Photo 6.1 The sign, in English and Hebrew, reads:
"This market was built on Jewish property stolen by Arabs after the 1929 massacre."
It hangs on the wall of a controversial Jewish settlement building in the West Bank
city of Hebron/Khalil. The area was previously part of a Palestinian market.

The first period of the revolt ended at the request of the newly formed Arab Higher Committee for Palestine (AHC), which urged Palestinians to wait for the outcome of deliberations by the Palestine Royal Commission, known as the Peel Commission, which was set up by Britain to investigate the situation. The revolt's second stage was sparked by the Peel Commission report recommending the partition of Palestine into two states in order to accommodate the competing claims of Palestinians and Jews, which resulted in further escalation of the situation, with Zionist, Palestinian, and British forces fighting for control. Given the fierce resistance to the plan among both Palestinians and Jews, Britain was eventually forced to abandon the 1937 partition plan.

Nevertheless, partition plans continued to surface; these became particularly popular and gained international legitimacy in the aftermath of World War II and the Holocaust, which resulted in the near destruction of the Jewish people in Europe, as well as Gypsies, homosexuals, disabled persons, and others deemed "undesirable" by the Nazis. The best known is the 1947 United Nations partition plan, also known as UN Resolution 181, which called for the creation of a Jewish state and an Arab state in Palestine. The plan, which indicated that the British mandate over the area was to end on May 15, 1948, "gave the new Jewish state 57 percent of Palestine, including the fertile coastal region." Palestinians viewed this proposal as fundamentally flawed and unjust since "at the time Jews represented only about 33 percent of the population and owned only 7 percent of the land." Indeed, UN estimates suggest that the division of territory spelled out in the 1947 partition plan would have given the Jewish state economic revenues three times as great as those of the Palestinian state. On November 29, 1947, the UN General Assembly voted in favor of this particular plan (Gerner, 1994:43).

The Zionist response to UN Resolution 181 was to endorse it with reservations, insisting that the "Jewish homeland" be distinctively Jewish rather than religiously and ethnically pluralistic. At the same time, Zionist leaders did not abandon the conviction that eventually all of Palestine should come under Jewish control. From the Palestinian perspective, the UN partition plan was an illegal and illegitimate attempt to divide Palestine. Moreover, Palestinians feared that the establishment of two states would result in the expulsion of Palestinians who lived in areas that fell within the designated territory of the Jewish state. But contrary to common representations of this event that tend to portray Palestinians as rejectionists unwilling to compromise, the Arab leadership in and outside Palestine did not simply reject the partition plan; it endorsed the alternative proposal of the UN Special Committee on Palestine, which called for a single, unified state in Palestine that would be democratic and secular and grant equal rights to all its citizens (cf. Flapan, 1987; Finkelstein, 1995).

The UN vote on partition sparked an unprecedented wave of violence, which escalated into a full-fledged war following the establishment of the state of Israel on May 14, 1948. The differences in the interpretations of history by Palestinians and Jews has been most evident in the ways in which they refer to this war. Jews refer to it as the War of Independence, marking the fulfillment of their national aspirations with the establishment of the state of Israel. For Palestinians, however, the 1948 war (known as El-Nakbah, which means the catastrophe) meant disaster and destruction. In the course of the war, the Palestinian community was virtually destroyed. Approximately 780,000 Palestinians became refugees as a direct result of Israel's establishment. Some Palestinians fled, others were driven out by force, and 418 Arab villages were destroyed or depopulated (Morris, 1988; 1990). The war ended with the establishment of Israel on roughly 77 percent of the total area of Palestine. The remaining 23 percent was divided between Jordan, which gained control over the West Bank (including East Jerusalem), and Egypt, which took upon itself the administration of the Gaza Strip (Muslih, 1992).

☐ International Conflicts

In most literature on the conflict, the years since the establishment of the state of Israel are often divided into three periods: May 1948 to June

1967, June 1967 to December 1987, and December 1987 to the present. During the first period, between 1948 and 1967, Palestinians were in a state of shock and despair. The difficult circumstances and the lack of political leadership and economic resources forced them into a state of dependency on neighboring Arab states. As a result, until 1967, with the exception of the establishment of the PLO in 1964, Palestinian nationalism was for the most part muted; resistance to Israel was expressed primarily by Arab leaders residing outside Palestine. Meanwhile, on the other side of the Palestinian-Israeli divide, Israeli Jews worked to build a Western-style Jewish state in the middle of the Arab world. Consequently, the Palestinians who remained in Israel after the 1948 war were viewed as a problem for the evolving Jewish state. They were placed under military rule until 1966 and subjected to a slew of discriminatory regulations under the pretext of Israel's "national security" (Gerner, 1994:47, 57–58; Lustick, 1980; Zureik, 1979).

The June 1967 war, also referred to as the Six Day War, is one of the most significant turning points in the history of the conflict. It dramatically changed the map of the Middle East, resulting in Israel's occupation of the West Bank and Gaza Strip, the Sinai, and the Golan Heights. Contrary to conventional Israeli interpretations, however, which have insisted that Israel occupied these territories in a war of self-defense, there is ample evidence that Israel initiated the war under the pretext of a "preemptive attack" (Zilka, 1992). At the conclusion of the war, it appeared that Israel's conquest was just temporary. In fact, on June 19, 1967, the Israeli cabinet voted unanimously to give back the Sinai to Egypt and the Golan Heights to Syria in return for demilitarization and peace. With regard to Jordan, Israel demanded border adjustments, citing security reasons, but the status of Jerusalem was considered nonnegotiable; the city was unified and declared an indivisible part of Israel (Zilka, 1992:33). But despite UN Resolution 242, which was unanimously adopted on November 22, 1967, and called for Israeli withdrawal from the territories occupied during the war, Israel objected to a complete withdrawal and refused to withdraw from any territory before a peace treaty was signed. Syria rejected the resolution altogether, and Egypt and Jordan refused to sign a peace treaty prior to Israel's withdrawal.

Israel's victory in the Six Day War and its conquest of the remaining 23 percent of Palestine left Egypt, Syria, and Jordan shocked and humiliated and turned Palestinians' hopes to a deep sense of despair. Those Palestinians who were not forced to flee (many for the second time) and become refugees in the surrounding Arab countries were subjected to harsh military laws imposed by Israel. In addition, large amounts of land were confiscated to build Jewish settlements in the West Bank and Gaza Strip, which Israeli officials started referring to by the biblical names of Judea and Samaria. Jewish settlement construction in the Occupied Territories began within six months and had massive government support.

Map 6.1 Israel/Palestine, Showing the 1947 Partition Plan, 1948 Boundaries, and Borders After the 1967 War

© Deborah J. Gerner

Photo 6.2 This woman and child live in Bureij Camp,
one of twenty-seven overcrowded refugee camps in the West Bank and Gaza Strip
that are home to nearly half a million displaced Palestinians.

The 1973 war represents yet another significant turning point in the history of the Israeli-Palestinian conflict, marking the last war between Israel and an allied Arab force. The war began on October 6, 1973, with a coordinated attack launched by Egypt and Syria. But after a massive airlift of advanced military equipment from the United States, Israel was able to turn things around. On October 24, at the conclusion of the war, Israel recaptured most of the Sinai territory from which it had had to retreat and solidified its hold over the Golan Heights. This military victory notwithstanding, the 1973 war was politically costly for Israelis; it ended the collective sense of euphoria created in the aftermath of the 1967 war and shattered the illusion of military invincibility, clearing the way for a more realistic and critical assessment of Israeli society and politics and especially of the Arab-Israeli conflict. For Palestinians, the 1973 war marked yet another chapter in their growing disillusionment with the ability of Arab states to lead the struggle over Palestine.

As a result of the 1967 war and especially in the aftermath of the 1973 war, Palestinians sought their independent representation through the national resistance movement led by the PLO. Yasser Arafat's election as chairperson of the organization in 1968 represented an important milestone in the Palestinians' struggle for self-determination, and international recognition of the PLO as the sole representative of the Palestinian people. By 1974, Palestinians were able to alert the international community to the plight of the Palestinian people; achieve independent representation in many international bodies, including the UN and its related organizations; and gain recognition on the world stage. Yet throughout this period, Israel refused to recognize Palestinians' existence and right of self-determination (Kimmerling and Migdal, 1993:209–239).

The civil war in Jordan in 1970, which was characterized by daily violent confrontations between Palestinians and the Jordanian regime, was a major setback in the Palestinian efforts to strengthen the national movement outside Palestine. The months of buildup escalated into eleven days of bloodshed, often referred to as Black September, which resulted in the killing of thousands of Palestinians and Jordanians, spoiled the relationship between the Palestinian leadership and the Jordanian regime, and destroyed the political and military infrastructure established by the PLO in Jordan (Tessler, 1994:460–462). Following these events, the PLO began building its bases in Lebanon. Meanwhile, the Palestinian resistance movement in the territories was growing. Its strength and organization were reflected in the results of the first municipal elections in the West Bank in 1976. But when Likud came to power in 1977, Israel moved against these elected mayors and the newly elected municipal councils, appointing instead people who were considered more "moderate" and easy to control (Gerner, 1994:91).

Contrary to the gloomy predictions of many analysts, the unexpected victory of the right-wing Likud Party in the 1977 elections resulted in a temporary de-escalation of the Arab-Israeli conflict. A few months after Likud came to power, Egyptian president Anwar Sadat surprised the Israeli government and public, as well as the Arab world and the international community, when he became the first Arab head of state to visit Jerusalem. Another event that both reflected and contributed to the de-escalation of the conflict was the emergence of a distinct peace movement in Israel— Peace Now. The group, founded in 1978 by reserve officers and soldiers, argued that the Israeli government was not doing enough to bring about peace with Egypt (Bar-On, 1985; Wolfsfeld, 1988). Although Peace Now could not take much credit for this development, the Israeli and Egyptian governments began direct negotiations that year, and in 1979 Israel signed a formal peace treaty with Egypt, often referred to as the Camp David Accords.

The Camp David Accords have been viewed as significant in the history of the Palestinian-Israeli conflict because of the problematic manner in which they addressed the Palestinian dimension of the Arab-Israeli conflict and because they enabled the United States to establish itself as a major "peace broker" in the region and thus increase its sphere of power and influence. The accords contained two documents; the one titled "A Framework for Peace in the Middle East" attempted to address the Palestinian problem. With its vague formulation regarding the nature of Palestinian autonomy and its failure to recognize the PLO as the official representative of the Palestinian people and thus as a party to the negotiations, the document provoked strong reactions from the Palestinians (Lesch and Tessler, 1989).

It soon became clear that the government of Menachem Begin had no intention of allowing the Camp David Accords to lead to an Israeli withdrawal from the West Bank and Gaza Strip. To the contrary, in the 1980s Israel pursued its plan to lay the foundation for the permanent retention of the Occupied Territories. The government expanded settlement construction; applied Israeli laws to Jews residing in these areas; and took additional steps in such areas as transportation, communication, and economic activity to link the West Bank and Gaza more closely to Israel and to blur the 1967 border, often referred to as "the Green Line" (Tessler, 1994: 519–521). For Palestinians, this period has been characterized by harsh economic conditions and growing dependency on Israel, a shortage of adequate housing, a crisis in education and deteriorating school facilities, and many other problems that have become more acute as a result of the Israeli occupation (Nakhleh, 1980; Tamari, 1980).

Its reservations regarding the Camp David Accords notwithstanding, during this period the PLO began to signal its readiness for a political settlement. Israel refused to acknowledge, let alone act upon, the softening in the PLO's public statements and political agenda; instead, it took actions to remove the remaining elected Palestinian leaders in the West Bank and Gaza Strip and to set up instead the Village Leagues, whose Arab members were appointed by Israel and thus lacked credibility among Palestinians. These actions prompted fierce resistance by Palestinians, resulting in serious clashes between Palestinians and Israeli soldiers in March, April, and May 1982. Another significant event during this period was the emergence of the popular committees, including women's groups and labor unions, across the West Bank and Gaza Strip. These local committees, most of which were affiliated with the various factions of the PLO, were established to address the service needs of the Palestinian community.

The Israeli invasion of Lebanon in 1982 marked a serious escalation of the Israeli-Palestinian conflict. The Israeli government's decision to inflict damage on the PLO's political and military bases in Lebanon stemmed directly from the insistence of most members of the Israeli government at the time that the PLO was the source of unrest and troubles in the West Bank and Gaza Strip. Nevertheless, the Israeli government's previous attempt, in 1978, to destroy the PLO's headquarters and bases in Lebanon not only failed but triggered the escalation of Israeli-Palestinian hostilities across the Israeli-Lebanese border and heightened tensions between Israel and the Arab states (Gerner, 1994:124–128; Tessler, 1994:568–599). In June 1982, Israeli troops invaded Lebanon for the second time, instigating what became the most controversial war in Israel's history.

The officially stated Israeli goals were to move Palestinian fighters out of range of northern Galilee and to eliminate the PLO's political and military infrastructure in Lebanon. Yet Israeli troops proceeded into Lebanon beyond the 25 miles initially announced, encircling and bombing Beirut in an effort to force the evacuation of Arafat and the PLO (Schiff and Ya'ari, 1984). Israel agreed to stop the bombing only after the completion of the PLO's evacuation in late August.

The cease-fire did not last long. In mid-September 1982, following the assassination of Beshir Gemayel, the newly elected Lebanese president, Israeli troops returned to Beirut, occupying the entire city and sealing off the Sabra and Shatilla refugee camps, home to many Palestinians and poor Lebanese. These actions precipitated one of the most tragic events in the history of the conflict: the Sabra and Shatilla massacre. The massacre was carried out by Lebanese Maronite Christians, who were known for their hatred of Palestinians, with Israeli knowledge and according to some accounts even tacit approval. Forty hours later, when the camps were finally unsealed, the body count reached 700–800 people, according to Israeli estimates, the majority of whom were civilians, including many women and children. Contending accounts indicated that the number of people murdered was perhaps as high as 1,500 or 2,000 (Schiff and Ya'ari, 1984; Tessler, 1994:590–599).

The Israeli invasion of Lebanon reinvigorated existing Israeli peace groups such as Peace Now and the Committee for Solidarity with Bir Zeit University (which decided to rename itself the Committee Against the War in Lebanon). In addition, the invasion triggered the emergence of new protest groups such as Parents Against Silence, Women Against the Invasion of Lebanon, and Yesh Gvul (literally, there is a limit) (Kaminer, 1996; Sharoni, 1995a:106–109). Questioning the legitimacy and morality of the war, Yesh Gvul called upon Israeli soldiers to refuse to serve in Lebanon. Not only did hundreds of soldiers sign petitions declaring that they were prepared to take this course of action, but also a significant number of soldiers were sent to jail for their "refusal to carry out an order" (Kaminer, 1996:36–38).

For the first time in Israel's history, Israeli citizens not only questioned their government's policies but also took to the streets to voice their discontent. From the beginning of the invasion, there was a flurry of protest activities: vigils and demonstrations in the streets and on university campuses, antiwar petitions, and letters to the editors. The first national demonstration against the war on June 26, 1982, drew approximately 20,000 Israelis, who demanded the immediate withdrawal of their country's army from Lebanon. A few months later, in response to the Sabra and Shatilla massacre, Israel witnessed its largest demonstration ever; according to Peace Now and media reports, about 400,000 people participated. Political protest intensified following the publication of the report by the Kahan Commission, a special inquiry commission set up to investigate Israeli involvement in the Sabra and Shatilla massacre (Kaminer, 1996:34–36). The commission's report and the public debates it triggered, coupled with the widespread antiwar demonstrations (which lasted until the partial Israeli withdrawal from Lebanon in 1985), signaled a gradual erosion of the Israeli consensus regarding issues of peace and security.

For Palestinians, the defeat of the PLO in Lebanon resulted in internal fragmentation and disputes among the different PLO factions as well as among the Arab countries that supported them. At the same time, the internal Palestinian leadership had been growing and organizing against the Israeli occupation. In fact, the destruction of the PLO infrastructure in Lebanon contributed to the emergence of a more organized grassroots, autonomous resistance movement in the West Bank and Gaza. This resistance movement gained prominence on the world's stage with the outbreak of the intifada in December 1987.

□ The Palestinian Uprising

The popular uprising was precipitated on December 8, 1987, "when an Israeli army tank transporter collided with a line of cars filled with Palestinian workers waiting at the military checkpoint at the north end of the Gaza Strip" (Gerner, 1994:97). The accident left four Palestinians dead and seven seriously injured, and rumors began to spread that the collision was not an accident but rather a deliberate act carried out by Israel in retaliation for the killing of an Israeli salesperson in Gaza a few days earlier. Thus, the funerals of the dead turned into a massive demonstration; Palestinians continued to protest the following day, and the demonstrations and resistance rapidly spread from the Gaza Strip to East Jerusalem and the rest of the West Bank. Although the accident is often viewed as the catalyst for the uprising, analysts agree that the conditions under which Palestinians lived resembled a pressure cooker, and thus an explosion was imminent.

The literal meaning of the Arabic word *intifada* is "shaking off." For Palestinians, this word has symbolized not only their determination to shake off the Israeli occupation but also their disillusionment with external forces—the United Nations, the United States, and the Arab states and

Arab League—and their resolve to take matters into their own hands. Palestinian mobilization was unprecedented not only in scope and magnitude but in organization as well. People who took part in the mostly nonviolent actions that characterized the intifada—from street demonstrations, tax resistance, and commercial strikes to the establishment of agricultural cooperatives and alternative education centers—were extremely disciplined and came from various socioeconomic backgrounds, political affiliations, and all walks of life. Within weeks, the focus of the conflict and the world's attention turned to scores of Palestinians in the West Bank and Gaza Strip, led by an indigenous leadership (the Unified National Leadership of the Uprising) who demanded the withdrawal of the Israeli military from their occupied land and a just and lasting solution to the conflict (Nassar and Heacock, 1991; Gerner, 1990; Brynen, 1991; Hunter, 1991).

On the other side of the Palestinian-Israeli divide, the Israeli government, which the intifada had caught by surprise, was trying with great difficulty to formulate a response to the uprising and at the same time to launch a public relations campaign designed to redeem Israel's image worldwide. Indeed, the intifada marked a significant shift in power relations between Israel and the Palestinians. Although in strategic terms the advantage still lay with the Israeli side, Palestinians had the moral high ground. For the first time in the history of the conflict, the David versus Goliath analogy was used in scholarly analyses and media reports, describing Israel as Goliath, the mighty aggressor, and the Palestinians as David, the underdog who is determined to win against all odds because his cause is just (Lockman and Beinin, 1989; Schiff, 1990; Perez, 1990).

But Palestinians were well aware that in order to fulfill their aspirations for self-determination, they needed to establish their own social, political, and economic infrastructure, a project prevented by the Israeli occupation. Toward this end, Palestinians established five principal popular committees to deal with agriculture, education, food storage, health care, and security. These committees, which operated both nationally and locally, soon became the most practical mechanism for political mobilization and for the preservation of the community. For many Palestinians, the committees represented the infrastructure of the future Palestinian state or, at least, transient democratic institutions designed to govern the community during the intifada. Palestinian women were actively involved in the establishment and operation of all the popular committees, which resembled the women's committees that had been active in the West Bank and Gaza Strip for more than a decade (Jad, 1990; Hiltermann, 1991; Sharoni, 1995a:72–73).

During the first two years of the intifada, the general atmosphere within the Palestinian community was extremely positive. The sense of purpose and self-reliance, coupled with the ability to forge unity within and mobilize international support for the Palestinian cause, empowered Palestinians and filled many with pride and hope that a diplomatic solution was in sight. Indeed, analysts agree that the intifada enabled Palestinians to renounce the armed struggle, recognize Israel's right to exist, and resolve to establish a Palestinian state in the West Bank and Gaza Strip alongside Israel (Tessler, 1994:717–725). This dramatic transformation became evident in November 1988, when Yasser Arafat formally and publicly endorsed the two-state solution and proclaimed the independent state of Palestine in the West Bank and Gaza Strip.

For the most part, the Israeli government ignored the significance of the 1988 declaration, and efforts to achieve a political solution foundered. Instead, the Israeli government and military continued to respond to the uprising with repression and intransigence. As happened during the 1982 invasion of Lebanon, the government's actions were met with growing public criticism and protest. Although the main currents in the Israeli peace camp had already acknowledged the destructive effects of the occupation on Israeli society long before the intifada began, the uprising was a watershed for political mobilization on the Israeli left. Women and groups who were previously involved in solidarity work with Palestinians led the struggle, which centered around one or more of the following messages: end the occupation, negotiate peace with the PLO, and create two states for two peoples (Kaminer, 1996:41–48). Although the peace movement was fairly successful in mobilizing public opinion, its efforts fell short of changing the Israeli government's policies. By late 1990, the Palestinian-Israeli conflict had settled into a grim war of attrition as the world's attention was diverted to the crisis in the Gulf (Hajjar and Beinin, 1990; Gerner, 1991).

☐ Palestinians and Israeli Jews in the 1990s

The Gulf crisis, which began on August 2, 1990, with the Iraqi invasion of Kuwait and escalated into a war in January 1991, represents another turning point in the history of the conflict (Bennis and Moushabeck, 1991; Sifry and Cerf, 1991; Hiro, 1992). Contrary to the common view among scholars and media analysts that Palestinians made a poor political choice by siding with Saddam Hussein, the Palestinian position was far more complex (Andoni, 1991). Throughout the crisis, the official Palestinian position underscored two principles: denunciation of the Iraqi occupation and opposition to a military solution to resolve the crisis (Ashrawi, 1991:191). But like many other societies, Palestinian society is not monolithic; there were Palestinians who expressed sympathy with Saddam Hussein for standing up to the Gulf states, the United States, and the West more generally and especially to Israel. Nevertheless, regardless of their view on the Gulf crisis, Palestinians criticized the explicit double standard of the international community that utilized the UN and appeals to international law to demand Iraq's immediate withdrawal from Kuwait but failed to apply the same measures to the Israeli occupation of the West Bank and Gaza Strip (Ashrawi, 1991:192–195).

The Gulf crisis and war contributed to the escalation of tension between Israeli Jews and Palestinians. When the U.S.-led air attacks on Iraq began, Israel imposed a twenty-four-hour curfew on Palestinians in the West Bank and Gaza Strip, which lasted a full month and a half. Iraq responded to the air attack with largely ineffective but frightening Scud missile attacks on Saudi Arabia and Israel. Although only two Israelis died directly as a result of those attacks, the country was in a state of panic, and thousands of Israelis fled from the urban areas to the countryside to avoid a possible missile attack. Israelis' sense of helplessness was compounded by the fact that they were asked not to retaliate against Iraq because the United States feared that an Israeli attack might break the already fragile coalition (Schiff, 1990). At the same time, on the other side of the Palestinian-Israeli divide, 1.5 million Palestinians were under total curfew, many on the verge of starvation, with no warning sirens against Scuds and no gas masks to protect them against the possibility of an airborne chemical attack (Strum, 1992:59–78; Sharoni, 1995a:82–83).

In addition to its effects on Israel and on Palestinian-Israeli relations, the Gulf War had grave implications for Palestinians both in the West Bank and Gaza Strip and in the Gulf. The long curfew caused great economic hardship, which intensified when Palestinians who had worked in Israel before the war discovered that their employers had replaced them with recent Jewish immigrants. Palestinians in the Occupied Territories were also affected by the fate of relatives who had been working and living in the Gulf. Close to 400,000 Palestinians living in Kuwait lost their livelihood and were forced once again to flee and look for refuge elsewhere. Since most of these people used to support family members in the West Bank and Gaza Strip, their unexpected displacement translated into a direct loss of income for many families. Moreover, external contributions from the Gulf states to the PLO and to Palestinian institutions such as hospitals, schools and universities, and social welfare organizations stopped almost instantly (Andoni, 1991).

In the aftermath of the Gulf War, the Arab-Israeli conflict was back on the agenda of the Unites States' Middle East policy. In October 1991, after months of intense and systematic shuttle diplomacy efforts carried out by U.S. secretary of state James Baker, an international peace conference was convened in Madrid, Spain, under joint sponsorship of the United States and the Soviet Union. The conference's participants included Egyptian, Syrian, Lebanese, and Israeli delegations and a joint Jordanian-Palestinian delegation because the Israeli government refused to accept an independent Palestinian delegation led by the PLO. These peace talks continued throughout 1992 and the first half of 1993 in Washington, D.C., and elsewhere on two parallel tracks: bilateral and multilateral. Despite the fact that no agreements were reached during that period and that by mid-1993 negotiations on the Palestinian-Israeli track reached a total stalemate, some analysts contend that the very fact that Palestinian and Israeli-Jewish officials were engaged in face-to-face negotiations was a major step forward in Palestinian-Israeli relations (Tessler, 1994:748–750).

The victory of the Labor Party in the 1992 Israeli elections triggered in many hopes for progress in the peace process. Another encouraging sign in this direction was the new government's introduction of a bill removing the ban on unauthorized meetings with members of the PLO. These developments notwithstanding, the situation in the West Bank and Gaza Strip continued to be tense, escalating into occasional violent clashes. Then in late August 1993 the world learned that secret negotiations between Israeli government officials and official representatives of the PLO had been taking place in Norway for many months. The announcement that the two parties signed a joint Declaration of Principles (also known as the Oslo Accords) was both surprising and encouraging. Soon thereafter the world witnessed PLO president Yasser Arafat and Israeli prime minister Yitzhak Rabin shaking hands at the conclusion of the signing ceremony of the Declaration of Principles at the White House in Washington, D.C.

On July 1, 1994, after twenty-seven years in exile, Arafat set foot on Palestinian soil, greeted by hundreds of thousands of Palestinians. Soon thereafter he formed the Palestinian National Authority, and the first democratic Palestinian elections were held in January 1996. Initially, the Oslo Accords enjoyed public support on both sides of the Palestinian-Israeli divide. Ordinary people, fed up with the cycle of violence that characterized the conflict, were quite eager to reap the benefits of peace promised to them by their leaders. But as negotiations dragged on and living conditions

© Deborah J. Gerner

Photo 6.3 Physician and political figure Haider Abdul-Shafi was one of the chief Palestinian negotiators during the Madrid peace process and in January 1996 was elected to the first Palestinian Legislative Council.

Photo 6.4 Palestinian president Yasser Arafat.

failed to improve, support for the agreement, and the peace process in general, declined. Moreover, the stalemate in the process and the failure of the leadership on both sides to keep the public informed about the dynamics and points of contention, coupled with the lack of improvement in Palestinians' living conditions, precipitated a new wave of violence.

The atmosphere of crisis strengthened the opposition to the Oslo Accords and exposed internal divisions and conflicts within both Palestinian and Israeli societies. These divisions, which became clearer following the signing of the Oslo Accords, involve questions of identity and community and contending views not only about the boundaries between Israel and Palestine and the relationship between them but also about the social and political character of each society. The sharp political divisions within Israeli society became evident in November 1995 following the assassination of Yitzhak Rabin by a fellow Jew who opposed Rabin's notion of peace.

But contrary to common perceptions, the Oslo Accords were not a peace treaty. Rather, they constituted an agenda for negotiations covering a five-year "interim period," which was expected to lead to a permanent settlement based on UN Security Council Resolutions 242 and 338. The accords called for a transitional period during which Israel would gradually withdraw its troops from major Palestinian centers in the Occupied Territories, beginning with Gaza and Jericho (Aruri, 1995; Usher, 1995a). In May 1994, nearly five months behind schedule, following the signing of the Cairo agreement that was designed to ratify the Declaration of Principles, the Israeli military began its redeployment as the Palestinian police began to move into the newly autonomous areas.

Presently, the Palestinians have full autonomy in 27 percent of the Occupied Territories (6.6 percent of the territory of historical Palestine). In the West Bank, this translated into 3 percent of the total surface area, whereas in Gaza the PNA presently controls 60 percent of the territory. In the West Bank villages, however, the PNA has only civil and police powers, and Israel remains responsible for "internal security," the meaning of which is open to interpretation. Furthermore, because the towns and

Map 6.2 Areas A, B, and C Within the West Bank

Area A
Major Cities

Area B
Clusters of Palestinian
Villages and Cities

Area C
Full Israeli Control

▲ Israeli
Settlements

JENIN

Mehola

TULKAREM

Salt

QALKILYA

NABLUS

Ariel

Elkana

Ma'aleh
Ephraim

Kiryat Sefer

RAMALLAH

JERICHO

JERUSALEM

Ma'aleh
Adumim

Beitar

BETHLEHEM

Tekoa

HEBRON

Karmel

Eshkolot

© Deborah J. Gerner

Photo 6.5 Israeli troops confront Palestinian demonstrators in the highly contested West Bank city of Hebron/Khalil. The Palestinians were protesting their lack of access to the Mosque of Ibrahim, known to Jews as the Cave of Machpelah, where the Prophet Abraham, Sarah, and their children are believed to be buried.

villages are mostly noncontiguous and Israel remains in command of the road network connecting them, all movement of goods and persons into and out of these enclaves as well as between them can be interdicted at will (Rabbani, 1996:4).

Further complicating the already delayed implementation of the Oslo Accords was the unexpected victory of the Likud Party, led by Benjamin Netanyahu, in Israel's May 1996 elections. Netanyahu argued, and many analysts agreed, that his policies of settlement expansion and the "judaization" of East Jerusalem merely followed those set by earlier Labor governments. Nevertheless, the blunt and uncompromising manner in which Netanyahu carried out these policies resulted in a serious escalation of Palestinian-Israeli relations and another major setback in, if not total collapse of, the peace process. The main disputes have revolved around two central issues: Jewish settlements and Jerusalem. Both of these issues, along with the questions of Palestinian refugees and final borders, were not addressed in the Oslo Accords but rather left to be discussed during final status negotiations, which were originally set to begin in September 1998 but had not started when the five-year Oslo transition period ended in May 1999.

■ ONE LAND, TWO PEOPLES: CENTRAL ISSUES AND POINTS OF CONTENTION

As the previous section illustrates, the dynamics of the conflict, the range of solutions, the role of outside actors, and the political positions of both Palestinians and Jews have dramatically changed throughout the course of the conflict. At the same time, the central issues underlying the conflict have not been dramatically transformed. One such set of issues involves the competing claims of two national movements for the same piece of land.

The Israeli-Palestinian conflict has served as both the catalyst and the touchstone for the consolidation of particular notions of national "imagined community" for Palestinians and for Israeli Jews. For Palestinians, the imagined community came to be seen as a future sovereign Palestinian state. Apart from differences concerning the territorial boundaries and the political and social character of their future state, there is a broad consensus among Palestinians that the principles of national self-determination and territorial sovereignty are inseparable and crucial to the survival of the Palestinian people. A consensus around the same principles has served as the basis for the Israeli-Jewish imagined community. Yet, although Jews realized their dream and established a Jewish state, this has come at the expense of Palestinians, whose desire to fuse national self-determination with territorial sovereignty remains unfulfilled. This turn of events has in many ways formed the basis for the present conflict.

The principles of national self-determination and territorial sovereignty underlie the early conflicts between Zionist settlers and the indigenous Palestinian population. The dynamics and intensity of the Israeli-Palestinian conflict and its significant military component over the years have contributed to the escalation of the conflict and reinforced sharp distinctions between "us" and "them." The establishment of the state of Israel further exposed the differences between Palestinian and Israeli nationalisms: first, the difference between institutionalized state nationalism and the nationalism of a liberation movement, and second, the disparities in power relations between an occupying state and a population struggling to rid itself of that state's rule.

The emerging Jewish state has placed a special emphasis on its national security. For Palestinians, however, national liberation has emerged as the most important focus of their collective identity, especially following the Israeli occupation of the West Bank and Gaza Strip in 1967 and the emergence of the PLO as a vehicle of national aspirations. Within Israeli-Jewish society, the constant invocation of Israel's security concerns has helped reinforce an overt and covert militarization of peoples' lives. But for Palestinians, the centrality of the conflict has manifested itself in the privileging of national liberation not only as the primary ideology of struggle against Israeli occupation but also as the principle discourse that shapes certain ideas and ways of thinking about Palestinian identity and community.

National security and national liberation doctrines are similar in that they view the potency and unity of the nation as superior to issues raised by private citizens and various social groups within that nation. As a result of the primary emphases on national security and national liberation, different social and economic problems within both communities have been put on the back burners until the Israeli-Palestinian conflict is resolved. Nevertheless, the differences between Israeli-Jewish and Palestinian nationalisms, which are often overlooked, are far greater than the similarities. They involve fundamental differences in the history and social context of the two national movements and, most particularly, striking disparities of power and privilege between the two communities.

In order to formulate a solution to this long-standing conflict that would be acceptable to both Palestinians and Jews, one should first identify the central issues for each party. During this process, it is important to pay attention to the changes that occurred in the parties' framing of issues over the years as well as to similarities and differences in the parties' perceptions of central issues. Following is a preliminary list of some of the issues that analysts view as central to a just and lasting resolution of the conflict:

- Fixed, agreed-upon borders between Israel and its neighbors
- The assurance of mutual security for all states and peoples in the region
- The status of Jerusalem
- Jewish settlements in the West Bank and Gaza Strip
- Compensation for Palestinians who were forced to leave their homes and property as a direct result of the Israeli-Palestinian conflict
- The political, civil, and national status of Palestinians who live in Israel and hold Israeli citizenship
- The economic viability of Israel, Palestine, and the other states in the region and the economic relations among them
- The allocation of resources such as water among the states of the region
- The role of the international community in peacekeeping, peacemaking, and peace building

It is important to note that these issues are not listed in any particular order. In fact, if Palestinians and Israeli Jews were asked to prioritize them, they would most likely come up with very different lists. Moreover, many of these issues are interrelated, and some have been addressed at least partially within the framework of the Oslo Accords. Other issues, however, such as settlements, final borders, the fate of Palestinian refugees, and the status of Jerusalem have been identified as issues to be discussed during final status negotiations. On these particular issues, it is interesting to note the difference between the official Israeli and Palestinian positions. For Palestinians, these are the main issues presently underlying the Israeli-Palestinian conflict. Concerned (for good reason) that the process may break down before these issues are discussed, Palestinians wanted to place these issues on the agenda from the start. Israel, however, preferred to defer the discussion of these four issues primarily because the resolution of any one of them would have been impossible without an Israeli concession. Although the decision to delay the discussion of these four critical issues was presented to the parties as a compromise, a careful study of the Israeli position reveals that Israel, the more powerful party in the negotiations, was able to impose its will on the Palestinians with the help of a third party who wanted to keep the peace process on track.

Another point to keep in mind in examining changes that occurred in the parties' positions over time involves the question of representation. More specifically, the changes occurred mostly in Israel's position, and they center mainly around Israel's willingness to finally accept the PLO as the legitimate representative of the Palestinian people. The negotiations that led to the signing of the Camp David Accords in 1978 did not treat the Palestinians as an autonomous party, nor did they acknowledge the PLO as their sole representative. At the time, many elected officials in Israel publicly denied the existence of a Palestinian people. This situation changed dramatically with the outbreak of the intifada. Yet until summer 1993, the Israeli government refused to negotiate with the PLO. This policy was particularly evident in the period preceding the Madrid conference in 1992, when the Israeli government vetoed certain Palestinian delegates because of their suspected affiliation with the PLO. Moreover, the Israelis refused to accept an independent Palestinian delegation and insisted on a joint Jordanian-Palestinian delegation instead. According to many analysts, the Oslo Accords were signed because Israeli officials who took part in the secret meetings with PLO officials realized that if Israel were serious about peace, it would have to negotiate directly with the PLO.

Finally, once the parties agree on a preliminary agenda and on who will be involved in the negotiations, they must address a set of very important procedural issues: when, where, and for how long negotiations will take place; whether the process requires a third party to mediate issues; and, if so, who that party should be. Before the parties meet at the negotiation tables, delegates must study the issues, prepare position papers, and review past attempts to resolve the conflict. A careful analysis of past and present conflict resolution attempts, their success (or failure), and the ways in which they were perceived in both communities may inspire new thinking and creative ideas for the resolution of the conflict.

■ THE ROCKY ROAD TO PEACE: PAST AND PRESENT ATTEMPTS TO RESOLVE THE CONFLICT

Since the turn of the century, there have been numerous attempts at resolution carried out separately and jointly by Palestinians, Jews, and various members of the international community. Following is a partial list of some of the major scenarios that have been proposed by various actors over the years:

- Two states for two people: a Palestinian state alongside Israel, in the West Bank and Gaza Strip
- Greater Israel: a Jewish state that would annex the West Bank and Gaza Strip and "transfer" the Palestinian population to Jordan and other Arab countries
- Greater Palestine: a Palestinian state on all the territory of historical Palestine, with no Israeli Jews except those whose families lived in Palestine before 1948
- Greater Israel: a Jewish state in all the territory of historical Palestine with Palestinians as citizens of the state
- Greater Palestine: a Palestinian state in all the territory of historical Palestine with Israeli Jews as citizens of the state
- A partial autonomy, more or less according to the terms described in the Oslo Accords: Palestine controls the civic affairs and internal security in its cities and villages, and Israel administers external security and controls the land and natural resources
- Return to the pre-Oslo situation: Israel continues to control the territories
- A binational state on the land of Palestine/Israel

It is important to distinguish between those attempts that have addressed primarily the needs and aspirations of one party to the conflict (Jews or Palestinians) and those that have sought to take into account the needs, aspirations, and preferred solutions of both Palestinians and Jews. According to some analysts, to come to terms with the contending conflict resolution perspectives on the Israeli-Palestinian conflict, it may be useful to place them along a continuum bounded by the terms *exclusivist* on one end and *accommodationist* on the other (Vitalis, 1992:290). This continuum clearly reflects the dominant view, according to which the conflict stems from competing claims of two peoples to the exclusive right of national self-determination and sovereignty rights on the same piece of land. According to this view, the single-state solutions—whether Jewish or Palestinian—are exclusivist in nature since they undermine the other party's vision and claims.

There is a tendency, especially among conflict resolution scholars writing about the conflict, to view the transition from exclusivist scenarios to accommodationist ones as a combination of historical progression and rational choice. Thus, the Zionist state-building project in Palestine, which led to the establishment of the Jewish state in 1948, completely undermining the existence of the indigenous Arab population, is often compared with the attempts in the 1950s and 1960s of Palestinians supported by Arab leaders to liberate their homeland.

According to this interpretation, with time and the impact of particular political developments, as both Israeli Jews and Palestinians concluded that their vision of an exclusive homeland was not likely to lead to peace, they gradually began to explore accommodationist scenarios. These scenarios reflected some willingness to compromise and acknowledge, although with many reservations, the other party's national aspirations and right to the land. This acknowledgment, which is particularly evident in such proposals as the two-state solution and the binational state, is praised in the literature as a "win-win solution" and presented as the best scenario for a peaceful resolution of the conflict (Kelman, 1982; Vitalis, 1992). However, such scenarios overlook the grave power differentials between Palestinians and the state of Israel, which are crucial to the understanding of the transition from exclusivist to accommodationist visions within both communities.

Another common continuum used to analyze conflict resolution attempts is that between violent and nonviolent attempts to resolve the conflict. Like the exclusivist-accommodationist categorization, this continuum has been inspired by a combination of rational choice theories with some historical analysis. Accordingly, over time, most Palestinians and Israeli Jews came to the conclusion that the conflict could not be resolved through military might and that diplomacy might be a better venue. Still, in most media accounts of the conflict, there has been a tendency to present Palestinians as more prone to violence and more reluctant to accept diplomatic solutions. This tendency also manifests itself in differential treatment of violence carried out by Palestinians, which is usually referred to as "terrorist attacks," whereas violence carried out by the state of Israel is said to be done in the name of "national security."

As critical scholarship on terrorism has underscored, rather than blaming the underdog in a conflict for resorting to violent means, we must examine the conditions under which certain groups see no other alternative but violence to achieve their goal. By pursuing this line of thinking, we do not condone violence but instead look beneath the surface for its root causes in an attempt to propose a more comprehensive and long-lasting solution (cf. Rubenstein, 1987). Thus in the context of the Palestinian-Israeli conflict, it seems that as the PLO achieved legitimacy on the world's stage and especially after it was recognized by Israel and the United States as the official representative of the Palestinian people, it gradually and willfully moved away from military struggle to pursue diplomatic means for the resolution of the conflict.

It is important to note that neither Palestinian nor Israeli collectivities are homogeneous; within both communities there are individuals and groups who still refuse to move away from exclusivist and militant solutions to the conflict. From a conflict resolution perspective, it would be a mistake to simply characterize these people as "enemies of peace" and suppress their activities. Rather, it is imperative that we examine the impetus behind these individuals' and groups' behavior and their contending solutions to the conflict.

What could further complicate the dynamics of the conflict and the prospects for its resolution is the role of outside parties, with their own agendas and definitions of peace. The United States has a long and complex history of vested economic and political involvement in the Middle East. Most U.S. administrations agreed that a resolution of the Israeli-Palestinian conflict was crucial to achieving a comprehensive peace in the Middle East. Peace was viewed as synonymous with stability, which is necessary for continued U.S. hegemony in the region. To further this end, the United States assumed the role of referee and principal negotiator.

Yet despite its self-portrayal and peacemaking initiatives, the United States hardly fit the role of an impartial third party. In fact, some analysts have argued that in the Middle East, as in many other parts of the world, the United States has acted more as a cobelligerent than as a peacemaker. As Israel's chief ally and protector, the United States was simply unable to discharge its self-assigned mission as a catalyst for peace; the tensions between such roles as mediator and those of Israel's chief diplomatic backer, bank-roller, and military supplier have surfaced quite often (Aruri, 1995:19–21). Moreover, due to the largely unchallenged U.S. insistence that it is the only party that can act as a mediator between Palestinians and Israeli Jews, the services of other potential third parties have been ignored or relegated to backstage initiatives. This trend has resulted in the marginalization of the United Nations as a potential peacemaker and in the abandonment of the once popular idea of convening a UN-sponsored international peace conference (Bennis, 1996:211–232).

When discussing past and present attempts to resolve the conflict, most media accounts, like the vast majority of scholarly literature on the

conflict, tend to focus on the activities of elected officials, thus overlooking attempts by citizens on both sides of the political divide to bring about
a peaceful resolution to the conflict. Some scholars have distinguished between peace-from-above and peace-from-below, or top-down and bottom-
up conflict resolution attempts (Falk, 1994:189; Sharoni, 1996). In the
context of the Israeli-Palestinian conflict, top-down conflict resolution
takes place primarily around negotiation tables, usually outside the region,
and is often characterized by attempts to apply generic, universal models
of conflict resolution to the conflict. Bottom-up peace initiatives, however,
tend to emerge from the "inside," from within Palestinian and Israeli societies and struggles. According to those who emphasize bottom-up solutions, social movements, protest, and grassroots activism are viewed as
crucial venues for peacemaking and conflict resolution (Sharoni, 1996).

Indeed, long before the much-celebrated handshake between Arafat
and Rabin, Palestinians and Israelis at the grassroots level had launched
both separate and collaborative initiatives designed to bring about a just
and lasting solution to the conflict. Despite their absence from the negotiation table, Palestinian and Israeli-Jewish women have played a significant
role in the struggle to end the Israeli occupation of the West Bank and
Gaza Strip (Hiltermann, 1991; Strum, 1992; Sharoni, 1995a; Emmett,
1996). Other examples of conflict resolution initiatives at the grassroots
level include such groups as Israeli-Palestinian Physicians for Human
Rights, which provides medical attention and services to Palestinians in
need, and joint educational projects and dialogue groups designed to
counter stereotypes and fear and establish conditions for coexistence between Palestinians and Israeli Jews (Abu-Nimer, 1993; Hurwitz, 1992;
Fernea and Hocking, 1992; Rosenwasser, 1992; Kaminer, 1996).

These initiatives clearly demonstrate that the expertise for resolving
conflicts peacefully does not reside solely with official government personnel or procedures. Rather, citizens and groups from a variety of backgrounds and with a variety of skills can play an important role in peacemaking and conflict resolution processes. Moreover, there is a growing
realization among conflict resolution experts and ordinary citizens alike
that formal, government-to-government official interactions between in-
structed representatives of sovereign nations are not sufficient to secure international cooperation or resolve deep-rooted conflicts. Even if the parties
to the conflict sign a peace agreement, its successful implementation depends on the support of grassroots constituencies on both sides of the political divide (Sharoni, 1996). In fact, one of the major shortcomings of the
Oslo Accords lies in the failure of both Palestinian and Israeli-Jewish officials to draw on the experience and expertise of peace and community
activists on both sides of the Palestinian-Israeli divide. This rupture in the
relationship between official and unofficial peacemakers may have its

© Deborah J. Gerner

*Photo 6.6 Israeli and Palestinian peace activists
often participated jointly in political demonstrations.*

roots in different definitions of peace that inform the groups' practices and
affect their relations with one another.

Indeed, one more way to examine various peace and conflict resolution initiatives is by focusing on the definition of peace that informs them.
One of the most popular distinctions in the field of peace and conflict resolution studies is that between negative peace and positive peace (Barash,
1991:529–590). Negative peace is defined merely as the absence of war or
direct violence, whereas positive peace requires the eradication of all
forms of violence, including structural violence, and a transformation of
society grounded in the principles of equality, social justice, and nonvio-
lence. In the case of the Palestinian-Israeli conflict, it seems that official
representatives of the two collectivities viewed peace mostly as the absence of war and direct violence (negative peace), whereas grassroots activists within both communities envisioned peace as a transformative
process grounded in the presence of justice (positive peace). The advantage of this distinction is that it enables us to come to terms with competing sets of values, experiences, and political discourses that inform various
definitions of peace.

For example, peace has been defined and envisioned differently by Israeli Jews and Palestinians both before and after the signing of the Oslo
Accords. Peace for Jews has primarily meant peace with security, although

since the signing of the Oslo Accords this formulation has been used interchangeably with terms such as *peace and stability* or *peace and prosperity*. For Palestinians, however, references to peace have almost always been accompanied by invocation of such terms as *justice, equality, liberation,* and *self-determination* (Sharoni, 1995b:400–401). The significant differences between them notwithstanding, these definitions are not mutually exclusive but rather interdependent. Both the two-state solution and the binational-state option can accommodate these contending visions of peace.

The main challenge, however, is not only for each collectivity to recognize the validity of the other party's vision. Because of the asymmetrical nature of the conflict, it appears that the fulfillment of these interdependent visions depends on the willingness of the stronger party to the conflict, the Israeli government, to take the first step and recognize the Palestinians' right of self-determination. To win the support of its electorate for such an act, the Israeli government must introduce it not as a unilateral concession but rather as an essential step toward long-lasting peace in the region. In accepting the two-state solution and recognizing Israel's right to exist, Palestinians have demonstrated their realization that the fulfillment of their national aspirations depends on Israel's sense of security. It is imperative now that Israeli Jews understand and publicly acknowledge that their quest for security, stability, and prosperity will not

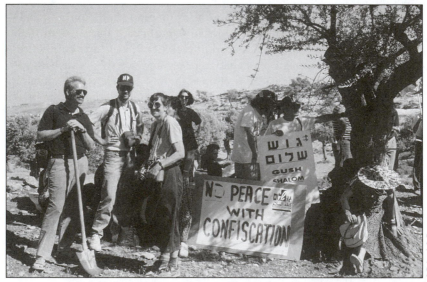

© Deborah J. Gerner

Photo 6.7 Israeli peace activists protest the building of a new Israeli settlement at Har Homa/Jebel Abu Ghneim, near Jerusalem and Bethlehem.

materialize as long as Palestinians' quest for justice, equality, and national self-determination remains unfulfilled.

■ CONCLUSION

It is clear that over the years both the Palestinian leadership and Israeli government have moved away from exclusivist military solutions to the conflict to more accommodationist diplomatic ones. At the same time, it is also obvious that the two national collectivities still hold very different definitions of peace, informed to a great extent by the power disparities between them that the Oslo Accords failed to address. This asymmetry in power relations has been reinforced by the failure of past and present conflict resolution attempts to successfully address the two central issues at the heart of the Palestinians' struggle—national self-determination and territorial sovereignty. Most Palestinians feel that they have already made a serious concession by giving up the dream to reclaim historical Palestine and instead accepting the two-state formula, that is, a Palestinian state in the West Bank and Gaza Strip, alongside Israel.

The implementation of the two-state solution, however, depends on a complete Israeli withdrawal from the territories it occupied in 1967 in violation of international law. So far, the Israeli government has refused to comply and return to the pre-1967 borders. The Oslo Accords offered a temporary cover-up of the situation by highlighting Israel's willingness to negotiate directly with the PLO and grant Palestinians limited autonomy to govern their internal affairs. At present, with the implementation of the Oslo agreements months behind schedule and no set date for the beginning of final status talks, Israel remains in control of most of the contested land, and Jewish settlements continue to expand. As a result, Palestinians across the West Bank and Gaza Strip who have seen very little improvement in their daily lives since the signing of the Oslo Accords in 1993 are growing more and more impatient. The Israeli government has continued to use its national security as a precondition for peace, failing to recognize that Israelis will not be secure until Palestinians fulfill their national aspirations through a political solution they deem just.

Rather than subsume alternative visions of what peace might look like under the narrow formulations of those presently in power, we ought to treat more seriously the divergent positions of the people—Palestinians and Israeli Jews—whose lives have been entangled in the conflict. Such voices and perspectives often point out that the Israeli-Palestinian conflict is more than simply an intractable territorial dispute between two national collectivities; it also involves contending visions concerning the resolution of the conflict and the future of the Middle East that have been the subject of

heated political debates and contestations within both Palestinian and Israeli-Jewish communities.

Finally, as citizens of the Middle East and as conflict resolution scholars, we would like to voice our skepticism regarding conflict resolution
initiatives carried out by such interested third parties as the United States
or a myriad of conflict resolution experts. Far from being neutral or impartial facilitators, these outside parties, whose intentions are sometimes
noble, tend to marginalize or altogether ignore the hopes and fears of ordinary people in the region while imposing their own conflict resolution
frameworks and visions of peace on the conflict. In contrast, we believe
that Palestinians and Israeli Jews, if not their present leaders, hold the key
to a just and lasting resolution of the conflict. The role of Middle Eastern
scholars and conflict resolution experts or the international community
more generally is not to bring peace to the Middle East, but rather to em-
power and support those people in the region who have long been involved
in the elusive search for peace.

■ BIBLIOGRAPHY

Abdo, Nahla. 1992. "Racism, Zionism, and the Palestinian Working Class, 1920–
    1947." *Studies in Political Economy* 37, no. 2:59–93.
Abu-Lughod, Ibrahim (ed.). 1982. *Palestinian Rights: Affirmation and Denial.*
    Wilmette, Ill.: Medina Press.
Abu-Lughod, Janet. 1987. "The Demographic Transformation of Palestine." Pp.
    139–164 in Ibrahim Abu-Lughod (ed.), *The Transformation of Palestine.*
    Evanston: Northwestern University Press.
Abu-Nimer, Mohammed. 1993. "Conflict Resolution Between Arabs and Jews in
    Israel: A Study of Six Intervention Models." Ph.D. diss., George Mason Uni-
    versity, Fairfax, Virginia.
Alcalay, Ammiel. 1993. *After Jews and Arabs: Remaking Levantine Culture.* Min-
    neapolis: University of Minnesota Press.
Andoni, Lamis. 1991. "The PLO at the Crossroads." *Journal of Palestine Studies*
    81:54–65.
Aruri, Naseer. 1995. *The Obstruction of Peace: The U.S., Israel and the Palestini-
    ans.* Monroe, Maine: Common Courage Press.
Ashrawi, Hanan Mikhail. 1991. "The Other Occupation: The Palestinian Re-
    sponse." Pp. 191–198 in Phyllis Bennis and Michel Moushabeck (eds.), *Be-
    yond the Storm: A Gulf Crisis Reader.* Brooklyn: Olive Branch Press.
Barash, David. 1991. *Introduction to Peace Studies.* Belmont, Calif.: Wadworth
    Publishing Company.
Bar-On, Mordechi. 1985. *Peace Now: The Portrait of a Movement* (in Hebrew).
    Tel Aviv: Hakibbutz Hameuchad.
Bennis, Phyllis. 1996. *Calling the Shots: How Washington Dominates Today's UN.*
    Brooklyn: Olive Branch Press.
Bennis, Phyllis, and Michel Moushabeck (eds.). 1991. *Beyond the Storm: A Gulf
    Crisis Reader.* Brooklyn: Olive Branch Press.

Brynen, Rex (ed.). 1991. *Echoes of the Intifada: Regional Repercussions of the Palestinian-Israeli Conflict*. Boulder, Colo.: Westview Press.

Cobban, Helena. 1984. *The Palestinian Liberation Organization: People, Power and Politics*. Cambridge: Cambridge University Press.

Davis, Ury. 1986. "Israel's Zionist Society: Consequences for Internal Opposition and the Necessity for External Intervention." Pp. 176–201 in Eaford and Ejaz (eds.), *Judaism or Zionism: What Difference for the Middle East?* London: Zed Books.

Eisenberg, Laura Zittrain, and Neil Caplan. 1998. *Negotiating Arab-Israeli Peace: Patterns, Problems, Possibilities*. Bloomington and Indianapolis: Indiana University Press.

Emmett, Ayala. 1996. *Our Sisters' Promised Land: Women, Politics, and Israeli-Palestinian Coexistence*. Ann Arbor: University of Michigan Press.

Evron, Boas. 1995. *Jewish State or Israeli Nation?* Bloomington and Indianapolis: Indiana University Press.

Falk, Richard. 1994. "World Order Conceptions and the Peace Process in the Middle East." Pp. 189–196 in Elise Boulding (ed.), *Building Peace in the Middle East: Challenges for States and Civil Society*. Boulder, Colo.: Lynne Rienner.

Fernea, Elizabeth Warnock, and Mary Evelyn Hocking (eds.). 1992. *The Struggle for Peace: Israelis and Palestinians*. Austin: University of Texas Press.

Finkelstein, Norman. 1995. *Image and Reality of the Israel-Palestine Conflict*. London and New York: Verso.

Flapan, Simha. 1987. *The Birth of Israel: Myths and Realities*. New York: Pantheon Books.

Gerner, Deborah J. 1990. "Evolution of the Palestinian Uprising." *International Journal of Group Tensions* 20, no. 3:233–265.

———. 1991. "Palestinians, Israelis, and the *Intifada:* The Third Year and Beyond." *Arab Studies Quarterly* 13, no. 3–4:19–60.

———. 1994. *One Land, Two Peoples: The Conflict Over Palestine*. 2d ed. Boulder, Colo.: Westview Press.

Grayzel, Solomon. 1968. *A History of the Jews*. New York: New American Library.

Greenstein, Ran. 1995. *Genealogies of Conflict: Class, Identity, and State in Palestine/Israel and South Africa*. Hanover and London: Wesleyan University Press.

Guyatt, Nicholas. 1998. *The Absence of Peace: Understanding the Israeli-Palestinian Conflict*. London and New York: Zed Books.

Hajjar, Lisa, and Joel Beinin. 1990. *Palestine and Israel: A Primer*. Washington, D.C.: MERIP.

al-Haq. 1988. "Repression of Education." Pp. 419–448 in *Punishing a Nation: Human Rights Violations During the Palestinian Uprising*. Ramallah, West Bank: Al-Haq.

Heller, Mark, and Sari Nusseibeh. 1991. *No Trumpets, No Drums: A Two-State Settlement of the Israeli-Palestinian Conflict*. New York: Hill and Wang.

Herzberg, Arthur (ed.). 1962. *The Zionist Idea: A Historical Analysis and Reader*. New York: Doubleday Press.

Hiltermann, Joost. 1990. "Work in Action: The Role of the Working Class in the Uprising." Pp. 143–158 in Jamal Nassar and Roger Heacock (eds.), *Intifada: Palestine at the Crossroads*. New York: Praeger.

———. 1991. *Behind the Intifada: Labor and Women's Movements in the Occupied Territories*. Princeton: Princeton University Press.

Hiro, Dilip. 1992. *Desert Shield to Desert Storm: The Second Gulf War*. London: HarperCollins.

Hirst, David. 1984. *The Gun and the Olive Branch: The Roots of Violence in the Middle East*. 2d ed. London: Faber and Faber.

Hunter, Robert. 1991. *The Palestinian Uprising*. Berkeley: University of California Press.

Hurwitz, Deena (ed.). 1992. *Walking the Red Line: Israelis in Search of Justice for Palestine*. Philadelphia: New Society.

Jad, Islah. 1990. "From Salons to the Popular Committees: Palestinian Women 1919–1989." Pp. 125–142 in Jamal Nassar and Roger Heacock (eds.), *Intifada: Palestine at the Crossroads*. New York: Praeger.

Kaminer, Reuven. 1996. *The Politics of Protest: The Israeli Peace Movement and the Intifada*. Sussex, UK: Academic Press.

Kelman, Herbert C. 1982. "Creating the Conditions for Israeli-Palestinian Negotiations." *Journal of Conflict Resolution* 26:39–75.

Khalidi, Walid. 1971. *From Haven to Conquest: Readings in Zionism and the Palestine Problem Until 1948*. Beirut: Institute for Palestine Studies.

Kimmerling, Baruch. 1983. *Zionism and Territory: The Socio-Territorial Dimensions of Zionist Politics*. Berkeley: University of California Press.

Kimmerling, Baruch, and Joel Migdal. 1993. *Palestinians: The Making of a People*. New York: Macmillan.

Legrain, Jean-François. 1990. "The Islamic Movement and the Intifada." Pp. 175–189 in Jamal Nassar and Roger Heacock (eds.), *Intifada: Palestine at the Crossroads*. New York: Praeger.

Lesch, Ann M., and Mark Tessler (eds.). 1989. *Israel, Egypt, and the Palestinians: From Camp David to the Intifada*. Bloomington and Indianapolis: Indiana University Press.

Lockman, Zachary, and Joel Beinin (eds.). 1989. *Intifada: The Palestinian Uprising Against Israeli Occupation*. Boston: South End Press.

Lustick, Ian. 1980. *Arabs in the Jewish State: Israel's Control of a National Minority*. Austin: University of Texas Press.

———. 1993. *Unsettled States, Disputed Lands: Britain and Ireland, France and Algeria, Israel and the West Bank and Gaza*. Ithaca and London: Cornell University Press.

Morris, Benny. 1988. *The Birth of the Palestinian Refugee Problem, 1947–1949*. Cambridge: Cambridge University Press.

———. 1990. *1948 and After: Israel and the Palestinians*. Oxford: Oxford University Press.

Moses, Rafael. 1990. "Self, Self-view, and Identity." Pp. 47–55 in *The Psychodynamics of International Relationships*. Vol. 1. Lexington, Mass., and Toronto: Lexington Books.

Muslih, Muhammad. 1992. "History of the Israeli-Palestinian Conflict." Pp. 62–79 in Elizabeth Warnock Fernea and Mary Evelyn Hocking (eds.), *The Struggle for Peace: Israelis and Palestinians*. Austin: University of Texas Press.

Nakhleh, Emile (ed.). 1980. *A Palestinian Agenda for the West Bank and Gaza*. Washington, D.C.: American Enterprise Institute.

———. 1988. "The West Bank and Gaza: Twenty Years Later." *Middle East Journal* 42:209–226.

Nakhleh, Khalil, and Elia Zureik (eds.). 1980. *The Sociology of the Palestinians*. New York: St. Martin's Press.

Nassar, Jamal R. 1991. *The Palestine Liberation Organization: From Armed Struggle to the Declaration of Independence*. New York: Praeger.

Nassar, Jamal, and Roger Heacock (eds.). 1991. *Intifada: Palestine at the Crossroads*. West Bank and New York: Birzeit University and Praeger.

Parkes, James. 1964. *A History of the Jewish People*. Baltimore: Penguin Books.

Perez, Don. 1990. *Intifada: The Palestinian Uprising*. Boulder, Colo.: Westview Press.

Quigley, John. 1990. *Palestine and Israel: A Challenge to Justice*. Durham: Duke University Press.

Rabbani, Mouin. 1996. "Palestinian Authority, Israeli Rule: From Transitional to Permanent Arrangement." *Middle East Report* (October–December):2–6.

Reich, Bernard. 1985. *Israel: Land of Tradition and Conflict*. Boulder, Colo.: Westview Press.

Rekass, Elie. 1989. "The Israeli Arabs and the Arabs of the West Bank and Gaza: Political Affinity and National Solidarity." *Asian and African Studies* 23, nos. 2–3:119–154.

Rosenwasser, Penny. 1992. *Voices from a "Promised Land": Palestinian and Israeli Peace Activists Speak Their Hearts*. Willimantic, Conn.: Curbstone Press.

Rothman, Jay. 1992. *From Conflict to Cooperation: Resolving Ethnic Conflict and Regional Conflict*. Newbury Park, London, and New Delhi: Sage Publications.

Rouhana, Nadim. 1989. "The Political Transformation of the Palestinians in Israel: From Acquiescence to Challenge." *Journal of Palestine Studies* 3:38–59.

Rubenstein, Richard. 1987. *Alchemists of Revolution: Terrorism in the Modern World*. New York: Basic Books.

Sachar, Abram Leon. 1964. *A History of the Jews*. New York: Knopf.

Said, Edward. 1980. *The Question of Palestine*. New York: Vintage.

Said, Edward, Ibrahim Abu-Lughod, Janet Abu-Lughod, Muhammad Hallaj, and Elia Zureik. 1990. *A Profile of the Palestinian People*. Chicago and New York: Palestine Human Rights Campaign.

Saunders, Harold. 1985. *The Other Walls: The Politics of the Arab-Israeli Peace Process*. Washington, D.C.: American Enterprise Institute for Public Policy Research.

Segal, Jerome. 1989. *Creating the Palestinian State: A Strategy for Peace*. Chicago: Lawrence Hill Books.

Schiff, Ze'ev. 1990. *Intifada: The Palestinian Uprising—Israel's Third Front*. New York: Simon and Schuster.

Schiff, Ze'ev, and Ehud Ya'ari. 1984. *Israel's Lebanon War*. New York: Simon and Schuster.

Shahak, Israel. 1995. *Jewish History, Jewish Religion: The Weight of Three Thousand Years*. London: Pluto Press.

Shapira, Anita. 1992. *Land and Power: The Zionist Resort to Force, 1881–1948*. New York: Oxford University Press.

Sharoni, Simona. 1995a. *Gender and the Israeli-Palestinian Conflict: The Politics of Women's Resistance*. Syracuse: Syracuse University Press.

———. 1995b. "Peace as Identity Crisis." *Peace Review* 7, nos. 3–4:399–407.

———. 1996. "Conflict Resolution and Peacemaking from the Bottom Up: The Roles of Social Movements and People's Diplomacy." Paper prepared for the fourth seminar of the International University of People's Institutions for Peace (IUPIP), Rovereto, Italy.

Shohat, Ella. 1988. "Sepharadim in Israel: Zionism from the Standpoint of Its Jewish Victims." *Social Text* 19, no. 10:1–35.

Sifry, Micah, and Christopher Cerf (eds.). 1991. *The Gulf War Reader.* New York: Times Books/Random House, 1991.

Smooha, Sammy. 1989. *Arabs and Jews in Israel*. Vol. 1: *Conflicting and Shared Attitudes in a Divided Society*. Boulder, Colo.: Westview Press.

————. 1992. *Arabs and Jews in Israel*. Vol. 2: *Change and Continuity in Mutual Tolerance*. Boulder, Colo.: Westview Press.

Strum, Philippa. 1992. *The Women Are Marching: The Second Sex and the Palestinian Revolution*. New York: Lawrence Hill Books.

Suleiman, Michael (ed.). 1995. *U.S. Policy in Palestine: From Wilson to Clinton*. Normal, Ill.: AAUG Press.

Swirski, Shlomo. 1989. *Israel: The Oriental Majority*. London: Zed Books.

Tamari, Salim. 1980. "The Palestinians in the West Bank and Gaza Strip: The Sociology of Dependency." Pp. 84–111 in Khalil Nakhleh and Elia Zureik (eds.), *The Sociology of the Palestinians*. New York: St. Martin's Press.

Taraki, Lisa. 1989. "The Islamic Resistance Movement in the Palestinian Uprising." Pp. 171–177 in Zachary Lockman and Joel Beinin (eds.), *Intifada: The Palestinian Uprising Against Israeli Occupation*. Boston: South End Press and MERIP.

Tessler, Mark. 1994. *A History of the Israeli-Palestinian Conflict*. Bloomington and Indianapolis: Indiana University Press.

Usher, Graham. 1995a. *Palestine in Crisis: The Struggle for Peace and Political Independence After Oslo*. East Haven, Conn.: Pluto Press in association with the Transnational Institute (TNI) and the Middle East Research and Information Project (MERIP).

————. 1995b. "What Kind of Nation? The Rise of Hamas in the Occupied Territories." *Race and Class* 37, no. 2:65–80.

Vitalis, Robert. 1992. "The Palestinian-Israeli Conflict: Options and Scenarios for Peace." Pp. 285–313 in Elizabeth Warnock Fernea and Evelyn Hocking (eds.), *The Struggle for Peace: Israelis and Palestinians*. Austin: University of Texas Press.

Volkan, Vamik. 1990. "An Overview of Psychological Concepts Pertinent to Interethnic and/or International Relationships." Pp. 31–46 in Vamik D. Volkan, Demetrios A. Julius, and Joseph V. Montville (eds.), *The Psychodynamics of International Relationships*. Vol. 1. Lexington, Mass., and Toronto: Lexington Books.

Wolfsfeld, Gadi. 1988. *The Politics of Provocation: Participation in Protest in Israel*. Albany: SUNY Press.

Yahya, Adil. 1991. "The Role of the Refugee Camps." Pp. 91–106 in Jamal Nassar and Roger Heacock (eds.), *Intifada: Palestine at the Crossroads*. New York: Praeger.

Zilka, Avraham. 1992. "History of the Israeli-Palestinian Conflict." Pp. 7–61 in Elizabeth Warnock Fernea and Mary Evelyn Hocking (eds.), *The Struggle for Peace: Israelis and Palestinians*. Austin: University of Texas Press.

Zunes, Steve. 1994. "Zionism, Anti-Semitism, and Imperialism." *Peace Review* 6, no. 1:41–49.

Zureik, Elia. 1979. *The Palestinians in Israel: A Study in Internal Colonialism*. London: Routledge and Kegan Paul.

▪ 7 ▪

The Economies
of the Middle East

Elias H. Tuma

This chapter examines the diverse experiences of states in the Middle East in order to gain insight into the processes of economic development in the region. The economies of the Middle East have come a long way since individual countries acquired statehood and became free of foreign occupation.[1] Some have achieved development and wealth, whereas others remain relatively poor; however, all face significant challenges as they look toward the twenty-first century.

There are twenty-four sovereign states in the Middle East and one potential state, Palestine, whose political status is still in limbo. These states vary widely in geographical area, population, resource endowments, levels of economic and human development, political and economic regimes, and in the ability to integrate into the global economy. Economists classify most of them as middle-income countries, although the range of per capita incomes is extremely wide. Thus, one sees significant contrasts in both the assets Middle Eastern countries have available for economic development and the levels of development they have managed to attain.

Several important features of this diversity may be gleaned from the available quantitative data. First, there is a wide variation in the natural and human resources available for mobilization by the states in the Middle East. The countries vary widely in population, from the tiny country of Bahrain, with perhaps half a million inhabitants, to Egypt, Turkey, and Iran, each with well over 60 million people. Virtually all have an extremely high rate of population growth that is due at least in part to immigration, whether temporary, as in laborers working in the Gulf states, or permanent, as in Israel's effort to gather in Jews from around the world.

In Chapter 2, Ian R. Manners and Barbara McKean Parmenter commented upon the diversity of Middle Eastern countries with respect to endowments of land and other resources. The largest country, Sudan, with more than 237,000,000 hectares (ha) of land, is more than 3,000 times larger than the smallest country, Bahrain, which has only 69,000 ha.[2] However, all the Middle Eastern countries except Lebanon and Turkey have predominantly arid environments and have little arable ground. For instance, less than 2 percent of the total territory of Bahrain and Kuwait is suitable for agriculture; Iran has 17,750,000 ha of arable land, or just over 10 percent of its total area. Turkey is the only country with a large portion of cultivable land, approximately one-third of the total.

Water resources are also limited: they are both scarce and unequally distributed. Iraq's and Syria's water sources originate in Turkey and are shared by all three countries, not always amicably. Iraq's water from the Tigris and Euphrates Rivers needs better management to avoid salinity and exploit the rivers' tremendous potential for energy generation. In addition, some parts of Iraq are flooded swamps, whereas other areas are desert. The other significant river, the Nile, is Egypt's, Sudan's, and Ethiopia's main water source for domestic and industrial uses; for growing cotton, rice, sugar cane, and vegetables; and for fisheries, recreation, and power generation. But the Nile too is suffering from overutilization and pollution.

Many Middle Eastern countries are able to exploit mineral deposits and other natural resources for economic development (see Table 7.1). Some countries are able to attract foreign tourists and their much-needed hard currency. Israel, Palestine, and Saudi Arabia have holy places that annually attract many religious pilgrims, and Egypt, Syria, Turkey, and Iraq have major historical sites that attract tourism and form an important economic resource. However, except for those countries with large oil reserves, the only really significant potential source of wealth for most Middle Eastern countries is embodied in the still-to-be-developed abundant human capital.

The countries of the Middle East also vary widely in the extent to which they have been able to develop economically. As Table 7.2 indicates, Middle Eastern economies range in size from several countries with a gross domestic product (GDP) of less than $5 billion per year to Saudi Arabia, which produces over $170 billion of GDP. As Table 7.2 illustrates, these countries also exhibit wide extremes of wealth per person. Comoros, Somalia, Sudan, and Syria each have a per capita GDP of less than $1,000 a year, whereas countries such as Bahrain, Kuwait, Israel, and the United Arab Emirates (UAE) have a per capita GDP equal to those of Western European countries. Other indicators of development, such as adult literacy rates and proportion of the population in urban areas, also exhibit considerable variation among countries.

In recent years, much criticism has been aimed at the use of income as a measure of economic conditions. Therefore, an index of human development

Table 7.1　Natural Resources

Country	Population[a]	Land Area (1,000 ha)[b]	Arable Land (1,000 ha)[b]	Natural Resources[a]	Principal Industries[a]
Algeria	29,539,400	238,174	7,521	oil, gas, iron	petroleum, light industries, natural gas
Bahrain	590,100	69	2	oil, gas, fisheries	petroleum, aluminum, ship repair
Comoros	569,300	223	78	agriculture	perfume, tourism
Djibouti	383,000	2,318	n/a	none	port and maritime support, construction
Egypt	63,575,000	99,545	2,800	oil, gas, iron	textiles, food processing, chemicals
Iran	65,780,000	162,200	17,750	oil, gas, sulfur	petroleum, textiles, cement
Iraq	21,422,000	43,737	5,500	oil, gas, phosphates	petroleum, petrochemicals, textiles
Israel	5,433,200	2,062	351	copper, phosphates, bromide	food processing, diamond cutting, textiles
Jordan	4,212,200	8,893	320	phosphate, potash	phosphates, petroleum, cement
Kuwait	1,950,100	1,782	5	oil, fisheries	petroleum, petrochemicals, desalination plants
Lebanon	3,776,400	1,023	186	limestone	food processing, cement, petroleum
Libya	5,445,500	175,954	1,815	oil, gas	food processing, petrochemicals, textiles
Mauritania	2,337,000	102,522	488	iron, gypsum, fisheries	iron and gypsum mining, fish processing
Morocco	29,779,000	44,630	8,806	phosphates, iron, manganese	phosphate mining, mineral processing, food processing
Oman	2,186,000	21,246	16	oil, gas, coal	petroleum, fisheries, copper smelting
Qatar	547,800	1,100	13	oil, gas, fisheries	petroleum, gas, fisheries
Saudi Arabia	19,409,100	214,969	3,700	hydrocarbons, iron, gold	petroleum, petrochemicals, cement
Somalia	9,639,000	62,734	1,000	uranium, timber, fisheries	sugar refining, tuna and beef canning, textiles
Sudan	31,065,000	237,600	12,920	oil, iron, copper	textiles, cement, cotton ginning
Syria	15,609,000	18,378	4,486	oil, gas, phosphates	petroleum, mining, manufacturing
Tunisia	9,020,000	15,536	2,842	oil, phosphates, iron	mining, petroleum, olive oil
Turkey	63,700,000	76,963	24,474	coal, chromite, copper	textiles, food processing, mining
UAE	3,057,400	8,360	35	oil, gas, cement aggregate	petroleum, light manufacturing
Yemen	17,300,000	52,797	1,440	oil, gas, gold	oil refining, food processing, textiles

Sources: a. Data for Comoros, Djibouti, Mauritania, and Somalia is from Ramsay, 1997. All others from Spencer, 1998.
　　b. FAO, 1999.

Table 7.2   Indicators of Development

Country	GDP (U.S.$ billions)	GDP Per Capita (U.S.$)	Percent Urban	Literacy Rate (%)	HDI Score	HDI Rank
Algeria	97	3,480	50	57	0.746	82
Bahrain	7	12,100	88	84	0.872	43
Comoros	<1	700	n/a	48	0.411	141
Djibouti	<1	1,200	77	48	0.324	162
Egypt	152	2,490	45	62	0.612	112
Iran	310	4,720	58	78	0.758	78
Iraq	n/a	n/a	70	89	0.538	127
Israel	70	13,880	90	95	0.913	22
Jordan	17	4,280	78	83	0.729	87
Kuwait	31	16,900	96	74	0.848	54
Lebanon	16	4,360	86	76	0.796	66
Libya	33	6,510	85	60	0.806	64
Mauritania	2	1,110	39	35	0.361	149
Morocco	88	3,060	47	50	0.557	125
Oman	17	10,020	12	40	0.771	71
Qatar	11	2,820	91	76	0.840	57
Saudi Arabia	173	9,510	79	79	0.778	70
Somalia	3	500	24	24	0.221	172
Sudan	24	870	23	27	0.343	157
Syria	14	850	51	64	0.749	81
Tunisia	37	4,200	60	57	0.744	83
Turkey	182	4,910	63	79	0.782	69
United Arab Emirates	63	22,480	82	71	0.855	48
Yemen	23	1,955	23	38	0.356	151

Sources: HDI score and ranking from UNDP, 1998, except Somalia, UNDP, 1997. Other data for Comoros, Djibouti, Mauritania and Somalia is from Ramsay, 1997. Data for all others from Spencer, 1998.

has been devised to measure a country's achievement in improving the quality of life for its people. The Human Development Index (HDI) ranks countries on a scale from zero to one, using three indicators: life expectancy, an education index that includes the adult literacy rate and school enrollments, and a measure of per capita income adjusted to reflect purchasing power.

The 1998 HDI ranks 174 countries. The lower the rank number, the higher the achievement or the better the quality of life in the respective country. For example, the United States ranked number 4 after Canada, France, and Norway. By comparison, eight Middle Eastern countries ranked below the top 100. Only Israel (rank 22), Bahrain (rank 43), and the UAE (rank 48) are among the top 50 globally. Overall, the HDI rankings indicate that Middle Eastern countries are well below international averages in achieving a decent quality of life for their citizens.

Given the wide diversity among the states of the Middle East, why, then, do we treat these countries as a unit, as is often the case in literature, world affairs, and this chapter? Perhaps the most obvious reason is intellectual inertia: the region has long been treated as a unit in academic, foreign policy, and journalistic writings. There are, however, more valid reasons for considering these states together. First, as Arthur Goldschmidt Jr. discussed in Chapter 3, they share numerous historical experiences, including (in most cases) rule by the Ottoman Empire. Common features of language, religion, colonial legacy, and proximity to each other are also important. Furthermore, with the possible exception of Turkey, these countries consider themselves parts of the Middle East. However, the implied unity of the region is deceiving since most countries follow their own interests. Even members of the Arab League rarely coordinate their policies effectively. (For a discussion of the economic experiences of individual countries, see Niblock and Murphy, 1993; Lavy and Sherrer, 1991; and Chaudhry, 1997.)

The conceptual framework that I employ here to analyze the economies of the Middle East is represented in the schematic analysis of economic and political change shown below as Figure 7.1.

I have reviewed most well-known models of development (e.g., Wilson, 1995:chap. 2) and found them to be too restrictive for this analysis. The basic idea of this chapter is that development policy emanates from the philosophy, or doctrine, on which the economic system is based. The philosophy guides the establishment of institutions that reflect and sustain it, and in turn, these institutions guide the creation of an administrative machinery that will formulate and implement policies. The administration supervises the field workers who also must be in favor of the policy for it to succeed. Thus, a favorable behavioral structure leads to the creation of a favorable development context: favorable population policy, stable and reliable government, an efficient infrastructure, and a favorable level of science and technology. A favorable development context promotes favorable expectations, which in turn encourage investment, capital accumulation, and elevation of the quality of human capital. This dynamic process allows for changing the economic structure, raising productivity, and improving per capita income. In contrast, failure to create favorable conditions at any level of this scheme can cripple the process of development and prevent a country from realizing its potential.

In light of this framework, a few observations will suggest the argument of this chapter. First, Middle Eastern countries entered the twentieth century with unfavorable behavioral structures and defective developmental contexts. The only exception to this observation was the presence of a favorable demographic context. Therefore, one could hardly have expected highly successful results from the economic development strategies pursued in the Middle East. The two processes, creating preconditions and embarking on development, overlap. They are dynamic and interdependent and reinforce or interfere with each other. Second, economic change in the

Figure 7.1 Schematic Analysis of Economic and Political Change

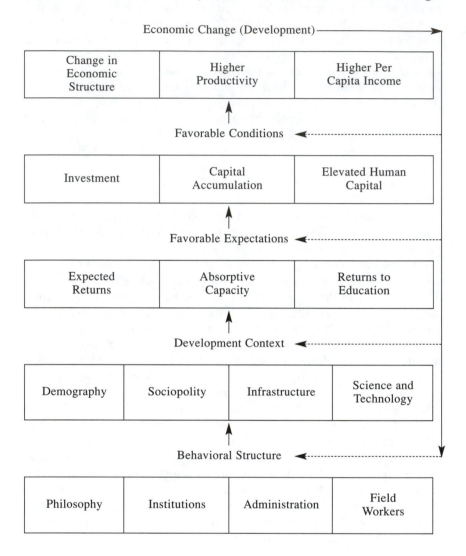

twentieth century has been discontinuous primarily because of extra-economic forces: foreign domination by one power or another, hot and cold wars, the oil price revolution, and intraregional and civil wars.

Because of the importance of historical patterns of development for understanding contemporary Middle Eastern economies, this chapter is organized by chronological phases or subperiods that are separated by recognizable benchmarks: 1918–1939 (initial conditions); the years of World War II, 1939–1945 (change of focus); 1945–1982 (postwar expansion and oil boom); and 1982 to the present (reassessment). In my concluding remarks, I suggest explanations for the differences among Middle Eastern states in terms of their current conditions and prospects for economic development in the future. In Chapter 8, Valentine M. Moghadam further develops several additional aspects of Middle Eastern economics at the turn of the millennium.

■ INITIAL CONDITIONS, 1918–1939

The defeat of the Ottoman Empire and its replacement by Britain, France, and Italy as colonial powers in the Middle East opened windows to the developed industrial world. This change had the potential to enhance economic development, transfer technology, and integrate regional economies into the international economy. The initial conditions, however, were somewhat restrictive.

The economies of the pre–World War II Middle East were sharply characterized by dualism. In a dualistic economy, two economies, one developed and the other underdeveloped, exist simultaneously. In the modern sector, wages are relatively high, high-skill occupations are common, and modern technology is employed. For most of the population, however, work is done in a traditional, inefficient manner, and poverty is ubiquitous. This economic duality continues to act as a barrier to development in most Middle Eastern countries today.

All Middle Eastern countries were underdeveloped; were almost completely dependent on agriculture; and had low levels of technology, segmented markets, widespread barter trade (that is, trade through the exchange of goods rather than using cash), and low per capita incomes, or purchasing power. All had very low rates of literacy. Several countries had unmarked boundaries, poorly defined political systems, and virtually no economic development. Titles to the land were often unsettled, and land-ownership was highly concentrated, with widespread absentee ownership and tenancy. By necessity, external trade relations were common since none of the countries was or could be self-sufficient in basic needs. Domestic industry and the levels of technology in general remained low, barely able to produce commodities that could compete on the international market.

On the positive side, Middle Eastern countries were relatively under-populated, with highly favorable resource to population ratios. Beginnings of urbanization were evident. A few capital cities had large concentrations of people. The following country profiles will illustrate these points.[3]

☐ North Africa

The North African region was still under colonial rule before World War II. Algeria, Tunisia, and part of Morocco were ruled by the French. Spain ruled part of Morocco as well. Tripoli (Libya) was an Italian protectorate. Despite the different colonizers, the territories of North Africa developed similar economic structures.

The economies of the region exhibited considerable dualism during this period, with colonial expatriates holding virtually all the positions in the productive modern economy and trade relations consisting primarily of ties to the colonial center. In Algeria, for instance, the majority of the Arab workforce was in agriculture, whereas the French labor force was concentrated in urban manufacturing and trade. (Most of the large farms and vineyards were in the hands of French farmers, whose property was several times greater than the average Arab farm.)

Algeria was considered an integral part of France, and most of its trade was with that country. Algeria's exports included flour and foodstuffs; vegetable fibers, especially esparto grass; and cork. Imports included live animals and animal products, vegetables, minerals, large and small manufactured products, coal, cotton goods, timber and other building materials, green tea, wool, glassware, paints, and other items. The economy functioned as a market system, although relations with France rendered it complementary to and dependent on the French economy. The other colonies in the region were not as completely integrated into the colonizer's territory as was Algeria; however, they had similar dependent economic relations.

All the territories in North Africa received development assistance in the 1920s: transportation infrastructure was built, health and sanitation programs were promoted, some industrialization occurred, and irrigation and technology applications increased agricultural yields. These development projects mostly benefited the colonial powers and their expatriates, however; very little development occurred in the traditional economy in which the Arab citizens lived and worked. Education policy benefited the European expatriates as well. Few of the students enrolled in upper-level educational institutions were of Arabic origin, preventing them from competing for lucrative opportunities in the modern sector.

The global economic depression of the early 1930s harmed the economies of North Africa considerably. Unemployment increased, wages were low, and credit was difficult to secure. Banks extended loans on security of land titles, but the benefits accrued mainly to expatriate farmers. The indigenous Arabs, largely uneducated in matters of banking and credit, mainly depended on informal-sector moneylenders, who often charged exorbitant rates of interest.

By the end of this period, the region's economic structure had hardly changed. Trade and production were roughly the same as they were at the beginning. Dualism still prevailed. Although roads, electricity, and housing were improved, the indigenous economy stagnated. Even Arab housing was little improved in terms of hygiene, comfort, or planning and design, although these features were evident in European housing. Although some industrialization had occurred, many enterprises failed during the Depression. Few were in the hands of indigenous owners and would not provide much of a base for development in the postcolonial era.

☐ Egypt

Egypt had a different experience from those of its neighbors to the west, but the result was similar: by 1939, Egypt was still underdeveloped, highly dependent on agriculture, and heavily influenced by foreign interests. Egypt was not colonized by European settlers; Britain was an imperial but not colonizing power in Egypt. Britain's impact was felt in Egypt even before it acquired a big share in the Suez Canal, but the canal gave it an excuse to land British troops in Egypt in 1882 to guard the trade routes to India.

Egypt, then as now, depended on the Nile, cotton, the Suez Canal, and tourism as sources of revenue and foreign exchange. Its population of 12.9 million in 1918 had grown to 16.3 million in 1938 (*International Historical Statistics*, 1998), but the qualifications of the labor force had changed very little. Following World War I, British expeditionary forces in Egypt gave the economy an impetus by their spending, providing a false impression of increased (but temporary) prosperity. In 1919 attempts were made to create an indigenous bank. A firm of "Egyptian" cotton exporters was established, and a cooperative society for marketing and credit was founded. Raw materials dominated exports, and processed goods dominated imports. An interesting feature of the early 1930s was the increasing frequency of barter transactions on the international level: cotton for machinery from Germany and for railway materials from Hungary and Sweden. (A similar trend prevailed in the second half of this century.)

In 1925 Egypt experimented with town planning and built Port Fuad as a modern town in the Suez region. Unfortunately, the experiment was not carried much farther. The creation of textile, cement, sugar, and tanning factories came out of the Depression of the early 1930s, but large businesses, including ship repair companies, were mostly owned by non-indigenous entrepreneurs. At this time, the government stepped in to prevent or slow down the forced sale of mortgaged peasant properties and to protect agriculture from foreign competition. Another interesting feature was the establishment of model industries by government: a carpet factory, a glass factory, and spinning and dyeing factories. The end of the decade saw increasing economic hardships for most Egyptians, even as expenditures on luxuries and movement by wealthy Egyptians to the more comfortable European districts were on the increase, continuing the dualistic nature of the economy. Opportunities were limited, however, and unemployment among educated people was on the rise.

By 1937, when the privileges granted to the European imperial powers were abolished, Egypt could feed but not clothe itself; cotton exports paid for manufactured imports. Revoking these privileges, however, did not end foreign influence and privilege. Unequal power and the 1936 Anglo-Egyptian Treaty were strong replacements. According to the treaty, Egypt had to erect roads and barracks for defense purposes, even though low cotton prices had pushed the economy into a slump.

□ Sudan

Sudan had been under a joint Anglo-Egyptian administration (the condominium) since 1890, which meant that economic decisionmaking was almost totally in foreign hands. Sudan's population around 1930 was somewhere between 5 and 6 million people. Its major economic resource was agriculture, which was dependent entirely on the Nile; the main export was gum arabic, for which Sudan supplied 85 percent of the world's production. Other important crops included *dura,* or millet (used mainly as a staple for breadmaking); doom-palm, or vegetable ivory (used by the United States in button manufacturing); and raw cotton, which irrigation had made an important cash crop. As in Egypt, Sudan's dependence on cotton made the economy vulnerable to fluctuations in cotton output and prices on the world market.

Although this vast country was greatly underdeveloped, there was a growing market for motorcars and machinery, mostly from Britain and the United States. Foreign trade was facilitated by improvements in Port Sudan on the Red Sea and construction of strategic railways to serve trade and the military. Other imports included basic needs, especially manufactured goods such as textiles and clothes, shoes, flour, tobacco, coffee, beer, fuel, and timber. Methods of production were mostly traditional, the population remained mostly illiterate, and duality was evident, especially between urban and rural and between peasant and absentee landlord.

□ The East

Moving east of the Mediterranean, a different experience in development was under way. As Goldschmidt discussed in greater detail, the Ottoman domains had been divided between Britain and France: Palestine,

Transjordan, and Iraq had come under British influence, and Syria and Lebanon were under French administration. Palestine and Jordan were formally separated, and by 1922 international borders between them had been established. Palestine came under a British mandate and a government commitment to facilitate the establishment of a Jewish national home in the country, without infringement on the rights of the indigenous people, as dictated by the Balfour Declaration of 1917.

Palestine. From that point on, the economic history of Palestine was in large measure the history of economic development in the Jewish sector. Early Jewish settlers came from Europe with high qualifications: education and skills as well as ideological commitment and determination. They also had the backing of the British and mandatory governments and the support of the world's Jews as well as many Western countries.

The population of Palestine in 1922 was about 757,000 people, rising to more than 852,000 in 1926. Of these, 628,000 were Muslim Arabs, 140,000 Jews, and 76,000 Christian Arabs; the rest were Druze Arabs. Native-born Jews were few, mostly urban, but new Jewish settlement of the land was a common pattern, even as urban population centers were growing. For both political and economic reasons, the goal of the Jewish community was to maintain for new immigrants a standard of living similar to what they had in their former home countries. To accomplish this, the community developed modern agricultural techniques, which, in the moshav (cooperative settlement) and the kibbutz (collective settlement), were advanced enough to compete on the international market. Industrial development was a mix of private and public or semipublic in ownership and management; it, too, was internationally competitive.

Roads, bridges, railways, and other construction projects were financed by advances from the British government. Jewish agriculture expanded both by learning from the indigenous Arab cultivators and by applying new techniques brought from Europe. Jewish farmers introduced new crops such as oilseeds, soybeans, fibers such as flax and hemp, and bananas. New factories were built, mostly but not exclusively in the Jewish sector, such as a silk factory in Tel Aviv, a match factory in Acre, and a cement factory in Haifa. Power stations were created, irrigation systems were established, and exploitation of the chemicals of the Dead Sea and the hydroelectric power of the Jordan River got under way. By the early 1930s, the manufacturing sector was quite diverse, producing a variety of products from soap and artificial teeth to pharmaceuticals. Even so, agriculture continued to be the main source of employment and income in the country.

Jewish labor was organized early in this period in the General Federation of Trade Unions, or Histadrut; however, the unionization of Arab labor was slow, spotty, and ineffective. Joint organization of Arab and Jewish workers existed only in government employment and public enterprises. Jewish labor was better educated, better organized, and paid thirty to fifty times more than Arab workers.

By the end of the 1930s, despite political conflict between Arabs and Jews and between both of them and the mandatory government, the Jewish economic sector was solidly established, with a harbor in Haifa, extensive drainage of swamps in the Huleh district, an oil refinery, expanded irrigation, and a flourishing citrus industry for exports. In contrast, with few exceptions, Arab agriculture still relied on established methods of cultivation: limited irrigation and traditional crops under traditional tenure systems. Except in the urban centers, which were often a mix of Arabs and Jews, the infrastructure in the Arab sector was poor, with few roads, no electricity, no running water, and limited facilities for credit, marketing, and education. Palestine was a small country with two virtually separate and unequal economies. The Arab economy had much in common with the economies of neighboring Arab states, whereas the Jewish economy more closely resembled those in Europe but with a big dose of creativity and initiative.

© Deborah J. Gerner

Photo 7.1 Palestinian women have found that small-scale economic activities such as sewing and embroidery allow them to earn much-needed money while preserving a part of their culture.

Iraq and Syria. Iraq was also placed under British supervision, although it had the semblance of an independent state. In 1922, under British guidance, Emir Faisal became constitutional monarch King Faisal I, supported by a Chamber of Deputies. Iraq was admitted to the League of Nations in 1932 after the 1930 Treaty of Alliance with Britain ensured the continuation of British influence and benefits from oil exploitation. Oil concessions were awarded to the Iraq Petroleum Company (IPC) and the British Oil Development Company. Iraq's commercial laws betrayed this influence; they were a mixture of provisions from prewar Ottoman laws, an Indian Company Act (basically British), and the British Patent or Trade Mark Law.

The government of Iraq offered tax exemptions and loans to stimulate industry, but the results were limited. A few factories produced cotton textiles, cigarettes, bricks, soap, canned fruit, and jute products. These factories were small, more like cottage industries in method, scale, and productivity. Agriculture was the main source of employment, but landownership titles were unsettled. Land registration was introduced in 1932, but the lack of adequate documentation gave powerful tribal chiefs great advantages in appropriating large areas at the expense of the peasants and sharecroppers.

The government took the initiative to build bridges, canals, and irrigation systems on the Tigris and the Euphrates Rivers. The port of Basra had already been built by the British army during World War I, as had railways for troop transportation. However, the maintenance of these facilities suffered during the Depression years and the end of the mandate. The country had some good roads, extensive river navigation, and a public airport that opened in 1933.

The country's known resources, other than oil, included salt and low-quality coal. However, agriculture and cultivable land were abundant relative to the population, which in the early 1930s was about 3 million people. Most of the labor force was illiterate. Sharecropping was common, and the economy was barely monetized. Even so, modern Western-style houses were being built, especially in Baghdad, Basra, and Mosul, but no sewage system or urban zoning existed.

Iraq produced grain, dates, and tobacco. The methods and technology of cultivation were changing slowly. The peasants were not accustomed to using bank facilities and therefore depended on moneylenders. The government did not have any plans for industrialization, but it built new roads and in 1926 decided to construct the Turko-Syrian railroad line.

After World War I and the exit of the Ottomans, Syria and Lebanon came under French mandate. The territory, then known as Syria, was segmented into districts or provinces: Beirut, Damascus, Aleppo, Latakia, and Jebel ed Druz. In addition to having internal ethnic conflicts, the Syrian nationalists never accepted the domination of the French. Therefore, political unrest was frequent. Economic activity responded to expenditures by the French army, but the economy depended mainly on agriculture, trade, and tourism, especially in Beirut and Aleppo. Wheat and other cereals were prominent crops. Local industry included weaving, tanning, dyeing, and the production of olive oil, soap, silk, and tobacco. Use of machinery had begun. The French promoted road building and constructed a railway to Damascus. Imports consisted mostly of food and consumer items such as clothing, petroleum, motor fuels, and motorcars. The major exports were dried fruits, pistachio nuts, olive oil, and live animals, which were primarily reexports from Turkey.

Among its resources, the Syrian region had gold, copper, iron, manganese, chrome, and gypsum. However, dependence on imports was increasing, especially hardware, machinery, paper, glass and china, hosiery, drugs, pianos, safes, clocks, and beer. Silkworm eggs came from France and were hatched into caterpillars and raised to maturity, and then the silkworm cocoons were reexported to France. Syria's economy was tied to that of France, both because of the mandate and because the Syrian lira was tied to the French franc. As a result, agricultural Syria shared the market fluctuations experienced by industrial France.

A significant development in this period was the separation of Syria and Lebanon and the adoption of new constitutions by both, still under French mandate. According to the 1936 treaty between France and both Syria and Lebanon, these two countries would be independent three years after signing the treaty. However, World War II delayed implementation of that treaty.

Interest in industry led to protectionism in Syria, the building of hotels in the cities, a free trade zone in Beirut, expansion of railways from the

© Thomas Hartwell

northern city of Aleppo to the borders of Iraq, and the building of roads. Air service was established to the French city of Marseilles in the west and the French colonial center of Saigon, Vietnam, to the east. A tobacco monopoly was granted to a private company.

The government also adopted five-year (spending) plans for the mandated territories. Among the new industries were factories for

Photo 7.2 A young woman weaves an ornate Persian carpet. Carpets are one of Iran's most important exports (after petroleum and petrochemicals).

perfume, blankets, ladies' hosiery, and cement tiles. Hemp, a widely used fiber-producing plant, was introduced in agriculture. Irrigation systems in Homs and the Ghab district were undertaken, but the Ghab project was abandoned when the end of mandate became imminent. Land reclamation and drainage of marshes also began. However, these small-scale projects were insufficient to significantly affect the economic structure. The economies of Syria and Lebanon remained primarily agricultural, under-developed, and service-oriented. Opposition between urban and rural, rich and poor, literate and illiterate, and Western and traditional continued to be evident.

Iran. Iran, or Persia as it was known at the time, was not dominated by a colonial power, but strong foreign influence was always evident. Although rich in resources, Iran depended heavily on the outside world for basic needs. Its imports included sugar, cotton, tea, rice, animals, metal goods, machinery, and implements. Exports included heavy oil and petroleum products, wool, carpets, opium, gum, raw tobacco, sheepskins, raw silk and cotton, pearls, drugs, rice, wheat, barley, and raw skins. A few new industries sprang up, such as leather, shoe, and button factories.

Iran had an underdeveloped infrastructure. Most people traveled by pack animals and carts, although a few roads were good enough for motorcars. Mining was done by concession, mostly granted to foreigners, and economic decisions were guided by a resident U.S. adviser. Almost 25 percent of the budget went to the military in the mid-1920s, and government efforts to increase funds by securing foreign capital fell short. At least two major banks existed, the Banque d'Escompte de Perse (taken over by the U.S. adviser) and the Imperial Bank of Persia, the state bank. The economy, however, was hardly monetized. The government resorted to unpaid labor (corveé) to build military and trade roads. Technical education was minimal, although a technical school was established by the government in the mid-1920s.

The second half of the decade witnessed increasing centralization, sometimes by ruthless means. Sugar and tea monopolies were created to generate revenues to subsidize railway building. A national bank was chartered by the Majlis (parliament) in 1927, to be capitalized by the sale of crown jewels and domains. Trade was limited by the poor infrastructure as well as the low purchasing power of the people. The poor transportation system delayed delivery to such an extent that the Union of Soviet Socialist Republics (USSR) imposed a boycott on Persian goods for more than two years.

The government promoted public education. Almost 500,000 students attended schools, both public and private, at various levels, in 1926–1927. Iran also had higher education institutions in medicine, fine arts, pedagogy,

law, political science, engineering, and military science. To promote economic independence, in 1928 Iran abolished the Capitulations system that
had given significant rights to Europeans and pursued nationalist economic
policies. However, most contracts for railway building were awarded to
foreigners, presumably because the local population lacked the skills and
equipment needed for large building and engineering projects.

In 1931 foreign trade monopolies were expanded, and exporters were
required to sell most of their foreign currency to the government. New monopolies were established to manage imports and exports of certain items,
including silk cloth and silk cocoons. Nevertheless, industry continued to
be underdeveloped, and dependence on the outside world remained. Carpets continued to be the major export and manufactured goods the major
import. Among these imports were textiles, matches, electric lights,
hosiery, leather, glassware, soap, and dried fruit. Special attention was devoted to agriculture, although irrigation systems and new cultivation techniques were not in evidence.

Iran was greatly influenced by appearances of modernity as reflected
in patterns of living. By the late 1930s, there were cinemas and theaters
but no broadcasting, although wireless radios were widely used. Finally,
although protectionism was widespread, Iran concluded bilateral trade
agreements (in 1935 with Syria and the USSR and in 1936 with Germany
and Austria) as well as multilateral ones (in 1937 with Argentina, Mexico,
and Turkey and with Iraq, Afghanistan, and Turkey). As the 1930s came to
an end, Iran's economy was still underdeveloped, dualistic, unevenly developed, and highly dependent on and influenced by foreign interests.

The Gulf. The Gulf countries had little development prior to World
War II. Kuwait, Bahrain, and Aden were transit centers and stations for
pearling, fishing, and repairing ships. There was little agriculture and
hardly any industry. Saudi Arabia, most of which is desert, had not yet
begun exploiting its petroleum deposits, although signs of the potential oil
wealth already existed. The most important source of revenue was spending by Muslim pilgrims coming to Mecca from all over the world. Agriculture was important on the east and west coasts of the region but not
enough in any of these countries to satisfy the needs of the population.
Population estimates for the Gulf region in this period are imprecise, but
there were probably less than 10 million people in all countries combined.

Turkey. Although not ruled by foreign powers, Turkey had been under
foreign influence for a long time, first under the centuries-old system of
Capitulations and then through heavy indebtedness to Western powers during the second half of the nineteenth century. The attempt to develop and

industrialize the economy took the form of a mix between private and public enterprise. Between 1922 and 1934, development was promoted through investment banks created by the state. In addition to the Agricultural Bank already in existence, the state created the Ish Bank, a private company set up to organize and finance business enterprises. The Industrial and Mining Bank of Turkey, a state bank, had the charge of managing state-owned industrial enterprises. As a result, many new industrial projects were established, aided by the state. The number of workers in industry increased from 17,000 to 62,000 between 1927 and 1933. The output of cotton yarn, woolen textiles, sugar, leather, and cement increased rapidly. Agricultural output also expanded sufficiently to the extent that Turkey could feed itself. The production of cereals, tobacco, vegetables, and fruits increased steadily during the 1920s and 1930s.

To conclude, Middle Eastern countries were only beginning to change their economies during this phase. Consumption of manufactured products was more evident than production. Agriculture was the main sector in virtually all the countries. Dualism prevailed, with only a small portion of the population involved in efficient, profitable production. With the exception of Palestine under the British mandate, which had begun industrializing rapidly, all countries had started on the road to industrialization and structural change, but only barely. The advent of World War II made a difference, to which we turn next.

■ THE WAR YEARS, 1939–1945

During World War II, Middle Eastern countries were allied (willingly or unwillingly) with one of the warring parties and therefore directly affected by the war machine. Their economies had to be reorganized to serve that machine. The Middle Eastern supply center for the Allies, headquartered in Egypt, took charge of coordinating the distribution of supplies, allocation of resources, maintenance of infrastructure, and encouragement of local production to substitute for imports and augment the war economy. That system of coordination treated the whole region as a unit. The coordination was so successful that it was optimistically perceived as a prototype of regional planning and development, but little came out of it after the war's end (Wilmington, 1971).

During the war, however, there was pressure to expand local production and produce imports in-country. In Egypt the industrializing trend that had started before the war was encouraged so that by the end of the war, Egyptian industry was able to satisfy 86 percent of its domestic needs for consumer nondurables, employ 8.4 percent of the labor force, and produce

12 percent of the GDP (Radwan, 1974:245). However, this level of industrial employment was the same as in 1937, which meant that little structural
change had taken place in the meantime.

Iran, in contrast, felt the negative shock of the war while experiencing
few positive effects. There was more pressure on the infrastructure but no
investment to maintain it. Foreign control directed all efforts toward war
objectives in which Iran had no interest (Bharier, 1969:88).

More significant war effects were felt in Iraq's economy. Production
of bricks, hand tools, oilseeds, tanning, and other traditional commodities
expanded, but no modern factories were created. Railroads were expanded
and maintained, as were roads and port facilities. Agriculture also benefited from the use of tractors, cultivators, and combines, in some places for
the first time. In 1941 a college of agriculture was established (Longrig,
1968:320–323). Such improvements, however, were not common. Only
Iran and Syria, like Iraq, expanded their rail system by more than 100 kilo-
meters between 1940 and 1945. In contrast, Algeria lost some rail, probably because broken tracks were not replaced.

Turkey, with its closer ties to Europe, had a unique experience. At the
end of World War I, it had just been reduced from a vast empire to a weak,
poorly organized, underpopulated country. Turkey had a split identity, part
European and part Asian. The revolution of the Young Turks and advent
of Mustafa Kemal Atatürk (father of the Turks) were perceived as the

© Thomas Hartwell

Photo 7.3 A traditional dhow boat passes an oil tanker in the Bahraini port.

mechanisms to create a unified identity, with a republican constitution, an industrialized economy, and independence from foreign influence.

The thrust of Turkey's development during the first half of the century came between 1934 and 1947. This period witnessed the evolution of state socialism, etatism, and economic planning. The five-year plan introduced in 1934 brought aid from the Soviet Union, both physical and managerial. Turkey chose to remain neutral during the war but still spent a great deal of money on armaments, presumably to protect its neutrality. The government emphasized industrialization, but agriculture seemed neglected.

The mining sector responded to state efforts. Production and export of coal increased. Electrical power generation increased from two stations in 1923 to 180 in 1945. Nevertheless, the movement to industrialize made few changes in the structure of the economy. As late as 1946, imports included machinery and processed goods, whereas exports included tobacco, cereals and legumes, dried fruits, nuts, raw cotton, wool, and live animals (Thornburg, Spry, and Soule, 1968:chaps. 1–3, Appendix).

In sum, the war period brought the state into a more active role in managing the economies of the Middle East. Similar positive and negative effects of the war could be found in most countries. People had jobs and money to spend but suffered shortages of consumer and producer goods since supplying the armies and the war machinery took priority. Prices, except of rationed goods, went up throughout the region. Controls were also imposed on the political movements for independence. The war did lead to an expanded market, experience with foreign management of the economy and industry, and knowledge of coordination of economic and military activities, but even so, no positive or lasting impact on economic development and structural change was evident. Two side-effects should be noted, however: a demonstration effect that introduced people to certain products and raised their expectations for the future and a kind of indebtedness by the colonial powers that may have expedited political independence and the end of colonialism.

■ POST–WORLD WAR II EXPANSION AND THE OIL BOOM, 1945–1982

The end of the war signaled a new world order for the countries of the Middle East. Colonialism formally came to an end, although several regimes were replaced by military regimes posing as republics or by monarchies supported by the former colonial powers. While peace prevailed in the West, the Middle East witnessed several wars, in 1948, 1956, 1967, 1973, 1980, 1982, and 1991; coups in Egypt, Syria, Libya, Iraq, Iran, and Sudan; wars of independence in Algeria, Tunisia, and Palestine;

and long periods of civil war in Algeria, Sudan, Yemen, Somalia, and Lebanon. New states came into being, including Israel, Djibouti, Somalia, and the Comoros.

Ambitious development programs were initiated throughout the region for agriculture and industry, education, technology transfer, and modernization. These programs complemented a strong tradition of government intervention:

> Public policy in the Middle East and North Africa is driven by the belief that the state is the most effective agent for stimulating economic development. . . . Accordingly, nationalization and public ownership of the means of production figure prominently in public policy, and the state has sought to become the primary supplier of investment. (Anderson and Martinez, 1998:179)

Another feature of the period was the increase in consumerism, even in relatively poor countries dependent on aid and loans. Finally, the oil price revolution of 1974 created a semblance of prosperity and growth for all, although the benefits were concentrated within the oil-exporting countries.

The Cold War between East and West had its impact, as countries of the Middle East were pressured to line up with one camp or the other. Egypt, together with India and Yugoslavia, initiated the Non-Aligned Movement to create a balance between the two superpower camps and promote neutrality for Third World countries. Following World War II, Turkey tried to remain independent and neutral, but the advent of the Cold War and temptations of economic aid from the United States changed this policy. The promise of aid through the Marshall Plan, membership in the North Atlantic Treaty Organization (NATO) to provide protection from the giant USSR, and the power of the World Bank and the International Monetary Fund (IMF) redirected Turkey's economic policies toward the West. The impact was most strongly felt during what became known as the democratic decade (1950–1960), when a democratic government was in office. However, the role of government in the economy remained significant. After 1960 Turkey faced military coups, which created a lasting role for the military in the economy.

During this period, the Middle Eastern countries varied in the extent to which they achieved economic development, industrialization, and structural change (Tuma, 1987:chaps. 6–8 provides an elaboration of the argument in this section; see also Wilson, 1995). On the whole, all countries except Israel remained underdeveloped and not much more industrialized than they were at the beginning of the period.

Agriculture continued to be a vital sector in most Middle Eastern economies as a source of employment and income for a large percentage of the steadily increasing population. Agriculture was also perceived as a stabilizing force within the economy because it could absorb surplus labor.

As late as 1978, agriculture employed more than 40 percent of the economically active population in twelve countries and more than 50 percent in eleven other countries. Only three countries employed less than 25 percent of the active labor force in agriculture.

Agricultural production increased in all countries of the region during the 1950s and 1960s, except Algeria. Taking 1952–1956 as the base period, Israel increased its agricultural output threefold by 1968. Lebanon, Libya, and Sudan almost doubled theirs; Iran and Iraq raised theirs by more than 50 percent;, and the remaining countries raised theirs by a little less than 50 percent. Somalia and Mauritania increased agricultural output by more than 2 percent annually between 1960 and 1975 (IBRD, 1988; see also FAO, 1987).

After 1969, however, the advance in agricultural output slowed somewhat. Libya more than doubled its output between 1968 and 1978; Syria, Tunisia, and Israel all expanded production one and a half times in the same period. However, agriculture almost stagnated in Morocco, the Yemen Arab Republic, and, to a certain extent, Egypt and Iraq.

Even in countries with steadily increasing agricultural productivity, it was impossible to meet the demands of rapid population growth. The change in per capita agricultural output was negative in a number of countries. For instance, in Jordan, Morocco, Iraq, and the Yemen Arab Republic, food production per person declined significantly. The most serious decrease probably took place in Jordan, presumably because of the loss of the West Bank to Israel in the 1967 Six Day War (Tuma, 1987:Table 1).

The increase in agricultural output between 1961 and the end of the 1970s was accompanied by expansion of the arable and permanent crop areas in all countries of the region (to various degrees) except in Syria. This was especially true in Algeria, Morocco, the People's Democratic Republic of Yemen (PDR Yemen), and Iraq. In spite of these gains in output and arable land, agriculture's relative contribution to the GDP remained small or decreased in most countries. Labor productivity in agriculture was relatively low, and therefore the share of GDP produced by agriculture was less than the proportion of the population engaged in agricultural production. To illustrate, 49 percent of the Algerian active labor force worked in agriculture in 1981, but their contribution to the GDP was only 6 percent; in Morocco 51 percent of the active labor force contributed only 14 percent of the GDP (Tuma, 1987:109). In Turkey 64.2 percent of the labor force worked in agriculture, contributing only 26.2 percent of GDP (Hale, 1981). The less than proportional contribution was evident in all countries except Lebanon, where 9 percent of the active labor force contributed 12 percent of the GDP (Tuma, 1987:109).

Improvements in agriculture could also be seen in the changes in yield per unit of land. Most Middle Eastern countries experienced increases in yield between 1969 and 1979 in the production of cereals, roots and tubers, tomatoes, and tobacco leaves. It is interesting to observe different patterns among these countries. For instance, only Lebanon, Israel, and Turkey experienced increases in yield in most crops and no declines in any. Egypt, Iraq, and Sudan each had declines in three or more products. Syria and Tunisia had declines in one crop each. However, the changes in yield varied widely from one crop or country to another. The UAE increased its yield of tomatoes by 391.4 percent, but the productivity of milk per cow declined by 43.6 percent. Iraq had a decline in the yield of seed cotton but an increase in the yield of tomatoes. Turkey's biggest gain was in the production of industrial crops rather than food crops. In general, the changes in agricultural yields were modest, definitely below the potential suggested by other realized advances in the region (Tuma, 1987:chap. 6).

The process of change and development was probably as significant as the actual effects. There were attempts to introduce major policies in agriculture to promote development and growth, equity, freedom, regime survival, and political stability. Policymakers sometimes had to trade economic efficiency for sociopolitical objectives.

Agrarian reform was introduced in almost all countries of the region, but most dramatically in Egypt, Syria, Iran, Iraq, Algeria, and PDR Yemen. In these countries agrarian reform covered land tenure, tenancy, and patterns of production and farm organization. Ceilings on landownership were established, and most of the land above those ceilings was expropriated and redistributed to landless former tenants and to those who had less land than a specified minimum. Compensation was usually paid for expropriated land, and recipients of the land usually paid for it in long-term installments.

By contrast, agrarian reform in Tunisia, Morocco, and Libya primarily involved appropriating land held by foreigners and distributing it to local farmers. Tunisia attempted to cultivate these lands collectively but was unsuccessful. Jordan and Sudan concentrated their efforts on specific projects such as management of the Gezira scheme in Sudan and development of the East Ghor district in Jordan. In Sudan the government took over management of the private irrigation system and tractor schemes to make sure the services reached the farmers who needed them. Turkey's agrarian reform concentrated on distribution of public land, expansion of irrigation, use of fertilizers, and acquisition of tractors. In Lebanon, Saudi Arabia, and the Yemen Arab Republic, the policy focused on land consolidation and reclamation of new land.

Distributive reform was accompanied in virtually all cases by the creation of agricultural cooperatives whose functions varied from providing credit and marketing services to overseeing production and management. In most reforming countries, the government established state demonstration farms, large-scale production units on the socialist pattern, or agribusinesses and farm corporate ventures, as in Iran and Saudi Arabia. Israel did not introduce agrarian reform because its Jewish agriculture was initially planned according to Zionist national objectives. Side by side with the small private Jewish agricultural sector, Israel established the moshav, in which farmers cultivated their individual farms but cooperated in major farm operations such as cultivation or marketing. Another form was the kibbutz, which was operated collectively as a large-scale farm, with the rewards distributed according to the members' needs. In contrast, Arab agriculture in Israel was similar to agriculture in the neighboring countries but with no reform or planning. Gradually, however, Arab farmers in Israel started to adopt more advanced methods of cultivation, but the system of tenure remained unchanged.

There were attempts to mechanize certain agricultural activities, increase irrigation, and increase consumption of fertilizers. Tractor use increased radically in Kuwait, the Yemen Arab Republic, Libya, Oman, Syria, and Iran. Turkey had a great opportunity to use tractors as part of the Marshall Plan, even though it lacked spare parts and facilities for maintenance. However, the distribution of tractors per unit of cultivated land varied widely from one country to another. Israel had one tractor for every 12 ha in 1980, whereas Sudan had one tractor for every 1,124 ha (Tuma, 1987:115).

An important feature of Middle Eastern agriculture in the post–World War II period was the building of large irrigation and hydroelectric projects. These projects had multiple objectives: to increase resources, enhance production, and show tangible results of government policy. The Aswan High Dam in Egypt, the Euphrates Dam in Syria, and the Hula-Negev project in Israel are only a few examples. These and similar projects helped to increase the cultivable land area in most countries. For example, Iraq increased its cultivable area by 130,000 ha between 1961 and 1977; Iran increased cultivated lands by more than 1 million ha; and Morocco added more than 280,000 ha in the same period. Even so, except in Egypt where agriculture was 100 percent irrigated, rain-fed agriculture remained the rule (Tuma, 1987:116).

Everywhere in the Middle East except in Israel's Jewish sector, agriculture continued to suffer from duality, with a large segment exhibiting backwardness, low productivity, small scale, and archaic techniques. A much smaller segment enjoyed advanced technology with relatively large-scale operations and management. The rates of growth in agriculture in general were modest and the policies only partially successful.

Interest in agriculture was strong, but industrialization had a magic of its own. The three decades following World War II were remarkable in the history of industrialization in the Middle East. The rates of growth of industry and manufacturing rose, industry increased its contribution to GDP, and a higher percentage of the labor force now worked in industry. By

© Thomas Hartwell

Photo 7.4 Drip irrigation makes agriculture possible even in the Egyptian Sinai.

1980, fully half of the countries of the region reported larger percentages of GDP originating in industry and manufacturing than previously.

Although industry and manufacturing increased their share of GDP between 1960 and 1981, the average annual rates of growth varied widely. Algeria's average annual growth rate of industry went down from 11.6 percent in the 1960s to 7.6 percent in the 1970s. The average annual growth rate of industry and manufacturing in Turkey was 9.6 percent between 1962 and 1978. In Iran and Syria it reached as high as 16.7 percent between 1970 and 1980 (Tuma, 1987:chap. 7). As Table 7.3 indicates, by the late 1980s industry had become an important factor in national wealth in several Middle Eastern countries.

The advance of industry was also demonstrated by increases in the consumption of industrial energy and rates of employment in industry and manufacturing. Energy consumption increased in all countries, dramatically in some, especially in the oil-rich countries. However, countries such as the Yemen Arab Republic and Sudan used very little energy due to their very low levels of industrialization.

The pattern and level of industrialization may also be explored by asking which country produced what and how much. A survey of twelve Arab countries (Shafii, 1978) in the late 1960s showed that the main industries were food processing, textiles, and light industries such as woodwork and printing. Machinery and basic metals were also produced in significant

Table 7.3 Contribution over Time of Agriculture and Industry to GDP (percentage)

Country	1958 Agriculture	1958 Industry	1968 Agriculture	1968 Industry	1978 Agriculture	1978 Industry	1988 Agriculture	1988 Industry
Algeria	25	20	n.a.	n.a.	7	49	7	52
Egypt	33	24	25	24	24	27	16	31
Iran	32	30	22	34	9	46	21	20
Iraq	20	50	15	43	7	67	15	39
Israel	12	32	8	34	4	23	3	20
Jordan	18	14	15	21	6	21	6	22
Lebanon	n.a.	n.a.	11	21	9	21	9	21
Libya	n.a.	n.a.	4	65	2	68	5	49
Mauritania	n.a.	n.a.	n.a.	n.a.	25	24	21	26
Morocco	35	26	32	29	18	33	17	33
Saudi Arabia	n.a.	n.a.	6	62	1	79	2	73
Somalia	n.a.	n.a.	n.a.	n.a.	55	10	63	9
Sudan	59	12	39	15	36	14	29	15
Tunisia	n.a.	n.a.	18	21	16	27	13	28
Turkey	30	28	25	27	17	37	41	14

Source: International Historical Statistics, 1998.
Note: n.a. Information not available.

numbers in some countries. Specialization and concentration of production were also apparent in the survey. For instance, Egypt produced 23.2 percent of all machinery manufactured in the twelve countries; 76.8 percent of all basic metals; 39.5 percent of all textiles; and 43 percent of all paper, publishing, and printing products. Algeria produced 27.5 percent of all machinery, 23.8 percent of all woodwork, and 16.9 percent of all nonmetallic industries. Lebanon produced 34.1 percent of all woodwork. Morocco produced 16.3 percent of all machinery; 28 percent of the processed foods; 24.3 percent of the paper, printing, and publishing materials; and 18.25 percent of all chemicals, petroleum, and coal products. Tunisia specialized in basic metals, providing 18.2 percent of the total produced by these twelve countries.

The specialization pattern within each country did not change much between the 1960s and early 1980s, with some exceptions. Major developments took place after 1975 in oil and petrochemical industries in the oil-producing countries; in car assembly in Iran and Egypt, vehicle assembly and component manufacturing in Tunisia, truck assembly in Turkey, and tractor assembly in Syria; and in the arms and mineral industries in Israel. In addition, food processing continued to grow in various countries of the region. The petrochemical industry acquired enough importance to be described as the key to Arab development. In Egypt a major effort for industrialization came from the military, which produced both civilian and military products, although not very successfully (Deaver, 1996).

The distribution of industrial projects within countries was concentrated in specific regions, either because of proximity to raw materials such as soil deposits or because of the development of infrastructure in and around the largest cities and near the coast. The few exceptions were Iran, which had the most dispersed industry among the large countries, followed by Egypt and Morocco, and by Israel, which had the widest dispersal of all in the region. In general, the pattern of industrialization within individual countries mirrored and reinforced the dualistic economic structures that had prevailed at the beginning of the period.

The development of industry and manufacturing was promoted by a combination of market control and planning activities. Most countries in the region were aware of their relative backwardness and were anxious to develop at relatively rapid rates, which made government intervention seem indispensable. All governments assigned high priorities to industrial production and often participated directly in the economy. In most Middle Eastern countries, until recently the state owned or controlled most of the natural resources and carried the responsibility for large sectors of the economy, whether the country considered itself "socialist" or "capitalist." Thus, government and public forces in both groups of countries were conspicuously responsible for industrialization policy.

A third group of countries eschewed too much government involvement in the economy and pursued industrialization through more market-oriented policies, such as Bahrain, Iran before the 1979 revolution, Jordan, Lebanon, Morocco, Tunisia, and the Yemen Arab Republic. The government intervened indirectly through taxation, subsidies, and protectionism. It is notable that Morocco and Lebanon achieved a fair degree of advancement in light industry. Government policy in these countries was one of facilitating industrialization by improving infrastructure and raising incentives through higher wages, traditional benefits, and appeals to nationalistic sentiment. By the late 1970s, even the socialist countries had shifted toward the market economy. Egypt introduced its Infitah (open door policy), and Algeria began to open up to the private sector to combat the apparent retardation of the economy.

In spite of their differences, the three groups of countries had certain policies and measures in common. For instance, all countries had indicative economic plans, rather than command plans to be implemented by government. Those plans specified the expected levels of expenditure in the main sectors of the economy, but the government had no way of enforcing those plans, nor were the people indoctrinated enough or always willing to adopt them.

Another common feature was a certain emphasis on large-scale turnkey industry. In such cases, contracts were concluded for establishing industries by foreign contractors who took responsibility for all construction activities, leaving little room for learning by doing by the domestic labor force. Still another feature was the concentration of industrial production and manufacturing in commodities for the domestic market, thus ignoring international standards of quality and efficiency. Finally, it seems evident that when government did not interfere directly, industry remained small and often more traditional than otherwise. In conclusion, industry and manufacturing made some progress during the three decades following World War II, but they did not achieve competitiveness on the world market. Nor, with the exception of Israel, did they become major sectors in the various economies in terms of contribution to GDP, productive employment of labor, or changes in the patterns of trade, as will be seen below.

From 1945 to 1975, the Middle East experienced rapid expansion in international trade. Direction and volume varied according to endowment, alliances, and economic and political ideologies and objectives. The oil-exporting countries had relatively abundant purchasing power to spend on trade, while other countries had to depend on economic aid, loans, and military alliances to finance trade deficits. The socialist governments used some degree of planning and thus were able to regulate both the volume and composition of trade and avoid deficits more than the others. Yet in all cases, trade was expanded or curtailed largely according to political and military alliances (or semi-alliances), rather than according to economic and market conditions.

All Middle Eastern countries increased their exports during the 1960s, although the increases varied widely. Sudan's exports increased only slightly, whereas Libya increased its exports enormously because of increased oil production and higher oil prices. Several other countries, including Israel, Jordan, Turkey, and Lebanon, had average annual increases in exports of more than 10 percent without the benefit of oil exports. Most countries were unable to maintain their position during the 1970s, however, when many suffered a decline. The same period witnessed absolute declines in exports in seven countries, five of which were oil producers and exporters.[4] Apparently Algeria, Iran, Iraq, Kuwait, and Libya reduced their exports intentionally as part of the reaction to the 1973 Arab-Israeli war and the oil price revolution. Egypt and Sudan needed foreign currency but were unable to sustain their level of exports because of a shift to production for the domestic market and low productivity.

The Middle East has not experienced a uniform regional increase in economic growth comparable to that of East Asia, Southeast Asia, or Latin America. Part of the problem may be the absence of a "lead economy" driving regional growth, as Japan did in Asia:

> Israel could potentially be seen in this role, but although it is the most developed country within the region on most criteria, its economy is small. Its supply capacity is very limited in comparison to Japan, and it lacks the purchasing power to transmit substantial multiplier effects to other Middle Eastern countries that would help their exports. (Wilson, 1995: 16–17)

Although exports declined in the 1970s in most countries, imports generally continued to increase. During the 1970s, only Israel and Lebanon had declines in imports. Again, war was a major factor in both countries. The increase in imports by the non-oil-exporting countries caused large deficits in the balance of trade that had to be financed by foreign aid, loans, and foreign investments. Primary commodities, fuels, minerals, and metals dominated exports between 1960 and 1980. Some manufacturing exports came from Jordan, and industrial and manufactured products from Syria and Tunisia, but all other countries except Israel continued to export the same goods they had exported in the past. Some of the industrial and manufacturing exports were often reexports by transit economies such as Lebanon, the UAE, and Jordan.

During this period, imports of machinery increased somewhat and imports of other manufactures decreased somewhat in Algeria, Egypt, Iran, Iraq, Morocco, Sudan, Syria, and Tunisia. Import substitution policies played a major role in that development. Israel, in contrast, reduced imports of machinery and transportation equipment and increased imports of other manufactures. It also increased the import and consumption of fuel, in the pattern of the industrialized countries. Turkey, however, increased its production and assembly of machinery and other manufactured goods and reduced imports of these items between 1962 and 1978.

The flow of trade within the region also was not uniform. It was common to see intraregional trade concentrated within subregions: the Gulf states, North African countries, western Asia, and so on. However, intraregional trade was relatively small compared with regional trade with other regions and countries. The reasons are clear. The countries of the Middle East duplicated each other's products and competed for markets and clients. Therefore, the region had to depend on imports of manufactured and industrial goods from outside the region, and export to those regions the raw materials and primary products that were not in demand within the region. The features of underdevelopment were as evident in the pattern of trade in the early 1980s as they were at the beginning of the period. The boom witnessed increased consumption, expanded infrastructures, and mounting debts. It also prompted modernization but little technology transfer, and expansion of trade but also dependency on foreign capital, technology, and markets (Roberts and Fowler, 1995). Therefore, when the developed countries suffered a recession in the mid-1980s and the price of oil declined in the 1990s, Middle Eastern countries began to suffer as well. In an extensive study of the effects of oil on the economies of the Gulf Cooperation Council, Hoosein Askari, Vahid Nowshirvani, and Mohamed Jaber ask,

> [H]as oil been a blessing or a curse? If the rate of private section growth is the basis for the answer, then oil seems to have been much more a curse than a blessing, especially for future generations of citizens. However, oil could be seen as a blessing because it affords the financial resources needed to support radical changes in policy. (Askari, Nowshirvani, and Jaber, 1997:96)

The tendency to change policy and try to integrate national economies into the new global economy created new burdens for which these economies were scarcely prepared. The mechanism for such integration, under pressure from the World Bank, the IMF, and the U.S. State Department, was to introduce structural reform and privatization. Freer trade, less protectionism, and denationalization became the motto at the end of the period, even though these countries could hardly compete on the international market. Compliance, therefore, was found to be difficult and costly but still attempted (Barkey, 1992; Niblock and Murphy, 1993; El-Ghonemy, 1998).

■ CONTEMPORARY MIDDLE EASTERN ECONOMIES, 1982 TO THE PRESENT

Given their diverse patterns of historical evolution, it is not surprising that contemporary Middle Eastern economies vary widely in their economic outlook and philosophy. Although under pressure to reform their economic structures, privatize public enterprise, and liberalize trade, most countries still maintain some version of a mixed economy. The dominant form of mixed economic system is one in which public and private sectors interact, but the public sector has more power than the private sector. This pattern exists in Algeria, Tunisia, Egypt, Syria, Iraq, Mauritania, Somalia, Comoros, Yemen, and Turkey. Israel is similar, except that increasingly the private sector has more influence than the public. Another unique feature of Israel is that its economic institutions are sufficiently well developed to permit economic management through the use of monetary and fiscal policies, rather than by direct government intervention.

Among the Gulf oil-exporting countries, the mixed economy takes the form of state capitalism. Here the royal families control power and oil wealth and dole out benefits to their subjects, who then practice some form of market capitalism. However, little decisionmaking takes place through popular participation in the market. The same applies in Libya, which has no royal family; oil revenues go directly into the state coffers of the only remaining "Arab socialist" regime in the region.

Although traditional monarchies such as Jordan and Morocco lean toward a competitive market system, their economic institutions are still too underdeveloped to allow the market to guide the economy. Hence government intervention, or management by the king, is not uncommon. Probably the closest to a free market approach exists in Lebanon and Bahrain. The Lebanese economy has been too chaotic since 1975 to be clearly defined, but signs of recovery are now abundant. And Bahrain depends heavily on offshore economic activities, to which domestic regulations do not apply, and therefore entertains free market practices in its domain (Edwards, 1996).

Finally, there is what has been called the Islamic economic system, primarily in Iran and Sudan; Saudi Arabia also claims to have an Islamic economic system. The main rules in this system are that there should be no interest charges on loans and all investment capital must come from shareholders, directly or through banks. The impact of Islamic economic institutions on economic development and growth has yet to be assessed. So far, the most effective economic model in the Middle East has been the mixed economy model, in which the weight of influence is concentrated in the public sector (Wilson, 1995).

Throughout most of the region, there is relatively low participation in paid labor in general and by women in particular. Although some countries, particularly Gulf states such as Kuwait, Qatar, or the UAE, can boast of relatively high rates of participation, at least of male labor, most of that labor is foreign. The exceptions to low workforce participation are the Comoros Islands, Israel, Turkey, and Mauritania. Active participation of female labor in the informal economy within households, although presumably high, has not been adequately recorded or analyzed, an observation more fully developed by Valentine Moghadam in Chapter 8 and Lisa Taraki in Chapter 10. The combination of relatively low workforce participation with high population growth means that these economies face high rates of dependency on foreign labor and low capacity to generate savings for investment.

A large percentage of the labor force is engaged in agriculture, although in many cases more than 50 percent of the potential workforce is in services, unemployed, or uncounted. The sectoral distribution of the labor force changed during the decade of the 1980s. A lower percentage of workers were engaged in agriculture and a higher percentage in industry in 1990 than in 1980. In contrast, agriculture's contribution to GDP increased in a few cases and declined in others. The same was true of the contribution of industry and manufacturing to GDP, which remained relatively low, especially if the shares of extraction industries, such as potash, oil, and rock quarries, are excluded. The late 1980s and early 1990s were not good years for income earners in the Middle East.

The income per capita in 1994, when adjusted for purchasing power, increased in only three of the reported countries, decreased in seven, and remained the same in one. This should not surprise us, however, given the effects of various wars, the decline in oil prices, and the general economic decline in various parts of the world. The average growth rate of gross national product (GNP) between 1985 and 1994 declined in eight countries, and in four others it was less than 0.5 percent. Only Egypt, Israel, Kuwait, Morocco, Tunisia, and Turkey had average growth rates higher than 1 percent. In contrast, annual growth rates in industrialized countries are typically between 2 and 4 percent, and rapidly developing countries can achieve growth rates of 5 to 10 percent. (On income levels and distribution, see El-Ghonemy, 1998, chaps. 4 and 11.)

Most countries of the Middle East do not report their patterns of income distribution, but those providing such information do not show unusual inequality compared with most other countries in the world, including the United States, as measured by the shares of the lowest 20 percent and highest 20 percent of income recipients. Nevertheless, there are differences within the region. For example, Israel's income distribution was far more equal than that of Jordan, Morocco, and Tunisia; the latter two had more equal distributions than Jordan did. Egypt had the most equal distribution in the region, as measured by both shares of the two income groups noted above and by the smaller gap between them (Eeghen, 1998).

The economic profile of the region may be understood more clearly by exploring the composition of trade and the direction of trade of the individual countries. The latest available data show a pattern of trade that is common among underdeveloped countries. Most exports are extractive products, raw materials, or agricultural commodities. The imports are mostly manufactured goods, processed chemicals, and appliances. In some cases, the imports are raw materials for processing.

To illustrate this point, we can consider the fact that petroleum, natural gas, and petroleum products are the main exports of Algeria, Bahrain, Egypt, Iran, Iraq, Kuwait, Libya, Oman, Qatar, Saudi Arabia, Syria, and the UAE. Little other specialization is evident in these countries. Egypt sells cotton, textiles, and fabrics and some engineering and metal products, but these are only a small percentage of total exports. Iran exports carpets and pistachio nuts. Syria exports fresh fruit, vegetables, and beverages in addition to petroleum products. Most other countries, such as the UAE, re-export nonpetroleum products, which appear as exports on the record (Edwards, 1996:600; Diwan, Yang, and Wang, 1998:53–56).

Other major exports of the region include vanilla and ylang-ylang from Comoros; live animals from Djibouti (including camels); machinery, worked diamonds, and chemicals from Israel; and phosphate, potash, and their joint products (fertilizers) from Jordan. Lebanon sells food and beverages, machines and appliances, textiles, and metal products. Fish and iron ore come from Mauritania; food and other consumer goods from Morocco; agricultural products and live animals from Somalia; and cotton, gum arabic, sesame seeds, and sheep and lambs from Sudan. Clothing and accessories come from Tunisia, and Turkey exports textiles and iron and steel products. Yemen exports food, live animals, and raw materials. Egypt and Turkey assemble cars, trucks, and other industrial products, but most of the output is designed for domestic use. Although the export of these agricultural products and raw materials may have the same effects on development as other exports, the value of exports is relatively small compared with the needs of the country to finance imports for consumption and investment capital.

The mix of products imported into the region is as telling as the types of exports. All countries import machinery, transportation equipment and parts, appliances, and other manufactured goods. Even industrialized Israel imports capital goods, mostly machinery. Most countries also import basic foods and consumer goods as well as industrial and manufactured items.

Regional underdevelopment is also reflected in the direction of trade. A large percentage of the trade is conducted with industrial and developed countries since no country in the region has the quantitative and qualitative capacity to satisfy regional demand for manufactured products. Furthermore, intraregional trade is small relative to total trade, largely because all the countries produce similar goods and a low level of industrialization is common to all of them. The fact that imports include industrial and investment capital may also be misleading because a large percentage of these imports consists of arms and military equipment that do little to enhance development and growth (Edwards, 1996).

■ CONCLUSION

Over the past four decades, efforts have been expended to develop and bring Middle Eastern economies to the level of developed economies. Yet development has been elusive except in Israel. Sustained underdevelopment is reflected in the relatively low levels of technology and labor productivity, dependence on economic rents and foreign aid, external borrowing, and a trade composition characteristic of underdevelopment and dependence.

The countries of the region have benefited in various degrees from international agencies, such as the United Nations, Food and Agriculture Organization, World Bank, and others, that have been willing to extend help when needed, under certain conditions. Bilateral agreements with developed countries were another mechanism that often brought easy credit, grants, trade agreements, and technology transfer to various states, especially during the Cold War. The oil price revolutions of 1973–1974 and 1979 generated large flows of capital into the region, primarily to the oil-exporting countries, but other countries benefited as well. Finally, new technologies were accessible upon request in most cases, at least for purposes of economic development.

Middle Eastern countries took advantage of these opportunities. Most states applied for some form of economic planning, subsidized private industry, created public enterprises, regulated their markets, or sometimes liberalized them. Policymakers also tried to encourage technology transfer through subsidy, education, foreign investment, and import substitution policies. Moreover, the Arab countries explored possibilities of an Arab common market. Even so, underdevelopment has persisted.

Development efforts faced many obstacles, both external and internal. Among the external obstacles was the legacy of colonialism, which bred economic duality and left most economies so far behind that it seemed virtually impossible to catch up. Wars of independence, civil wars, and intraregional wars were another type of obstacle that taxed virtually all economies by wasting resources and detracting attention from economic development. The Cold War, although helpful in some cases, handicapped development because some of the policies applied often were mandated by one or the other of the dominant powers. Finally, intervention by international agencies and pressure to change policy, reform the economic structure, privatize public enterprise, liberalize trade, and let the market guide the economy were not always timely or helpful. On the contrary, such pressures often interrupted the process of development and misdirected energies and resources away from development (Chossudovsky, 1997).

However, the main obstacles were internal. First, most countries of the region are resource poor, in both materials and human capital. Second, virtually all countries started at a relatively low level of development; thus the preconditions for development were totally lacking. But the most serious internal obstacle was the unfavorable behavioral structures and developmental contexts that discouraged development and change (see Figure 7.1; see also Tuma, 1987:chap. 9; Tuma, 1988). In all countries except Israel, these structures were not favorable to development. The philosophy that prevailed in these countries privileged political, religious, cultural, and regime survival objectives over economic development and industrialization. The institutional framework was underdeveloped, as was the administrative machinery that would guide development. These handicaps were aggravated by equally defective developmental circumstances that could hardly generate enough optimism or high expectations to attract investment and technology transfer. For example, demographic conditions worsened as uncontrolled population growth required that resources be divided among more citizens. Government stability and popular participation in decisionmaking remained below the minimum necessary for successful economic development and growth plans.

The infrastructure also remained underdeveloped. Transportation, communications, utilities, and marketing and financial facilities offered limited services relative to the needs of developing economies. This often caused segmentation of the market, raised the costs of production, and reduced the competitive power of these economies in the international market. Finally, most states failed to create a literate, highly skilled, and professional labor force that would meet the demands of development without depending on foreign expertise and technologies. Thus, brain drain and capital outflows were common whenever opportunities existed elsewhere, and technology transfer was minimal. Development efforts were handicapped, and underdevelopment remained the rule.

The only exception to this pattern was Israel. The Israeli commitment to development resulted in the building of institutions and administrations that reflected the philosophy of development and allocated resources to promote it. As the population grew, especially through immigration, the Israelis made sure that resources would flow in as well. They built a democracy, at least for the Jewish people, which encouraged participation and guaranteed political stability. They built the infrastructure fast enough and broadly enough to facilitate development and integrate Israel's economy

Photo 7.5 *The influence of U.S.-based multinational corporations can be seen throughout the Middle East. This McDonald's fast food outlet is in the Tel Aviv Central Bus Station in Israel.*

© Deborah J. Gerner

into the international economy. And, most important, Israel exploited the high-quality human capital that came in the form of immigrants and also made sure to produce high-quality human capital in the domestic institutions of learning. These conditions, the combined favorable behavioral structure and development context, were conducive to development.

Thus Israel was able to develop economically even though it had lived in a state of war during much of the period following independence. Israel had two unique advantages: access to large amounts of capital and a highly skilled labor force that could take advantage of scientific and rational approaches to development. However, other countries in the region—for example, Iraq, Iran, and other oil-exporting countries—also had large sums of capital available to them but not the commitment or the skills to develop their economies. These countries have adopted tradition, confessionalism, and conformity as their guiding principles. Their economies had no chance to develop to the levels they aspired to because they were unwilling to take the necessary steps.

■ **NOTES**

This chapter was written with the assistance of Tanya Wanchek, to whom I am grateful.

1. Iran and Turkey were not ruled by other countries, but their economies were influenced by foreign powers through the Capitulations, a series of treaties granting residency and economic rights to Europeans (Tuma, 1989).

2. For comparison, 1 hectare is equal to 2.47 acres; 1 square mile contains 259 hectares.

3. Unless explicitly stated, the rest of this section is based on Britain's Department of Overseas Trade Reports series and the U.S. Department of Commerce Reports series.

4. Based on data from *International Historical Statistics,* 1998.

■ **BIBLIOGRAPHY**

Anderson, Robert E., and Albert Martinez. 1998. "Supporting Private Sector Development in the Middle East and North Africa." Pp. 178–193 in Nemat Shafik (ed.), *Prospects for Middle Eastern and North African Economies: From Boom to Bust and Back?* New York: St. Martin's Press.

Askari, Hoosein, Vahid Nowshirvani, and Mohamed Jaber. 1997. *Economic Development in the GCC: The Blessing and Curse of Oil.* Greenwich, Conn.: JAI Press.

Barkey, Henri J. 1992. *The Politics of Economic Reform in the Middle East.* New York: St. Martin's Press.

Bharier, J. 1969. *Capital Formation in Iran: 1900–65.* Ph.D. diss., University of London.

Calhoun, David (ed.). 1997. Britannica *Book of the Year: Events of 1996.* Chicago: Encyclopedia Britannica.

Chaudhry, Kiren Aziz. 1997. *The Price of Wealth, Economies and Institutions in the Middle East.* Ithaca and London: Cornell University Press.

Chossudovsky, Michel. 1997. *The Globalisation of Poverty: Impacts of IMF and Work Bank Reforms.* Atlantic Highlands, N.J., and London: Zed Books.

Deaver, Michael V. 1996. "Military Industrialization of Egypt: Development, Debt, and Dependence." Pp. 127–148 in Karen Pfeifer (ed.), *Research in Middle East Economics.* Greenwich, Conn., and London: JAI Press.

Diwan, Ishac, Chang-Po Yang, and Zhi Wang. 1998. "The Arab Economies, the Uruguay Round Predicament and the European Union Wildcard." Pp. 47–95 in Nemat Shafik (ed.), *Prospects for Middle Eastern and North African Economies: From Boom to Bust and Back?* New York: St. Martin's Press.

Edwards, Glenn M. (ed.). 1996. Britannica *Book of the Year: Events of 1995.* Chicago: Encyclopedia Britannica.

Eeghen, Willen van. 1998. "Poverty in the Middle East and North Africa." Pp. 226–261 in Nemat Shafik (ed.), *Prospects for Middle Eastern and North African Economies: From Boom to Bust and Back?* New York: St. Martin's Press.

FAO (Food and Agriculture Organization). 1987. *1948–1985 World Crop and Livestock Statistics.* Rome: FAO.

———. 1998. Website: http//apps.fao.org. Last updated May 1998.

El-Ghonemy, Riad. 1998. *Affluence and Poverty in the Middle East.* London and New York: Routledge.

Hale, William. 1981. *The Political and Economic Development of Modern Turkey.* London: Croom Helm.

IBRD (International Bank for Reconstruction and Development). 1988. *Social Indicators of Development.* Washington, D.C.: IBRD.

————. 1997. *World Development Indicators.* Washington, D.C.: IBRD.

International Historical Statistics: Africa, Asia, Oceania, 1750 1993, 3d ed. 1998. London: Macmillan Reference.

Issawi, Charles. 1995. *The Middle East Economy: Decline and Recovery* Princeton, N.J.: Markus Wiener Publishers.

Lavy, Victor, and Eliezer Sherrer (eds.). 1991. *Foreign Aid and Economic Development in the Middle East: Egypt, Syria, and Jordan.* New York: Praeger.

Longrig, Stephen Hemsley. 1968. *Iraq, 1900–1950: A Political Social, and Economic History.* Oxford: Oxford University Press.

Niblock, Rim, and Emma Murphy (eds.). 1993. *Economic and Political Liberalization in the Middle East.* London and New York: British Academic Press.

Pfeifer, Karen (ed.). 1996. *Research in Middle East Economics.* Greenwich, Conn., and London: JAI Press.

————. 1997. *Research in Middle East Economics.* Greenwich, Conn., and London: JAI Press.

Radwan, Samir. 1974. *Capital Formation in Egyptian Industry and Agriculture 1882–1967.* London: Ithaca Press.

Ramsay, F. Jeffress (ed.). 1997. *Global Studies: Africa.* 7th ed. Guilford, Conn.: Dushkin/McGraw-Hill.

Roberts, Gwilym, and David Fowler. 1995. *Built by Oil.* Reading, England: Garnet Publishing.

Shafii, Irfan. 1978. "Processing Industry in the Arab World: Incentives and Objectives." *Journal of Social Sciences* (Arabic) 6, no. 1.

Shafik, Nemat (ed.). 1998. *Prospects for Middle Eastern and North African Economies: From Boom to Bust and Back?* New York: St. Martin's Press.

Spencer, William. 1998. *Global Studies: The Middle East.* 7th ed. Guilford, Conn.: Dushkin/McGraw-Hill.

Thornburg, Max Weston, Graham Spry, and George Soule. 1968. *Turkey: An Economic Appraisal.* New York: Greenwood Press.

Tuma, Elias. 1987. *Economic and Political Change in the Middle East.* Palo Alto, Calif.: Pacific Books.

————. 1988. "Institutionalized Obstacles to Development. The Case of Egypt." *World Development* 16, no. 10:1185–1198.

————. 1989. "The Economic Impact of the Capitulations: The Middle East and Europe. A Reinterpretation." *Journal of European Economic History* 18, no. 3:663–682.

UNDP (United Nations Development Programme). 1997. *Human Development Report 1997.* New York: Oxford University Press.

————. 1998. *Human Development Report 1998.* New York: Oxford University Press.

Wilmington, Martin W. 1971. *The Middle East Supply Center.* Ed. Laurence Evans. Albany: State University of New York Press, and London: University of London Press.

Wilson, Rodney. 1995. *Economic Development in the Middle East.* London and New York: Routledge.

■ 8 ■

Population Growth, Urbanization, and the Challenges of Unemployment

Valentine M. Moghadam

The Middle East has been experiencing rapid rates of urbanization and population growth over the past several decades. Although countries are at different levels of urbanization, the region as a whole is expected to have about 60 percent of its population living in urban areas by the year 2000—up from 25 percent in 1960. At the same time, population growth rates in the Middle East–North Africa (MENA) region are among the highest in the world, second only to those in sub-Saharan Africa, although fertility rates have been falling, especially among young, educated women in urban areas. The population is expected to swell to 576 million by 2025—more than double the current size. Given the aridity of much of the region, these growing numbers will place increasing demands on water and agricultural land, and urban services, currently strained, will need to be vastly expanded and improved.

Rapid urbanization and rapid population growth have transformed the structure of the labor force. In many countries, the population has shifted from one engaged predominantly in rural and agrarian production systems to one involved in various types of urban industrial and service-oriented economic activities. Moreover, because of previously high fertility rates, the age structure of the labor force is skewed toward the under-twenty-five group. Meanwhile, due to both economic and demographic factors, urban labor markets have been unable to absorb the growing labor force. This has resulted in the expansion of the urban informal sector, income inequalities, urban poverty, and rates of unemployment that are among the highest in the world. In particular, women's unemployment rates are exceedingly high.

Photo 8.1 Ramallah, located just north of Jerusalem in the West Bank, is one of hundreds of rapidly growing towns and cities in the Middle East.

This chapter examines the interrelated processes of urbanization, population growth, employment challenges, and poverty in the Middle East and North Africa. For ease of exposition, we examine each separately, even though the issues are linked. Furthermore, to reflect differences in population and labor force size as well as income levels, we frequently refer to the region in terms of two sets of countries: the small, oil-rich states that belong to the Gulf Cooperation Council (GCC), including Bahrain, Kuwait, Oman, Qatar, Saudi Arabia, and the United Arab Emirates (UAE); and the larger and more diversified countries (Algeria, Egypt, Iran, Iraq, Israel, Jordan, Lebanon, Libya, Morocco, Syria, Tunisia, Turkey, and Yemen). To the extent possible, we shall also include the West Bank and Gaza Strip in the analysis.

■ URBANIZATION

The urban population of the region has been growing rapidly since 1950. Its share of the total population has grown from 24 percent in 1950 to 57 percent in 1990 (Omran and Roudi, 1993:21). The most rapid growth in urbanization occurred in the oil-exporting countries; the population doubled between 1960 and 1980 in Saudi Arabia, Oman, Libya, and the UAE and between 1950 and 1985 in Iran and Iraq (Assaad, 1995:21). Among countries that are not already highly urbanized, the slowest rate of urbanization was in Egypt, whose urban share increased from 32 percent in 1950 to 44 percent in 1990; Iran, Turkey, and Egypt, with large populations and extensive land, were still 40 to 55 percent rural. Their large rural populations constitute a pool of future rural-to-urban migrants (Omran and Roudi, 1993:20). Oman and Yemen (especially the north) have the lowest levels of urbanization in the region, whereas Kuwait, Qatar, and Bahrain are virtually city-states.

Table 8.1 illustrates the varying levels of urbanization across the region. It should be noted that after Latin America, which is 71 percent urbanized, the region has the highest level of urbanization in the developing world.

Urbanization is a key aspect of social change and of economic development. It entails the implementation of policies leading to the growth of

Table 8.1 Population and Urbanization in the Middle East and North Africa

Country	Population (in millions) 1996	Percent Urban 1996	Percent Urban 1990	Percent Urban 1950
Algeria	29	56	51.7	22
Bahrain[a]		n.a.	83.0	64
Comoros[a]		n.a.	27.8	3
Djibouti[a]		n.a.	80.7	41
Egypt	59	45	46.7	32
Gaza Strip[a]		n.a.	94.0	50
Iran	63	60	56.7	27
Iraq	21	75	71.3	34
Israel	6	91	92.0	65
Jordan	4	72	68.8	35
Kuwait	2	97	95.6	59
Lebanon	4	88	83.7	23
Libya	5	86	70.2	19
Mauritania	2	n.a.	46.8	2
Morocco	27	53	48.0	26
Oman	2	77	11.0	2
Qatar[a]		n.a.	89.5	63
Saudi Arabia	19	83	77.3	16
Syria	15	53	50.5	31
Tunisia	9	63	54.3	31
Turkey	63	70	61.4	21
United Arab Emirates	3	84	77.8	25
Republic of Yemen	16	34	28.9	6

Sources: UN (1993a); World Bank (1998).
Notes: a. Bahrain, Djibouti, and Qatar have populations of under 600,000; Comoros, 820,000; and the Gaza Strip, 764,000.
n.a. Information not available.

cities and rural-to-urban migration. The latter is typically fueled by both push and pull factors: the push of population pressure on natural resources and the lack of economic opportunity in the rural areas and the pull of perceived economic opportunity and a better lifestyle in the big cities (Omran and Roudi, 1993:21). The continuing growth of cities and of rural-to-urban migration is often exacerbated by the "urban bias" of government policies and development strategies, which leads to underdevelopment of rural areas, greater investment in urban infrastructure, and income gaps between rural and urban workers.

International migration can also play a part in urbanization. For example, in the case of Israel, immigration by Jews from other countries has contributed to the growth of Tel Aviv and West Jerusalem, and in the case of the small, oil-rich GCC countries, labor migration from other Arab countries contributed to the rapid rates of urbanization, especially during the 1970s.

Between 1950 and 1980, there was tremendous growth of the large cities in the region, including Tehran, Cairo, Istanbul, and Baghdad, as a result of both high fertility rates and rural-to-urban migration. In 1950 there were only four cities with populations exceeding 1 million; by 1970 there were nine (Assaad, 1995:22). By 1990 the number of such cities had exceeded twenty. Megacities such as Cairo, Tehran, and Istanbul have seen the growth of their populations during the 1980s, but so have a second tier of cities, such as Alexandria, Esfahan, Mashhad, Ankara, and Adana (see Table 8.2). Some of the megacities, and especially Cairo, have extremely high population densities, severe shortages of housing and services, and lack of regulation of construction and urban development. Indeed, the economies of the cities cannot absorb their large urban populations, leading to unemployment, underemployment, and poverty among urban populations. Other problems include a shortage of clean drinking water, the growth of slums or shantytowns, polluted air, and inadequate waste disposal systems (Omran and Roudi, 1993:30).

■ POPULATION GROWTH

According to theories of epidemiological and demographic transitions, a population's fertility and mortality will decline from high to low levels as a result of economic and social development. The decline in mortality usually precedes the decline in fertility. This transition occurred in the European countries during the nineteenth century and in the developing world during the twentieth century. Currently, the countries of the Middle East and North Africa are differentially situated along the transition continuum and are characterized by varying levels and combinations of mortality and fertility.

Table 8.2 The Middle East and North Africa:
Cities with Populations over 1 Million, 1995

Country	City	Population (millions)
Algeria	Algiers	3.7
Egypt	Cairo	9.6
	Alexandria	3.5
Iran	Tehran	7.7
	Esfahan	1.9
	Mashhad	2.0
	Shiraz	1.0
	Tabriz	1.4
Iraq	Baghdad	4.4
Israel	Tel Aviv	2.2
Jordan	Amman	1.1
Kuwait	Kuwait City	1.0
Lebanon	Beirut	1.8
Libya	Benghazi	1.0
	Tripoli	3.2
Morocco	Casablanca	3.2
	Rabat	1.5
Saudi Arabia	Jeddah	1.4
	Riyadh	2.5
Syria	Aleppo	1.8
	Damascus	2.0
Tunisia	Tunis	2.0
Turkey	Adana	1.0
	Ankara	2.8
	Bursa	1.0
	Istanbul	7.8
	Izmir	2.0

Source: UN (1995a).

In the 1950s there was a population explosion in the Middle East and North Africa, a result of high fertility and declines in the crude death rate, although infant mortality rates were still very high. In the 1960s the region had the world's highest fertility rate among developing regions, but since about 1970 fertility has been falling rapidly, and fertility rates in sub-Saharan Africa have now surpassed those in the Middle East. At the same time, the infant mortality rate, which was as high as 200 per 1,000 live births in 1955, began to decline quite rapidly in 1960. By 1990 it had reached about 70 per 1,000 live births, still higher than Latin America, East Asia (which has seen the most dramatic drop), and the developed countries but lower than South Asia and sub-Saharan Africa. The total fertility rate for the region has gone from 7 children per woman in the 1950s to 4.8 in 1990 and is expected to decline further to 3.8 by the year 2000. As one analyst notes, "The trend has been similar to that in Latin America, albeit at a higher absolute level" (Assaad, 1995:5). The fertility decline reflects in part the steep falls in Egypt, Tunisia, and Turkey, which are associated with an effective family planning campaign and increases in women's education and employment (see Table 8.3).

Following the analysis by Abdel R. Omran and Farzaneh Roudi (1993) but with some modifications, we may divide the countries of the Middle East and North Africa into four groups based on the trends in birth and death rates and their socioeconomic settings. Group 1 is characterized by persistent high fertility and declining mortality among middle-income and poor countries in an intermediate-to-low socioeconomic setting and includes Jordan, Iraq, Syria, Yemen, and the West Bank and Gaza Strip. Group 2 is characterized by declining fertility and mortality among middle-income countries in an intermediate level of socioeconomic development and includes Egypt, Lebanon, Turkey, Iran, Morocco, and Tunisia. A third group of countries, made up of the rich GCC countries, is characterized by

Table 8.3 The Middle East and North Africa: Basic Demographic Indicators

Country	Annual Population Growth Rate (%)		Total Fertility Rate[a] (%)		Average Age at First Marriage[b]	Contraceptive Prevalence 1990–1996[c]
	1980–1996	1996–2010	1980	1996		
Algeria	1.3	1.9	6.7	3.4	21.0	51
Bahrain	4.0	2.3	n.a.	3.0	25.5	53
Egypt	2.3	1.6	5.1	3.3	21.9	48
Iran	2.9	1.9	6.1	3.8	22.0	52
Iraq	3.1	2.8	6.4	5.3	22.3	14
Israel	2.4	1.7	3.2	2.6	24.0	n.a.
Jordan	4.3	2.6	6.8	4.4	22.8	35
Kuwait	3.3	2.1	5.3	2.9	22.4	35
Lebanon	1.9	1.4	4.0	2.7	n.a.	n.a.
Mauritania	6.7	3.7	6.3	5.1	23.1	n.a.
Morocco	2.1	1.6	5.4	3.3	22.3	50
Oman	4.2	3.8	9.9	7.0	19.2	9
Saudi Arabia	4.6	3.3	7.3	6.2	21.7	n.a.
Syria	3.2	2.3	7.4	4.0	21.5	40
Tunisia	2.2	1.4	5.2	2.8	24.3	60
Turkey	2.1	1.3	4.3	2.6	21.5	78
UAE	5.5	1.9	5.4	3.5	23.1	n.a.
West Bank and Gaza	4.0	3.5	n.a.	n.a.	n.a.	n.a.
Yemen	3.8	3.3	7.9	7.2	19.1[d]	n.a.

Sources: World Bank (1998); UN (1995b); UNDP (1998).
Notes: a. Births per woman.
b. Females.
c. Percentage of women ages 15–49.
d. Refers to the former Yemen Arab Republic (North Yemen).
n.a. Information not available.

high fertility amid rapidly declining mortality in a high socioeconomic setting. Finally, Israel is the only country in the region that follows the European-style transition of low fertility and mortality in an upper-middle-
income and above-average socioeconomic setting.

Iran and Turkey have had some volatility in their demographic transitions. Turkey began its transition earliest, in the 1950s, only to experience
a kind of baby boom in the early 1970s. Iran's total fertility rate declined
during the 1970s but increased during the 1980s following the Iranian revolution. The dramatic population growth rate of the 1980s is attributed to
the pro-natalist policies of the new Islamic regime, which banned contraceptives and encouraged marriage and family formation (Moghadam,
1993:chap. 6), but it may also be a result of rural fertility behavior, which
was slow to decline during the 1970s. Since the reversal of the pro-natalist
policy following the results of the 1986 census and the introduction of an
aggressive family planning campaign after 1988, there has been a change
from the fertility and population growth trends of the 1980s. In the mid-
1990s, fertility declined again.

In some countries, fertility rates are considerably higher in rural areas
than urban areas, as confirmed by recent Demographic and Health Surveys
(DHS).[1] For example, in Egypt fertility rates remain very high in the rural
areas of Upper Egypt, where infant and under-five mortality rates also are
high. A 1992 DHS measured a total fertility rate of 2.9 children per woman

*Photo 8.2 Children sift through a garbage dump in a poor part of Cairo,
looking for clothing and other salvageable items.*

in urban Egypt, compared with 4.9 children in rural areas. A 1990 DHS in Jordan found that women in the largest cities had 4.8 children on average, those in smaller urban areas had 5.6 children, and women in rural areas had 6.9 children. In Yemen a 1991–1992 DHS measured a total fertility rate of 5.6 among urban women, compared with 8.1 among rural women (Omran and Roudi, 1993:13).

Like the World Fertility Survey of the late 1970s and early 1980s, the more recent DHS research has confirmed the link between mother's education and total fertility rate: the higher the educational attainment, the smaller the number of children. In Jordan, for example, women with no formal education had an average fertility rate of 6.9, whereas the figure for those with a secondary or higher education was 4.1 per woman. Still, Jordan is unique in its relatively high fertility rate among highly educated women; this may be a function of the very low labor force participation of women.

In Morocco, Tunisia, and Turkey, fertility has also declined faster in urban than in rural areas, suggesting the effect that urbanization and its correlates—mainly, female education, employment opportunities, delayed marriage, and access to contraceptives and family planning information—have had in those countries. But, in Turkey and Tunisia and to a lesser degree in Morocco, fertility declines are being registered in rural areas as well, partly due to the availability of contraception, suggesting that these countries may be well on their way in the demographic transition.

Nevertheless, decades of high birth rates have helped to keep the population of Middle Eastern countries young. More than 40 percent of the region's population is under fifteen years of age, whereas only 4 percent is over age sixty-five. These percentages are similar to the average for all developing countries but very different from the pattern in industrial countries. There are also variations across the region. The percentage of population under age fifteen ranges from 28 percent in Qatar to over 50 percent in the West Bank and Gaza. The percent of the population aged sixty-five or older ranges from 9 percent in Israel to 1 percent or less in the Gulf states (Omran and Roudi, 1993:15). These differences in age structure are tied to the different birth rates across the region.

Countries with young populations exhibit a high dependency ratio and small tax base, a situation exacerbated by the low labor force participation of women in nonagricultural and modern occupations. We turn to the subject of workforce participation in the next section.

■ LABOR FORCE GROWTH AND EMPLOYMENT CHALLENGES

Despite growing urbanization in the Middle East and North Africa, roughly one-third of the total population still depends on agriculture for its livelihood. The proportion of the labor force in agriculture varies from around 50 percent in Turkey, Yemen, and Syria to less than 5 percent in Israel and the small Gulf states. Economic modernization, however, has resulted in changes in the sectoral distribution of the labor force, with a growing proportion of workers involved in services and, to a lesser degree, in industry. The emergence of the services sector has been especially evident in Jordan, where the share of agriculture in total employment declined from 42 percent in the 1960s to less than 7 percent in the early 1990s (Shaban, Assaad, and al-Qudsi, 1995:71). Although the services sector has been expanding and thriving throughout the region, the manufacturing sector has not fared as well, partly due to the reliance on wealth generated from oil exports. Still, in a number of countries, the economic development strategy of the time, which included protection and promotion of the manufacturing sector, did lead to increases in (mostly male) employment in industry. Throughout the region, the structural transformation of the regional economy was accompanied by the emergence of a female labor force, but it has remained a relatively small percentage of the total salaried workforce. Although labor force statistics in the region are not always exact, and women's economic activity outside the formal and modern sector has tended to be underestimated, it appears that a large part of the female population in many of the countries, such as Turkey, Syria, and Iran, remains rooted in agriculture.

Table 8.4 provides data on the sectoral distribution of the labor force in the countries of the region, divided into the oil-rich and labor-poor GCC countries and the larger and more diversified economies. In terms of the differences among the countries, in the highly urbanized GCC countries of Bahrain, Kuwait, Qatar, and the UAE, the agricultural workforce is quite small. There is greater involvement in agriculture in Oman and Saudi Arabia, but more so on the part of men than of women, which raises the question of whether women's agricultural activity is properly measured. In the GCC countries, with the exception of Oman, the vast majority of the female workforce (nationals) is engaged in service-sector work. Less prestigious service work is performed by imported female labor. The involvement of women in industry is negligible, except in Oman.

Among the larger and non-GCC countries, the majority of women are engaged in agriculture in Iran, Iraq, Turkey, Syria, and Yemen. Turkey remains anomalous, in that it is the most modernized of the countries of the region and yet the one where women are most likely to be found in agriculture. In Algeria, Egypt, Jordan, Lebanon, and Libya, the majority of the female measured workforce is concentrated in the services sector. Only in Morocco and Tunisia are large percentages of the female workforce involved in the industrial (manufacturing) sector. In all countries, the male workforce is more evenly distributed across the sectors and more likely to be found in modern occupations. As can be readily seen from Table 8.4,

**Table 8.4   Distribution of the Labor Force by Sex and Female
Share of Salaried Employment, 1990–1994
(percentage)**

	Agriculture		Industry		Services		Female Share of Total Employees
Country	Female	Male	Female	Male	Female	Male	
GCC							
Bahrain	0	3	4	39	96	58	12
Kuwait	0	2	2	36	97	62	21
Oman	12	45	39	25	49	30	n.a.
Qatar	0	3	0	30	100	67	10
Saudi Arabia	16	34	6	20	79	46	n.a.
UAE	0	4	7	40	93	56	5
Non-GCC							
Algeria	10	16	21	34	69	51	10
Egypt	8	42	20	25	71	33	16
Iran	69	22	15	40	16	38	10
Iraq	68	18	9	26	23	56	11
Israel	4	4	17	37	79	59	43
Jordan	1	11	7	27	92	62	9
Lebanon	16	6	22	32	62	62	n.a.
Libya	32	16	15	30	54	53	n.a.
Morocco	27	35	46	30	28	34	18
Syria	60	18	14	39	26	43	15
Tunisia	47	25	44	46	10	28	17
Turkey	84	27	6	30	10	43	18
Yemen	45	58	6	14	49	28	6

Source: UN (1995b), Table 12.
Note: n.a. Information not available.

the female share of the total salaried workforce is very small, under 20 percent. Clearly, salaried work is a male domain in the region.

At the height of the region's oil-based economic development during the 1970s, an unprecedented form of intraregional labor migration began, characterized by a massive outflow of surplus labor from countries such as Egypt, Jordan, the West Bank, Tunisia, Yemen, and Lebanon to capital-rich and labor-deficit GCC countries, as well as to Libya and Iraq. These countries also imported non-Arab workers, including Koreans, Filipinos, Sri Lankans, and Yugoslavs, who were attracted by the high wages offered in the capital-rich Arab countries. In 1975, foreign labor constituted 47 percent of the labor force in the Gulf countries, and by 1990 the figure had increased to 68 percent. In Kuwait in 1990, fully 86 percent of the workforce was foreign (ESCWA, 1993). Remittances from nationals working abroad became especially important to the economies of Egypt, Jordan, and Yemen.

Jordan was unique among Arab countries in being a labor-exporting country that also imported labor. It exported skilled workers and educated professionals to the rich Gulf states, but it also imported unskilled and low-wage workers for construction, domestic services, and some public services that Jordanian nationals would not perform, such as waiting tables, cleaning buildings, and cleaning streets. Most of the imported Arab labor was (and remains) Egyptian. Almost all domestic workers are from the Philippines. A rather peculiar result has been the underutilization of an educated population of Jordanian women, who in the absence of labor force attachment tend to have more than four children, as we saw above (see also Moghadam, 1998).

The labor migration patterns of North Africans and Turks have been different. Their preferred destination has been Europe, notably Germany for Turks and France for Algerians, Moroccan, and Tunisians (although Tunisians also went to Libya, as mentioned above). Furthermore, labor migration began earlier, during the 1950s and 1960s, in response to European guest worker programs. In the 1970s, European countries began to reduce the influx of guest workers, although the number of Turks in Germany has continued to grow through a combination of natural increase, family reunification, and illegal immigration (OECD, 1992; Omran and Roudi, 1993:24). Tunisian emigrants continued to head to Europe in the 1980s, and in a new development, the migration streams have started to include women on their own.

In Arab countries, political and economic instabilities have resulted in a reduction of intraregional labor flows, affecting mainly Jordanian, Palestinian, and Yemeni workers working in Kuwait and Saudi Arabia. The expulsion of the expatriate workers was a punishment for their countries' stance on the 1991 Gulf War, revealing once again the facade of Arab unity. At the same time, Kuwait and Saudi Arabia rewarded Egypt for its position against Iraq and in favor of the war by replacing expelled Jordanians, Palestinians, and Yemenis with Egyptian workers. Still, a large number of Egyptians left the Gulf and returned to Egypt as a result of the Gulf War. The Economic and Social Commission for West Asia (ESCWA) has estimated the total number of returnees at 2 million people. Most returnees were nationals of Yemen (732,000), Egypt (700,000), and Jordan (300,000, including Palestinians). The return of expatriates has been a mixed experience; in some cases returnees contributed to a boom in the construction industry and in small businesses (especially in Jordan), but in other cases returnees have experienced unemployment, slow absorption into the local labor market, or poverty. Poverty has been especially acute for Yemenis, who were largely unskilled workers unable to find employment at home.

■ **RISING UNEMPLOYMENT**

Thus, by the mid-1990s, the demographic transition characterized by high fertility, rural-to-urban migration, and changes in the pattern of intraregional labor migration had led to rapid growth of the labor force. In a situation of economic stagnation, this resulted in high rates of unemployment, especially in urban areas.

The unemployment situation is a shock to the educated population in particular, which has come to expect guaranteed jobs in the public sector. During the 1960s and 1970s, state-sponsored economic development resulted in an expansion of public-sector employment. For example, Egypt had a policy of guaranteeing public-sector jobs to graduates of vocational secondary schools and universities. Morocco had a similar scheme, albeit one that provided "temporary employment" to graduates. As a result of these policies, some countries, such as Egypt, Jordan, and Algeria, employed more than 50 percent of the labor force in the public sector. A majority of the workforce in the GCC countries was also employed in the public sector.

As a result of the recessionary conditions experienced in the region since the mid-1980s and structural adjustment policy prescriptions to contract the public-sector wage bill, public sectors are no longer hiring as expansively as before, although they are not yet laying off large numbers of workers (as has occurred in Latin America and sub-Saharan Africa, where structural adjustments had been implemented earlier). Indeed, due to political and social concerns, governments have preferred the strategy of wage deterioration or encouragement of early retirement rather than outright layoffs. Of course, economic restructuring in the private sector has resulted in worker layoffs in Tunisia, Morocco, and Turkey. But for the most part, the current unemployed population consists of first-time job seekers, mainly but not exclusively secondary school graduates, male and female alike, who are seeking jobs out of economic need.

The contraction of public-sector employment and declines in government social spending have forced real wages and, as a result, household incomes to fall substantially in many countries (Karshenas, 1994). For example, the real wage rate in Jordan increased by 45 percent over the period 1975–1987, but by 1990 it had declined to roughly its value in 1975 (Shaban, Assaad, and al-Qudsi, 1995:74). The drop in real wages has not, however, been accompanied by an increase in job creation or the demand for labor or by a decrease in the unemployment rates. This suggests that the problem in the labor market is not high wages (as in the past) but perhaps a lack of competitiveness and productivity and inefficient utilization of human resources. It also suggests the underdevelopment of the private sector in the region and its inability to absorb the growing labor force.

Except in the GCC countries, unemployment rates are very high in the Middle East and North Africa by international standards, and they are exceptionally high for women. Unemployment is often difficult to measure in developing countries. Most of the countries in the Middle East have only recently started to count those who are either unsuccessfully seeking jobs for the first time (as with high school and college graduates) or who have lost jobs due to enterprise restructuring (a far smaller proportion). Measured unemployment is usually urban, although countries are now increasingly including the rural areas in their enumeration; thus some countries now disaggregate unemployment by urban or rural area as well as by gender.

Urban unemployment rates began increasing in the 1980s and have reached highs of 10–18 percent in Algeria, Tunisia, Egypt, Jordan, Iran, Turkey, and Yemen. According to ESCWA, the rates may be as high as 30 percent in Yemen, the West Bank, and Gaza. As mentioned previously, unemployment is age-specific, with most of it consisting of new entrants to the workforce in the age groups fifteen to nineteen and twenty to twenty-four. Unemployment rates vary by educational attainment, but in some countries college graduates experience high rates of unemployment. Unemployment rates among high school graduates are between 17 percent and 29 percent in Algeria, Egypt, Jordan, Morocco, and Tunisia; college graduates show unemployment rates of 15 percent and 23 percent in Egypt and Morocco, respectively; and among workers with primary education or less, unemployment rates are 17–27 percent in Algeria, Morocco, and Tunisia (ILO, 1993).

Female unemployment rates are as high as 25 percent, indicating a growing supply of job-seeking women, in contrast to an earlier pattern of "housewife-ization." Only in Algeria is women's unemployment lower than men's (17 percent female compared with 21.7 percent male in 1991). Yet given that Algerian women constitute a mere 10 percent of the labor force, their unemployment rate is disproportionately high. This is also the case in Iran. Women's high unemployment rates appear to be a function of both women's preferences for public-sector jobs, which are not available, and the private sector's discrimination against women, ostensibly due to maternity leave requirements in labor law. The feminization of unemployment, therefore, is a defining feature of the urban labor markets of the Middle East and North Africa (see Table 8.5).

How do the unemployed—those who expect jobs in the formal sector but do not find them—fare in countries where unemployment insurance is not in place or is not available to new entrants? It appears that some of the job seekers—and especially the men—have gravitated to the urban informal sector, which by all accounts has grown tremendously in the region. Informal-sector workers may include taxi drivers, construction workers, domestic workers, people who work in souks and bazaars (the traditional markets in the Middle East), hairdressers, barbers, seamstresses, tailors, workers in or owners of small industrial or artisan workshops, hawkers of sundry goods, repairmen, and so on. It also includes home-based female pieceworkers, such as women in Turkey, Syria, and Jordan who are engaged

**Table 8.5 Unemployment Rates in Selected Countries, by Sex
and Year**

Country	Year	Male	Female	Total
Algeria	1991	21.7	17.0	21.1
Egypt	1991	5.9	21.3	9.6
Iran	1991	10.0	25.0	17.5
Morocco	1991	15.1	22.6	17.0
Syria	1991	5.2	14.0	6.8
Tunisia[a]	1989	13.9	20.9	15.3
Turkey[b]	1992	9.8	20.5	11.7

Source: ILO (1994), Table 9A.
Notes: a. Tunisian figures are from official sources (see Moghadam, 1998: chap. 3).
   b. Data for Turkey are from a national report prepared for the Beijing Conference (see Moghadam, 1998:chap. 4). The figures are for urban areas only and are not exact.

in sewing and embroidery for a contractor or subcontractor. The nature and function of the informal sector has been much debated; although it is agreed that it serves to absorb the labor force and to provide goods and services at relatively low cost, it is also unregulated and untaxed, leading to poor labor standards and income (such as the wealth of many merchants) that is not distributed. The informal sector both contributes to, and is a reflection of, income inequality in the society.

■ POVERTY AND INEQUALITY

Poverty and inequality are measured by household income and consumption and by quality-of-life indicators. A distinction is also made between "absolute poverty," characterized by hunger and destitution, and "relative poverty," which measures where households are situated in relation to an established "poverty line." There has been considerable improvement over time in standards of living in the Middle East and North Africa, as measured by such social indicators as life expectancy, infant mortality, maternal mortality, access to safe water, adequate sanitation facilities, rising age of first marriage, fertility rates, literacy, and school enrollments, as well as by wage rates and household incomes. However, gender gaps exist, and given the income levels of many countries in the region, the social indicators should be better. Moreover, it appears that although levels of absolute poverty have been decreasing in some parts of the region, poverty has actually been increasing in other parts. This is mainly a function of high population growth, but is also due to the creation of new poverty groups in urban areas caused by economic recession, rising prices, deteriorating wages, and unemployment. This shift has been occurring since the mid-1980s, when the price of oil and hence gross national product (GNP) declined, the external debt rose, and government spending was reduced.

According to the World Bank and as noted also by ESCWA, the number of poor people in the Middle East and North Africa increased from an estimated 60 million in 1985 to 73 million in 1990 or from 30.6 percent to 33.1 percent of the total population (World Bank, 1993:5; ESCWA, 1993:121; see also ESCWA 1995b, 1995c). Poverty assessments prepared by the World Bank, which have been derived from living standards surveys undertaken within various countries, reveal growing poverty in Egypt and Jordan and the emergence of urban "working poor" in Tunisia and Morocco. According to official statistics, 23 percent of the population in Egypt in 1991 and 18 percent of the population in Jordan in 1993 were considered to be living under the poverty line. It is widely believed that the poverty incidence could be as high as 30 percent in both countries (Moghadam, 1997, 1998). In both countries poverty is largely rural, and the rural poor are small landholders and tenants, landless agricultural workers, and pastoralists (ESCWA, 1993:6). In Egypt the urban poor include the unemployed and female-headed households. In all countries, because of gender differences in literacy, educational attainment, employment, and income, women are especially vulnerable to poverty during periods of economic difficulty or in the event of divorce, abandonment, or widowhood.

The increase in poverty and inequality should be understood in the context of both the new economic policies of structural adjustment and trade and price liberalization, as well as the old policies of high military spending and inadequate taxation. Military expenditures remain very high in absolute terms in many countries of the region. In Iraq, Oman, Saudi Arabia, Syria, and Yemen, military expenditures in 1990 far exceeded expenditures on education and health (see UNDP, 1996: Table 19). In the case of Iraq, of course, war and economic sanctions have exacerbated the situation of the poor and have also created new poverty-stricken groups. The destruction of Iraq's infrastructure by U.S.-led coalition bombings in January 1991 (see Drèze and Gazdar, 1992), the shortage of medical supplies and of foodstuffs caused by the long sanctions regime, and the collapse of public services have completely transformed a country that was once urbanized, mechanized, and prosperous.

In Lebanon, the main factors behind the alarming increase in the incidence of poverty are the civil war and misguided economic policies, including tax write-offs for large firms engaged in the country's reconstruction and the absence of any property taxes. According to ESCWA, about 1 million people in Lebanon are living below the poverty line, representing

28 percent of the population, and some 75 percent of the poor are urban dwellers. The country's unemployment rate reached 15 percent in 1996, compared with 8.1 percent of the workforce in 1975, before the country's long civil war began. The ESCWA report singled out the absence of government social spending and "unjust wealth distribution" as the factors behind the rise in nutritional deficiencies, lack of hygiene in poor areas, and the lowering of teaching and health standards (*Middle East Times,* 1996:19).

In the large and diversified economies, inequalities (or indicators of relative poverty) are quite pronounced—and have been growing—in Turkey, Lebanon, and the Islamic Republic of Iran. The persistence of absolute poverty, mainly in rural areas, is a problem in such low-income countries as Egypt, Yemen, and Morocco, and perhaps also in the Gaza Strip. Social indicators on health, safe water, and sanitation reflect the quality of life of citizens as well as urban-rural disparities. Although urbanization has brought about access to health, safe water, and sanitation for residents in most of the countries, some countries—including Algeria, Syria, and Yemen—continue to have difficulties in the provision of such urban services, as was noted earlier in this chapter. In other countries there are distinct rural-urban disparities, as seen in Table 8.6. (The high rates of rural access to health, water, or sanitation reported by some of the countries in Table 8.6 should be viewed with some skepticism.) From the perspective of access to services, urban living is definitely superior to rural living, but population increases and decreases in government social spending are straining the quality and quantity of urban services. These pressures are not conveyed by the statistics but are best discerned by visits to and stays in the nonelite sections of the cities of the Middle East and North Africa, where overcrowding, rundown and inadequate public transportation, streets in disrepair, polluted air, high noise levels, and lack of building codes are only some of the problems that low-income urban dwellers endure.

We end this section with profiles of poverty and inequality in Morocco, Tunisia, Egypt, and Palestine (the West Bank and Gaza). These profiles are largely derived from the World Bank poverty assessments, themselves based on living standards measurement surveys or income studies carried out in the countries. Another source is a Norwegian-funded study of living standards of the Palestinian population in the West Bank, Gaza, and Arab Jerusalem. The profiles show that in addition to external factors such as occupation, war, or unfair terms of trade, crucial internal factors in the creation or perpetuation of poverty and inequality are state policies, class structure, and the status of women.

Morocco's 1991 living standards measurement survey counted 2.5 million poor, of whom 72 percent lived in rural areas and more than half were extremely poor. The highest poverty levels are among rural wage

**Table 8.6   Indicators of Urban–Rural Disparities, Selected
Countries: Percent of Population with Access to
Services, 1985–1993**

Country	Health Urban	Health Rural	Safe Water Urban	Safe Water Rural	Sanitation Urban	Sanitation Rural
Algeria	90	38	50	24	56	67
Egypt	100	99	95	86	80	26
Iran	95	65	100	75	100	35
Iraq	97	78	93	41	96	n.a.
Jordan	98	95	100	97	100	100
Lebanon	98	85	95	85	94	n.a.
Morocco	100	50	92	14	95	38
Oman	100	94	91	77	75	40
Saudi Arabia	100	88	100	74	100	30
Syria	96	84	90	58	84	82
Tunisia	100	80	100	74	100	30
Turkey	n.a.	n.a.	95	63	n.a.	n.a.
United Arab Emirates	100	100	100	30	93	22
Yemen	81	32	61	30	87	60

Source: UNDP (1995).
Note: n.a. Information not available.

earners, and females are the most disadvantaged. In urban areas, the poor
are mainly self-employed. The typical poor worker earns one-third the average wage or one-half the legislated minimum wage; poor women get as
little as half the wage rate per hour earned by poor males. During the
1980s, as Moroccan exports expanded, women's employment grew, especially in the most competitive sectors of clothing, food, leather, and shoes.
But these sectors offered very low wages. Unemployment is high in Morocco, especially among the poor and among women. Some 30 percent of
the urban poor are unemployed, and women in the poorest households experience the highest rates of unemployment in urban areas. In the mid-
1990s, Morocco did not have a system of social protection in place to address poverty or unemployment.

The new economic policies of the 1980s, although promoting growth
through increased production and exports, also brought about rising prices,
a deterioration of wages, and cuts in social spending by the government.
Not enough of the national income has been channeled into categories of
public spending—basic health care, schooling, and essential infrastructure
services—that improve the well-being of the poor (World Bank, 1994:
180). In the 1980s, poor parents were forced to withdraw their children
from school. Indeed, enrollments in primary education actually declined
after 1982, recovering only in 1990. As late as the mid-1990s, Morocco

still did not have universal primary and secondary school enrollments, and the gender gaps in school enrollments continued to be very wide (see World Bank, 1998: Table 2.12).

Rural women in Morocco are largely unpaid family workers. By contrast, men tend to work as independent, small-scale farmers or in commerce, and 25 percent are wage earners. The structure of rural social relations and its gender dimension in Morocco is captured in the following observation: "While women rarely obtain a job of their own for a wage, they often share in their husband's work outside the household farm. And having command over family labor, women and often children, gives a laborer a competitive edge in the labor market" (World Bank, 1994:vol. 1, p. 48). Clearly what Morocco needs is more social investment by the government to create a skilled, educated, and better-paid labor force, to raise female literacy and educational attainments, and to reduce rural-urban gaps.

In *Tunisia,* poverty is predominantly rural, but a growing percentage of poor households are in urban areas. According to the 1990 Household Consumption Survey, about 600,000 people, or 7 percent of the population, have annual expenditures below the poverty line, and another 7 percent are "near poor." Most of the urban poor are wage earners in the construction sector with little or no formal education. Others are involved in temporary, low-wage, and low-skill employment in the expanding sectors of tourism and textiles (World Bank, 1995a). Still others are unemployed. As we have seen earlier in this chapter, unemployment is high in Tunisia; as in Morocco, it is especially high among the poor, youth, and women. And because of the sluggish growth of the private sector, there is also a high incidence of unemployment among skilled workers.

In contrast to Morocco, however, Tunisia has demonstrated a commitment to social spending and has been expanding its social insurance program. The Tunisian government cut social expenditures less than other expenditure categories during its period of fiscal restraint. The social security system covers wage earners in both the public and private sectors, including self-employed workers and government employees. Furthermore, there are two types of social assistance programs to alleviate poverty—direct transfers and consumer subsidies. Free health care and schooling are available to all. Among countries of the Middle East and North Africa, only Tunisia has established effective social programs to tackle poverty, increase employment through public works, and encourage employment among women.

In *Egypt,* poor households constitute 20–25 percent of the total, most of which are concentrated in Upper Egypt, where women and children are the most vulnerable. Female-headed households are poorer than male-headed households in both rural and urban areas. Labor among children under twelve years of age is very high, especially in rural areas, and there is a high prevalence of anemia among women and small children. The poor are agricultural laborers or farmers with little or no land. In urban areas, the poor are construction workers or service workers and include "a significant number of government employees" (World Bank, 1991:35), partly because of the drastic deterioration in real wages that the government has allowed in the public sector. Wages have fallen especially dramatically in sectors where women predominate. Interestingly enough, although casual labor appears to be the most important source of employment for poor males in both the urban and the rural sectors, such is not the case for women. A higher proportion of poor women are employed as salaried workers, and more poor females are found working in community services and in trade and services than is the case for men, which indicates the very low wages working women must accept. What is more, unemployment rates are strikingly higher for females than for males, as we saw earlier. Poor women are also less literate and educated than poor men. Whereas poor men tend to have 5.77 years of schooling, poor women have 3.09; 63 percent of poor men can read and write, but only 33 percent of poor women can (Jolliffe, 1997).

Unsurprisingly, given the gender gaps in Egypt, widows and members of multiple-person female-headed households constitute two of the most economically vulnerable groups of people.

> Even the youngest widows have no realistic prospect of making anything but the most casual and intermittent earnings, and the more elderly none whatsoever. Despite the traditional custom of support for widows through transfers from family members, even if they do not live in the same household, many widows in practice are not adequately supported by members of their family. They are destitute and depend on casual charity from neighbors to survive. Field reports from charity organizations operating in Cairo reveal that elderly widows form the single most important client group. Non-governmental organizations recognize them as a group prone to poverty and in need of special assistance. (World Bank, 1991:11)

According to official statistics, about 12 percent of households in Cairo had a female head in 1988, although this figure now may be as high as 18 percent. Egyptian sociologist Iman Bibars has studied the growing phenomenon of female-headed households. This category "is not exclusive to widows, divorcees and the deserted but to a new rising category of wives of 'useless' husbands" (Bibars, 1996:13), including men who are imprisoned, terminally ill, disabled, or unemployed. In one study of a poor urban quarter in Cairo, women headed 29 percent of the sampled households. The majority of those women were illiterate and either widowed or divorced. They tended to have half the disposable income of poor male-headed households, lived in poorer housing units, and owned very few consumer durables (Fergany, 1994). Egypt has an inadequate system of social protection, and many poor women have difficulties dealing with the bureaucracy. Thus they often turn to charitable foundations—many of which are now run by Islamist organizations.

Among *Palestinians,* Gaza is the region worst off in the Occupied Territories, which is closely related to its high share of economically deprived refugees. The most important type of household income—earnings from labor activity—is rendered unstable by curfews, strikes, and restrictions on employment in Israel. But even among Palestinians, who already suffer injustices and hardships, women's lot is especially dire. Gender discrimination and social controls on women make them especially vulnerable to poverty. One factor is the very high fertility rate, which keeps women tied to the home and increases pressures on the household budget. In 1992, a survey by the Fafo Institute for Applied Social Science in Oslo, Norway, estimated the total fertility at 6.84 births per woman. This estimate was based on "unsupported evidence of a rising trend in early marriages since the outbreak of the Intifada and a general tendency among Palestinians in the occupied territories to have more children during the last five-year period" (Heiberg, et al., 1994:65). In Gaza, more than a third (37 percent) of the entire female population got married under the age of seventeen—the legal minimum marriage age for women. The data also suggest that women are the most frequent early school dropouts. Among women, early marriage seems to be a factor in leaving school, but for both men and women, especially in the lower-income households, the direct costs and opportunity costs of education (e.g., lost labor) were cited as the major cause inhibiting the continuation of schooling.

The Fafo survey found a female labor force participation ratio of only 14 percent, indicating that most Palestinian women work in household production and in the domestic sphere rather than in paid employment outside the home. Examples of work in the family sphere done by housewives are contract/piecework, involvement in a family business or shop, and work on the family farm. Employment outside the family sphere requiring education and training or involvement in unskilled paid labor is relatively limited. Female labor force participation is especially low in Gaza and in the refugee camps, although these areas offer very weak employment possibilities for men as well. Divorced and separated women and wealthy and educated women have the highest labor force participation rates. Many women accept low-paid piecework at home rather than participation in the Israeli labor market.

In a social context in which so few women directly participate in the labor force, it becomes important to assess other means through which individual women get access to economic resources and thus avoid poverty. One source is the dowry. The Fafo study found that although jewelry constitutes the major form of women's independent property ownership in the West Bank, Gaza Strip, and Arab Jerusalem, women do own other forms of property, such as land, although to a much lesser degree. Most women sampled claimed they had nothing to sell or mortgage in case they needed money badly. Over time, women's dowry jewelry is gradually dissipated to pay for various investments for the family, husband, or children (Heiberg, et al., 1994:295–300).

■ CONCLUSION

This chapter has surveyed trends in population growth, urbanization, labor force growth, rising unemployment, and poverty. These social and demographic trends have implications for household well-being, individual capabilities, and political stability. Although urbanization holds many promises for people, including a wider range of options, activities, and services, unchecked population growth has created enormous pressures on urban services. At a time of reduced government spending, these demographic pressures on health, education, and utilities are likely to increase inequalities and deprivation. High fertility rates have resulted in the emergence of a large population of young people who are seeking but not finding jobs. In a context of reduced government spending and rising unemployment, poverty increases rather than diminishes. Although poverty and inequality are social phenomena, reflecting a class structure and skewed distribution of income, wealth, and opportunities, it appears that women are more vulnerable to poverty and more subject to inequality than are men.

The countries of the Middle East and North Africa, therefore, are faced with a number of social and demographic challenges that require concerted action among governments, nongovernmental organizations, citizen groups, and international organizations. Identifying problems and solutions will require short-term, medium-term, and long-term perspectives informed by both developmental imperatives and the social entitlements of citizens. These include policies and measures to enhance women's access to education and jobs as a way of stabilizing population growth and reducing fertility rates as well as expanding women's capabilities and raising household incomes; investments in the physical and social infrastructure to upgrade urban services as well as create employment; enhancement of the legal and regulatory framework to improve labor and environmental standards as well as to improve the system of taxation; and community development programs that involve high school and college graduates, as a way of mitigating youth unemployment, alleviating urban poverty, and instilling solidarity.

■ **NOTE**

1. The Demographic and Health Surveys (conducted during the 1990s) and the earlier World Fertility Surveys (conducted during the late 1970s and early 1980s) are international surveys undertaken by governments but coordinated by a central body elsewhere, which also undertakes the cross-national analyses and global assessments. The DHS is coordinated by Macro International Inc., in Maryland, in the United States, and the World Fertility Survey was coordinated by the International Statistical Institute in the Netherlands. The World Fertility Survey sought to examine trends in fertility and its correlates (contraceptive use, mother's education, child health, mother's health); the DHS similarly has been designed to collect data on fertility, family planning, and maternal and child health.

■ **BIBLIOGRAPHY**

Assaad, Ragui. 1995. "Urbanization and Demographic Structure in the Middle East and North Africa with a Focus on Women and Children." Population Council, Regional Papers no. 40 (January).

Bibars, Iman. 1996. "Women: Reconciling Contradictory Roles." *Civil Society* 5, no. 56 (August):13.

Drèze, Jean, and Haris Gazdar. 1992. "Hunger and Poverty in Iraq." *World Development* 20, no. 7.

ESCWA (Economic and Social Commission for West Africa). 1993. *A Conceptual and Methodological Framework for Poverty Alleviation in the ESCWA Region*. New York: UN (January 19).

———. 1995a. *Statistical Abstract of the ESCWA Region 1984–1993*. 15th issue. New York: UN.

———. 1995b. *Women and Poverty in the ESCWA Region: Issues and Concerns.* Series of Studies on Arab Women and Development, no. 22. New York: UN.

———. 1995c. *Survey of Economic and Social Developments in the ESCWA Region, 1994*. New York: UN.

Fergany, Nader. 1994. *Urban Women, Work and Poverty Alleviation in Egypt*. Pilot Study sponsored by ILO/UNDP. Cairo: Al-Mishkat Research Institute.

Heiberg, Marianne, et al. 1994. *Palestinian Society in Gaza, West Bank and Arab Jerusalem: A Survey of Living Conditions*. Oslo: Fafo Institute for Applied Social Science.

ILO (International Labor Organization). 1993. *World Labour Report 1993*. Geneva: ILO.

———. 1994. *Yearbook of Labour Statistics 1994*. Geneva: ILO.

Jolliffe, Dean. 1997. "What Do We Know About Poverty in Egypt? An Analysis of Household Survey Data for 1997." Paper presented at the annual meeting of the Middle East Studies Association, San Francisco, November 22–24.

Karshenas, Massoud. 1994. *Structural Adjustment, Wages, and Employment in the Middle East*. World Employment Program Working Paper. Geneva: ILO.

Middle East Times. November 3–9, 1996.

Moghadam, Valentine M. 1993. *Modernizing Women: Gender and Social Change in the Middle East*. Boulder, Colo.: Lynne Rienner.
———. 1997. "The Feminization of Poverty? Notes on a Concept and Trends." Illinois State University, Women's Studies Program, Occasional Papers no. 3 (August).
———. 1998. *Women, Work, and Economic Reform in the Middle East and North Africa*. Boulder, Colo.: Lynne Rienner.
OECD (Organization for Economic Cooperation and Development). 1992. *Trends in International Migration*. Paris: OECD.
Omran, Abdel R., and Farzaneh Roudi. 1993. "The Middle East Population Puzzle." *Population Bulletin* 48, no. 1 (July).
Shaban, Radwan A., Ragui Assaad, and Sulayman S. al-Qudsi. 1995. "The Challenge of Unemployment in the Arab Region." *International Labour Review* 134, no. 1:65–81.
UN (United Nations). 1993a. *The Sex and Age Distribution of the World's Populations: The 1992 Revision*. New York: UN.
———. 1993b. *World Urbanization Prospects: The 1992 Revision*. New York: UN.
———. 1995a. *World Urbanization Prospects: The 1994 Revision*. New York: UN.
———. 1995b. *The World's Women 1995: Trends and Statistics*. New York: UN.
UNDP (United Nations Development Programme). 1995. *Human Development Report 1995*. New York: OUP.
———. 1996. *Human Development Report 1996*. New York: OUP.
———. 1997. *Human Development Report 1997*. New York: OUP.
———. 1998. *Human Development Report 1998*. New York: OUP.
UNESCO (United Nations Educational, Scientific, and Cultural Organization). 1995. *World Education Report*. Paris: UNESCO.
World Bank. 1991. *Egypt: Alleviating Poverty During Structural Adjustment*. Washington, D.C.: World Bank.
———. 1993. *Implementing the World Bank's Strategy to Reduce Poverty: Progress and Challenges*. Washington, D.C.: World Bank.
———. 1994. *Morocco: Poverty, Adjustment, and Growth, Vols. 1 and 2*. Washington, D.C.: World Bank.
———. 1995a. *Republic of Tunisia: Poverty Alleviation: Preserving Progress While Preparing for the Future*. Washington, D.C.: World Bank (August).
———. 1995b. *World Development Report: Workers in an Integrating World*. New York: OUP.
———. 1998. *World Development Indicators*. Washington, D.C.: World Bank.

■ 9 ■

Kinship, Class, and Ethnicity

Laurie King-Irani

"So, Khalid," my husband George said, accepting a demitasse of strong, black, Turkish coffee from Hussein, our waiter, "I guess Adnan told you all about his adventures in Lebanon during his first visit in fifteen years. He sure was received like royalty—I don't think that he paid for a single meal the entire month he was there!" Khalid smiled broadly at George and replied, "Oh, I think that there was at least one meal that he definitely paid for! Has Adnan told you that he will soon be going back to Beirut?" All eyes turned to Adnan for clarification of this surprising piece of news. With the San Francisco Bay forming a backdrop to his happy face, Adnan leaned back in his chair and tried unsuccessfully to repress a grin. "Well, you might as well hear it from the source: I am going to get married in Lebanon next month!" Adnan announced with evident satisfaction.

"Mabruk!" (congratulations), my husband and I answered as one. "Who is the lucky bride?" I asked, wondering to myself what had happened to Adnan's American girlfriend, Lisa, a rising young graphic designer. "Laila Karam," he answered. "She's the sister-in-law of my cousin Rima, *bint 'ammi* (daughter of my father's brother). I met her at a family picnic up in the Shuf [a mountainous area in south-central Lebanon], near the village where her family used to live before the war and the massacres in 1983, and then I went to see her with some other cousins a few more times after that. She's twenty-six, really pretty and clever, and a terrific cook as well!

"During my last week in Beirut, amm Waseem accompanied me to her father's house. We made the formal request for her hand in marriage, and after we had worked out all of the logistical details and decided on the *mahr* [the dowry paid by the groom's family to the bride's family], we celebrated our *khitbe* [formal announcement and celebration of an engagement] with a big dinner—the one I paid for! So it's official: We will be married at the end of October in my family's church, the big Melkite

263

[Greek Catholic] cathedral above the city of Jounieh. You are, of course, going to receive a formal invitation from Laila's family. They are Maronite Christians, like my mom's family. I hope that will be a good basis for Laila and my mother to start their relationship, because after the honeymoon, I will be bringing her back here to live with me and my mom in a house I just bought near Palo Alto."

"Will Laila work here?" George asked. "No," said Adnan. "First, she'll have to learn English; she's French-educated. Maybe she can help me and Khalid out at the office, since she has an associate's degree in accounting, but I think we are going to be focusing on starting a family in the very near future."

"The guy's in a hurry!" said Khalid with a wink to me and George, before saying, half-jokingly, "Hey, Adnan, I just thought of a potential problem: Laila's a Maronite—does she know that I, your best friend and business partner, am a Palestinian Muslim from Jerusalem? Maybe she won't be so happy about that!" Adnan dismissed his question with a smile and a wave of his hand, answering, "Look, as long as you're not a Druze [a religious sect that broke away from Islam in the eleventh century], I don't think she'll mind!"

After the waiter had brought us baklava (sweet Arabic pastry), I turned to Adnan and said, "I am really happy for you, but I have to admit that this is a big surprise. Forgive me for prying, but what happened to Lisa?" Adnan took a deep breath, pushed his empty dessert plate aside, and lit a cigarette. "A lot of people are surprised, and many have asked me the same question. It is a complicated story; I guess it all began back in April of this year. One morning I woke up, and realized that it was twenty years to the day since my dad was killed by a sniper in Beirut during the second year of the war. Then I realized that I am the same age now as he was then: thirty-six. When he was my age, he had already been married for sixteen years and had a fifteen-year-old son and two small daughters; it made me realize how fast time passes, and I started to wonder what I was doing with my life. Okay, I have an M.A. in computer programming, and *nishkur' allah* (thank God), I have a very successful business, but if I knew I was going to die tomorrow, I would have one very big regret: I don't yet have any kids.

"Later that same day, I turned on the news, and heard that Beirut had been bombed for the first time in fourteen years by the Israeli Air Force. Lisa and I were having a dinner party that evening, and I was in a bad mood from remembering my father's death and hearing about the attack on Beirut. Our guests noticed I wasn't my usual happy and hospitable self. When I tried to explain that I was upset about what I'd heard on the news, they didn't really seem too sympathetic. One of Lisa's colleagues, who, as I later discovered, thought I was Mexican, even said, 'Well, that's the Middle East;

what do you expect? All those people over there are just a bunch of warring tribes!'

"After the guests had gone, Lisa and I were cleaning up and I told her that her colleague's comment had really bothered me; she said I was being too sensitive. I also told her that I felt it was about time I got married and had children, since the family name and line will die out if I don't perpetuate it. My dad is gone, his two male cousins died during the war, I am the only son, and all my father's brothers had only daughters. After I explained all of this, Lisa just looked at me like I was crazy, and said, 'I hope you have a candidate besides me for childbearing, because I don't plan on sacrificing my art career for motherhood—not now or ever!' That was the beginning of the end of our relationship. Two weeks later, when the hostilities in Lebanon had ended, I called my uncles in Beirut and told them to expect me for a long visit in July."

Khalid, who had been listening sympathetically, looked at me and said, "I don't know how it is for other immigrants to the U.S., but if you're an Arab in America, you can never forget where you come from. Every day, something on the news, or someone's question about your accent, or some remark on television or in a movie about Arabs being terrorists, will always remind you of who you are. Adnan and I have been American citizens for more than a decade, and this is a great country which has given us so many opportunities, for which we are grateful, but his heart will always be in Beirut, and mine in Jerusalem. You can never forget your people; their joys are your joys, and when they suffer, you suffer. Any time you can do something for them, whether here or back home, you don't hesitate. Adnan has now realized this, as I did during the intifada. You should hear the waiter, Hussein's, story of how he felt during the Gulf War. He's a Shi'ite from southern Iraq, and even though he hates Saddam Hussein, he was outraged to see the U.S. and its allies attacking Iraq so forcefully; he took it personally, like his whole self and heritage were being attacked. Once, he was almost beaten up by some American teenagers who started a fight with him on the bus during the war. The poor kid went through a real identity crisis that year!"

Silence enveloped our table as Adnan stared pensively at his empty coffee cup. Dispelling the somber mood, Khalid informed us in a cheerful voice, "Okay, now we are going to tell you how, with the help of Laila's family in Syria and my relatives in Israel, our company is going to corner the computer games market in the new Middle East!" Adnan chuckled and looked at George, who was raising his eyebrows in surprise and curiosity. "If they ever work out a peace agreement in the Middle East," said Adnan, "Khalid and I will have all our networks in place. Some of his cousins are Palestinian citizens of Israel living in Nazareth, one of whom is a computer programmer who's thinking of opening up a computer supplies store and training center. Laila's mother is Armenian, and most of her family lives in Syria, especially in Aleppo and Damascus, where they manage a number of bookstores, and from what I hear, business has been very slow there the last couple of years. So, what could be more natural than forming a regional marketing and distribution network with *ibn khal* [male maternal cousin] Khalid in Nazareth and *ibn khal* Laila in Syria? If all goes well, we could make millions!" exclaimed Adnan. "And then we'll make another couple of millions by selling our company to one of the big multinationals that will be eager to get into the Middle East market after a peace agreement!" added Khalid. "If we're lucky, we can both retire before we're fifty, go back to Jerusalem and Beirut, build nice houses, and raise our kids in a cultural environment that has stronger family values than they have here in the U.S.!"

"Insha'allah!" (if God wills it), said George with a smile. "Yes, *insha'allah!"* echoed Adnan and Khalid.

Although this conversation among friends took place half a world away from the Middle East, it provides some insights into the prevailing social, cultural, political, and economic realities of an important but troubled region of the contemporary world. Adnan's story and Khalid's comments illustrate the crucial role of kinship and marriage in Middle Eastern societies and also highlight the political and psychological dynamics of ethnicity while hinting at the existence of conflicts within and between countries of the region. Their future business plans highlight mercantile economic patterns and social class structures characteristic of the Middle East, and Khalid's observation about the interests of multinational corporations indicates the extent to which the Middle East is, or soon may be, firmly incorporated into complex global markets that could have a profound impact on the way the peoples of this region, be they Arabs, Turks, or Iranians, Jews, Christians, or Muslims, live their lives in the coming century.

This chapter employs an anthropological perspective on kinship, ethnicity, and social class in the contemporary Middle East in order to illustrate the relationships among these three domains of social reality as well as their connections to other trends and institutions. We will examine how individuals and groups use kinship and ethnic identity to access networks of affiliation and assistance not only to make a living, but just as important, to make a meaning, in the face of the rapid changes, conflicting cultural values, and pervasive uncertainties characteristic of the late twentieth century. Although economic pressures and political instability are certainly not unique to the Middle East, the strategies chosen by the peoples of this region to respond to contemporary challenges draw on a particular constellation of historical experiences, cultural traditions, religious values, and modes of socioeconomic organization, all of which distinguish the Middle East from European, Asian, or African sociocultural systems.

■ PERSISTENT CHALLENGES AND ADAPTIVE STRATEGIES: THE ENVIRONMENTAL AND HISTORICAL CONTEXT

The peoples of the Middle East are no strangers to harsh and uncertain environments, whether natural, economic, or political. Inhabiting an ecological zone characterized by aridity, steep valleys, rugged mountains, few rivers, scant rainfall, and poor soils, Middle Eastern communities traditionally had no choice but to combine a variety of difficult modes of subsistence, such as pastoral nomadism, small-scale agriculture, commerce, and fishing, in order to make a living. Groups dwelling in this arid and semiarid region also developed distinctive cultural patterns and sociopolitical institutions that served to minimize the hardships and uncertainties arising from the conditions of their natural environment and the implications of some of their modes of economic production. Up until today, the peoples of the Middle East remain justly famous for their loyal attachment to their families, distinctive rituals of hospitality and conflict mediation, and effective and flexible kin-based collectivities, such as the lineage and the tribe, which until quite recently performed most of the social, economic, and political functions of communities in the absence of centralized state governments.

Although far-flung empires and tribal confederations in the Middle East were replaced by clearly bounded nation-states earlier this century and even though the vast majority of nomadic peoples have been sedentarized—settled into villages and cities where, thanks to new techniques of irrigation, they can earn a modest living as farmers, skilled laborers, or professionals—everyday life in the modern Middle East continues to be difficult and uncertain for many and occasionally dangerous for some. The contemporary Middle East is a region of rich civilizational heritage and immense human potential. It is also a region beset by political volatility, economic disparities, and ecological vulnerability. Despite the fact that the state bureaucracies of most countries in the region are well entrenched and heavily subsidized, few have succeeded in distributing resources equitably, administering justice fairly, protecting and advancing the interests of the majority of the people, and thereby winning public support and popular participation through legitimate means. Most states in the Middle East serve narrow elite interests rather than the common good (Sharabi, 1990; Tibi, 1990; Barakat, 1993; Makiya, 1993).

The overwhelming majority of the region's population does not participate in the economic and political decisionmaking processes that will greatly influence their lives and their children's lives. Middle Eastern states usually rule rather than govern their populaces, employing coercion, manipulation, and co-optation to achieve control and compliance. Consequently, the peoples of the Middle East have learned to place their trust in those whom they know well and with whom they share similar interests, goals, and characteristics: their relatives, neighbors, friends, and members of their own ethnic, religious and linguistic groups. The Middle Eastern nation-state, an externally imposed and new system of sociopolitical organization, still cannot claim the same kind or degree of support, loyalty, and legitimacy that Middle Eastern kin and client networks have always claimed. Even a half-century after the nation-state's advent in the region, kinship relations (or relations modeled on a kinship pattern) mediate individuals' personal, economic, and political lives to an extent almost unimaginable to anyone who has grown up in Western Europe or North America.

For example, individuals' interactions with state bodies and governmental bureaucracies take place primarily through patron-client relationships mediated by ties of kinship (actual or fictive), political party membership, or ethnic and sectarian affiliation (Cunningham and Sarayrah, 1993). In most Middle Eastern societies, governmental services are available only to those who have connections (*wasta* in Arabic; *protektzia* in Hebrew). Citizenship, an identity category that derives its significance from the jural relationship of each individual to the nation-state, carries much less emotional, moral, legal, and political weight in the Middle East than do identity categories such as kinship, ethnicity, and religion.

Understanding the reasons citizens of Middle Eastern nation-states persist in clinging to pre-state social and political institutions such as the family, lineage, tribe or sect, and primary (i.e., kinship, ethnic, and religious) affiliations will help us understand the causes of intrastate turmoil and interstate hostilities in a more objective manner than did Adnan's insensitive dinner guest. Discovering how Middle Eastern peoples strategically invoke and manipulate kin ties, ethnic affiliations, and patron-client relationships will give us a new appreciation of the creative and effective means individuals and groups have developed in order to survive and thrive in a challenging socioeconomic environment while preparing for future contingencies. To analyze the interrelationship of kinship, ethnicity, and social class formation in the context of the contemporary Middle East, let us first review some key anthropological viewpoints on these three categories, which profoundly influence the everyday activities and choices of Middle Eastern peoples.

■ KINSHIP

At first glance, it seems self-evident that kinship is a naturally occurring phenomenon, not a cultural construct. After all, every living person has or had kin (relatives), linked to him or her through blood and probably through marriage, too. Common sense tells us that biological relationships are a human universal; even "test tube" babies have biological parents, regardless of whether or not they have ever met them. Anthropologists, though, are forever questioning the easy assumptions underlying "common sense." Instead of appraising human phenomena according to its obvious surface characteristics, anthropologists look at human beings and their behavior holistically and relativistically, that is, from every possible angle and in every relevant context, in an effort to understand the totality of human experience and behavior. The anthropologist's goal is to decipher the meanings of the underlying concepts, attitudes, and values that guide people's choices and interactions. These meanings are not visible; they must be inferred from carefully observed behavior over time. Whereas a geneticist would examine DNA (deoxyribonucleic acid) to determine kinship, an anthropologist attends simultaneously to the biological and the cultural, economic, moral, and political dimensions of kin ties. Indeed, one anthropological definition of kinship is that it concerns "biological relationships, culturally defined" (Keesing, 1975). Hence, an anthropologist investigating the kinship system of a particular community will be less concerned with discovering the actual genetic links between individuals than with ascertaining how individuals in this community conceive of kinship connections and the extent to which these cultural conceptions shape actual social interaction among individuals who consider themselves kin.

Although the act of sexual procreation and the phenomenon of birth are human universals, not all human societies interpret and value biological connections in precisely the same way. In societies characterized by bilateral kinship systems, such as North America, individuals recognize and value their links to relatives on both their mother's and father's sides of the family equally. In other societies, classified as matriarchies, only an individual's maternal relatives will be recognized for economic, social, and political purposes.

In North American society, individuals consider children of their mother's siblings (i.e., maternal cousins) to occupy the same social category as children of their father's siblings (paternal cousins). A particular set of cultural expectations and values guide interactions between cousins in North America (Schneider, 1968). Cousins are people you enjoy seeing; you feel a connection to them that is stronger than friendship but not as complicated or demanding as the tie between siblings. Very few people in North America would contemplate marrying a first cousin. In fact, such a marriage would be illegal in some U.S. states.

In the Middle East, however, people can and do marry their first cousins; in some rural areas, the union of a man and his father's brother's daughter is still considered to be the preferred marriage choice (Murphy and Kasdan, 1959; Abu-Lughod, 1986). Maternal and paternal cousins are considered to be distinctly different categories in the Middle East; an individual will behave differently toward his female paternal cousin than he does toward his female maternal cousin, and the tone of his relationship to a male paternal cousin is likely to be more formal, reserved, and subdued, whereas mutual affection and joking usually characterize his relationship with a male maternal cousin.

Anthropologists researching Middle Eastern societies as widely separated as Morocco and Iran have noted several key characteristics of kinship in the region. Middle Eastern kinship systems are extended, patriarchal, hierarchical, patrilineal, and often endogamous (Patai, 1971; Geertz, 1979; Barakat, 1993). The extended family plays a crucial economic, political, and socializing role in Middle Eastern societies. Within the family, authority and respect are accorded to men and elderly family members of both sexes, who, occupying the top positions in the family hierarchy, wield more power, prestige, and rights than female family members and children of either sex.

The Middle Eastern family is not an egalitarian structure. Men's and women's roles are considered to be complementary and integrative, not equal. Men are the primary decisionmakers, although women exercise much more power within the family "behind the scenes" than is immediately apparent (Abu-Lughod, 1986; Geertz, 1979; Mundy, 1995; Peteet, 1991; Sayigh, 1994; Singerman, 1995). Traditionally, a man's overarching responsibility has been to lead, protect, and provide for his family completely. A woman's primary role has been to make a comfortable home, oversee all aspects of the private, domestic sphere, and bear and nurture children.

Gender roles in the Middle East, as in the rest of the world, are undergoing rapid changes as a result of increased education, rapid urbanization, new economic relationships, and the employment of women. Nonetheless, Middle Eastern men and women continue to place a high value not on their own personal achievements, but rather on their family affiliations in general and on their roles as generators of new families in particular. In other words, men's and women's roles as parents are more important and valued than any other role they can fulfill. Young people in most Middle Eastern societies are not considered to be truly adult until they have completed the important rites of passage of marriage and parenthood. Westerners visiting Middle Eastern societies are invariably asked about their marital status, and women who are still unmarried or married and not yet mothers after the age of twenty-five, will find themselves repeatedly explaining their unusual single or childless state to their concerned Middle Eastern hosts (Fernea, 1969; Singerman, 1995).

An oft-noted cultural particularity of Middle Eastern kinship systems is the practice of endogamous marriage, or marriage between men and women belonging to the same kinship group. As previously mentioned, a preferred form of marriage in the Middle East has traditionally been that between a man and his father's brother's daughter (*bint 'amm* in Arabic), henceforth abbreviated as FBD. Because Middle Eastern kinship systems are patrilineal, that is, based on ties of agnation and descent traced through paternal relatives, a man and his FBD are always members of the same patrilineage. In anthropological terminology, cousins in this category of relationship to each other are known as parallel cousins. The daughters of a man's mother's brother do not belong to his patrilineage; anthropologists refer to this category of cousins as cross cousins.

Marriages can and do take place between both categories of cousins in the Middle East, and many scholars have noted that endogamy refers more to an ideological preference than an actual practice. For instance, the Lebanese anthropologist Fuad Khuri, conducting research among Muslim residents of Beirut in the late 1960s, discovered that only 11 percent of marriages in his sample were endogamous (FBD) marriages (Khuri, 1970). My research among Palestinian citizens of Israel in Nazareth in 1992 indicated that less than 5 percent of a sample of 341 households consisted of spouses who were parallel cousins.

Given the prevalence of labor migration and rapidly increasing urbanization in the region, extended families of grandparents, parents, brothers, sisters, cousins, aunts, and uncles living under the same roof are less and less common. In the major cities of the Middle East, where the bulk of the region's people live, anthropologists have discovered that unions between members of the same neighborhood, sect, ethnic group, and social class form the overwhelming majority of marriages. Hence, a form of sociocultural, if not familial, endogamy still persists in the contemporary Middle East because families prefer that their sons and daughters marry individuals whose social backgrounds and kinship networks are well known to them (Al-Akhras, 1976; Singerman, 1995). Adnan's fiancée's family, for instance, readily accepted his proposal of marriage, despite the short amount of time that Adnan and Laila had known one another. Such acceptance would not have been forthcoming if Adnan had not been a part of Laila's kinship network.

Endogamous marriage patterns, which are practiced by very few cultures outside the Middle East, stem not from exotic cultural beliefs, a peculiar mentality, or unquestioned obedience to ancient traditions, but from a desire to enhance and strengthen group solidarity. Endogamy is a strategy for retaining individuals' loyalty and commitment, as well as their wealth (whether in the form of bridewealth, productive property, or inheritances), within the family circle, widely defined. Such desires and strategies are indices of a long historical experience of economic scarcity, harsh environmental conditions, political uncertainty, and pronounced competition for limited resources in this vast, semiarid zone. The interplay of these

ecological, political, and economic factors has at times engendered an atmosphere of unpredictability and mistrust in Middle Eastern societies
(Schneider, 1971; Meeker, 1979).

In examining the patrilineal nature of Middle Eastern kinship systems,
we must look beyond the domain of the nuclear family's domestic concerns to the public realm of the community's political and economic interests, which are greatly affected and conditioned by the natural and human
environments. As one anthropologist notes, "kinship is the dominant mode
of forming the larger groupings central to social and political life in pre-
industrial societies. Kinship provides solutions to ecological and organizational challenges in space and time" (Keesing, 1975:8).

The choice of the patrilineage as the key sociopolitical mode of organization in the Middle East was not arbitrary, since

> unilineal descent groups [whether matrilineal or patrilineal] were a cru-
> cial development in the evolution of tribal societies. They provided an
> adaptive solution in different ecological settings to the problem of main-
> taining political order and defining rights to land and other resources
> across the generations. (Keesing, 1975:24)

The ecological realities of the Middle East have given rise to three key
modes of subsistence: nomadic, village, and urban. Although communities
of bedouins, farmers, and city-dwelling merchants and artisans were historically distinct from one another, they were nonetheless economically interdependent. Their lives were always in actual or potential contact, and
their respective interests were often in conflict (Ibn Khaldun, 1967; Nelson, 1973).

In the absence of a strong, centralized governmental administration,
well-armed, roving bedouin tribes (i.e., coalitions of patrilineages claiming
descent from a common, distant ancestor) could easily sweep into poorly
defended agricultural settlements mounted on their formidable camels and
take goods, crops, livestock, and other forms of wealth by force. Some nomadic tribes coalesced into powerful federations capable of extracting payments of tribute (in effect, protection money) from sedentary villagers
over a very wide area. In some cases, wealthy urban elites formed alliances with leaders of bedouin tribal federations in an effort to extract
maximum economic resources from the land and people in the countryside, thus controlling the political dynamics of an entire region (Khoury
and Kostiner, 1990; Barakat, 1993).

Pastoral nomadism has become increasingly rare as a viable mode of
subsistence following the advent of nation-states demarcated by closed
borders and the rapid and dramatic urbanization and proletarianization of
the region's population. Nonetheless, nomadic peoples and their traditions

have left a deep imprint on Middle Eastern culture, society, and politics. One anthropologist hypothesizes that the characteristic form of pastoral nomadism that developed in this semiarid zone accounts for the strikingly similar cultural orientations found throughout the vast area of the Middle East:

> In the Near East today we find a remarkable similarity among the traditions of many people throughout a large region. The explanation for such a phenomenon among peoples who have never been politically united in an important way and who have never been part of a tightly organized economic order indicates that a force was at work all over the arid zone and only in that zone. Islamization, the spread of a religious faith, is often offered as an explanation for this uniformity. But could Islam by itself have become so deeply rooted among the diverse peoples of such a vast area, unless it was somehow a response to a life experience which all of these people shared in common? . . . Extreme arid conditions resulted in independent little herding groups dispersed across the desert and steppe. The domestic wealth of such groups was that much more vulnerable because the strategy of organizing scattered and independent little groups in protective political alliances was less effective. This situation is reflected in the atomistic form which political alliances tended to take. (Meeker, 1979:7)

The patrilineal descent groups found in every Middle Eastern society, whether Arab, Turkish, or Persian, had their genesis thousands of years ago as an adaptive response to the interrelated ecological and political conditions of the region (Schneider, 1971; Meeker, 1979). Pastoral nomadism is a strenuous mode of subsistence; it both demands and frustrates cooperative, interdependent social relations. Pastoral nomadism requires the careful and timely coordination of different activities by different people. If the needs of the herds and flocks are not met, they and the human community dependent upon them for its livelihood can easily perish. Members of nomadic groups are thus willing to pitch in for the common good and extend themselves magnanimously if the situation demands brave and generous behavior. But in this arid and unpredictable ecological zone, people must also be selfish and calculating at times in order to survive. This fact "places heavy burdens on interpersonal relations, for everyone must think first of his immediate household's interests and needs and resist undue claims for assistance from kinsmen and friends" (Schneider, 1971:5). Among pastoral nomads, the need for water may well outweigh the claims of blood.

The natural environment in which pastoral nomads live is clearly harsh and uncertain. The social environment is also threatening since it is highly competitive. It is thus imperative for all pastoral nomadic peoples to institute

> organizational solutions to the compelling ecological problem of regulating access of humans and animals to natural resources. . . . Migratory groups cannot establish rights to land on a permanent basis, or fence it off against incursions. Raiding and animal theft are therefore endemic. . . . The determination of boundary lines is subject to continual human intervention; the definition of the group is problematic as well: social boundaries are difficult to maintain, and internal loyalties are questionable. . . . Individuals and groups are at once . . . vulnerable and opportunistic. (Schneider, 1971:24)

The organizational solution instituted by peoples of the Middle East to the challenges presented to them by their difficult environment consisted of adopting a social, political, and moral idiom of paternal blood relationship: the patrilineage. Members of a patrilineage could invoke their blood connections to other individuals and groups in order to obtain mutual support, defense, assistance, and protection in their unending struggle to eke a living out of the harsh environment. Patrilineal principles also facilitated the equitable division of wealth in inheritances, thus limiting the likelihood of contention and destructive conflict among surviving heirs, whose continuing cooperation was imperative for their own and their families' survival.

Depending on the need or the task at hand, nomadic peoples could employ an idiom of patrilineal relationships to mobilize groups ranging from a person's immediate male kin (brothers, father, grandfather, sons, uncles, and cousins) to a huge tribal federation numbering thousands of individuals representing many different patrilineages related through a distant founding (or "apical") ancestor. But because the natural environment could not support a large number of nomads and their animals living at the same place for any significant length of time, Middle Eastern patrilineages never developed into the sustained, enduring, clearly bounded unilineal descent groups found in more temperate and fertile ecological zones. Rather than becoming corporations, Middle Eastern kin groups were shifting coalitions that could be forged and broken, quickly and repeatedly, according to the relevant context and prevailing interests. Anthropologists term this process *segmentation,* and many social scientists characterize Middle Eastern societies as segmentary because of the prevalence of many similar yet differentiated components (e.g., families, lineages, guilds, ethnic groups, or sects) that can coalesce to cooperate or fragment to fight in the unending struggle for scarce and valuable resources.

Kinship, as an idiom of identity and social organization no less than as a basis of affiliation, protection, and cooperative action, is just as important in the Middle East today as it was hundreds of years ago. A person's identity as a member of a kin group entitles him or her to rights and services, just as it entails making considerable sacrifices for the sake of the group. In spite of the establishment of nation-states in the postcolonial period, the primary identification of the peoples of the Middle East is not civil, religious, or even ethnic but familial. For instance, the kingdom of Saudi Arabia is one large extended family whose members prefer endogamous marriages. Both Syria and Iraq are run by tightly knit, patrilineal coalitions of the brothers and cousins of Hafez al-Assad and Saddam Hussein, respectively; indeed, the Iraqi government is referred to in diplomatic circles as "the Takriti regime" after the name of the Sunni Muslim village in north-central Iraq from which Saddam Hussein and his family hail. It is instructive to note that both al-Assad and Hussein are members of religious minority groups in their own countries. Sunni Muslims are the majority community in Syria, where al-Assad's Alawite community holds all the decisive reins of power; in Iraq, a majority population of Shi'ites have lived under the rule of Hussein, a Sunni, for nearly two decades. These two leaders' rise to and continuing retention of the top posts in their countries in spite of their minority status speaks volumes about the strength and efficacy of family ties in Middle Eastern societies and polities.

As a strategy for survival, the patrilineal kinship system has certainly proved flexible and effective over many centuries under a variety of social, economic, and political conditions in the Middle East. What began as an adaptive response to ecological and social limitations gradually became a valued institution embodying a rich cultural complex of expectations, attitudes, values, beliefs, rituals, and behaviors. The distinctive kinship systems and practices of the Middle East are part of the region's civilizational heritage. Kinship is implicated in nearly every aspect of life and most social institutions, including religion and morality. Michael Meeker speculates that "the cultural uniformity which we now find in the arid zone does not reflect the traditions of a people bent on violence. On the contrary, it reflects . . . a moral response to the threat of political turmoil" (1979:19). Despite urbanization, modernization, and emigration, individuals are still judged primarily by how they perform their family duties. An individual's identity, decisions, and social reputation are profoundly influenced by his or her kin group. Adnan, for instance, makes a decision to marry not for love but to discharge his responsibilities to his family, since he is the sole surviving male capable of carrying on his patrilineage's name, a decision that his American girlfriend finds strange.

Let us now examine another adaptive strategy of contemporary Middle Eastern societies that, like kinship, centers on the individual's identification and affiliation with extensive networks. Through these connections, he or she can construct meaningful moral boundaries while obtaining access to power, protection, and resources in a highly competitive socioeconomic and political environment.

■ ETHNICITY

It is easy to assume that ethnic differences are essentially racial differences and thus to conclude that ethnic groups are determined and delimited largely by biological criteria such as hair, skin, and eye color, height, and physique, and only further distinguished by such characteristics as language, cultural patterns, and religious faith. Scholars examining the phenomenon of ethnicity, however, note that it is a strategic, more so than a genetic, phenomenon (Cohen, 1978; Royce, 1982; Anderson, 1993). Ethnic identity, whether referring to subjective criteria (an individual's awareness of and feelings about his or her membership in a particular ethnic category) or objective criteria (others' categorization of an individual on the basis of physical or cultural characteristics), cannot exist in a homogeneous society in which everyone shares the same cultural, religious, class, and linguistic background. Ethnicity and ethnic identity are oppositional phenomena; they emerge only in societies comprising different types of peoples from a wide variety of backgrounds. Ethnicity is a product of plural societies characterized by cultural, economic, linguistic, or religious heterogeneity. Due to migration from rural to urban areas and the impact of enhanced communications and transportation systems, individuals and groups from a wide variety of cultural, linguistic, socioeconomic, and religious backgrounds are suddenly brought into contact.

In the rapidly growing cities of the Middle East, various ethnic groups interact and compete with one another in a new and often alienating sociopolitical context characterized by economic scarcity and uneven development. The recognition of ethnic differences thus implies the recognition of economic and political differences as well. The ensuing awareness of relative and absolute economic differences can easily lead to conflict, competition, and opposition organized along ethnic lines. As anthropologist Ronald Cohen notes, "Ethnicity is . . . one of the many outcomes of group interaction in which there is differential power between dominant and minority groups. From this perspective, ethnicity is an aspect of stratification, rather than a problem on its own" (1978:386).

The categorization of individuals or groups according to their ethnic identity and membership is a salient feature of most contemporary complex societies. One of the greatest analytical and methodological challenges facing sociologists and anthropologists conducting research on societies of the non-Western developing world lies in determining the dividing lines (if any) between ethnic groups, kinship groups, and socioeconomic classes (Barakat, 1993). Ethnicity in the Middle East presents many definitional and methodological challenges for researchers since ethnic groups often behave like kin-based tribal groupings, especially in the way they mobilize their members by invoking a shared identity. At the same time, ethnic differences seem to correspond closely to socioeconomic distinctions.

For instance, in Israeli society, Western-oriented Ashkenazi Jews, although numerically the minority community, are the dominant class in terms of wealth and control of the state's decisionmaking bodies in comparison with the more numerous Sephardic (or Mizrachi) Jews, who come from Arab countries and whose cultural attitudes and practices have long been looked down upon by Ashkenazi Jews. Prior to the convulsions of the Lebanese civil war (1975–1990), the wealthy power brokers and owners of factories, banks, and businesses in Lebanon were invariably Maronite Christians, whereas the poorer, less powerful, agricultural communities in Lebanon tended to be populated by Shi'a Muslims.

There are, of course, exceptions to these correlations between class, ethnicity, and kinship. Only sustained and fine-grained research can elucidate the dynamic interrelationships of kinship, class, and ethnicity in the contemporary Middle East. Most social scientists consider ethnic political organizations and activities key phenomena of the modern world. Some scholars forecast the further solidification and entrenchment of ethnic and cultural identities as competition and conflict over limited goods increases throughout the world (Huntington, 1996). These recent predictions of social unrest and political violence between different cultural groups stand in stark contrast to the expectations of an earlier generation of academics and policymakers who, in the post–World War II era, expressed confidence that the universal adoption of a modernizing, liberal, secular, and technologically advanced culture and social system would facilitate homogenization and harmonization between different peoples within and between states. What these optimistic observers left out of their social equations were cultural dissonance, alienation, relative and absolute economic deprivation, the unequal distribution of resources, and differences in the types and amounts of power available to various ethnic groups in any given society. It is not the differences in cultural practices, religious beliefs, or linguistic characteristics that cause friction between members of opposing ethnic communities. Rather, "inequality, not ethnicity, is the basis of social stratification" and thus, conflict (Cohen, 1978:400).

If Middle Eastern kin-based institutions like patrilineage and the tribe were the primary adaptive responses to the ecological challenges and socioeconomic problems of intense competition over scarce resources in a harsh natural environment, then the ethnic group is the chief survival strategy of the politically marginalized individual in the harsh social and economic environments of the contemporary Middle East. Torn loose from the familiar moorings of village, home, and family as a result of poverty or war; struggling to make a decent living in crowded, impoverished, and poorly serviced cities; and underrepresented by or provided for by a concerned

A fraction of the ethnic diversity that is in the Middle East

Photo 9.1

Photo 9.2

Photo 9.3

Photo 9.4

Photo 9.5

Photo 9.6

Photo 9.7

government, the average individual in the contemporary Middle East is likely to feel lost, lonely, alienated, and powerless. If he or she cannot find kin or people from his or her region to provide guidance, mutual assistance, and support, an uprooted individual will most likely turn to other individuals and groups with whom he or she shares some common background characteristics, values, orientations, and goals: hence, the ethnoreligious group, which performs some of the same functions as the tribe but is neither based entirely on blood relationships nor as clearly bounded in terms of its membership as is the tribe. An organized and mobilized ethnic group or religious sect serves the economic, social, and political needs of its members far better than any state apparatus of the modern Middle East. This is a primary reason for the growth of so-called fundamentalist Islamic organizations in such urban centers as Cairo, Algiers, Istanbul, and Khartoum. These cities are filled with millions of young, unskilled, unmarried young men who have left an agricultural lifestyle in the countryside in the often vain hope of making a better living in the city.

At the beginning of the twentieth century, city-dwellers accounted for less than 10 percent of the total population of the Middle East. As Moghadam described in Chapter 8, urbanization has increased dramatically in recent decades, and recent studies by the UN predict that urban populations will reach 80 percent of the total for the Middle East within the next decade. Thus, the current trend of relying on family and ethnoreligious ties to survive in Middle Eastern cities is likely to continue. Cohen succinctly describes how comforting and empowering an ethnic reference group and support network can be to such displaced young people:

> If alienation is a malfunction of modern society, then ethnicity is an antidote. . . . Ethnicity provides a fundamental and multifaceted link to a category of others that very little else can do in modern society. . . . In a multiethnic society in which a plurality of groups, ethnic and non-ethnic, vie for scarce rewards, stressing individual human rights leads ultimately to unequal treatment. . . . Individuals are fated to obtain more rewards because of their group identities. Organized ethnic groups can fight for equal rights. (1978:401–402)

In other words, an ethnic group is not a racial unit or a cultural unit but a political unit. Ethnic groups are interest groups; they are structured to serve the various needs of affiliated members while competing with other interest groups for the limited resources to be obtained within the framework of the modern state. The group that can mobilize the greatest numbers of supporters and patrons, deliver the highest number of voters during elections, forge the strongest links with powerful groups within or without the society, and devise the most compelling and convincing arguments to advance its rights to resources, political posts, or economic redress will take the lion's share of the services, governmental posts, protection, and wealth that can be extracted from the state. Indeed, in the Middle East, a well-organized and ambitious ethnic or religious group can even take complete control of the entire state apparatus, as did the Alawites of Syria and the Sunnis of Iraq in the early 1970s.

■ THE HISTORICAL CONTEXT OF ETHNICITY

In the Middle East, ethnic groups and officially recognized ethnoreligious identity categories predate the creation of the region's nation-states. Prior to the advent of the nation-state system in the Middle East and even before the colonial era, most of the peoples of the region (with the exception of those living in Morocco and Iran) lived under Ottoman rule in the sociopolitical framework of a vast empire. Day-to-day matters of administration and basic governance were in the hands of local political elites chosen by the Ottoman leadership, as well as the local clergy. As an empire, the Ottoman system was organized not according to ethnic or national principles and categories but according to religious distinctions. Individuals living in the Ottoman Empire did not identify themselves as Ottomans, Turks, Arabs, or Kurds, but rather as Muslims, Christians, Jews, or Druze. Within this system of organization, Muslims were in the majority, both in terms of absolute numbers and in terms of privilege, rank, status, and opportunities. Christians and Jews were formally recognized as religious minorities.

Considered "Peoples of the Book" and categorized as *dhimmih* communities (literally meaning "on the conscience" of the larger and more powerful Muslim community), Christians and Jews were supposed to be protected from harm or persecution by the majority Muslim community in return for their acceptance of a subordinate status, payment of a special tax (*jizyah*), and abstention from any public display of their religious practices such as processions and liturgical ceremonies. As long as the non-Muslim communities obeyed Ottoman laws and paid their taxes, they were supposed to be left unmolested to conduct their lives alongside the Muslim community. *Dhimmih* communities were under the jurisdiction of Islamic courts in criminal cases and some property disputes but obeyed the jurisdiction of their own communities' religious laws and precepts concerning any issues related to religious and family matters. As non-Muslims, Christians, Druze, and Jews were not subject to the rulings of Shari'ah (Islamic law) in matters of personal status such as marriage, divorce, inheritance, and other family issues. Instead, Christian sects and Druze and Jewish communities sought guidance, mediation, and rulings from their own religious hierarchy, the leaders of which had the power to make binding judicial decisions in the domain of family law and to legally represent their religious communities in official dealings with the Ottoman authorities. This system of legally recognized non-Muslim communal autonomy was known as the *millet* system (meaning "people" or "community" in Turkish).

This brief historical overview indicates that the Middle East has always been culturally heterogeneous. The pronounced cultural and religious differences between the various ethnic groups of the region are not new or modern phenomena. The ecological characteristics of the region, combined with the prevalence of rugged mountains, deep valleys, and virtually impassable desert expanses ensured that different communities lived in small, close-knit groupings that were widely separated from each other. Until the advent of advanced communications technology and the construction of paved roads and railways, some areas of the Middle East were almost inaccessible. Existing independently of each other for so many centuries, it was only natural that noticeable linguistic, cultural, and religious differences would develop among the dispersed human populations of the Middle East. During the Ottoman era, the rugged mountainous areas of the Eastern Mediterranean became a refuge for a variety of Christian and Islamic religious sects and splinter groups seeking to escape persecution by orthodox religious authorities. Dwelling high atop these mountains, minority groups such as the Maronites, Druze, Shi'ites, and Alawites could pursue their religious traditions free of interference from either Christian or Muslim authorities.

Middle Eastern cities were always culturally and religiously heterogeneous. The plural nature of Middle Eastern urban areas is inscribed in the very towers, walls, and gates that marked off the various named quarters of traditional urban settlements, such as the "Muslim Quarter," "Armenian Quarter," "Jewish Quarter," "Orthodox Quarter," and so on, as we find in such ancient cities as Jerusalem, Cairo, Damascus, Istanbul, and Baghdad. The spatial separation of different religious and ethnic groups in the traditional Middle Eastern city was paralleled by a division of labor between these distinct communities. Christians, Muslims, and Jews occupied different professional categories in the Ottoman social and economic structure. The traditional city's division of labor was usually characterized by accommodation, complementarity, and integration rather than by competition and conflict. Muslims held positions in religious courts and schools as well as in the military and in local governmental administration, and non-Muslims served primarily as doctors, merchants, advisers, artisans, and religious and legal specialists for their own sectarian communities. The Ottoman division of labor is recorded to this day in the names of many Christian families from Lebanon, Palestine, and Syria, which designate the professional and artisan roles that their ancestors played in Ottoman society: *sabbagh* (dyer), *hakim* (doctor), *khabbaz* (baker), *banna* (builder), *sayigh* (goldsmith), *hayek* (weaver), *najjar* (carpenter), *khoury* (priest), and *shammas* (sexton).

The cultural and religious heterogeneity of the Middle East thus did not result from rapid urbanization or the establishment of nation-states in this century, nor is it a byproduct of colonialism (although colonial powers certainly employed tactics based on a policy of "divide and rule" to consolidate their control of local political systems). Different ethnic and religious groups have been living side by side in the Middle East for centuries, sometimes in conflict but more often than not in harmony. What is new in the ethnic and religious configuration of the contemporary Middle East is the social, political, and economic framework in which different groups live, work, and struggle. The relatively recent historical processes, which led to the region's incorporation into the global economy and the establishment of nation-states, altered the traditional balance of power and the system of accommodation that had prevailed during the Ottoman era. Although the Ottoman Empire was hardly a model of economic efficiency or social justice, it nonetheless encouraged a relatively viable form of accommodation and cooperation among the region's diverse ethnic and religious groupings.

To understand how the various ethnic and religious communities of the Middle East became embroiled in conflicts that are still continuing, we must now examine the historical processes of social class formation, which exacerbated competition and thus engendered conflicts between the different ethnic communities of the region.

■ SOCIAL CLASS

Unlike the identity categories of "kinship" and "ethnicity," social class is not based on biological or cultural criteria, but rather on economic and political differences. Like ethnic groups, social classes are oppositional phenomena: a social class cannot exist except in relation to other social classes, since the idea of a class entails a hierarchical arrangement of groups based on differences of wealth, power, and control over resources. A society whose members all share the same resources equally, own wealth in common, participate fully in all decisionmaking, and have equal rights and duties in relation to one another would be a classless society. The distinguishing criteria of any social class structure are inequalities of wealth and differential access to resources and means of economic production. Thus, class distinctions entail relationships of dominance and subordination between different competing groups, each of which continually strives to improve its relative position, or having attained a position of relative advantage, struggles to retain it.

According to the social historian Philip Khoury, the social class structure of the Middle East was relatively simple and stable until the middle of
the nineteenth century. Just 150 years ago, the Middle East began to be integrated into the capitalist world system. Consequently, new social classes
gradually emerged as a result of changing modes of economic production
and new forms of ownership and control of resources (Khoury, 1983). The
most significant economic change during the nineteenth century was the
advent of new forms of landownership. Following a series of military and
economic defeats at the hands of rising European powers, the Ottoman
leadership decided to institute a number of administrative reforms in an effort to improve and strengthen the Ottoman system by imitating European
societies and governments.

Chief among these reforms were new land laws that encouraged private, rather than communal, ownership of productive property. Muslim and
non-Muslim elites favored by the Ottoman rulers benefited from these reforms by taking control of formerly communal properties, on which they
planted cash crops such as tobacco in place of subsistence crops. This agricultural regime served the interests of international markets, not the local
populace. At the same time, merchants in cities such as Beirut, Damascus,
Acre, and Ladhakia began to earn a considerable profit as middlemen
overseeing trade between European producers of goods and newly wealthy
Middle Eastern consumers of fine furnishings, clothing, household equipment, and medicines. This shift from local to foreign markets for consumer
goods had a debilitating effect on local artisans and manufacturers, who,
along with peasants displaced from agricultural lands by private landownership, high taxation, and wars, became members of a new social class formation: the urban proletariat. This period marked the advent of a sharply
pyramidal class structure characterized by the political and economic domination of a large mass of impoverished people by a handful of extremely
wealthy landowning families.

Although markets and modes of production have changed dramatically
since the mid-nineteenth century, the social and economic class structure of
the Middle East is still profoundly pyramidal. Despite the omnipresent
stereotype of the super-rich Arab oil shaikh, the vast majority of people in
the region live at or below the poverty line, and only a handful of people
own and control considerable wealth derived from the oil industry, its sub-
sidiaries, and the consumption habits of the oil-producing elite. Economic
activity in the region as a whole consists of consumption more than production, and the exchange of goods and services between countries of the
region is limited, resulting in poor regional economic integration and
heightened dependency on Western goods and services (World Bank, 1996).

A close examination of the economies of the region quickly reveals a
glaring absence of industry and manufacturing in most countries, with the

exception of oil-related industries in the Gulf region, computer and military industries in Israel, and a variety of industrial activities in Turkey. By and large, the countries of the region consume much more than they produce. Agriculture is underdeveloped in Lebanon and Syria, countries that could technically produce significant amounts of agricultural goods; hence, most foodstuffs are imported and therefore too expensive for the average family to afford on a daily basis (World Bank, 1996).

Investments of oil revenues within the region are limited. The well-to-do oil-producing countries prefer to invest their money in Europe and North America (Makdisi, 1991), so there is little economic diversification or expansion of bases of production in the region. Commercial revenue from tourism has been limited due to a series of wars and continuing political tensions. The pronounced reliance on oil revenue has increased the region's economic vulnerability to external developments and decisions. Indeed, the countries of the Middle East are very dependent on economic and political decisions emanating from outside the region. Hence,

> their economic autonomy, defined as their ability to develop independently and/or to take policy actions without regard to developments and reactions elsewhere, is greatly constrained. . . . This economic dependence implies political dependence. (Makdisi, 1991:133)

As a result of the poor performance of the oil sector since the mid-1980s, countries throughout the region have felt the effects of falling oil prices in the form of decreasing remittance payments sent back to countries such as Syria, Lebanon, Egypt, and Jordan by migrant workers in the Gulf. Even before the fall in oil prices, poverty in the region was already pronounced: in 1980, approximately 44 percent of the population in Morocco and Egypt were living below the poverty line (Barakat, 1993); the situation has hardly improved much since then. During the last two decades, the Arab world has seen a

> progressive decline, or perhaps near elimination, of subsistence production, massive occupational shifts from agrarian to service . . . activities; a massive exodus of surplus rural labor to urban conglomerations [while at the same time witnessing] the rise of a new Arab bourgeoisie, a class of contractors, middlemen, brokers, agents of foreign corporations, and wheeler-dealers . . . typically engaged in nonproductive work. (Farsoun and Zacharia, 1995:73)

In the narrow space between the upper class (those few who possess and control great wealth) and the lower class (the millions of impoverished former peasants who are constantly streaming into the crowded urban areas of the region), we find the only productive sector of Middle Eastern society: a relatively small middle class composed primarily of small-scale commercial enterprises, self-employed merchants, repairmen, artisans, teachers, some white-collar professionals, and government employees. The members of this weak and vulnerable socioeconomic formation have discovered that remaining middle class requires a concerted family effort. Hence, the patrilineal kinship group that emerged as a strategic adaptation to desert conditions so long ago is once again the basic productive unit among the urban middle classes in the modern Middle East. As Farsoun notes,

> [R]ent income, small business income, and income from wages and other labor have emerged as key sources for an increasing number of multiple income families. . . . Most of these petty economic activities are traditional in style of organization and in the social relations of work, i.e., patriarchal and patronage. (1988:224)

■ KINSHIP, ETHNICITY, AND CLASS IN CONTEXT: STRATEGIES OR STRAITJACKETS?

Negatively affected by social and political transformations and economic restructuring at the local, regional, and international levels, particularly in the post–Cold War era, individuals in the Middle East have turned to their nuclear and extended families for support and mutual assistance. They have reactivated and emphasized traditional family structures, kinship networks, affiliations to ethnoreligious groups, and ties of patronage even as they have embraced the latest developments of modern technology, such as cellular telephones and the Internet. Consequently, the contemporary Middle East is a world of startling contradictions and ironic juxtapositions.

Halim Barakat notes that it is very difficult for observers to interpret socioeconomic developments in the region because "the contemporary Arab economic order is a peculiar cluster of different modes of production, all operating at once, which renders it simultaneously semi-feudal, semi-socialist, and semi-capitalist" (1993:77). The existence, side-by-side, of patrilineages and multinational corporations, rationalized bureaucracies and religious fundamentalism, modern nation-states and tribes, and traditional practices and cosmopolitan attitudes, which the political scientist Bassam Tibi refers to as "the simultaneity of the unsimultaneous" (1990:127), illuminates the extent to which the nation-state has failed in the contemporary Middle East while also revealing the degree to which the peoples of the region have compensated for this failure by adapting and revitalizing traditional sociocultural modes of survival.

> Unlike the imperial and the territorial dynastic states that were familiar in Middle Eastern history, the externally imposed new pattern of the nation state is defined as a national, not as a communal, polity. Its underlying

concept is sovereignty, which not only presupposes the capability of the
central power to establish itself over the entire territory, but also requires
established citizenship and a corresponding national identity and loyalty.
In varying degrees, all states of the Middle East lack this infrastructure.
. . . In most of the states of the Middle East, sovereignty is nominal. The
tribal ethnic and sectarian conflicts that the colonial powers exacerbated
did not end with the attainment of independence. The newly established
nation states have failed to cope with the social and economic problems
created by rapid development because they cannot provide the proper institutions to alleviate these problems. Because the nominal nation state
has not met the challenge, society has resorted to its pre-national ties as
a solution, thereby preserving the framework of the patron-client relationship. (Tibi, 1990:147–149)

Perhaps it is not too far-fetched to argue that extensive networks of
overlapping kin- and ethnic-based patron-client relationships linking those
in the government with those outside of it constitute the actual "glue" that
holds the Middle Eastern nation-state together. Rather than being sustained
by a sense of shared identity and a commonality of interests and goals, the
nation-state in the Middle East survives because of the public's considerable investment of time, energy, resources, and money in the cultivation
and maintenance of innumerable dyadic relationships with influential in-
cumbents of the governmental bureaucracy. Although patron-client relations "play an important role in facilitating the distribution of goods and
services among the population and harnessing popular support behind
leaders" (Khoury and Kostiner, 1990:18), ties of patronage are essentially
asymmetrical: perpetuating these relationships also perpetuates and reinforces unequal power structures in the starkly stratified societies of the
contemporary Middle East. Patron-client ties ensure that people are kept
"in their place": the rich and powerful maintain their dominant positions,
from which they have the advantage of becoming even more rich and powerful, and the less fortunate are kept in their subordinate position of dependency, remaining powerless over the decisionmaking processes and
larger forces that shape their lives.

Although resorting to primary identities and traditional relationships in
order to survive in a challenging world can be interpreted as logical and
strategic, it also entails costs and consequences that can have negative
repercussions on individuals and collectivities in the region. Relying on kin
rather than the state, affiliating with narrowly defined ethnoreligious groups
rather than forming broad-based coalitions and solidarities, and participating in patron-client exchanges of goods and services that perpetuate socioeconomic inequalities while consolidating age-old forms of political
domination impede economic, cultural, and political integration on the national and regional levels and discourage processes of empowerment, the
attainment of social justice, and the implementation of democratic reforms.
Farsoun enumerates the extent to which the popular cure for the problems

of the region only serves to sharpen the challenges facing Middle Eastern societies:

> Patriarchy, patronage, and the mercantilist spirit became intertwined with new capitalist social relations to produce a unique amalgam, which manifests itself in the behavior and values of contemporary Arab society. The resultant heterogeneous and fragmented class structure . . . produces fragmented and heterogeneous social views and social action. This fragmented urban mass . . . is less likely to engage in national or class organizations, and more likely to engage in social and political action based on kinship, neighborhood, ethnic, and religious organizations. (1988:229)

Turning inward to family, clan, or confessional sect is a valuable method of coping with a variety of daily challenges, but in so doing, the peoples of the region may lose sight of the common interests and goals that could unite them on bases of affiliation and organization that are much wider and potentially more effective than the narrow foundations provided by primary identities of blood and faith. Hence, Middle Eastern peoples may remain unaware of opportunities for large-scale cooperation and coordination to improve some of the difficult circumstances of their lives, particularly in areas such as environmental conservation and economic integration. Also, a public that has fragmented into separate, segmentary groups of kinsmen and co-religionists is facilitating its own control, exploitation, co-optation, and manipulation by repressive state governments. A divided population is much easier to rule, as the colonial powers so deftly proved.

The institutionalization of ethnic and religious identities for legal and administrative purposes, seen most clearly in states such as Lebanon and Israel, is a double-edged sword. Although official recognition of cultural heritage and religious laws may provide answers to individuals' psychological needs and communal organizational problems, it can also trap individuals in the vise of inflexible identity categories not of their own choice or making, thus limiting their personal options and opportunities while preventing the development of a more inclusive sense of overarching national loyalty and identity. The most extreme example of the triumph of the ethnic group over both the individual citizen and the overarching state is that of Lebanon, a state composed entirely of seventeen officially recognized ethnoconfessional groups, membership in which defines Lebanese individuals' rights and duties in the context of the state. The Lebanese sociologist Samir Khalaf notes that the tragedy of Lebanon lies in the fact that

> the very factors that account for much of the viability, resourcefulness, and integration of the Lebanese are also the factors that are responsible

for the erosion of civic ties and national loyalties. . . . In short, the factors that enable at the micro and communal level, disable at the macro and national level. This is, indeed, Lebanon's predicament. (1986:14)

Or, in the words of Ziad Rahbani, the bard of the Lebanese civil war whose captivating music and ironic lyrics allowed the Lebanese to look at themselves with jaundiced but compassionate eyes: yaa zaman at-ta'ifiyya! ta'ifiyya, ta'ifiyya / kheli eidek 'alal-howia; shidd 'alaiha qad ma fiik! ["Oh, these are confessional times, such confessional times! / so best keep your hand on your identity [card]; and grasp it for all that you are worth!"].

The song refers both to the wartime retreat into primary identities and the horrifying practice of political murders perpetrated by militiamen who routinely killed civilians on the basis of their religious confession, which is recorded on every Lebanese citizen's identity card.

Another danger posed by the current inward-looking tendencies and the resultant social and political fragmentation of Middle Eastern societies is that individuals and groups in this region will be unprepared to deal with the multifaceted challenges posed by media and market globalization. The Middle East, already economically marginalized and dependent in the current world economic system, may be at risk of being even further sidelined by the coming global restructuring of economic and political relationships. To succeed in the new global markets, Middle Eastern countries should be integrated into a regional economic framework, rather than being more closely linked to the West and its markets than they are to one another. In our opening story, Adnan and Khalid are clearly looking forward to regional economic integration as the condition of their own hoped-for personal success and familial happiness. But so long as mistrust, uncertainty, scarcity, poverty, and regional conflicts drive Middle Eastern peoples further into the traditional refuge of kinship, ethnicity, and patronage, the peoples of the region will be unlikely to achieve national and regional integration and the resulting levels of cooperation and coordination needed to meet so many of their interrelated economic, ecological, and political challenges.

The problems of the contemporary Middle East are not cultural ones centered on the resilience of traditional practices and primary identity categories in a modern world. Rather, the region's political and economic problems center not only upon the weaknesses and deficiencies of an imposed nation-state system that is not meeting people's basic needs, but just as important, on regional hostilities rooted in historical injustices and short-sighted policies initiated by Western powers from the colonial period until today. The Middle East is a region in which citizenship and its accompanying rights and duties have little meaning, but where

membership in kin-based groups is the individual's chief guarantee of security and access to resources—hence the necessity for strong group
maintenance mechanisms. Arab familism (or tribalism) must be viewed,
not as a cultural trait, but as a very ancient adaptive response to insecu-
rity; group cohesion is as important for survival under state oppression as
it is for survival in the absence of the state. (Sayigh, 1981:267)

■ CONCLUSION

Beginning with a lively conversation among American, Lebanese, and
Palestinian friends in an Arabic restaurant in California and ending with an
abstract observation about the deficiencies of the nation-state in its Middle
Eastern incarnation, this chapter has attempted to analyze and interpret
kinship, ethnicity, and social class in the contemporary Middle East by
showing how these sociocultural phenomena are related to ecological, eco-
nomical, psychological, administrative, and political realities and how they
interact with and shape one another. We have learned that social, political,
and cultural behaviors in the Middle East have historically been greatly affected by the limitations of a harsh natural environment in which economic
scarcity and pronounced political competition were constants, whereas
sustained relationships of mutual trust and permanent, broad-based, sociopolitical formations were not. Furthermore, we noted that the region underwent rapid economic and political changes in the nineteenth century,
permanently altering the traditional class structure and giving rise to sharp
socioeconomic inequalities that were exacerbated by colonialism and the
incorporation of the region into a competitive world capitalist economy.
These inequalities remain unresolved to this day.

Lacking assistance from the nation-states of the region, Middle Eastern peoples have turned to their primary identity categories and traditional organizational structures in an effort to make a living—and to make
a meaning—in the challenging world that confronts them. Although they
have succeeded in this effort, it has not been without costs and consequences. In the long run, resorting to kinship, ethnicity, and patronage
could have a negative effect on societies that may soon be forced to reconcile their segmented and fragmentary nature with increasing political
and economic pressures for integration, coordination, and cooperation
in the globalizing economy. There is much room for optimism, however.
The scholars we have cited, no less than Adnan and Khalid's conversation, show that the peoples of the Middle East are talented survivors possessing an exceptionally rich and resilient cultural heritage that
can be adapted to serve them in all political, economic, and temporal
environments.

■ BIBLIOGRAPHY

Abu-Lughod, Lila. 1986. *Veiled Sentiments*. Berkeley: University of California Press.

———. 1990 "Anthropology's Orient." Pp. 81–131 in Hisham Sharabi (ed.), *Theory, Politics and the Arab World*. London: Routledge.

Al-Akhras, Muhammad Safouh. 1976. *The Structure of the Arab Family*. Damascus: Ministry of Culture.

Anderson, Benedict. 1993. *Imagined Communities*. London: Verso.

Barakat, Halim. 1993. *The Arab World: Society, Culture, and State*. Berkeley: University of California Press.

Bosworth, C. E. 1982. "The Concept of Dhimma in Early Islam." Pp. 37–54 in Benjamin Braude and Bernard Lewis (eds.), *Christians and Jews in the Ottoman Empire*, Vol. 2: *The Arabic Speaking Lands*. New York: Holmes and Meier.

Cohen, Ronald. 1978. "Ethnicity: Problem and Focus in Anthropology." *Annual Review of Anthropology* 7:379–403.

Cunningham, Robert B., and Yasin K. Sarayrah. 1993. *Wasta: The Hidden Force in Middle Eastern Society*. Westport, Conn.: Praeger.

Farsoun, Samih K. 1988. "Class Structure and Social Change in the Arab World." Pp. 221–238 in Hisham Sharabi (ed.), *The Next Arab Decade: Alternative Futures*. Boulder, Colo.: Westview Press.

Farsoun, Samih K., and Christina Zacharia. 1995. "Class, Economic Change, and Political Liberalization in the Arab World." Pp. 261–282 in Rex Brynen, Bahgat Korany, and Paul Noble (eds.), *Political Liberalization and Democratization in the Arab World*, Vol. 1: *Theoretical Perspectives*. Boulder, Colo.: Lynne Rienner.

Fernea, Elizabeth Warnock. 1969. *Guests of the Sheikh*. New York: Doubleday.

Geertz, Clifford. 1973. *The Interpretation of Cultures*. New York: Basic Books.

Geertz, Clifford, Hildred Geertz, and Laurence Rosen. 1979. *Meaning and Order in Moroccan Society*. New York: Cambridge University Press.

Geertz, Hildred. 1979. "The Meaning of Family Ties." Pp. 315–391 in Clifford Geertz, Hildred Geertz, and Lawrence Rosen (eds.), *Meaning and Order in Moroccan Society*. New York: Cambridge University Press.

Harik, Iliya. 1972. "The Ethnic Revolution and Political Integration in the Middle East." *International Journal of Middle Eastern Studies* 3:303–323.

Huntington, Samuel. 1996. *The Clash of Civilizations and the Remaking of World Order*. New York: Simon and Schuster.

Ibn Khaldun. 1967. *The Muqaddimah: An Introduction to History*. Trans. Franz Rosenthal. Princeton: Bollingen Series, Princeton University Press.

Karpat, Kamal. 1982. "Millets and Nationality: The Roots of the Incongruity of Nation and State in the Post-Ottoman Era." Pp. 141–170 in Benjamin Braude and Bernard Lewis (eds.), *Christians and Jews in the Ottoman Empire*, Vol. 2: *The Arabic Speaking Lands*. New York: Holmes and Meier Publishers.

Keesing, Roger. 1975. *Kin Groups and Social Structure*. New York: Holt, Rinehart, and Winston.

Khalaf, Samir. 1986. *Lebanon's Predicament*. New York: Columbia University Press.

Khoury, Philip. 1983. *Urban Notables and Arab Nationalism: The Politics of Damascus, 1860–1920*. Cambridge: Cambridge University Press.

Khoury, Philip, and Joseph Kostiner. 1990. *Tribes and State Formation in the Middle East*. Berkeley: University of California Press.

Khuri, Fuad. 1970. "Parallel Cousin Marriage Reconsidered: A Middle Eastern Practice That Nullifies the Effects of Marriage on the Intensity of Family Relationships." *Man* 5:596–618.

Makdisi, Samir. 1991. "The Arab World and the World Economy: An Overview." Pp. 123–146 in Hala Esfandiari and A. L. Udovitch (eds.), *The Economic Dimensions of Middle Eastern History: Essays in Honor of Charles Issawi*. Princeton, N.J.: Darwin Press.

Makiya, Kanan. 1993. *Cruelty and Silence: War, Tyranny and Uprising in the Arab World*. New York: W. W. Norton.

Meeker, Michael. 1979. *Literature and Violence in North Arabia*. Cambridge: Cambridge University Press.

Mundy, Martha. 1995. *Domestic Government: Kinship, Community and Polity in North Yemen*. London: I. B. Tauris.

Murphy, Robert, and Leonard Kasdan. 1959. "The Structure of Parallel Cousin Marriage." *American Anthropologist* 61:17–29.

Nelson, Cynthia (ed.). 1973. *The Desert and the Sown: Nomads in the Wider Society*. Berkeley: Institute for International Studies, University of California.

Patai, Raphael. 1971. *Society, Culture, and Change in the Middle East*. Philadelphia: University of Pennsylvania Press.

Peteet, Julie M. 1991. *Gender in Crisis: Women and the Palestinian Resistance Movement*. New York: Columbia University Press.

Royce, Anya Peterson. 1982. *Ethnicity: Strategies of Diversity*. Bloomington: Indiana University Press.

Sayigh, Rosemary. 1981. "Roles and Functions of Arab Women: A Reappraisal." *Arab Studies Quarterly* 3:258–274.

———. 1994. *Too Many Enemies: The Palestinian Experience in Lebanon*. London: Zed Books.

Schneider, David M. 1968. *American Kinship: A Cultural Account*. Englewood Cliffs, N.J.: Prentice-Hall.

Schneider, Jane. 1971. "Of Vigilance and Virgins: Honor, Shame, and Access to Resources in Mediterranean Societies." *Ethnology* 10:1–24.

Sharabi, Hisham. 1990. *Theory, Politics and the Arab World: Critical Responses*. New York: Routledge.

Singerman, Diane. 1995. *Avenues of Participation: Family, Politics and Networks in Urban Quarters of Cairo*. Princeton: Princeton University Press.

Tibi, Bassam. 1990. "The Simultaneity of the Unsimultaneous: Old Tribes and Imposed Nation-States in the Modern Middle East." Pp. 127–152 in Philip S. Khoury and Joseph Kostiner (eds.), *Tribes and State Formation in the Middle East*. Berkeley: University of California Press.

World Bank. 1996. *Middle East and North Africa*. Washington, D.C.: World Bank.

▪ 10 ▪

The Role of Women

Lisa Taraki

Approaching the study of women in the contemporary Middle East is a difficult and challenging task. Decades of orientalist scholarship and popular and journalistic writing have left their indelible mark on the representation of the women of the Middle East. A priori assumptions, preconceptions, and stereotypes regarding Middle Eastern women abound, and generalizations about women in a region as internally diverse as the Middle East continue to predominate in current discourse. Scholars and others attempting an objective study of Middle Eastern women thus have a heavy intellectual legacy to contend with, and it is not surprising that much of the energy of scholars today is directed at challenging long-standing preconceptions and stereotypes concerning Middle Eastern women.

The more intractable of the impediments to understanding the reality of women living in the Middle East are lodged at the level of culture. What may be termed a "culturalist" bias presents a major challenge to those interested in the objective study of women's lives in the Middle East. Culturalists have approached issues such as women's labor force participation, status within the family, marriage patterns, fertility behavior, educational attainment, and political participation from within the broad framework of an unchanging and essential "Islamic" value system in the Middle East, which is assumed to hold a firm grip not only in matters of belief and attitude but also in practice and in the conduct of everyday life.

This chapter is based on the premise that, as in all societies, a multiplicity of social, economic, political, and cultural forces and factors have shaped the statuses, experiences, and living conditions of Middle Eastern women. We also stress the fact that just as an ahistorical conception of Islamic values as determinants of practice does not advance our understanding of complex historical processes, so too will the use of the unitary concept of the "Middle Eastern woman" obscure the rich diversity in women's lives across the Middle East. Important regional differences exist within the broad area covered in this book. In addition, within regions and countries, women's life chances, experiences, and status diverge and are shaped by a number of important factors, the most significant of which are class and place of residence (primarily urban or rural); ethnicity, refugee or non-refugee status, and religious affiliation also have important effects. Attributes pertaining to women as individuals, such as age, marital status, and number of children, also determine women's differential status, power, and access to opportunities within households, kinship groups, communities, and even the labor force.

■ THE MODERN NATION–STATE

We begin our discussion of the realities of women's lives with an examination of the relationship between women and the state in the modern Middle East. Recent scholarship has stressed the importance of understanding the relationship between women's status, rights, and position within society and state-building projects in the region (Kandiyoti, 1991c; Moghadam, 1993, 1995; Joseph, 1991; Molyneux, 1991). Whether states adopt positive strategies that effect changes in women's status or choose not to upset what is perceived to be the status quo has important implications for society in general and women in particular. The postcolonial state in the Middle East has had to face choices not only on the economic and political-strategic levels but also in relation to the kind of society it envisions for its citizens, both female and male.

As discussed in Chapters 3 and 4, the emergence of the modern nation-state in the Middle East in the twentieth century was accompanied in most instances by a modernizing agenda by which state elites attempted to transform or modify basic relations in society, including prevailing gender relations. A variety of legal-administrative measures, social policies, and a modernizing nationalist ideology were deployed to weaken the grip of primordial loyalties and affiliations, build the construct of *citizen* in the modern sense, and launch programs of social and economic development.

Education is perhaps the one domain where almost all Middle Eastern countries have achieved remarkable successes as a result of direct state policy. Although reforms in areas pertaining to personal status and political rights for women have been very uneven, the trend toward increasing educational levels for both women and men has been nearly universal. One measure of this success is that Arab states have made some of the greatest gains in women's education anywhere in the world, more than doubling women's literacy rate in the two decades from 1970 to 1990. These states also nearly doubled female primary and secondary enrollment, from 32 percent in 1970 to 60 percent in 1992 (UNDP, 1995:29).

In contrast, reforms of legislation and policies pertaining to women's rights within the family have been the subject of great debate and controversy all over the Middle East. Primarily because family legislation has historically been grounded in Islamic law (the Shari'ah), most state elites (with the exception of Turkey) have been very hesitant to introduce significant changes that would challenge prevailing gender hierarchies and the sexual division of labor that these laws took for granted.

Turkey was the first state in the Middle East to introduce legal and administrative reforms aimed at developing the economy and altering prevailing social relationships. The replacement of Islamic law with the Civil Code of 1926 and the enfranchisement of women in the early 1930s were measures undertaken by the new republic under Mustafa Kemal Atatürk (Father of the Turks) to change gender relations. Women became citizens of the republic, and the new laws banned polygamy and gave divorced women more rights. A modernizing nationalist ideology stressing women's equality with men was promoted by national ideologues and feminist writers and activists. This ideology has been viewed by some scholars as part of the arsenal of the new secular republic against the caliphate as an institution and as proof that Turkey was a democratic country, unlike the dictatorships in Germany and Italy with which it was allied (Kandiyoti, 1989:127).

In the decades that followed, Turkey continued on its trajectory as a modernizing and secular state, expanding civil and social liberties in the Constitutions of 1961 and 1982. However, the Civil Code, although more progressive than those in surrounding countries, still grants privileges to men in the areas of child custody, determination of place of residence, and personal freedom (Arat, 1996:29). Turkey is often singled out as the Muslim Middle Eastern country to have achieved the greatest levels of "modernization" and "Westernization." If progress is measured by basic indicators, however, we find that this leadership position is not warranted. Adult female illiteracy is still high (28 percent of women were illiterate in 1995, compared to only 8 percent of men) and reflects a significant gap between urban and rural areas. Labor force participation rates and school enrollment figures are also modest (Arat, 1996:30; UNDP, 1998:132).

The case of Israel is unique in the Middle East and presents some contradictions. The secular political elites of the immediate post-state period were in a most favorable position to build a modern nation-state in line with the democratic and secular principles they claimed formed the basis of the new society and polity. In addition to being culturally and politically hegemonic in the new state, they were not saddled by the heavy weight of entrenched traditional institutions (such as a powerful religious institution) and did not have to face traditional and conservative groups with a vested interest in maintaining the status quo. An examination of legislation affecting women, however, reveals that not all the opportunities were seized. The Women's Equal Rights Law of 1951, although abolishing blatant discrimination against women embodied in Ottoman law, was intended to protect the rights of women as mothers and wives, not as citizens; thus, a whole range of rights outside the domestic domain—such as in employment—were left out of the law (Berkovitch, 1996:20–21).

In the area of family status, Israel is much more in line with its neighbors in the region. It has not adopted secular laws, and the religious establishment exercises considerable influence. For instance, marriages can be contracted and dissolved only in religious courts. Women are not allowed to become judges in the orthodox rabbinical state courts, and as a rule, their evidence is not accepted, especially if there are male witnesses (Yuval-Davis, 1989:105). The army is another institution in which women do not enjoy equal opportunities with men. At least 70 percent of women in the military are trained to occupy traditional women's roles; furthermore, despite the mandatory recruitment law, only 65 percent of Jewish Israeli women serve in the army. The rest either opt out on religious grounds or fall under various categories of women exempted from military service (Sharoni, 1995:45–47; see also Yuval-Davis, 1982; Swirski and Safir, 1991).

Iran under Reza Shah was also among the first of the Middle Eastern states to articulate a modernizing agenda including the emancipation of women. However, unlike the Turkish republic, which was avowedly secular, the Iranian state in the early decades of this century was more mindful of powerful religious institutions, and thus the pace and nature of the changes were more modest. The major reforms and developments affecting women were introduced in the 1960s. Women were enfranchised in 1962, and significant gains in women's education were made during the 1960s and 1970s. In 1967 the new Family Protection Act gave women expanded rights within marriage and the family. In the early years of the Islamic Republic, however, several of these reforms were revoked, and an ideology stressing women's domesticity was articulated and encouraged.

Iran's situation calls into question some of the prevailing assumptions about the relationship between Islam and women's status. Although "Islamic," contemporary Iran has reconsidered certain postrevolutionary policies concerning women's rights within the family and the public domain. For example, although the Family Protection Act of 1967 was revoked after the revolution and replaced by legislation dating back to the 1930s, eventually the government responded to the agitation of Islamist women activists and revised the law to grant women more rights. Under legislation passed in 1992, for instance, divorced women are granted half of the wealth accumulated during the marital union, as well as wages for housework performed during the marriage (Hoodfar, 1995:124). Postrevolutionary population policy is another example. After dismantling family planning centers after the revolution, within a few years the state was actively reconsidering its pro-natalist policy. In 1989, the state ratified a new birth control policy and launched a national campaign to convince the population to accept and practice family planning (Hoodfar, 1995:108–109). Policies in education provide a further illustration. After initially setting a maximum limit for female university applicants in a wide range of scientific and professional fields, most of the quotas were removed in 1989 (Moghadam, 1993.187).

Most of the Arab states began to articulate and implement their social agendas during the second part of this century, in the aftermath of achieving national independence and following the consolidation of a new state elite. As in the case of Turkey and Iran, state elites introduced reforms in family law, encouraged women's education, and in some cases sought an increased female presence in the state bureaucracy and the labor force. Egypt, Iraq, Tunisia, and the People's Democratic Republic of Yemen (1967–1987) stand out as the pioneers, with the last instituting the most far-reaching reforms. Exceptions to this trend include Saudi Arabia and some of the Gulf states, where the pace of reforms has been very slow.

Of the three countries of the Arab Maghreb Union emerging as independent states following colonial rule (Tunisia, Algeria, and Morocco), Tunisia was the leader in introducing significant changes. The Personal Status Code of 1956, amended in 1964, 1966, and 1981, is the most progressive in the Arab world, outlawing polygamy and granting expanded rights to divorced women; labor legislation enacted in 1966 provides some protection for working mothers (Galal, 1995:63–64). In Algeria, however, reform came much later and was more modest in its content. Although the state abolished all colonial legislation pertaining to family matters in 1975, it was not until 1984, after considerable agitation by Algerian women, that a new family code was finally enacted. This code, like those in all Arab countries, was enacted within the framework of Shari'ah and offered only limited reforms in marriage, divorce, and custody (Lazreg, 1994:150–157; Hijab, 1988:26–29). Morocco has perhaps been the slowest country in the Arab Maghreb Union to respond to pressures for change in matters of family law. New legislation was enacted in 1957–1958 and granted women some rights in the matter of divorce, but it was not far-reaching and has remained virtually unchanged during more than four decades (Mir-Hosseini, 1991).

Recent research on the integration of women into the nation-state in the Middle East through reforms at the state level recognizes the limits of state-sponsored policies and legislation in bringing about significant changes in social relations in general and gender relations in particular. It may be argued that, despite the adoption of policies drawing women into the labor force and increasing women's education in several countries, wide gaps continue to exist between men and women in terms of labor force participation, educational attainment, and access to resources and opportunities.

This brings us to the crucial issue of the uneven manner in which state policies and reforms affect women. If we examine women's education and employment, we find that rising educational levels for women have generally been accompanied by an increase in the participation of women in the nonagricultural labor force, primarily in the service sector. Because most service jobs are concentrated in urban areas, women's increased participation in such work indicates that educational gains for women have been greater in urban areas and have prepared women to join occupations unrelated to the agrarian economy. These observations underline the fact that recent decades have witnessed a tremendous expansion of urban centers and an increasing differentiation between the city and the countryside. The consolidation of an urban middle class throughout the Middle East has had as an important component the increased visibility of women in the educational system, the labor force, and the public domain in general. It is these women who have been the main beneficiaries of state policies in education, labor, and other public services, which points to the fact that urban middle-class (and upper-class) women have been most positively affected by state policies. Women marginalized in the state modernization project, mainly peasant and poor urban women, live different realities and have not been able to benefit from state reforms on a wide scale.

■ ECONOMIC ACTIVITY

As Valentine M. Moghadam pointed out in Chapter 8, measuring the economic activity of the population in the Middle East, as in many other Third World countries, is fraught with difficulties. Women's economic activity is particularly elusive, and it is widely acknowledged that national labor force figures and other statistics do not represent the true magnitude of women's role in the economy. The reasons for this situation are many. First, women's unpaid domestic labor is unregistered and unquantified; the long hours and hard work that women expend in raising children and in household management are not reflected in national statistics. Second, the contribution of women to the household economy in the form of provision of home-use items is also largely unrecorded. This is due both to biases in data collection systems and also to the perceptions of respondents in national surveys concerning economic activity. (For instance, a woman who produces food and sews clothing for her family as an economizing measure will not likely be perceived by herself or a male household member to be economically active.) Third, and most important, women's economic activity in the informal sector is largely unmeasured in standard labor force statistics. This sector is an important component of the economy throughout the Middle East and includes a wide array of activities, many of them carried out by women, either within the household or on the streets and workplaces in the public sphere.

Due to the inadequacy of data on economic activity in the Middle East, it is indeed difficult to gain an accurate understanding of the magnitude of women's participation in the national economies of the region. Although small-scale studies of women's informal-sector activities in several countries have enriched our knowledge of the various strategies that households and women within them deploy to deal with economic hardship, we still have only formal labor force statistics—with all their weaknesses—as the most reliable cross-national indicators of women's economic activity.

Even though the participation of women in the formal labor force in the Middle East is still small compared to that in other world regions, it has been steadily increasing since the 1960s (Moghadam, 1993:31). Factors such as the tremendous expansion of the state bureaucracy and related services (especially in education, health, and social services), economic development, falling fertility levels, the rising age at first marriage, rapid urbanization, increased educational levels for women, and male labor migration from the poor to the oil-rich countries of the Gulf all played a part in encouraging the increase in rates of female employment. How these dimensions have come together in a given national setting has varied, however, and the outcomes in terms of participation levels have also been very different.

Women's share of the adult labor force in the Middle East in 1995 ranged from less than 15 percent in Oman, Qatar, Saudi Arabia, and the United Arab Emirates to more than 30 percent in Israel, Kuwait, Morocco, Tunisia, and Turkey (UNDP, 1998:164–165).

In terms of the distribution of the female labor force by occupation, the highest percentages are found in the public service sector, a pattern found the world over, with high percentages in agriculture found only in Egypt (41 percent), Morocco (32.5 percent), Syria (44 percent), and Turkey (72 percent). As Moghadam has pointed out, however, in some countries women in agriculture are not counted as part of the labor force, which explains the low figures for this sector of economic activity (Moghadam, 1993:45, 50–51). Only in Morocco and Tunisia do we find more women in industry than in services (Moghadam, 1993:45). Furthermore, with the exception of Turkey and Israel and to a lesser extent Tunisia, Kuwait, and Qatar, the female labor force tends to be concentrated among those aged fifteen to twenty-nine (Moghadam, 1993:43).

What do these figures tell us about working women in the Middle East? First, the high concentration of women in public services (occupations such as teaching and nursing) reinforces occupational stereotyping (Moghadam, 1993:50), by which certain occupations become identified as women's occupations. Second, women from well-off families are most likely to be formally employed, especially in the Gulf states (Moghadam, 1993:51). Other relevant conditions include the compatibility of some occupations (particularly teaching) with women's reproductive roles as mothers and domestic caregivers and the fact that most women in these occupations work in the public sector, where working women's rights (such as paid maternity leave) are generally better protected than in the private sector.

The concentration of younger women in the formal labor force is another reflection of the organic link between women's reproductive and productive activities. We can assume that most women in this age group are either single or newly married with few children and are therefore more free to take on employment outside the home. Furthermore, based on educational data for the region, these women also have the highest rates of educational achievement. Indeed, in the Middle East, employment in the formal nonagricultural labor force is positively linked to education (Moghadam, 1993:18).

An important determinant of women's formal labor force participation is the degree of public investment in working women with children, both in the provision of child care services and in the enactment and enforcement of labor laws protecting these women's rights. Three demographic characteristics of the region are relevant in this regard: first, a substantial proportion of the female population is in the reproductive age group; second, the great majority of women is married; and third, fertility rates are high (Zurayk and Saadeh, 1995:38). These attributes, which Huda Zurayk and Fadia Saadeh cite with respect to the Arab world, apply to Iran and Turkey as well; however, the demographic profile is different in Israel.

The implication of these demographic attributes is that some of the impediments to women's labor force participation could be attenuated by increased public and private investment in child care facilities for working women and, more important, by the enactment and enforcement of labor laws favorable to working women with children. As long as women's reproductive tasks are not socially supported and are considered private burdens, many women will not be encouraged to join the paid labor force. A further factor inhibiting women's employment is the relatively high cost of those child care facilities that do exist (whether public or private) as compared with the low wages that women command in the market, thus making the option of employment outside the home unattractive to women and their families.

Another consideration that influences women's formal labor force participation is located at the level of the family and household. Seteney Shami (1990) has proposed that women's work should be viewed as part of the strategies deployed by families and households for adapting to the circumstances of their class. In this view, families of modest means diffuse economic risk by diversifying the employment of family members: men and boys enter the more remunerative activities due to their higher education levels, whereas women tend to enter the informal sector or become the mainstay of subsistence agriculture. Thus, women perform activities related to family survival while men enter areas of the economy leading to family mobility. In those cases where women seem to be offered the opportunity for mobility, women do participate in the formal labor force and become a further economic asset to the family (Shami, 1990:xiv–xv).

It has become clear that a number of factors come together to condition and determine the extent and nature of women's economic activity in the Middle East. The lack of public support for women's employment, demographic factors such as those cited above, and issues having to do with the structure of the labor market and the household together are necessary to explain the low labor force participation of women.

What becomes of the widely held view that conservative attitudes deriving from an Islamic worldview constitute the major impediment to women's work in the public domain? Although it would be incorrect to dismiss the relevance of conservative attitudes—whether derived from a religious ethos or not—it is more reasonable to assume that a host of factors having to do with the structure of the economy, the educational system, population characteristics, and state policies are equally, if not more, influential in determining the magnitude and distribution of women in the labor force. It is true that rationales and justifications for women's exclusion from employment are often part of popular idiom and are couched in religious terms, but it is important to recognize how widely they are overlooked or disregarded in practice in the Middle East. Any person familiar with urban life in the Middle East will be struck by the numbers of women engaged in some kind of employment outside the home, whether they are women bosses (*mu'allimat*) on Cairo's streets, or female vegetable peddlers in the markets of Arab Jerusalem, or the armies of young women coming out of sewing workshops at the end of a day's work in Istanbul.

■ FAMILY AND KINSHIP

The preceding discussion has highlighted some features of Middle Eastern society relevant not only to the economic activity of women but also to dynamics within the family. We now examine some of the major features of familial gender relations.

It may be useful to begin our examination of the family with the concept of patriarchy, which in broad terms refers to a system that privileges males and elders and justifies this privilege in kinship terms (Joseph, 1994:2). The anthropologist Deniz Kandiyoti finds the clearest instances of "classic patriarchy" in North Africa, the Muslim Middle East, and southern and eastern Asia. Under this system, girls marry young into households headed by their husbands' fathers and are subordinate there to all men and to the more senior women, especially their mothers-in-law. Women frequently do not inherit from their fathers, although their access to resources and control over the *mahr* (bride price) and property can be highly variable (Kandiyoti, 1991b:31–32).

Patriarchy, representing a gender and age hierarchy based on the household as a productive unit, has been seriously challenged in recent decades by social transformations sweeping the regions in which it prevails. Wage labor opportunities outside the household (mostly for young men but also for a growing segment of urban women), the breakup of the extended family, the increasing age of marriage for both women and men, the rise in educational levels, and rural-to-urban migration, among other factors, have begun to erode some of the foundations of this system.

Households headed by women due to divorce or death of the husband, those in which men are away for extended periods for work, or situations in which women earn wages outside the home all present problems for patriarchy. The economic independence of sons and their move away from the natal household after marriage also challenge gender and age hierarchies, both in the case of the sons vis-à-vis their fathers and in the case of the sons' wives in relation to their mothers-in-law.

It is important to note, however, that certain circumstances can mitigate against the breakdown of patriarchy and in some cases may actually strengthen it. Let us take the example of the persistence in functional terms of the extended family household, despite the setting up of nuclear family households by married sons. Although this arrangement, which is an adaptation to the absence of social security and other state assistance to the elderly, may give sons authority over their fathers, it may also solidify the position of elder working sons vis-à-vis their sisters and brothers still at home, thus preserving gender and age hierarchies in another form. In the same vein, although the sons' wives may be liberated from the direct and daily control of domineering mothers-in-law, they may be dependent upon them if they go out to work. In the absence of adequate public facilities, women often rely on their mothers-in-law for child care, and may have to put up with the burdens—and interference in their children's upbringing— that this arrangement entails.

The preceding discussion has touched upon the issue of women's position within the household, and it is to this that we now turn. As with labor force participation, a number of factors help determine women's position—and particularly their authority—within the household. Age and marital status are two important determinants of women's position; a young wife is decidedly at a disadvantage compared to an older one, especially a mother-in-law, and unmarried women generally have less authority than married ones. However, unmarried women with access to financial resources such as income from property or employment may wield considerable authority over members of the household, including their parents and younger siblings. Divorced women, unless they have adequate resources, are among the more vulnerable, and may be almost totally dependent on their fathers and brothers in financial terms, even if they do not live with them in the same household.

The number of children—especially sons—a woman bears is another determinant of her status in the household. This feature of Middle Eastern family life has often been highlighted in accounts of the region and requires an explanation. Rather than understanding the preference for male children as a timeless cultural value derived from some primordial valuation of male offspring by Middle Easterners, it is more useful to view it as essential to the survival of the informal system of social security in Middle Eastern societies. In most societies in the Middle East, male children not only contribute their labor or income for the welfare of the household but also are a source of old-age security for their parents and any unmarried sisters in the absence of state-supported pensions and other compensations for the elderly and retired. For women, who are likely to be widowed earlier than men, the presence of sons is not so much a source of status—although it is expressed as such in the cultural idiom—but a form of security for which no real alternatives yet exist in the public sector.

Another important determinant of status is access to or control over economic resources. Literature on the Middle East often mentions that women, although entitled by law to a share of their fathers' estates (albeit unequal to that of their brothers), are routinely deprived of the right to inherit this property. Although it is undoubtedly true that Middle Eastern women continue to be disinherited in this sense—often with their own "consent"—it is important to understand the social and cultural logic behind what appears to be a flagrant violation of basic rights.

The material foundation of classic patriarchy, as discussed earlier, is the patrilocally extended household (Kandiyoti, 1991b:31). Within it, older males are regarded as having responsibility for the economic welfare of all members of the family, including women marrying into the household. Daughters marrying out become members of their husbands' households and are considered part of their responsibility. However, married women maintain a special relationship with their brothers, upon whose support they can count when facing marital problems, financial distress, or in the extreme case, divorce or abandonment. Clearly, this system rests on the assumption of female dependence on men, whether these men are husbands or brothers. Denial of inheritance to women is affirmation of this fact and is based on the widely acknowledged belief that men require the inherited property to meet the family obligations women are not expected to shoulder.

As patriarchy as a system erodes due to the social transformations mentioned earlier, challenges also begin to face the inheritance system. Working women who contribute their incomes to family welfare or self-supporting single women are realities with which this system increasingly has to deal. However, even within the sexual division of labor assumed by the inheritance system, it has not always been the case that all women have not been granted or claimed their inheritance.

Research findings from Palestine may be indicative of wider patterns. Anthropologist Annelies Moors has shown, for instance, that the crucial factors determining whether Palestinian women in the Nablus region receive or claim their share of inheritance are marital status, social class, and position in the family. Brotherless daughters and their widowed mothers show the most interest in claiming their shares; daughters from wealthy families are also in a better position to inherit some of the family property. In the case of the majority, that is, married women from families of modest means who do have brothers, the situation is different. Here, sisters refrain from claiming their share in favor of their brothers as part of an optimizing strategy: being ultimately dependent on their kin for their socioeconomic security, it makes sense for women to relinquish their inheritance in order to highlight their kin's obligations toward them (Moors, 1996:69–84).

The preceding discussion has shown that within the patriarchal family structure, denial of inheritance to women is not tantamount to a denial of all their rights to family resources. However, it must be realized, as Moors has pointed out, that women's dependence on men, which is the basis of this system as discussed earlier, may be increasingly becoming shaky; as the conjugal (husband-wife) tie becomes more important (Moors, 1996:83) and as the extended family becomes more fragmented, women will be left without the "protections" that the inheritance system entailed for them, and their vulnerability may increase.

■ **VALUES AND NORMS**

The idea that traditional norms and values surrounding women and the family dictate current social practices and serve to limit women's freedom and opportunities has become part of the commonsense understanding of gender relations in the Middle East. Many scholarly and popular works by Westerners and Middle Easterners alike routinely attribute women's low labor force participation or educational achievement, for example, to the hold of traditional conceptions of family honor and conduct appropriate to women.

It may be useful to take note of two features of explanations of social practices and behavior that refer to "tradition." First, such explanations deal almost exclusively with non-Western societies. The assumption appears to be that non-Western and particularly Islamic Middle Eastern societies are still under the grip of immutable traditional value systems. The almost mandatory prefacing of many examinations of women's current realities by a discussion of the traditional context is an outstanding example of this approach. It would indeed be very strange to see a discussion of French, Swedish, or North American women's lives framed similarly, implying that we could not hope to understand their current realities before first setting out the *traditional* context of gender relations. Second, the reference to traditional norms and values is almost invariably produced when matters concerning gender relations, roles, and identities are at issue.

How can we understand social practices and behavioral patterns that appear on the face of it to be dictated by traditional values and norms? To address this question, we must first recognize that norms and values are historical constructs above all, that in no society are they "handed down" from generation to generation without undergoing redefinition and reformulation. This process of transformation is conditioned by changing social realities and reflects the struggle between different social groups and collectivities in pursuit of their particular and common interests.

A prime example is the presumably timeless "honor code" believed to regulate women's conduct in Muslim Middle Eastern societies. An examination of social practices and values in these societies reveals that the meaning of *honor* has changed considerably over the past decades, as has what constitutes the violation of the honor code. Practices and conduct that may have been viewed as a grave breach of the honor code decades ago do not produce similar reactions today. Segregation of men and women, which is often regarded as an underpinning of the system of honor, is one example of a practice that has been seriously undermined if not swept away by the major social transformations taking place in the region. Although it is still a subject of debate among contending social forces, hundreds of thousands of Middle Eastern women today work and study in mixed-sex institutions without social censure or opprobrium. Even Islamists, interestingly, have reinterpreted supposedly fixed honor codes such as those forbidding the mixing of men and women by adjusting them to the exigencies of modern life, as in women's participation in the labor force or study at universities. Such accommodation to modern society by Islamists is the norm rather than the exception today, as we have tried to show in the discussion of Iran above.[1]

As noted earlier, and as in any society, contending social and political forces as well as individuals are constantly negotiating the definition and boundaries of honor. The great diversity in women's dress in the Middle East today can be regarded as a reflection of this silent struggle. Large

Middle Eastern women and girls
are as varied in appearance as females anywhere in the world

Photo 10.1

Photo 10.2

Photo 10.3

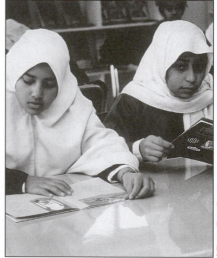

Photo 10.4

numbers of urban women have adopted various versions or degrees of "Islamic" dress; there are equal numbers dressing in variations on international styles. All of these women are mindful of proper and improper ways of dressing but are by their choices defining the different—and differing— codes of modesty and decorum. We thus witness the almost daily setting of new standards and norms by which women are continually negotiating and stretching the boundaries of the supposedly immutable codes of honor.

We must also consider the possibility that certain values and norms are group- or class-specific and not generalizable at the level of whole societies, let alone the region. How the process of generalization takes place is itself a subject for investigation since a host of factors come into play in the designation of values and norms as universal. For instance—and contrary to the impression given in much of the Western popular press— women's seclusion in the domestic sphere has not been the practice for the majority of women in Middle Eastern societies, whether in rural or urban areas. One of the main requirements for seclusion is the freedom from labor in the field, the neighborhood, or other public spaces; this is not an option for many women, even if it is viewed as preferable.

Judith Tucker's historical research in Egypt and Palestine, for example, has shown that in the nineteenth century in Cairo and Nablus, adherence to the modesty code was tempered by class: among the upper class, notions of women's honor were important, and women were confined to the harem, but for the poor, women were very much part of a public work life that precluded all but the most formal adherence to the ideal of female seclusion (Tucker, 1993:205). Agricultural communities could afford the seclusion of women even less. The pioneering research of Richard Antoun in a Jordanian village in the 1960s showed that peasant women's labor was crucial to the survival of dry-cereal farming in the village. This entailed women's presence in public space alongside men of their own families as well as unrelated men. Thus the agricultural regime and the sexual division of labor whereby women played an important part in agriculture were among the major factors that undermined adherence to the modesty code, even though it was upheld as an ideal in local discourse (Antoun, 1968:681–682).

■ POLITICS

Middle Eastern women's organized participation in the political process dates to the early years of the twentieth century and was linked from the start with two major overlapping currents sweeping the region, the drive for modernization and social reform and the nationalist struggle for independence from colonial domination.

The "woman question" has been an important component of the ideologies of reformist and nationalist currents throughout the Middle East.

The first organized women's movements with a feminist agenda took shape in Turkey, Iran, and Egypt in the first decade of the twentieth century. Their agenda included demands for education and work opportunities and for reform of legislation governing matters such as marriage, divorce, child custody, and inheritance (Graham-Brown, 1993:2). The first women's organizations were established in Turkey and Iran in the first decade of the twentieth century (Kandiyoti, 1991a:29; Afary, 1989:66), followed by the rapid expansion of women's organizations all over the Middle East.

It is important to note that the founders and, to a large extent, the members of the earlier women's organizations were drawn from the upper and middle classes; frequently they were wives, daughters, and sisters of men prominent in public life. Many of these women were also engaged in charitable work in their societies, a pursuit consistent with their status and privilege and part of a pattern found the world over. Despite these commonalities, women's participation in politics in the Middle East has not been restricted to activism within the framework of women's organizations agitating on women's issues. A rich diversity in forms and modes of women's participation exists; it is to this that we now turn.

Several different forms and modes of women's participation in politics can be identified in the Middle East. The first is women's participation as fighters and support staff in national liberation struggles or revolutionary movements, notably in the Algerian war of independence, the Palestinian resistance, and the Iranian revolution. The second mode of women's political activism is that of women forming "arms" or "branches" of political parties and fronts. Third, women participate as members of political parties and formations. Fourth, women have been active also in women's organizations created or sponsored by ruling parties and states, such as women's federations in many Arab countries and Iran. The fifth mode of women's political activism is in independent (but not necessarily apolitical) organizations whose agendas are greatly variable in terms of the nature and content of their activism on gender issues and causes. Although organizations such as these, in the form of charitable societies and the like, have existed in the Middle East for several decades, we focus on the new, more gender-conscious organizations of the 1980s and 1990s. Finally, the sixth mode of women's participation in politics is in the form of participation in the electoral process as voters and candidates and in responsible positions in governments.

This typology of modes of women's participation in politics must be treated with caution, however, since the categories are not exclusive, and considerable overlap between them may be found. For example, many Palestinian women participated in military and paramilitary activity within the framework of the Palestinian resistance in the 1970s, while at the same time being members of political parties *and* affiliated with the women's organizations of those parties.

☐ National Liberation and Revolutionary Movements

The best-documented cases of women's participation in national liberation struggles and popular revolutions are those of Algeria, Iran, and Palestine.[2] Despite many similarities in these and other cases, it is very difficult to generalize about the role and status of women in such struggles. Algeria's and Iran's struggles were carried out on national soil, but Algeria's was an armed struggle, whereas the revolution in Iran—and women's participation in it—was not of a military nature. (It must be noted, as Hammed Shahidian [1997] points out, that Iranian women *were* active in guerrilla organizations—primarily the People's Mujahidin Organization of Iran and the Organization of People's Fida'i Guerrillas—under the shah's rule in the 1970s, and also after the revolution and until the mid-1980s.)

In Palestine, most of the guerrilla activity was based outside Palestine in the 1970s, whereas inside, in the Occupied Territories, military struggle was crushed and did not have a popular mass base as in Algeria. Furthermore, Palestinians' struggle during the uprising of the late 1980s and early 1990s had mass support but was largely nonmilitary.

What is common to each of these examples is that women of all social classes, both urban and rural, participated in the struggles, although the balance was always in favor of women of more modest means. In addition, women did not have decisionmaking or frontline military positions in any of these revolutionary movements. Most of the tasks assigned to women were of a support nature. Even in Algeria, where women played an important and crucial role in the liberation war, including in the military arm of the National Liberation Front (FLN), paramilitary acts of destruction of civilian targets involved barely 2 percent (or sixty-five) of the women who joined the movement (Lazreg, 1994:124).

☐ Women's "Front" Organizations

The creation of women's "front" organizations or branches by parties and movements in order to mobilize women for the larger national cause is a well-known pattern in the Middle East. The relationship between the Sudanese Communist Party and the Sudanese Women's Union is one example; in the Palestinian case, the women's organizations attached to the various political parties and fronts in the Occupied Territories and the diaspora are another.[3] From Iran comes a further example of women's organizations affiliated to political movements before and during the revolution.

In general, women's organizations affiliated with political parties have had little autonomy; this has meant, in the majority of cases, that feminist concerns have been subordinated to larger national ones and that women's energies have not been primarily concentrated upon representing and fighting for the interests of women as women. This situation is not surprising, however, especially in the case of parties engaged in popular struggles for independence, such as in the Palestinian case.

☐ Political Parties

Not much research exists on women's participation in political parties. A general familiarity with the major political parties in the region shows, however, that women have not achieved leadership positions in either ruling or opposition parties across the Middle East. The lone exceptions are Israel and Turkey, where Golda Meir in the early 1970s and Tansu Çiller in the 1990s led political parties and headed their countries' governments. Political parties have thus been true bastions of male privilege and exclusivity in the Middle East, with little difference between liberal or leftist and more conservative right-wing parties.

One factor that accounts for the paucity of information on women's— or men's—participation in political parties is that the democratic process, whereby contending parties compete for constituencies, is still not the norm in many countries of the Middle East. Political parties are thus quite restricted in size, since they are robbed of their raison d'être, which is to represent their constituencies' interests in a political contest for power.

☐ "Establishment" Women's Organizations

Many feminists have argued that women's organizations in the Middle East have not developed autonomously, that is, their agendas and activism have been dictated either by political parties or, more important, by the state. A review of the major women's organizations in the various countries of the Middle East bears out this observation. Historically, we have shown how the first women's organizations arose out of the nationalist and reformist movements of the early twentieth century and articulated demands and goals consistent with the agendas of the modernizing elements within these movements.

In the decades following the establishment of the first women's organizations, we see that with few exceptions, women's organizing energies were harnessed by the state and in some cases made part of its state-building project. In Iraq, for example, the ruling Ba'th Party created the General

Federation of Iraqi Women in 1968 as a female arm of the party, with the aim of drawing women into the state and as part of its drive toward the re-socialization and mobilization of women. The federation has been funded by the state, and leadership positions are held by party members (Joseph, 1991:182). Iran is another case of a centralizing state attempting to contain and control women's organizing energies. In the 1960s, under Mohammad Reza Shah, the state began to solidify its control over women's organizations, ending in the establishment of the influential Women's Organization of Iran, with significant power and resources at its disposal (Najmabadi, 1991:60–61). Algeria is a further example. After independence, the ruling National Liberation Front set up the National Union of Algerian Women to represent the women of Algeria.

The drive to set up national women's organizations was given a great boost by the UN Decade for Women launched in 1975. Governments were thereafter required to send delegates to the successive world conferences on women and the growing number of international and regional conferences organized to discuss women's issues. The question, therefore, of how the country and its progress in achieving women's rights was to be represented acquired great importance. Many Middle Eastern countries were represented at the official level by their women's federations, which were by and large state-controlled. Forums for nongovernmental organizations were made available at the world conferences, however, and provided an opportunity for women in independent organizations to voice their concerns, which at times conflicted with the official line presented by the official delegations.

☐ Independent Women's Organizations

The 1980s and 1990s have witnessed the emergence of a new and diverse body of independent and semi-independent women's organizations in the Middle East. Although many are not overtly political in the conventional sense of the term and most do not have a grassroots constituency, all may be viewed as engaged in gender politics of one kind or another. The growth of these organizations (particularly in Egypt, Tunisia, Morocco, Jordan, Palestine, and Lebanon) is part of a wider development at the level of civil society in the Middle East, represented by the proliferation of nongovernmental organizations of various sorts. Human rights groups, development and social policy institutes, research centers, and legal assistance services are just some examples.

The new women's organizations can be distinguished from the more politicized women's "front" organizations, state-controlled women's federations, and traditional charitable organizations by their membership profile, their social and political agenda, and the range of their contacts within and outside the region. Founded and staffed mainly by middle-class professional women (such as lawyers, physicians, and academics), these organizations are attempting to formulate a feminist agenda around such issues as political and legal reform, social policy, reproductive health and population policy, domestic violence, and other issues of concern to women. Their members also have high visibility in international and regional forums convened to discuss such issues. These organizations have thus been vying with the official women's federations of their countries for attention in the national and international arenas and have been successful due to their familiarity with the international women's discourse and their considerable professional skills. The social impact of these organizations at home, however, remains limited, since many do not have access to the sources of power in society and are largely removed from the mass of women in their own societies.

☐ Women in the Electoral Process and in Government

Accurate data on women's participation in the electoral process are patchy. We do know that in most countries, women's participation in national and local elections is moderate to substantial (with the exception, of course, of those countries that do not have electoral processes or where women are not enfranchised).

Women's representation in state structures, primarily parliaments and governments, however, is quite limited. There are fourteen women among Israel's 120 members of the 1999 Knesset, including one who is a Palestinian citizen of Israel. Among parliaments in the Arab states, the highest percentages of female representation in parliament are found in Iraq (10.8 percent), Sudan (8.2 percent), Syria (8 percent), Algeria (7 percent), and Tunisia (6.7 percent). In Iran, Lebanon, and Jordan about 3 percent of representatives are women, but the numbers are still lower in Egypt (2.2 percent) and Turkey (1.8 percent) (UNDP, 1995:60–62; UNDP, 1996:141–142).

Women's presence at the ministerial and subministerial levels is even less significant. Figures for 1995 show no women at the ministerial level in the Gulf states, Saudi Arabia, Libya, Sudan, Morocco, Iraq, Lebanon, Algeria, and Iran; in other countries, Israel has the highest percentage (13 percent), followed by Syria at 6.8 percent and Jordan at 3.2 percent. The situation at the subministerial level is slightly better, where several countries, including some Gulf states, show some women's representation (UNDP, 1996:156–157).

These figures must be viewed in context, however. In the United States, only 10.4 percent of representatives are women, and in Japan barely 7 percent of parliamentary seats are occupied by women. This is in

Photo 10.5   Palestinian Samiha Khalil, head of the charitable society In'ash Al-Usra, ran against Yasser Arafat in the 1996 presidential election.

sharp contrast to world pioneers in the field: Norway (39.4 percent) and Finland (33.5 percent) (UNDP, 1995:60–62; UNDP, 1996:141–142).

☐ Islamist Women's Activism

Feminist activism in the Middle East has had an uneasy relationship with Islam since the beginning of this century. The engagement with Islam could not be avoided in societies where many of the laws affecting women's personal status were based upon the Shari'ah and where state elites were not keen on antagonizing the religious establishment or adopting positions that might offend what were perceived to be prevailing religious sensibilities. From the very beginning, then, feminists—as well as state institutions—sought to show that Islam was not opposed to women's education, enfranchisement, participation in the public domain, and work outside the home. However, even though Islam may have been invoked to justify women's emancipation, most feminists have been secular in their pursuits, lifestyles, and political convictions.

The growth of Islamist forces throughout the Middle East has posed a challenge to secular feminism and, more important, has led to the emergence of what may be called Islamist feminist currents. These currents receive state sanction in Iran, Sudan, and some Gulf states, and in the rest of the Middle East they are emerging as significant social and ideological forces in the political arena, competing with secular feminism for women's sympathies and support.

Islamist women do indeed pose a challenge to secular feminists. Since Islamist women activists are by and large educated and professional women and not obscurantist male theologians or ideologues, they cannot be dismissed as archaic or irrelevant by secular feminists. Moreover, in countries all over the Middle East, ranging from Iran to Kuwait, they are gaining more visibility and entering the public political arena. Although on the whole Islamist women have not publicly challenged the Islamist construct of the ideal Muslim woman or the prevailing sexual division of labor, they are, by their own lifestyles and professional and political pursuits, departing in many ways from the ideal. Now, at the beginning of the twenty-first century, a new model is being offered to young women, the model of an educated, professional, "Muslim" woman.[4]

In Iran, the role of Islamist women in challenging postrevolutionary state policies that restricted women's rights has been unique and noteworthy. After the revolution, the state encouraged the development of an Islamic women's movement to counter the threat from secular feminism; very soon, however, Islamist women began to voice their criticism of some Islamization policies, such as Islamist dress codes, leading in the late 1980s to the emergence of an Islamist feminist opposition. Islamist feminists have campaigned for issues relating to rights within the family, dress codes, employment, political participation, and education (Paidar, 1996:59–62).[5]

■ CONCLUSION

This chapter has attempted to highlight the diversity of women's status and realities in the Middle East while at the same time underlining the broad similarities in the social, economic, and political circumstances under which women live their lives. As we have seen, state-building projects have had important consequences for women's status in society and for the rights of which they are deprived or enjoy.

We have also seen that Middle Eastern women have been active in the political arena, a role not consistent with commonsense representations of Middle Eastern women as passive political subjects locked into the domestic arena. The massive participation of Iranian women in the revolution, for instance, flies in the face of such conceptualizations of Middle Eastern women as being outside the domain of politics.

Furthermore, we have tried to show that women's lives in the Middle East, as elsewhere in the world, are shaped by a multiplicity of influences and factors. Concrete material factors related to socioeconomic realities and state policies explain social practices and institutions better than do monolithic belief systems. These belief systems, although important in the overall scheme of things, are variable, flexible, and dynamic.

■ NOTES

1. Research by the author (Taraki, 1996) in Jordan supports these conclusions about Islamists' accommodation to the requirements of life in a rapidly changing society. For further discussion and analysis of Jordanian and other Islamists' preoccupation with women's conduct in modern society, see Taraki (1995).

2. Useful sources for the study of women's participation in revolutionary movements are Peteet (1991), Sayigh (1993), and Jad (1990) for Palestine; Lazreg (1994) for Algeria; and Nashat (1983), Ferdows (1983), and Shahidian (1997) for Iran.

3. See Hale (1996:151–183) for a discussion of this history.

4. An interesting volume including articles on women and Islamist movements in Sudan, Tunisia, Algeria, Egypt, Turkey, and Iran is Moghadam (1994).

5. It is important to caution against viewing Islamist women in Iran as a monolithic group, however. See Moghissi (1996) for a discussion that distinguishes between "conservative" and "reformist" Muslim elite women. The conservatives, apologists for the clerical state, occupy prominent public posts, are almost all related to powerful male elites, and are the main beneficiaries of financial and ideological support from the state. The reformists represent a growing disenchantment with the legal system and government policies in education and employment, although it appears that they are of the same social class and background as the conservative group.

■ BIBLIOGRAPHY

Afary, Janet. 1989. "On the Origins of Feminism in Early 20th Century Iran." *Journal of Women's History* 1, no. 2:65–87.

Antoun, Richard. 1968. "On the Modesty of Women in Arab Muslim Villages: A Study in the Accommodation of Traditions." *American Anthropologist* 70: 671–698.

Arat, Yesim. 1996. "On Gender and Citizenship in Turkey." *Middle East Report* 198 (January-March):28–31.

Berkovitch, Nitza. 1996. "Women and the Women's Equal Rights Law in Israel." *Middle East Report* 198 (January-March):19–21.

Ferdows, Adele. 1983. "Women and the Islamic Revolution." *International Journal of Middle East Studies* 15:283–298.

Galal, Salma. 1995. "Women and Development in the Maghreb Countries." Pp. 49–70 in Nabil Khoury and Valentine Moghadam (eds.), *Gender and Development in the Arab World*. London and Tokyo: Zed Books and United Nations University Press.

Graham-Brown, Sarah. 1993. "Women and Politics in the Middle East." Washington, D.C.: Special MERIP Publication no. 2.

Hale, Sondra. 1996. *Gender Politics in Sudan: Islamism, Socialism, and the State*. Boulder, Colo.: Westview Press.

Hijab, Nadia. 1988. *Womanpower: The Arab Debate on Women at Work*. Cambridge and New York: Cambridge University Press.

Hoodfar, Homa. 1995. "Population Policy and Gender Equity in Post-Revolutionary Iran." Pp. 105–135 in Carla M. Obermeyer (ed.), *Family, Gender, and Population in the Middle East*. Cairo: American University in Cairo Press.

Jad, Islah. 1990. "From Salons to the Popular Committees: Palestinian Women, 1919–1989." Pp. 125–142 in Jamal Nassar and Roger Heacock (eds.), *Intifada: Palestine at the Crossroads*. New York: Praeger.

Joseph, Suad. 1991. "Elite Strategies for State-Building: Women, Family, Religion and State in Iraq and Lebanon." Pp. 176–200 in Deniz Kandiyoti (ed.), *Women, Islam and the State*. London: Macmillan.

———. 1994. "Gender and Family in the Arab World." Washington, D.C.: Special MERIP Publication no. 4.

Kandiyoti, Deniz. 1989. "Women and the Turkish State: Political Actors or Symbolic Pawns?" Pp. 126–149 in Nira Yuval-Davis and Floya Anthias (eds.), *Woman-Nation-State*. London: Macmillan.

———. 1991a. "End of Empire: Islam, Nationalism and Women in Turkey." Pp. 22–47 in Deniz Kandiyoti (ed.), *Women, Islam and the State*. London: Macmillan.

———. 1991b. "Islam and Patriarchy: A Comparative Perspective." Pp. 23–42 in Nikki Keddie and Beth Baron (eds.), *Women in Middle Eastern History: Shifting Boundaries in Sex and Gender*. New Haven and London: Yale University Press.

———. 1991c. "Women, Islam and the State." *Middle East Report* 173 (November-December):9–14.

Lazreg, Marnia. 1994. *The Eloquence of Silence: Algerian Women in Question*. New York and London: Routledge.

Mir-Hosseini, Ziba. 1991. "Contrast Between Law and Practice for the Moroccan Family: Patriarchy and Matrifocality." *Moroccan Studies* 1:39–52.

Moghadam, Valentine. 1993. *Modernizing Women: Gender and Social Change in the Middle East*. Boulder, Colo.: Lynne Rienner.

——— (ed.). 1994. *Identity Politics and Women*. Boulder, Colo.: Westview Press.

———. 1995. "The Political Economy of Female Employment in the Arab Region." Pp. 6–34 in Nabil Khoury and Valentine Moghadam (eds.), *Gender and Development in the Arab World*. London and Tokyo: Zed Books and United Nations University Press.

Moghissi, Haideh. 1996. "Public Life and Women's Resistance." Pp. 251–270 in Saeed Rahnema and Sohrab Behdad (eds.), *Iran After the Revolution: Crisis of an Islamic State*. New York: I. B. Tauris.

Molyneux, Maxine. 1991. "The Law, the State and Socialist Policies with Regard to Women: The Case of the People's Democratic Republic of Yemen 1967–1990." Pp. 237–271 in Deniz Kandiyoti (ed.), *Women, Islam and the State*. London: Macmillan.

Moors, Annelies. 1996. "Gender Relations and Inheritance: Person, Power and Property in Palestine." Pp. 69–84 in Deniz Kandiyoti (ed.), *Gendering the Middle East: Emerging Perspectives*. London: I. B. Tauris.

Najmabadi, Afsaneh. 1991. "Hazards of Modernity and Morality: Women, State and Ideology in Contemporary Iran." Pp. 48–76 in Deniz Kandiyoti (ed.), *Women, Islam and the State*. London: Macmillan.

Nashat, Guity (ed.). 1983. *Women and Revolution in Iran*. Boulder, Colo.: Westview Press.

Paidar, Parvin. 1996. "Feminism in Islam in Iran." Pp. 51–67 in Deniz Kandiyoti (ed.), *Gendering the Middle East: Emerging Perspectives*. London: I. B. Tauris.

Peteet, Julie. 1991. *Gender in Crisis: Women and the Palestinian Resistance Movement*. New York: Columbia University Press.

Sayigh, Rosemary. 1993. "Palestinian Women and Politics in Lebanon." Pp. 175–192 in Judith Tucker (ed.), *Arab Women: Old Boundaries, New Frontiers*. Bloomington and Indianapolis: Indiana University Press.

Shahidian, Hammed. 1997. "Women and Clandestine Politics in Iran, 1970–1985." *Feminist Studies* 23, no. 1:7–43.

Shami, Seteney. 1990. "Introduction." Pp. xiii–xix in Seteney Shami, Lucine Taminian, Soheir A. Morsy, Zeinab B. El Bakri, and El-Wathig M. Kameir, *Women in Arab Society: Work Patterns and Gender Relations in Egypt, Jordan and Sudan*. Providence and Paris: Berg/UNESCO.

Sharoni, Simona. 1995. *Gender and the Israeli-Palestinian Conflict: The Politics of Women's Resistance*. Syracuse: Syracuse University Press.

Swirski, Barbara, and Marilyn Safir (eds.). 1991. *Calling the Equality Bluff: Women in Israel*. New York: Teachers College Press.

Taraki, Lisa. 1995. "Islam Is the Solution: Jordanian Islamists and the Dilemma of the 'Modern Woman.'" *British Journal of Sociology* 46, no. 4:643–661.

———. 1996. "Jordanian Islamists and the Agenda for Women: Between Discourse and Practice." *Middle Eastern Studies* 32, no. 1:140–158.

Tucker, Judith. 1993. "The Arab Family in History: 'Otherness' and the Study of the Family." Pp. 195–207 in Judith Tucker (ed.), *Arab Women: Old Boundaries, New Frontiers*. Bloomington and Indianapolis: Indiana University Press.

UNDP (United Nations Development Programme). 1995. *Human Development Report 1995*. New York and Oxford: Oxford University Press.

———. 1996. *Human Development Report 1996*. New York and Oxford: Oxford University Press.

———. 1997. *Human Development Report 1997*. New York and Oxford: Oxford University Press.

———. 1998. *Human Development Report 1998*. New York and Oxford: Oxford University Press.

Yuval-Davis, Nira. 1982. *Israeli Women and Men: Divisions Behind the Unity*. London: Change Publications.

———. 1989. "National Reproduction and the 'Demographic Race' in Israel." Pp. 92–109 in Nira Yuval-Davis and Floya Anthias (eds.), *Woman-Nation-State*. London: Macmillan.

Zurayk, Huda, and Fadia Saadeh. 1995. "Women as Mobilizers of Human Resources in Arab Countries." Pp. 35–48 in Nabil Khoury and Valentine Moghadam (eds.), *Gender and Development in the Arab World*. London and Tokyo: Zed Books and United Nations University Press.

▪ 11 ▪

Religion and Politics in the Middle East

John L. Esposito and Mohammed A. Muqtedar Khan

As previous chapters have repeatedly illustrated, the contemporary Middle East is a highly contested sociopolitical arena. Despite the efforts of numerous politicians and social elites, modernity has failed to establish its hegemony completely throughout the region (Gellner, 1992; also see Mahallati, 1996). Secularism, individualism, democracy, economic rationality, and constitutive institutions of modernity such as the nation-state have failed to gain as much currency there as they have in North America, East Asia, and Europe. The region remains a combination of modernity (artificial nation-states, authoritarianism, secularism) and vestigial traditions, reflected in cultural and religious practices and institutions (Marcus, 1989).

Religion and politics enjoy a special place in the history and politics of the Middle East. The homeland for three of the world's great religions, the Middle East is strategically located between the West and East and oversees important trade routes on land and sea. Today, the global resurgence of religion, with its influence on politics, often reveals itself most spectacularly in the Middle East.

Religion and traditional forms of governance were never as discredited in the Middle East as in Europe; they were merely marginalized. In Europe, the experiences of the Renaissance, Enlightenment, and Protestant Reformation were indigenous and precipitated the secularization of politics in the West. Secularism, the separation of religion and politics, came to be accepted as the norm in political development by many governments, policymakers, experts, and the media.

In contrast, secular values came to the Middle East through European colonization. Tradition and religion, however, continued to play a major role in society and politics. There was no mass intellectual and political movement that explicitly sought to secularize the Middle East. European colonial governments attempted to impose secular political institutions on the Middle East, and in response, some wars of independence were waged as jihad (divine struggle) against European secularism, as in Algeria and Sudan (Lewis, 1993).

After World War II when much of the Middle East became independent, religion and tradition were often marginalized in state formation. This pattern was set in the 1920s when Turkey, under Mustafa Kemal (later called Atatürk, "Father of the Turks"), became secular. Then in the post–World War II era, many other states like Tunisia, Egypt, Iran, Syria, and Iraq, although recognizing Islam as a state religion, limited its status and role in politics and society. In contrast, however, Saudi Arabia was established as a self-proclaimed Islamic state, and Pakistan, created in the name of Muslim nationalism, took the title Islamic Republic of Pakistan. At the same time (1948) the modern nation of Israel was established as a Jewish state.

In a sense the Middle East exists on the borderlines, between modernity and tradition, religion and politics, East and West, autonomy and dependency, independence and imperialism, and authenticity and uncritical emulation of the West. It is in this at once new and old Middle East that religion and politics dance the tango. This chapter plots this fascinating relationship across space and time and across faiths, tracing the interaction of religion and politics in the Middle East from its historical origins to its contemporary resurgence. Just as power and knowledge are inextricably intertwined in the modern world, in the Middle East power and religion often seem to be similarly inseparable.

■ THE HISTORICAL ROLE OF RELIGION IN THE MIDDLE EAST

The history of the Middle East is in many ways the history of monotheism, the belief in a single, supreme God. First Judaism, then Christianity, and later Islam have been a defining presence in the region. Islam spread throughout the Middle East, culturally expanding the territorial frontiers of the ancient Middle East to include North Africa, Iran, Turkey, Pakistan, and central Asian regions such as Uzbekistan, Turkmenistan, and Tajikistan. At present, a majority of the Middle Eastern population is Muslim. Jews are concentrated in Israel, with tiny minorities in Iran, Tunisia, Syria, Morocco, and Egypt. The most significant presence of Christian minorities in the Arab world is in Lebanon, Syria, Egypt, and Iraq.

□ Judaism

Judaism is a 4,000-year-old faith. The origins of the Jewish community can be traced back to Moses, who, according to Hebrew traditions, rescued the Jewish people from slavery in Egypt and brought them to the Holy Land to establish a kingdom of God (about 1450–1250 B.C.E.). The Torah, which includes the first five books of the Hebrew Bible, was revealed to Moses as a guide for the Jewish people. It is from the Torah and the Talmud (a secondary text that compiles interpretation of the Torah and Jewish law, the halakah) that the Jewish people derive their religious principles. Jews have always believed themselves to be a "chosen people" who would eventually establish God's domain on Earth, and this belief has informed their modern national self-consciousness. Jews represent a religious-racial community that values and guards its communal identity (Cavendish, 1980:133–170).

Just as in early biblical conflicts, when Jewish religious identity and political aspirations intertwined with war and peace, so too religion and politics in the late nineteenth and twentieth centuries merged to create a unique form of nationalism—Zionism—that is often simultaneously religious and secular. This convergence of religion and politics was finally manifested in the creation of the state of Israel. For those Israelis on the religious right, the Jewish nature of the state of Israel refers primarily to its faith; for those on the left, the Jewish nature of the state is the glue that cements a community. In either case, Judaism is a source of identity. An understanding of these religious beliefs and their appeal cannot be divorced from any contemporary understanding of the region's politics or society.

Historically, all three Abrahamic faiths—Judaism, Christianity, and Islam—have used religion to justify and legitimate expansion and warfare. Although much has been written and continues to be written about the significance of holy wars to Islam (jihad) and Christianity (Crusades), the importance of holy war in Judaism has received less attention. Yet it has influenced political affairs in the past and present. The idea of holy war occurs early in Jewish belief and history. Like Christianity and Islam, Jews associated holy war with divine guidance and mission. Thus, in the Hebrew Bible, whenever they fought against the enemies of Zion, God (Yahweh) fought on their side (Esposito, 1998). In the first two centuries of the second millennium B.C.E., Jews waged wars against the Canaanites who lived on the land Jews believed God had intended for them, gradually capturing enough territory to establish the first kingdom of Israel. These early holy wars are, in the eyes of many believers, likened to the 1947 and 1948 Zionist capture of territory from Arabs to build the new Israel (Armstrong, 1991:7–12).

After their dispersal from Jerusalem and Judea, Jews preserved and sustained their identity by belief in their divine election and distinctiveness and adherence to religious law and ritual practices. For more than 2,000 years the Jewish people lived in a diaspora—exiles from the land of Israel—and were marginalized and often persecuted in the Christian West. In contrast, during the Islamic age in Spain and in other parts of the Muslim world, Jews enjoyed some degree of tolerance and flourished there as a religious community as well as a cultural entity (Cavendish, 1980:165). In the late nineteenth century, a new wave of violence and discrimination against Jews in Europe compelled some Jewish leaders to once again search for a national solution. A Jewish activist, Theodor Herzl (1860–1904) renewed the call for the establishment of a Jewish state, giving the Zionist movement great momentum in the realization of the national aspirations of world Jewry (Cleveland, 1994:223–225).

The first Zionist congress met in 1897. It was after this meeting that the idea of a Jewish state captured the imagination of Jews in eastern as well as western Europe. The end of World War I saw the defeat of the Ottoman Empire and its subsequent dismemberment by Britain and France, which placed most of Palestine under British control. Leaders of the Zionist movement convinced the British to draw up the Balfour Declaration in 1917, which essentially approved the establishment of a Jewish state in Palestine. The League of Nations accepted the Balfour Declaration, and hundreds of thousands of Jews migrated to Palestine. In 1947, the United Nations (UN) passed a resolution for the division of Palestine and the creation of the state of Israel. Between that date and May 15, 1948, when the British mandate over Palestine was scheduled to come to an end, the Zionists and the Arabs in Palestine fought a civil war that drove many Palestinians into exile by the time Israel's independence was declared on May 15.

The establishment of the state of Israel marked a watershed in modern Middle Eastern politics. Israel was not only a reminder that religious identity could mold and motivate a modern nation-state but also a challenge to the predominantly Moslem states of the region. The conflicts between Israel and its neighbors, as well as with Palestinian Arabs displaced by these conflicts, would dominate much of the politics of the region for the remainder of the twentieth century.

□ Christianity

Christianity is the largest religion in the world, with more than 1.5 billion adherents. The origins of Christianity can be traced to the teachings of Jesus of Nazareth. Born in Bethlehem, he was crucified by the Romans in Jerusalem and was declared as Messiah and as a son of God by his followers. From its Jewish roots, Christianity spread first throughout the Mediterranean and subsequently has attracted followers on every continent. Christianity has had a major impact on the social and political development of the West and a significant, although somewhat lesser, impact on the rest of the world.

The expulsion of Jews from Jerusalem in 70 C.E. had put the city in Roman hands. Even though Christian Scriptures espoused the separation of church and state—"Render to Caesar the things that are Caesar's and to God the things that are God's" (Mark 12:17, Bible, King James Version)— the religion was viewed as a threat to the unity of the Roman Empire. For more than 300 years Christians suffered repression at the hands of Roman authorities. The faith, however, acquired followers rapidly, and within a hundred years (313 C.E.) Christianity was declared an officially tolerated religion by Constantine I. By 380 C.E., through the edict of Theodosius I, it became the official religion of the Roman Empire, inaugurating a new phase in the history of Christianity that reflected the confluence of religion and politics. From that point until the advent of Islam, Christianity thrived in what is the contemporary Middle East.

With the conquest of the Middle East by Islamic forces in the seventh century, the focus of Christianity shifted to Europe. By the twelfth century under Pope Innocent III (pope from 1198–1216), Christianity, as epitomized in the papacy, reached the zenith of its political power, deeply involved in politics through its control of vast territorial resources, its near-monopoly on education, and its influence on the appointment and legitimacy of many political positions. In this golden age of the papacy, Europe came closest to being a Christian empire. This was the period when the papacy, kings, and emperors struggled for sovereignty over land and people, a struggle that eventually precipitated the Protestant Reformation (1500–1650).

□ The Crusades

The increase in the influence of the Church in European politics led to the launch of the Crusades. In 1096, responding to the summons of Pope Urban II, Christian armies from Europe began a series of holy wars against Muslims to gain control of the Holy Land and once again establish the kingdom of God in Jerusalem.

The Crusaders enjoyed successes but failed either to regain the Holy Land permanently or to drive Islam out of it. The power of Islam continued unabated until the fifteenth century. The Crusades, however, remain a landmark event in Christian politics in the Middle East. They are the beginning of external Christian influence on politics in that region.

In 1099, the Crusaders captured Jerusalem and established a Christian kingdom in the Holy Land. The Crusaders accepted the Muslims' surrender and then proceeded to massacre all Muslim survivors, including women and children.[1] They desecrated Muslim religious sites, including the Dome of the Rock, which was converted into a church, and they made the al-Aqsa Mosque the residence for the Christian ruler after renaming it the Temple of Solomon.

But Christian control was relatively short-lived. In 1187, Saladin recaptured Jerusalem but, unlike the Crusaders, spared all Christian civilians

Photo 11.1   *Qabat al-Bahr (the Sea Castle), in Sidon, Lebanon, is a thirteenth-century Crusader fortress built on the site of an older temple dedicated to Baal.*

and left churches and shrines untouched.[2] The Third Crusade, under Richard the Lion-Hearted of England, attempted to regain control of Jerusalem but failed even to reach the walls of the city. By 1291, the last Crusader stronghold at Acre was captured by Muslim forces, and this era of Christian political influence ended.

The Crusades expanded and strengthened the Islamic world. Muslim armies not only defeated the Crusaders, but the Crusades themselves actually weakened Christian influence in the region. In 1204, Crusaders captured and sacked Constantinople, capital of the Christian (Greek Orthodox) Byzantine Empire, further weakening this outpost of Christian influence in the region. In 1453 Constantinople fell to Muslim armies and was renamed Istanbul. Memories of the Crusades, both real and mythical, would continue to influence relations between Islam and Christianity, the Muslim world and the West, down through the centuries.

☐ European Colonialism

Since the eighteenth century, first the British and the French and later the United States have politically dominated the Middle East. The British, and to a lesser extent the French, reorganized the Middle East into a number of nations and kingdoms. Along with the United States, they also supported the creation of the Jewish state of Israel in 1947. In addition, Christianity remains a force with certain interests in the Middle East, including Israel, Jerusalem, and the survival and welfare of Christian minorities.

European colonization of the area, many scholars believe, was inspired more by secular motives of national pride and trade than by any religious impulse. However, Christian missionaries benefited from the patronage of European imperial powers in their efforts to proselytize Muslims and spread European Christianity.[3] The collaboration between the cross and the crown was a subtheme of the colonial experience that led many Muslims to view the colonial conquests as a continuation of Christianity's Crusades against Islam. It is not coincidental that many of the wars of independence against colonial rule were fought in the name of religion (Esposito, 1999).

Christian missionaries accompanied the European soldiers and bureaucrats. The relationship between government officials and missionaries was celebrated by France's marshal Thomas-Robert Bugeaud de la Piconnerie as a *"grand rapport,"* and he commented that the clergy "gain for us the hearts of the Arabs whom we have subjected to force of arms." The missionaries opened schools, hospitals, and publishing houses. They sought to supplant not only local religion but Arabs' historical understanding of themselves, their culture, and their language (Esposito, 1999).

European successes were interpreted as the result of Christianity's superiority, and Muslim defeats were seen as a result of the inferiority of Islam by colonial powers. With the seizure of the Grand Mosque of Algiers and its conversion into the Cathedral of Saint-Phillippe, the French flag and the cross on its minaret symbolized the close relationship between the crown and the cross under colonialism. Thus in the short term, Christianity gained from the colonial conquests even though much of the rationale for European imperialism was political and economic.

Contemporary historians and social scientists, who often share a secular worldview, sometimes deemphasize the role and activities of missionaries in the former colonies. But in the Muslim mind, the threat of Christianity was foremost. Thus, it was fear of losing their faith—in addition to well-justified skepticism about European motives—that led to a policy of withdrawal and noncooperation with European efforts at development and modernization.

☐ Islam

In the early seventh century, Muhammad of Mecca (570–632 C.E.) declared himself the prophet of God (610 C.E.) and united the tribes of Ara-

Photo 11.2 Mosque at Job's Tomb near Salalah, Oman.

bia under the banner of Islam. Muhammad claimed to be a prophet like the biblical prophets Abraham, Moses and Jesus. He maintained that his message was the same as that revealed to Abraham and the rest of the prophets: that there is only one God, and no other god is worthy of worship. The simplicity of Muhammad's message and the fervor of his followers made Islam a major force in the region and globally.

Within seventy-five years of Muhammad declaring himself the prophet of God, the followers of Islam had extended their control from Arabia to Morocco. It was as early as 637 C.E. that the entire Holy Land, including Jerusalem, came under Islam. Many of the Jews and Christians who lived under Muslim rule eventually adopted the new faith or prospered in its relatively more tolerant environment in which, in sharp contrast to Europe, followers of other monotheistic religions did not suffer systematic repression.

Islam expanded beyond Arabia and soon Islamized as well as Arabized most of the Middle East. (Iran was a major exception, accepting Islam but retaining Persian language and culture.) The advent of Islam had a profound cultural and political impact on the Middle East, giving the varied peoples and societies of the region a common heritage. By the sixteenth century, Islam consisted of three great empires: the Ottoman, the Safavid in Iran, and the Mogul on the Indian subcontinent.

In the early centuries of Islam, Muslims created great centers of higher learning. They acquired and revived the lost wisdom of the classical period of Greek and Roman civilization (Lindhom, 1996). Poetry, literature, art and architecture, medicine, mathematics, chemistry, and philosophy all thrived and contributed to the cultural enrichment of the region from the seventh to the fifteenth centuries. The creation of universities spread Islam and brought the learning of other societies to the Islamic world. A rich synthesis of peoples, cultures, and knowledge took place under the umbrella of Islam. To a great extent, Islamic civilization and Middle Eastern political power reached their peak at the same time. In the following centuries, the decline and fragmentation of Islamic empires led to the gradual decline in the region's power and culture.

☐ Islam and Public Life

For many Muslims, Islam is a complete way of life that provides guiding principles for the personal and the public, for the individual and the community, for state as well as society (Hamidullah, 1979; Zubaida, 1993; el-Awa, 1980; Esposito, 1991). Muslim tradition teaches that the purpose of Islamic law (Shari'ah) is to establish peace and justice, forbid evil, and enjoin the good. The purpose of politics in Islam is for governments to provide ethical governance in consultation (*shurah*) with their citizens. Although Islam is not particular about the *form of government*, it is clear about the *purpose as well as ethics of governance* (Osman, 1994; Ahmad, 1986; Adams, 1983; Turabi, 1983). For many Muslims, this quality makes quranic injunction relevant to politics and society regardless of time and space. Thus politics and power have always been central to Islam, in contrast to early Christianity. The impact of European colonialism and the influence of a post-Enlightenment understanding of the nature of religion increasingly limited Islam to the private domain, but the continued political dimensions of Islam can be seen in a variety of events (Haynes, 1994: 1–21).

Long before the Islamic Republic of Iran made a traumatic entry into world politics, Saudi Arabia had been created by the House of Saud as an Islamic state (Esposito, 1998:96–157). The Khilafat (caliphate) movement in India, the creation of a Muslim Pakistan, and the use of Islamic symbolism

Photo 11.3 Ommayad Mosque in Damascus, Syria.

that accompanied the struggles for freedom from European colonialism (Libya, Algeria, Morocco, Sudan, and Pakistan) are all indications of how Islam played a major role in mass mobilization in moments of political crisis. Similarly, the use of *Allah-u-Akbar* (Allah Is Great) as the slogan of the Egyptian military in the Egyptian-Israeli war of 1973 and then by the secular Iraqi leader Saddam Hussein (in 1990, the slogan was hastily added to the Iraqi flag when it became evident that the U.S.-organized coalition would strike) underscores the importance of religion in popular politics in the Middle East.

This fusion of religion and politics is a characteristic feature of the contemporary resurgence of Islam. Islamic activists believe that once Islam is restored to its rightful place, at the center of all human affairs, the Muslim world will in turn regain its rightful place in international politics.

☐ Jerusalem: The Convergence of Power and Religious Symbolism

The present struggle for sovereignty over Jerusalem is symbolic of the convergence of the spiritual and the physical, the religious and the political in the Middle East. This "holy" city is historically as well as scripturally claimed by Jews, Muslims, and Christians. For the Jews, Jerusalem is the "mountain of the Lord." The Mishnah (second-century compendium of Jewish laws) asserts that the divine presence (*scechina*) has never left the Western Wall (Breger, 1996:91–118). Jerusalem has become the symbol and source of Jewish religious as well as nationalist identity.

In 70 C.E. the Romans destroyed the Second Temple in Jerusalem and expelled its Jewish population. Jews scattered throughout the world. Although many assimilated into the countries of their diaspora, they retained their faith and Jewish identity. Each year, Jews across the world conclude the Passover ceremonies with the determined wish, "Next Year in Jerusalem." The prophetic idea of an eventual gathering of all Jewish exiles into the land of their origin has influenced the attitudes of Westerners, Jewish as well as Christian, toward Jerusalem. The repeated assertion by Israeli leaders that a united Jerusalem is the eternal capital of Israel is an articulation of this biblical belief translated into a political vision. For 2,000 years, Jews have nursed the idea of returning to reclaim Jerusalem.

For Christians, Jerusalem is the site of their faith's origins and early history, where Jesus preached his message, was crucified, died, and was buried. It was there that in Christian belief Jesus was miraculously resurrected from the grave and ascended into heaven. The religious significance of Jerusalem was translated into the political when Pope Urban II summoned the First Crusade to recover Jerusalem and establish a Christian kingdom there (Runciman, 1992).

Christian political interest in Jerusalem was manifest more recently in the British mandate over Palestine and in continuing U.S. support for Israel. Christian groups and institutions such as the World Council of Churches and the Vatican have also maintained keen interest in the status of Jerusalem. Most important, Jerusalem and Palestine continue to be the home of Arab Christians, who have lived there for centuries. It is also significant to the many Christians who make pilgrimages to the historical Christian churches and sites in Jerusalem.

Jerusalem is one of the three most sacred places of Islam. It was the first city to which Muslims turned in prayer (subsequently changed to Mecca), and in Muslim belief, it is the place from which the Prophet Muhammad ascended to the heavens (*miraj haqq*) on a winged horse. According to Muslim eschatology (an aspect of theology that addresses the final events of human history), Jerusalem is the place where the end of time commences. Today, the loss of control of Jerusalem indicates to Muslims their ultimate defeat in what many regard as the unending Crusades launched by Christians against Islam. Failure to regain sovereignty over Jerusalem, they believe, is indicative of the decline of Islamic civilization and the failure of Palestinian aspirations to decolonize their land.

Jerusalem has also become a symbol of Western imperialism for many Muslims who see the continued expansion of Israel as a Western plot to dominate their lands and destroy Islam. They fear that under Israeli rule, Islam's third most important mosque (al-Aqsa/Bait-ul-Maqdis) will eventually be destroyed. Indeed some Jewish religious leaders and groups have expressed plans to rebuild the temple of King Solomon on that very site (Sprinzak, 1991:3–7; see also Mergui and Simonnot, 1987; Lustick, 1988; Friedman, 1990).

The continued settlement of Jews in Arab East Jerusalem and the forced evacuation of Palestinians, both Christian and Muslim, have only reinforced Muslim fears. Muslims see themselves as the inheritors of Judaism and Christianity. For them Islam bears the same message as Judaism and Christianity. They believe that Islam is a continuation and completion of Abraham's faith and that the Quran is the final revelation sent by the same God who sent his revelations through Moses and Jesus. In that same vein, many believe that they are the true inheritors of the Holy Land, symbolized by the conquest of Jerusalem by Umar ibn al-Khattab, the second of the "Rightly Guided Caliphs," in 637 C.E.

The struggle for Jerusalem is indeed representative of the intersection of religion and politics in the Middle East. It is in Jerusalem that the temporal, spiritual, political, cultural, and territorial converge. Jerusalem is both modern and traditional. It is modern in its status as the aspiration of Jewish and Palestinian nationalism, and it is traditional in its sacred significance to three religions. For many there can be no political solution for

Jerusalem without a religious solution (Friedland and Hecht, 1995; Esposito, 1998:99–157). In Israel, where Zionism fuses religion and nationalism, the modern and the traditional are not distinguishable; neither are the religious and the political (Liebman, 1990; Liebman and Don-Yehiya, 1983). Thus Jerusalem symbolizes the significance of religion in the politics of the Middle East.

■ THE CONTEMPORARY ROLE OF RELIGION IN MIDDLE EASTERN POLITICS

Religion continues to play a significant role in contemporary Middle Eastern politics. In Lebanon, Egypt, and Sudan, Christian minorities face issues regarding their status and role within Muslim majority societies. Jewish fundamentalism is altering the political equations in Israel and influencing the direction of the Arab-Israeli peace process. In terms of breadth of political impact, Islamic movements have often occupied center stage in attempts to transform the political and religious landscape of the Middle East.

□ Christianity and Contemporary Politics

Christians in the Middle East constitute a diverse group spread widely across the Muslim world (Cragg, 1991). Because of their minority status in the states of the region, Christians have often espoused sharing power either through a quota system of proportional representation (Lebanon) or through secularization (Sudan) since it is only in secular or pluralistic societies that Middle Eastern Christians can hope to share power. Christians have made their presence felt politically in Egypt, where Egyptian Copts are often the standard for measuring the tolerance and pluralism of Egyptian society. The issue of Christians in Egypt has often been synonymous with the status of religious minorities within Islam (Haddad, 1995). Copts, whose presence in Egypt predates the advent of Islam, make up about 10 percent of the Egyptian population. They have heightened concerns about freedom of religious practice and protection from religious extremists such as the Gamaa Islamiyyah (Islamic Group) who target Copts and their businesses.

In Lebanon the political system until recently favored Christian dominance. Today Muslims and Christians struggle to redefine their situation politically and socioeconomically. Lebanese Christians are significant in numbers, are politically very active, and share power with Sunni and Shi'a Muslims. Lebanon is a pluralist, multiethnic, and multireligious society that has experienced a fifteen-year civil war. Today the propensity for religious communities and political leaders to have their own armed militias is further compounded by the actions of Syria and Israel, who have occupied parts of the country in order to extend their influence and interests. Indeed, the term *Lebanization* has come to equal the older term *balkanization* as symbolic of widespread violence, political fragmentation, identity conflicts, and chaos (Salibi, 1981; Entelis, 1981).

In Sudan, resistance to the Islamization and Arabization policies pursued by the fundamentalist Sudanese government has produced an uneasy (and internally divided) alliance among Christians, moderate Muslims, and followers of traditional religions. Factions of this alliance have pursued both political resistance and civil war since then president Jaafar Nimeiri's declaration of Islamic law in 1983 (Voll, 1991). In Sudan as well as Lebanon, Christian politics is also the simultaneous manifestation of sectarian, ethnic, and ideological cleavages.

Christian intervention in Middle Eastern politics today occurs on two levels. First, domestic Christian lobbies in the West pressure governments to accommodate religious considerations in their foreign policy (Spiegel, 1982–1983; Haynes, 1994; Thomas, 1995). Second, international actors such as the World Council of Churches and the Vatican have direct contact and influence with foreign governments and their constituencies to advance Christian interests. The contemporary concerns of Christian politics in the Middle East include (1) protecting the interests of the Christian minorities in Muslim states, (2) moderating Zionist and Israeli extremism in the Holy Land, and (3) preaching and proselytizing wherever and whenever possible (Breger, 1996:113).

☐ Jewish Fundamentalism in Israel

Judaism, like Islam, has a religious-political tradition. Just as Islamic law (Shari'ah) has been preeminent within Islamic traditions, so has Jewish law (halakah) been very important in the practice of the Jewish faith (Sivan, 1990a:3). Jewish politics today is a complex convergence of ethnicity, nationalism, and religious communalism.

In Israel, there is the presence of both Jewish nationalism and Jewish communalism. Israel's dominant ideology has been Zionism, a form of socialism that has provided a common nationalist identity to religious as well as secular Jews from various ethnic backgrounds such as Africa, the Middle East, Russia, Eastern and Western Europe, Palestine, and North America. It is an ideology driven by existential concerns to create a religious polity, Israel, that would guarantee the survival and future of the Jewish people (Vogel, 1986).

In recent years there has been a perceptible growth in Jewish radicalism and fundamentalist movements (Sprinzak, 1991). Religion and politics were fused in the conception of a Jewish/Zionist state, its secular and so-cialist ideology notwithstanding. The contemporary resurgence of hyper-Judaism in the Jewish right goes beyond the preexisting fusion of religion and politics. Fear that the territorial gains made in 1967 to realize the bib-lical or greater Israel of Judea and Samaria will be squandered and a grow-ing disenchantment with the failure to institutionalize more fully the Jew-ish religious identity of Israel are two of the driving forces behind the contemporary resurgence of the Jewish right. The combination of this group's religious beliefs with their political interpretations are today a sig-nificant force affecting the Middle Eastern crisis (R. Friedman, 1992; M. Friedman, 1992; Hertzberg, 1992; Damant, 1995).

The various meanings of the diverse, sometimes contradictory beliefs incorporated in Jewish fundamentalism provide an important guide to un-derstanding the changing political climate in Israel. Although Jewish fun-damentalists may disagree on important matters, all agree on their people's right to their homeland. The cleavages in Jewish society have been identi-fied by Ian Lustick (1988:1–17) as separating Jews into three groups: sec-ular Zionists, Orthodox Jews, and Jewish fundamentalists.

Traditional Zionists, as discussed earlier, are basically secular Jews who connect the future of Jewish identity to the existence of a strong and independent Jewish nation-state. Their Jewish identity is a source of Jew-ish nationalism, which was harnessed for generating the political momen-tum necessary for the creation and sustenance of a Jewish state (Lustick,

© Thomas Hartwell

Photo 11.4 Orthodox Jewish youth praying at the Western Wall in Jerusalem.

1988). Historically, these individuals have tended to associate with the Labor Party in Israel.

The Haredim (literally meaning the fearful or God-fearing ones) constitute Orthodox Jewry.[4] They do not actively engage in politics in order to achieve rapid and comprehensive change in Israel. Their primary focus is that of religious observance, fulfilling the many and detailed rules and rituals that constitute Jewish law, the halakah. Wearing distinctive garb, they live in segregated neighborhoods and either isolate themselves from or oppose Zionism. However, their strong support for right-wing religious parties, their frequent confrontations with more secular Jews over issues of public religious observance, and their substantial financial support from the United States make them a significant force that can radicalize and desecularize Israeli politics (Ravitsky, 1993; see also Lustick, 1988; and Sprinzak, 1991).

Jewish fundamentalism is epitomized in Gush Emunim (the bloc of the faithful). The Gush Emunim believe that Jews are special and different because they are the "chosen people" selected by God to lead humanity in religious redemption. They do not consider Israel to be an ordinary nation-state. For them it is the divinely mandated state intended by God for a chosen people according to the Torah (Silberstein, 1993). Thus, they believe, Jews need to possess the land of Israel without remorse and self-doubt as they did more than 2,000 years ago through holy wars against the Canaanites. Indeed, many prominent leaders of Gush Emunim publicly refer to present-day Palestinians as Canaanites. They believe that Palestinian nationalism must be destroyed and view Arabs as the present manifestation of evil that must be conquered in order to establish the will of God and assert Jewish sovereignty over Israel (Lustick, 1988:72–91).

For the Gush Emunim, commitment to the realization of biblical political and territorial goals is a greater measure of faith than the Haredim's pursuit of ritualistic perfection. The Gush Emunim have strong symbiotic relations with the conservative Likud Party in Israel. They reinforce each other's political aspirations and in the process strengthen each other (Ravitsky, 1993).

From the early 1980s, a series of events pointed to the existence and growth of the Jewish right. On April 27, 1984, a plot to blow up five buses full of Arab passengers was discovered. This was followed by the discovery of a plan to destroy the Dome of the Rock using twenty-eight precision bombs. In both cases the would-be terrorists were members of Gush Emunim. These events were followed by the election to the Knesset of the late rabbi Meir Kahane, founder and leader of the aggressive and violent fundamentalist Jewish movement Kach (Thus), who advocated the violent expulsion of all Arabs from his vision of "Greater Israel" (Sprinzak, 1991:3–7).[5] In 1995, the assassination of Israeli prime minister Yitzhak

Rabin by a right-wing Jewish extremist, who cited Jewish religious law to justify his actions (*New York Times,* November 19, 1995:1), stunned Israelis and the international community.

The Jewish right is primarily a domestic force within Israel. However, its opposition to any reconciliation with the Palestinians or the Arabs made it a regional player in Middle Eastern politics. The unwillingness of the religious right to support negotiations on the status of Jerusalem proved to be a major hurdle to a peaceful solution of the Arab-Israeli conflict. For the religious right to renegotiate what they believe is a religious mandate is to compromise religion for politics. Religion, they say, should dictate politics, not vice versa.

☐ The Resurgence of Political Islam

The contemporary resurgence of Islam and its impact on regional and world politics has generally overshadowed Christian and Jewish religious politics in the Middle East. It has transformed the basic character of two prominent states—Iran and Sudan—and significantly influenced many others. Political Islam has seriously challenged the seventy-year-old secular trajectory of Turkey (Khan, 1996), and in December 1991 and January 1992 the Islamic Salvation Front (FIS) would have won parliamentary elections in Algeria if not for the intervention of the secular military elite. Islamic nationalist movements such as Hamas and Hezbollah, using Katyusha rockets and suicide bombings, have compromised Israeli security in Lebanon and Israel/Palestine. Egypt, Saudi Arabia, Tunisia, Bahrain, and Jordan have experienced Islamic resurgence and, at times, its challenge to the legitimacy of their political regimes (Esposito, 1999; Ayubi, 1991; Keppel, 1985; Abu-Amr, 1994).

The Islamic resurgence is a response to an amalgam of crises in the Middle East. Because of a crisis of identity, Muslim societies are caught between traditional loyalties, secular nationalism, and modern Islamic thrusts toward Islamic nationalism (Esposito, 1999; Choueiri, 1990; Husain, 1995). In the crisis of modernization, top-down attempts at modernization have led to urbanization but limited economic development, resulting in a large, educated, urban class disaffected by high unemployment, a growing gap between rich and poor, and widespread corruption. A crisis of change has occurred because decolonization from the West, although successful, resulted in regime change but very little system change (Rahnema, 1994; Sidahmed and Ehteshami, 1996). People found themselves under authoritarian and military rule, in states where the ruling elites equated modernization with Westernization. Critics dismissed secular Westernized elites as "Westoxicated" or the product of "Westruckness." Finally, a crisis of power was engendered by conflict with Israel. The failure to recover territories from

Israel and its continued expansion, including its control over Jerusalem, has merely underscored for many the inability of Muslims to protect their lands and their religion from the repeated assaults of an imperial West (Esposito 1983, 1995:11–24).

Thus the current Islamic resurgence is a broad-based grassroots response to multiple crises. It is a struggle for both cultural authenticity and self-determination (Ayubi, 1991:214–220; Esposito, 1998; Haynes, 1994: 66–94). Some have described it as "civil society striking back" at incompetent and inefficient yet authoritarian and dictatorial states (Sivan, 1990b; Fuller, 1995). In many places it plays role similar to that of a state by providing health care, education, and economic assistance. Some see moderate Islamic movements as not just an institution of civil society but as the authentic impulse of the masses to democratize Muslim polities. Others in the West as well as in the Muslim world fear that democratization will facilitate Islamization in the Middle East, destroying regimes, threatening access to oil, and undermining the Arab-Israeli peace process (Pipes, 1995:57; Miller, 1993; also see Rodman, 1994).

Islamic movements and organizations, both moderate and extremist, have become major actors and agents of change. They have established modern political and social organizations and embrace modern means to disseminate their messages in the media, in audio- and videotapes, through faxes, and over the Internet. The majority of them function within civil society as social and political activists. The Muslim Brotherhoods of Egypt and Jordan, Pakistan's Jamaat-i-Islami, Turkey's Refah Party, Tunisia's al-Nahda, and Algeria's Islamic Salvation Front, to name a few, eschew violence and participate in electoral politics. They build schools, hospitals, clinics, and banks; offer inexpensive legal and social services; and are leaders in politics and in professional associations of doctors, lawyers, engineers, and teachers.

At the same time, a minority of extremists seek to overthrow regimes and impose their own brand of Islam. Egypt's Gamaa Islamiyyah, Algeria's Armed Islamic Group, and jihad organizations in many countries have engaged in violence and terrorism that has threatened the stability and security of many regimes and extended its reach to Europe (bombings in Paris) and the United States (World Trade Center bombing).

Islamic movements aim to liberate Muslim societies from Western (European, Soviet, and U.S.) colonial domination as well as from cultural imperialism (Esposito, 1999). Some seek to revive Islamic values in order to establish Islamic states as first steps toward the higher end of establishing a global Islamic *umma* (community) (Abu-Rabi, 1994). Political Islam has not opposed modernization, but it does oppose the Westernization and secularization of society. It embraces modern technology and science but rejects Western secular and cultural values. Islamists see no necessary

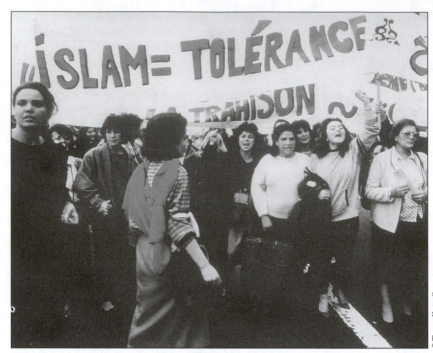

*Photo 11.5 In Algiers, Algeria, women march to protest
the policies of Islamic militants.*

linkage between technological advancement and economic development
on the one hand, and Western secular modernization on the other (Voll,
1994; Esposito, 1998). They believe that the primary interest of the West
in the Middle East lies in exploiting the natural resources of the Muslim
world, notably oil. They see the threat from the West as one of political
domination and cultural penetration (Abu-Rabi, 1996; Esposito, 1999).

The role of Islam in contemporary Middle Eastern politics is unlikely
to wane in the near future. It is gaining strength across social and economic strata in many Muslim societies. Many governments are plagued by
issues of legitimacy, authoritarianism, failing economies, maldistribution
of wealth, corruption, and human rights abuses. Although the impact of
change is felt by almost all, the benefits of modernization have been
shared by very few. Many of the younger generation resent existing
regimes and their failure to deliver on their promises and are more critical
of political, economic, and cultural dependence on the West. Secular elites,
a minority often blamed for the failures of their societies, are increasingly
challenged by the emergence of an alternative elite, more educated, more

Islamically oriented, and more critical of the failures and excesses of modernity.

■ UNDERSTANDING THE ROLE OF
RELIGION IN MIDDLE EASTERN POLITICS

The study of religion has once again become important in the late twentieth century, especially with the end of the Cold War. During the Cold War (1945–1989), the study of developing societies by most social scientists and other experts proceeded from a Eurocentric assumption that sooner or later the Middle East, like the rest of the Third World, would resemble the West in its modern and secular outlook. This precluded any systematic study of religion and its political potency (Appleby, 1994:chap. 1).

The study of religion and politics was left to sociologists and historians of religion (Mottahedeh, 1985; Voll, 1994). The failure of most political analysis to take religion seriously was exposed when the Iranian revolution exploded on the scene of world politics in 1979 (Esposito, 1990). Since then the religious resurgence of Islam in the Middle East has provided the necessary impetus for political scientists to study the contemporary ascendance of religion in the political sphere (e.g., Ayubi, 1991; Zubaida, 1993; Burgat and Dowell, 1993; Fuller and Lesser, 1995; Esposito, 1998; Sivan, 1985; Munson, 1988; Choueiri, 1990).

The global resurgence of religion shattered the expectations of most experts who had assumed that the rest of the world would duplicate the Western experience of political development (Thomas, 1995:289). None had anticipated the force with which religion would once again enter the realm of politics. William Swatos, a sociologist, expressed the sentiments of the academic community:

> There is no weapon in the theoretical arsenal of the social scientific study of religion or of political science that can attack the problem of worldwide religious resurgence. The two primary theories of "modernization"—development or exploitation—both proceed from the assumption that religious "prejudices" hamper "progress" and are disappearing throughout the world. (Swatos, 1989b:1)

Scholars had allowed their bias for secularism to incapacitate their disciplines when it came to the study of religion, transforming a theory into a dogma. Jeffery Hadden, in his 1986 presidential address to the Southern Sociological Society, noted that "in form and its genesis" secularization constituted a "*doctrine* more than a theory," based upon presuppositions that represent a "taken-for-granted *ideology*" of social science "rather than a systematic set of interrelated propositions." He further argued that over time, *"the idea of secularization became sacralized,"* that is, it became a belief system accepted "on faith" (Swatos, 1989a:146).

In a powerful indictment of social scientists' antipathy for religion, Fred Von Der Mehden (1986:13–19) argues that not only are these scholars alienated from religion but are also hostile toward it. He also points out that theoretical conclusions about the relations of tradition and religion to modernization, particularly in the Third World, were often drawn without any firsthand experience of or familiarity with the regions, religions, or traditions.

This blind faith in secularization has had two negative impacts on the study of religion and politics. First, religion was either excluded or boxed in the amorphous category of "culture," along with ethnicity, tradition, and tribalism, only to be taken seriously after unexpected events such as the Islamic revolution in Iran. Second, this ideology has led to an a priori delegitimization of ideas such as the Islamic state or Islamic governance because they challenge the dominant faith in secularization. Some scholars of international relations, who faced a similar crisis at the failure of their theories to anticipate the Cold War, mused:

> Theory is supposed to free scholars from their political, generational, and cultural biases. But social theory inevitably reflects these biases. It does a disservice when it confers an aura of scientific legitimacy on subjective political beliefs and assumptions. (Lebow and Risse-Kappen, 1995:5).

Thus a belief in secularism, or what some have called "secular fundamentalism," as a necessity for development prevented many analysts from appreciating the significant role that religion plays in Middle Eastern politics.

■ CONCLUSION

Religion has once again become a major theme in the study of world politics, particularly in the context of the Middle East. Rather than receding, religion has returned to the center stage. History is not progressing according to the script that modernity had envisaged for the region. The region is developing both in political as well as economic terms, but not along the lines that Western social sciences had predicted. The long history of the nexus between power and religion and current conditions in the Middle East suggests that Western-style secularism will continue to be challenged by the contemporary religious resurgence.

A particular reading of postcolonial history created the false expectation that the Middle East was well on the way toward secularization. In recent years, new Islamic republics have been declared in Iran, Sudan, and

Afghanistan. In Morocco, as in Saudi Arabia, the monarchy is strongly legitimized by its close association with Islam. In Jordan, King Hussein never forgot to mention his lineage, which he traced back to the Prophet Muhammad. Muslim rulers remain acutely sensitive to the power of religion, and opposition movements also appeal to Islam for legitimacy and popular support.

Similarly, Israel's very existence and identity remains tied to Judaism. Many believers base their political agenda on issues and sites that their faith holds sacred. Whether to defend the status quo or to condemn it, politicians in the Middle East, Jews as well as Muslims, invoke religious categories. The difference between the role of religion in contemporary politics, in politics in the precolonial past, and in politics in the postcolonial secular era has been one of degree, not of kind.

In the twenty-first century, religion will continue to be a major driving force in global politics. It performs many political functions, just as politics serves many religious functions in the traditional land of God, the Middle East. Religion is a source of identity as well as signification, providing symbols of authentication and meaning for social and political existence. It is the basis for states as well as a source of civil society. It is invoked to give legitimacy to systems and regimes and to provide revolutionary fodder to challenge the legitimacy of states, systems, and regimes. Jerusalem represents the locus where all three Abrahamic faiths have come together in the past and remains the subject of common and at times competing claims. The challenge for the religious politics of the Middle East in coming years, as with the issue of Jerusalem, will be developing a pluralistic mode of existence based on the recognition of shared principles, values, and interests amid acknowledged religious and political differences.

■ NOTES

1. For a graphic description of the massacre in Jerusalem, see Runciman (1992:187–188) and Mayer (1988).

2. Islamic traditions refer to Jews and Christians as "People of the Book" and recognize the common origins of the Torah, the New Testament, and the Quran.

3. Ironically, considerable missionary efforts were expended in Arab communities that had been Christian for centuries but that followed ancient branches of Christianity not fully understood by nineteenth-century Western churches.

4. The Islamic equivalent of this term is Mutaqqi, also meaning the God-fearing.

5. In March 1994, following the massacre of twenty-nine Muslim worshipers in Hebron by a Kach follower, Kach and another Kahane-inspired organization were banned by the Israeli government under its antiterrorist laws.

■ BIBLIOGRAPHY

Abu-Amr, Ziad. 1994. *Islamic Fundamentalism in the West Bank and Gaza: Muslim Brotherhood and Islamic Jihad.* Bloomington: Indiana University Press.

Abu-Rabi, Ibrahim (ed.). 1994. *Islamic Resurgence: Challenges, Directions and Future Perspectives.* Tampa: World and Islam Studies Enterprise.

———. 1996. *Intellectual Origins of Islamic Resurgence in the Modern Arab World.* New York: State University of New York Press.

Adams, Charles. 1983. "Maududi and the Islamic State." Pp. 99–133 in John Esposito (ed.), *Voices of Resurgent Islam.* Oxford: Oxford University Press.

Ahmad, Mumtaz (ed.). 1986. *State Politics and Islam.* Indianapolis, Ind.: American Trust Publications.

Appleby, Scott R. 1994. "The Surprising Resurgence of Religion." In *Religious Fundamentalisms and Global Conflict.* New York: Foreign Policy Association.

Armstrong, Karen. 1991. *Holy War: The Crusades and Their Impact on Today's World.* New York: Doubleday.

el-Awa, Muhammad. 1980. *On the Political System of the Islamic State.* Indianpolis, Ind.: American Trust Publications.

Ayubi, Nazih. 1991. *Political Islam: Religion and Politics in the Arab World.* London: Routledge.

Breger, Marshall. 1996. "Religion and Politics in Jerusalem." *Journal of International Affairs,* 50, no. 1:91–118.

Burgat, François, and William Dowell. 1993. *The Islamic Movement in North Africa.* Austin: University of Texas.

Cavendish, Richard. 1980. *The Great Religions.* New York: Arco Press.

Choueiri, Youssef. 1990. *Islamic Fundamentalism.* Boston: Twayne.

Cleveland, William L. 1994. *A History of the Modern Middle East.* Boulder, Colo.: Westview Press.

Cragg, Kenneth. 1991. *The Arab Christian: A History in the Middle East.* Louisville, Ken.: John Knox Press.

Damant, Peter. 1995. *Jewish Fundamentalism in Israel: Implications for the Mideast Conflict.* Jerusalem: Israel/Palestine Center for Research and Information.

Entelis, John. 1981. "Ethnic Conflict and the Reemergence of Radical Christian Nationalism in Lebanon." Pp. 227–246 in Michael Curtis (ed.), *Religion and Politics in the Middle East.* Boulder, Colo.: Westview Press.

Esposito, John L. (ed.). 1983. *Voices of Resurgent Islam.* Oxford: Oxford University Press.

——— (ed.). 1990. *The Iranian Revolution: Its Global Impact.* Miami: Florida International University Press.

———. 1991. *Islam: The Straight Path.* 2d ed. New York: Oxford University Press.

———. 1998. *Islam and Politics.* 4th ed. Syracuse: Syracuse University Press.

———. 1999. *The Islamic Threat: Myth or Reality?* 3d ed. New York: Oxford University Press.

Esposito, John L., and John Voll. 1996. *Islam and Democracy.* London: Oxford University Press.

Friedland, Roger, and Richard D. Hecht. 1995. "The Politics of Time and Space in Jerusalem: Interest, Symbol and Power." Pp. 373–424 in Sabrina P. Ramet and Donald W. Treadgold (eds.), *Render unto Caesar: The Religious Sphere in World Politics.* Boston: American University Press.

Friedman, Menachem. 1992. "Jewish Zealots: Conservative Versus Innovative." Pp. 159–176 in Lawrence Kaplan (ed.), *Fundamentalism in Comparative Perspective*. Amherst: University of Massachusetts Press.

Friedman, Robert. 1990. *The False Prophet: Rabbi Meir Kahane from FBI Informant to Knesset Member*. Chicago: Lawrence Hill Books.

———. 1992. *Zealots for Zion: Inside Israel's West Bank Settlement Movement*. New York: Random House.

Fuller, Graham. 1995. "Has Political Islam Failed?" *Middle East Insight* (January-February):8–11.

Fuller, Graham, and Ian Lesser. 1995. *A Sense of Siege: The Geopolitics of Islam and the West*. Boulder, Colo.: Westview Press.

Gellner, Ernest. 1992. *Postmodernism, Reason and Religion*. London: Routledge.

Haddad, Yvonne. 1995. "Christians in a Muslim State: The Recent Egyptian Debate." Pp. 381–398 in Yvonne Haddad and Wadi Haddad (eds.), *Christian-Muslim Encounters*. Miami: University Press of Florida.

Hamidullah, Muhammad. 1979. *Introduction to Islam*. London: MWH London Publishers.

Haynes, Jeffrey. 1994. *Religion in Third World Politics*. Boulder, Colo.: Lynne Rienner.

Hertzberg, Arthur. 1992. "Jewish Fundamentalism." Pp. 152–159 in Lawrence Kaplan (ed.), *Fundamentalism in Comparative Perspective*. Amherst: University of Massachusetts Press.

Huntington, Samuel. 1968. *Political Order in Changing Societies*. New Haven: Yale University Press.

Husain, Mir Zohair. 1995. *Global Islamic Politics*. New York: HarperCollins College Publishers.

Keppel, Gilles. 1985. *Muslim Extremism in Egypt: The Prophet and Pharaoh*. Los Angeles: University of California Press.

Khan, Mohammed A. Muqtedar. 1996. "Turkey Returns." *The Message* (August): 15–17.

Lamb, Harold. 1930. *The Crusades*. New York: International Collectors Library.

Lebow, Richard Ned, and Thomas Risse-Kappen (eds.). 1995. *International Relations Theory and the End of the Cold War*. New York: Columbia University Press.

Lewis, Bernard. 1968. *The Emergence of Modern Turkey*. London: Oxford University Press.

———. 1993. *Islam and the West*. New York: Oxford University Press.

Liebman, Charles. 1990. "The Jewish Religion and Contemporary Israeli Nationalism." Pp. 77–94 in Emmanuel Sivan and Menachem Friedman (eds.), *Religious Radicalism and Politics in the Middle East*. New York: State University of New York Press.

Liebman, Charles, and Eliezer Don-Yehiya. 1983. *Civil Religion in Israel*. Los Angeles: University of California Press.

Lindholm, Charles. 1996. *The Islamic Middle East: An Historical Anthropology*. Oxford: Blackwell.

Lustick, Ian S. 1988. *For the Land and the Lord: Jewish Fundamentalism in Israel*. New York: Council on Foreign Relations.

Mahallati, Mohammad. 1996. "The Middle East: In Search of an Equilibrium Between Transcendental Idealism and Practicality." *Journal of International Affairs* 50, no. 1:119–141.

Marcus, Abraham. 1989. *The Middle East on the Eve of Modernity*. New York: Columbia University Press.

Mayer, H. E. 1988. *The Crusades.* New York: Oxford University Press.

Mergui, Raphael, and Philippe Simonnot. 1987. *Israel's Ayatollahs: Meir Kahane and the Far Right in Israel.* London: Saqi Books.

Miller, Judith. 1993. "The Challenge of Radical Islam." *Foreign Affairs* 72, no. 2:43–56.

Minault, Gail. 1974. "Islam and Mass Politics: The Indian Ulama and the Khilafat Movement." Pp. 168–182 in Donald E. Smith (ed.), *Religion and Political Modernization.* New Haven: Yale University Press.

Mottahedeh, Roy. 1985. *The Mantle of the Prophet: Religion and Politics in Iran.* New York: Pantheon Books.

Munson, Henry, Jr. 1988. *Islam and Revolution in the Middle East.* New Haven: Yale University Press.

Osman, Fathi. 1994. *Sharia in Contemporary Society: The Dynamics of Change in Islamic Law.* Los Angeles: M. V. International.

Pipes, Daniel. 1995. "There Are No Moderates: Dealing with Fundamentalist Islam." *National Interest* 41:57.

Rahnema, Ali (ed.). 1994. *Pioneers of Islamic Revival.* London: Zed Books.

Ravitsky, Aviezer. 1993. *Messianism, Zionism, and Jewish Religious Radicalism.* Chicago: Chicago University Press.

Rodman, Peter. 1994. "Co-opt or Confront Fundamentalist Islam?" *Middle East Quarterly* 1, no. 4:61–64.

Runciman, Steven. 1992. *The First Crusade.* Abridged ed. New York: Cambridge University Press.

Salibi, Kamal. 1981. "The Lebanese Identity." Pp. 217–226 in Michael Curtis (ed.), *Religion and Politics in the Middle East.* Boulder, Colo.: Westview Press.

Shahin, Emad Eldin. 1995. "Under the Shadow of the Imam." *Middle East Insight* 11:40–45.

Sidahmed, A. Salam, and A. Ehteshami (eds.). 1996. *Islamic Fundamentalism.* Boulder, Colo.: Westview Press.

Silberstein, Lawrence (ed.). 1993. *Jewish Fundamentalism in Comparative Perspective: Religion, Ideology and the Crisis of Modernity.* New York: New York Press.

Sivan, Emmanuel. 1985. *Radical Islam: Medieval Theology and Modern Politics.* New Haven: Yale University Press.

———. 1990a. "Introduction." Pp. 1–9 in Emmanuel Sivan and Menachem Friedman (eds.), *Religious Radicalism and Politics in the Middle East.* New York: State University of New York Press.

———. 1990b. "The Islamic Resurgence: Civil Society Strikes Back." Pp. 96–108 in Lawrence Kaplan (ed.), *Fundamentalism in Comparative Perspective.* Amherst: University of Massachusetts Press.

Spiegel, Steven. 1982–1983. "Religious Components of U.S. Middle East Policy." *Journal of International Affairs* 36, no. 2:235–246.

Sprinzak, Ehud. 1991. *The Ascendance of Israel's Radical Right.* New York: Oxford University Press.

Swatos, William, Jr. 1989a. "Losing Faith in the 'Religion' of Secularization: Worldwide Religious Resurgence and the Definition of Religion." Pp. 147–154 in William Swatos Jr. (ed.), *Religious Politics in Global and Comparative Perspective.* New York: Greenwood Press.

———. 1989b. "The Kingdom of God and the World of Man: The Problem of Religious Politics." Pp. 1–10 in William Swatos Jr. (ed.), *Religious Politics in Global and Comparative Perspective.* New York: Greenwood Press.

Thomas, Scott. 1995. "The Global Resurgence of Religion and the Study of World Politics." *Millennium: Journal of International Studies* 24, no. 2:289–299.

Turabi, Hassan. 1983. "The Islamic State." Pp. 241–251 in John Esposito (ed.), *Voices of Resurgent Islam.* Oxford: Oxford University Press.

Usher, Graham. 1996. "Picture of War." *Middle East International* 535:3–5.

Vogel, Manfred. 1986. "The State as Essential Expression of the Faith of Judaism." Pp. 11–20 in Nigel Biggar, Jamies S. Scott, and William Schwieker (eds.), *Cities of God: Faith, Politics, and Pluralism in Judaism, Christianity, and Islam.* Westport, Conn.: Greenwood Press.

Voll, John (ed.). 1991. *Sudan: State and Society in Crisis.* Bloomington: Indiana University Press.

———. 1994. *Islam: Continuity and Change in the Modern World.* Syracuse: Syracuse University Press.

Von Der Mehden, Fred. 1986. *Religion and Modernization in Southeast Asia.* Syracuse: Syracuse University Press.

Zubaida, Sami. 1993. *Islam, the People and the State: Political Ideas and Movements in the Middle East.* London: I. B. Taurus.

■ 12 ■

Middle Eastern Literature
miriam cooke

In this chapter, we discuss the emergence of literature in the Middle East as a new art form. European modernity hit the countries of the Middle East hard. Everything formerly accepted as normative came under question, nothing more so than literature. Traditional notions of what literature was and what function it should fulfill in the life of the individual and society changed. No longer the repository for all knowledge, *adab* (literature) branched out into the various genres of drama, short story, novel, and a radically new conception of poetry.

It is not possible to understand the role of literature in the Middle East without first glancing at its history and, above all, its evolution during the first half of the twentieth century. Although Middle Eastern literatures have become privileged sites for recording and engaging with sociopolitical tensions and conflicts, this was not always the case. In the medieval and early modern periods, Middle Eastern literatures had been the preserve of the elite, providing them with literary frames in which they might elaborate an already familiar tradition and demonstrate formal skills and erudition. Popular literature such as *A Thousand and One Nights* also relied on the already known. The roles of the imagination and of social commentary were generally downplayed in the Middle Eastern context.

■ EUROPEAN COLONIALISM AND ITS DISCONTENTS

The arrival in the late eighteenth and nineteenth centuries of the French and British colonial expeditions, with their technological, cultural, and intellectual institutions, forced a new look at society and culture. Contact with European modernity cast Islamic cultures in a poor contrastive light. Egyptians in particular, because they were the first to experience

French colonialism, became concerned to learn about Western culture and science.

Under such Ottoman rulers as Muhammad Ali Pasha and his son Ibrahim Pasha, groups of male scholars traveled to Western Europe, and particularly to France, to study scientific texts and to translate them into Arabic. Because of the enormity of the task, these scientific missions might stay in Europe for months on end. When they were not squirreled away in the libraries or archives, they were in the theaters watching plays by French playwrights like Jean-Baptiste Molière or in their rooms reading short stories in French by such writers as Guy de Maupassant or the Russian Anton Chekhov in French translation. The genre that was the newest and the most intriguing was the novel, and these men returned with translations of European masterpieces by Honoré de Balzac, Gustave Flaubert, Leo Tolstoy, and Ivan Turgenev, to mention only a few.

Some of these intellectuals understood that the writing and function of literature in the Middle East had to change to accommodate the new realities in their lives. They knew, however, that those who were unfamiliar with the new genres of short story, novel and play, and modern poetry might resist their introduction. The apparent focus of European fiction writers on entertainment at the expense of traditional education, on communication of sociopolitical messages of current concern and not so much on literary artifice and excellence was indeed greeted by some with the skepticism reserved for the introduction of anything new anywhere. Like the reactionary defenders of the Western canon, who in the 1980s announced the end of civilization as we know it if subaltern, marginalized literatures were to replace some of the time-tested writings of dead white Western men, the conservative elites of the region warned of civilizational decline, even extinction. Some feared that the great classical literatures of the Arabs, Persians, and Turks might not survive the invasion into literature of the trivia of the modern world. Literary practitioners would surely lose their storehouse of classical knowledge if they did not continually tap into it and thus renew it. They would lose their verbal agility if they turned from the eloquent description of great events in history to the banality of the world around them. Others saw in the dialogue between their own cultural traditions and those of the Europeans the possibility of reimagining national identity within a common modernity.

Whether they were closed or open to the outside, Middle Eastern intellectuals became engaged in the question of language as central to the process of modernization. They questioned, first of all, the boundary between the high-culture languages and the vernaculars, as well as the question of importation of foreign words. In Iran, the historian Mohamad Tavakoli-Targhi explains, the key was to disassociate from the Islamic past and to project a "pure" national origin. Arabic words that had been part of the language for half a millennium

> were purged, and "authentic" Persian terms were forged, and neologisms and lexicography were constituted as endeavors for "national reawakening." . . . The invention of an idealized past was contemporaneous with the restyling of language, which was achieved in a dialogic relationship with Iran's Arab-, European-, and (the often ignored) Indian-Other. . . . The Persian language was reconstituted as the essential component of Iranian national identity. (Tavakoli-Targhi, 1990:77, 86)

Language reform "was not an aftereffect of the constitutional revolutions in Iran and the Ottoman Empire but a prelude to them. Purists constituted language as the essential component of the national identity" (Tavakoli-Targhi, 1990:91). History could not be reconceived without a radical transformation of the language and its grammar.

In the case of Turkish and Arabic, the linguistic situation was more extreme because of the distance between the classical and the colloquial languages. Indeed, in both cases there had emerged a kind of bilingualism. The written language of the Turks was so different from the spoken that it was even named differently: it was called Ottoman Turkish. Written in the Arabic script and filled with Persian and Arabic vocabulary—as much as 75 percent—this Ottoman Turkish had to be learned as an entirely distinct language with its own rules of grammar (Halman, 1982:36). Paradoxically, the poetry of the mystic Yunus Emre (d. ca. 1321), written before the Turks' importation of a foreign lexicon (partly as a result of their embracing Islam), is more accessible to Turks schooled in the post-Atatürk era than the literature they learned from their grandparents. Atatürk's Westernization campaign in the 1920s that entailed the eradication of Islamic elements in the language put an end to the bilingual situation that had pertained in Turkey for centuries.

There has been no comparable revolution in the Arab world, and so the split between the classical and colloquial Arabic languages persists until today. The codification of the spoken language is still tentative because the Arabic of the Quran retains its place of honor as the literary medium of expression. Conservative Arab intellectuals feared that the use of colloquial expressions in literature, particularly since there was no consensus over the way in which the colloquial should be codified, might herald the demise of the scriptural language; it might put an end to a pan-Arab literature, because these vulgar languages would create a tower of Babel in which multiple, mutually incomprehensible local literatures would vie for a small spot on the grand stage of what had once been a great and unified literary tradition.

Such anxieties notwithstanding, some Middle Eastern intellectuals, particularly those who had traveled to Europe with the scientific missions, turned their attention to the great French, English, and Russian writers of the day. Indeed, French had become the lingua franca in many Middle Eastern countries, even in those like Turkey that had not experienced the *mission civilisatrice* (civilizing mission). Flaubert and Maupassant, Charles Dickens and Percy Bysshe Shelley, as well as Chekhov and Tolstoy in French translation, all provided models of how the crises and concerns of the modern world could be turned into works of literary merit. During the earliest periods, these modernist intellectuals translated nineteenth-century European literature into their own languages. By the 1880s, however, some were experimenting with this new kind of writing. The Syrian-Lebanese Jurji Zaydan (1861–1914), for instance, wrote a series of historical novels and even a short autobiographical piece. Despite the general disapproval of writing one's own life, Zaydan published the story of his education during a time of major upheaval, having recognized in his experiences those of others.

■ **CULTURAL FERMENT AT THE
TURN OF THE TWENTIETH CENTURY**

Early-twentieth-century Egypt provided the regional context for literary experimentation and excitement. Middle Eastern intellectuals who did not go to Paris might move to Cairo to participate in the excitement of cultural innovations and transformations. Literary salons convened men and sometimes even women to discuss the new trends in politics and literature. At a time when most middle- and upper-class women were confined to their homes, these gatherings of intellectuals were almost the only places where women could appear with men. Literary schools in Egypt, such as the Diwan School, the New School, and the Apollo School (none of which included women among their numbers), encouraged the production of new kinds of writing that were then often published in their own journals and newspapers. These debates and their publication produced a new space, that of the public sphere. Discussions about national identity and the new roles women and men were expected to play in the nation of the future became matters concerning everyone and not merely a restricted community of scholars, often religious scholars. In the process, new conceptions of literary criticism appeared.

The new critics' insistence on the centrality of the imagination in works of art and the need for the work to interact with and hopefully to change society influenced a new generation of critics and writers. The notion that criticism should be neither descriptive nor evaluative but rather investigative led to some radical critical writing. Taha Husayn (1889–1973), the Egyptian author of dozens of books, including novels, works of philosophy, and his own autobiography entitled *The Days* (1929), published in 1926 his *On Pre-Islamic Poetry*, which calls into question the dating of some of this poetry. There was an uproar because this poetry, composed before the time of the Prophet Muhammad, was considered to be the paragon of literary expression, and with the Quran, it was cherished as the perfect classical Arabic language that the Prophet spoke. To cast doubt on its authenticity was to throw into turmoil other certainties connected to the founding moment of Islam. New literary critical tools were opening up new ways of approaching old texts, and above all they were revolutionizing literary production.

Simultaneous with this literary activity in Egypt, two revolutions broke out in Turkey and Iran. Young Turks and Iranians brought up on Enlightenment ideals rebelled against autocratic, self-indulgent rule by the last rulers of the Ottoman and the Qajar Empires. Between 1919 and 1922 Mustafa Kemal (1881–1938, also known as Atatürk after 1933), waged his war of independence against the British, French, Italians, and Greeks. The expulsion of these foreigners was followed by a series of revolutions that continued beyond the 1923 founding of the Turkish republic. Upon assuming national leadership, Atatürk abolished the Ottoman caliphate in 1924 and then implemented his secularization program. He introduced a new Europeanized dress code and declared illegal the wearing of Islamic dress, such as the veil. Most traumatic for traditional litterateurs, in 1928 he replaced the Arabic-based Ottoman script with the Latin alphabet. Yakup Kadri Karaosmanoglu (1889–1974) is the writer who best encapsulates the mood of the times, which Talat Halman describes as being marked by "the disintegration of Ottoman society, ferocious political enmities, and the immoral lives of religious sects, as well as the conflicts between urban intellectuals and poverty-stricken peasants" (Halman, 1982:29). Karaosmanoglu saw himself as a representative of the new cultural revolution that had to be spread throughout the country. His book *The Outsider* tells a typical story of the alienation of the Middle Eastern government official when confronting rural peoples to whom he has been sent. But in this case, Karaosmanoglu adds to the sense of rejection and disappointment. He describes the failure of the city intellectuals to convey the meaning and passion of the revolution and the new Turkish nationalism to the farmers.

In 1905, Iran was rocked by its constitutional revolution. Nationalists confronted the British and the local feudal landlords, demanded a constitution that would vouchsafe them democracy and justice, and eventually agreed on a compromise. The period was rich with new kinds of writing, most of it referred to as *pishru* (progressive). These liberal and often socialist writings depict the turmoil of the period. They reacted against the purple prose and the social irrelevance of the Qajar writers. After his coup in 1921, Reza Shah became absolute monarch of Iran. He introduced strict censorship and centralized control, but he also concerned himself with the position of women. In 1936, perhaps in response to Atatürk's recent prohibition on the wearing of the veil, the shah enforced unveiling. Some see this measure as helpful to women, whereas others recognize in it yet another violence done to women in the name of progress. To force a woman who is not ready to reveal her face to unveil is tantamount to asking her to strip publicly. Many writers have dealt with the topic.

Such legislation against veiling should be seen against the background of late-nineteenth-century debates about feminism that were going on throughout the Middle East and beyond. Claims on behalf of women's education were entering the public sphere. Recent research by feminist scholars both in the Middle East and elsewhere has revealed that it was women themselves who were the first to raise the issue of women's absence in decisionmaking positions at the national or local levels. Yet it was not until the men took up the "woman question" that it became a matter for common concern.

In 1899, the Egyptian reformer Qasim Amin (1865–1908) had published his controversial book *The Liberation of Women,* in which he called for the education of women, as the mothers of the next generation, as well as for their unveiling and greater participation in the life of the nation. Along with other modernist reformers of the period who emphasized companionate marriage and nuclear families in a world where all individuals had the right to freedom and equality, Amin was drawing attention to the fact that when half a people does not engage in the activities of the other half, then the whole suffers. This emphasis on women as the gauge of a society's progress seems to reflect James Stuart Mill's reference in 1817 to India's barbarity being demonstrated by the fact that "women were in a state of abject slavery." As employee of the East India Company, Mill clearly felt himself authorized to make such pronouncements. The Western, colonial origin of these ideas was not lost on the more conservative Middle Eastern intelligentsia.

It was not only in his native Egypt but throughout the Middle East that Amin's treatise was influential. In 1900, *The Liberation of Women* was partially translated into Persian. Its publication in Iran did not launch the kind of debate about the rights and roles of women that it had in Egypt because it fell on fallow ground (Najmabadi, 1998:100–104). In 1921, Mohammed Ali Jamalzadeh (b. 1892) had brought out his first collection of stories, entitled *Once upon a Time.* The collection is as famous for its introduction, which explains the new function of literature as a mirror for the times, as it is for its satirical descriptions of Shi'ite scholars and its sympathetic portrayals of the lives of ordinary women and men (Daragahi, 1984:104–123). The following year, Morteza Moshfeq Kazemi published his two-volume *Horrible Teheran,* which takes up the cause of women by describing the numerous abuses they routinely suffer.

Atatürk may not have been directly influenced by the Middle Eastern debates surrounding the "woman question," but his fascination with the West, where feminists were beginning to attract attention, had predisposed him to be a strong advocate of women's rights. After coming to power, he gave them the vote and placed some women in parliament. One of the women whom he supported was Halide Edip Adivar (1884–1964), an ardent revolutionary who was pictured during the occupation of Istanbul preceding the war of independence lecturing crowds of men even while veiled. Journalist, feminist activist, literary critic, and novelist, her 1926 autobiography describes her adventures with the nationalists, which included the experience of cross-dressing so as to be able to fight in the army with the Young Turks. Her best known work is *The Clown and His Daughter,* a work that appeared first in English in 1935 and a year later in Turkish.

During this same period, the European Zionist movement was beginning to become active as Jews emigrated from Europe to settle the land of Palestine. Zionism at that time was a socialist ideology owing more to Russian-inspired communism than to Judaism. As such it must have looked to the inhabitants of Palestine much like the *missions civilisatrices* that the French and the British had been dispatching to the Middle East since the eighteenth century.

These alarming developments in the region gave rise to fledgling Islam-inspired reform movements throughout the Middle East. Their members warned against unthinking mimicry of the West and urged the virtues and relevance of Islam as nations strove to become part of the modern world.

■ THE SHORT STORY AS LITERARY PIONEER

First the short story and later the novel provided frames within which intellectuals could address the problems of their age. The short story, said to have Middle Eastern precedents in folk literature such as *A Thousand and One Nights,* developed most rapidly as a local genre. It was well suited to the needs of writers who had urgent sociopolitical messages they wanted to convey in a succinct and persuasive manner. Quickly written and read, the short story became an important vehicle for socially engaged intellectuals to communicate with people beyond their immediate circle of friends and colleagues.

☐ **Egyptian Stories**

It was in Egypt that the Arabic short story first took hold, and therefore its history there can be considered to be exemplary. Lawyers like Yahya Haqqi (1905–1991) and Tawfiq al-Hakim (1898–1987), who is better known for his drama, turned some of their cases into stories that became part of a general debate about modernization. Haqqi's "The First Lesson," published in 1926, is a powerful example of naturalist criticism of the new that was often symbolized by the train. Preparing for his first day in school, the son of the station master of a remote, rural, milk-train stop, watches the Nubian station guard, a deeply spiritual man and his only friend, slip off the platform and roll under the wheels of the train. The tragedy does not interrupt the day's program. He goes to school, sits at his new desk, and tries to fulfill the teacher's first assignment to the pupils: write an essay on the advantages of the train. Twenty-seven years later, Haqqi returned to the theme of the destructiveness of the railway in his indictment of the 1952 Free Officers' Revolution. *Good Morning!* is a novel, the only one Haqqi wrote, that contrasts the fullness of the lives of a few villagers before the introduction of the train into their lives with the pain and the suffering they experience after the station is built in their village.

Engineers and doctors also turned their professional experiences into the stuff of fiction. Whether they felt real sympathy or not is less crucial than the fact that they made the lives of the urban and rural poor available and sometimes even important for their mostly middle-class readers. The engineer Mahmud Tahir Lashin (1894–1954) wrote several stories about his professional visits to government offices, popular cafes, and also the countryside. His 1929 story, "Talk of the Village," which has been described as marking the maturation of the Arabic short story (Hafez, 1992:274), confronts an urban intellectual with the reality of the romanticized village. This is no utopia but rather a place of primitive passions and traditions.

Mahmud Taymur (1894–1973), from an upper-class family of litterateurs, was drawn to the simplicity of the life of the poor but also to the injustices to which they were exposed. To write about them convincingly he had to use their language. He is considered to be one of the pioneers in the literary usage of the colloquial. He told stories about women's abuse at the hands of unscrupulous men. He described young girls condemned to marry men older than their fathers and women paying food bills with their bodies so as to keep their families alive. The most prolific and best known of these early short story writers, Taymur kept his readers informed about the terrible lives women were leading and how the tragedy of such lives was not restricted to the individual but had implications for society as a whole.

The most diverse and complex of Arabic short story writers was Yusuf Idris (1927–1991). He was a medical doctor who had spent years practicing medicine when he turned to story writing. Like his professional forebears, he brought his experience in the clinic to his creative work. Like them also, he drew special attention to the ways in which the bad situation of women impacts everyone. His first collection of short stories, *The Cheapest Nights* (1954), deals not only with the customs and traditions but also the diseases of the fellahin (peasants). The title story is almost a manifesto on behalf of family planning. A villager comes home one night after searching in vain for affordable entertainment, and he produces another mouth to feed! In "The Dregs of the City," Idris turns to the city to present a middle-aged, middle-class man preying on his servant, her theft of his watch, his humiliating recovery of the watch, and her consequent ejection to walk the streets as a prostitute. The storyline is not new; what is different and moving is the narration of inevitable destruction. In his many other collections of stories, as in his novels and plays, Idris examines the lives of his compatriots, dissecting those elements that lead people to destroy each other.

☐ Iranian Stories

At the end of the nineteenth century, the encyclopedist Ali Akbar Dehkhoda launched the short fiction piece with the publication of some satirical articles. However, it was Jamalzadeh who turned this journalistic precedent into a local literary genre. The critic Heshmat Moayyad has referred to the 1921 introduction to *Once upon a Time* as "a manifesto for modernist Persian prose writing" (Moayyad, 1991:31). The stories in the collection provided Iranian intellectuals with a model of how to integrate this new genre into the repertoire of a transformed national literature.

The first Iranian to succeed in writing a fully developed short story in an accessible language was Sadeq Hedayat (1903–1951). Born into the Iranian nobility, he was educated in Paris, where he was deeply engaged by surrealism. His early work described Iran's great past, whereas his later writings, which were influenced by European writers and particularly by Franz Kafka, were as dark and despairing as his life. He committed suicide in 1951. Hedayat wrote novels, critical essays, and plays, but above all short stories that portrayed with sympathy the life of the destitute in Iran's cities. He, too, used colloquial expressions, but his goal was more political than artistic: literature needed to participate in the fight against tradition and particularly religious customs as the nation strove to become part of the modern world. During the 1930s and 1940s, he published three collections, including *The Stray Dog* (1942). Through the eyes of a dog, Hedayat told a story of rejection and alienation. The use of an animal as a protagonist goes back to a strong tradition of animal fables.

Sadiq Chubak (1916–1998), a younger friend of Hedayat who is best known for his novels, and the social critic Jalal Al-e Ahmad (1923–1969) elaborated what Hedayat began. It was Chubak who first experimented artistically with the use of the colloquial in formal writing. In *The Puppet Show* (1945), he strove to render the rhythm of the spoken language and not merely to include dissonant vernacular vocabulary for political effect. Like others, he was committed to describing and hoping to change the situation of women.

The son of a Muslim Shi'ite cleric, Al-e Ahmad focused on political oppression and, in the early stages of his writing career, on religious hypocrisy. The title story of his first collection, *Exchange of Visits* (1946), cynically describes a pilgrimage to a saint's tomb in Iraq. He has, however, been most closely associated with the notion of "Westtoxification," the title of a book he wrote in 1962, which was used as a slogan against the shah in the 1960s. For Al-e Ahmad, as for many of his contemporaries, the greatest danger was the cultural, economic, and political subordination of countries like Iran to the West. As Tavakoli-Targhi says in an interview, Al-e Ahmad "envisaged an alternative modernity informed by Islam. This work became important for Ayatollah Khomeini and other Iranian religious scholars who viewed Islam as the foundation of Iranian cultural independence" (Tavakoli-Targhi, 1999). This book may be seen as an early warning of the growing conservatism and anti-occidentalism that led to the Islamic revolution of 1978.

During the 1960s, many new short fiction writers appeared, most notably Gholam Hosayn Saedi (1935–1985). Trained as a psychiatrist and practicing in Tehran, he applied his clinical experience to his thirty volumes of stories, plays, essays, and ethnographies. Like Al-e Ahmad, he is severe in his criticism of the Westernization of Iranian society. Yet once the Islamic government was in power, he did not hesitate to criticize it in drama. His 1984 *Othello in the Wonderland* was performed in Paris, where Saedi ran less immediate risk for his mocking portrayal of the system's obsession with covering women's bodies.

The Islamic revolution produced a new generation of writers, many of whom are women. Critics like Moayyad praise these writers, whether they called for the overthrow of the monarchy or not, for their brave stand against a corruption that had seemed endemic and unassailable for centuries. However, for some the fight became too difficult during the 1980s, and many have chosen exile (see below).

□ Turkey's Master Story Teller

One of the earliest Turkish writers of short stories is Sait Faik Aziz Abasiyanik (1906–1954). Like his counterparts in the rest of the Middle East, Abasiyanik was interested in daily life both in the cities and outside. It is Aziz Nesin (1915–1995) who is the most prolific and admired short story writer in Turkey, as well as in Iran, where many of his works were translated into Persian. He has been called the twentieth-century Nasreddin Hoca, a witty, eloquent folk hero. He has written dozens of books, including *Elephant Hamdi* and *Madmen on the Loose*. His stories are marked by a sharp wit and concision. In "House on the Border," a Kafkaesque story about a tenant, the six thieves who prey on him, and their final forced collaboration to fight injustice, he takes on the repressive government apparatus. Nesin depicts the bumbling attempts of an alienated hero to find protection and justice from institutions that were established to protect the people but that refuse to become accountable.

Nesin's activity on behalf of the translation and publication of Salman Rushdie's controversial *Satanic Verses* almost cost him his life. He is one of the few Middle Eastern writers who made a handsome living from his writings; most others have had to rely on income from other professions such as journalism to allow them to write. After his death, his family established the Nesin Foundation, which supports literary activity as well as social projects.

☐ Women's Stories

Several women writers chose the short story as their frame for literary expression. As early as 1929, the Egyptian Suhayr Qalamawi had published a collection of short stories entitled *Grandmother's Tales*. The figurative use of the "grandmother" became popular as women sought models of feminine strength and stability in a patriarchal past. The piety of the grandmother was ambivalently presented: it could be a sign of blind faith and superstition or a trace of a time when there was safety and security from outside forces threatening one's belief system. Many women have followed in Qalamawi's steps, claiming that this short genre is perfectly suited to the life of a mother and housewife, where opportunities for concentration on a protracted plot are limited.

Three Syrian women are exemplary. Ulfa Idilbi (b. 1917) did not start publishing until the early 1950s, but she, too, described the problems women confront in a conservative society poised on the edge of change. Ghada al-Samman (b. 1940) wrote a collection of stories under the title *Your Eyes Are My Destiny* (1961), in which she explored the possibilities for women in a male-dominated world. Colette Khoury (b. 1937), more romantic but no less revolutionary, published *Days with Him* (1959), in which the heroine rebels against men's automatic reduction of women to mothers and hostesses and insists on her dignity and worth as an individual.

One of the most famous—and notorious—short stories of the Arab world is "Spaceship of Tenderness to the Moon" (1964) by the Lebanese writer Layla Baalbaki (b. 1936). The story of an early morning moment in the life of a couple, it reveals their erotic love for each other and their conflict over the desire for a baby. A trial was held to assess whether the story was pornographic or not. Baalbaki was finally acquitted, but the controversy has entered the history of twentieth-century Middle Eastern literature. In most of these women's writings, the heroine is defeated by the struggle against patriarchy. Whether she gives in to a man or abandons him, the final decision brings no satisfaction. A single woman cannot defy all with whom she comes into contact when the society is not yet ready to incorporate her into its fabric.

In 1947, with the appearance of *Fire Quenched,* Simin Daneshvar (b. 1921) became the first woman in Iran to publish a collection of short stories. Farzaneh Milani has praised her for creating women who are not simply victims of an overbearing patriarchy, but rather active human beings struggling to give meaning to their lives. In the later work of women like Shahrnush Parsipur (b. 1946) and Goli Taraqqi (b. 1939), Milani recognizes Daneshvar's focus on the disappointments inherent in mostly middle-class relationships in transitional societies, where individualism is in tension with traditional values (Milani, 1992:199).

Women have written about how their domestic responsibilities restrict attention and preclude sustained invention. They have also written about wars. Emily Nasrallah (b. 1938) wrote prolifically on the devastating effects of the Lebanese civil war, particularly as it affected women's lives. Her three collections of war stories capture moments of horror and loss that other genres could not quite encompass. In Iraq during the war with Iran from 1980 to 1988, Aliya Talib and Daisy al-Amir published their daring criticisms of an autocratic regime in the succinctness of quirky tales.

■ FRANCOPHONE NOVELS IN NORTH AFRICA

In the countries of North Africa that the French colonized in the nineteenth century (Algeria in 1830 and Tunisia in 1881), the first novelistic attempts appeared at the beginning of this century in French. In Tunisia, Jewish intellectuals like Jacques Victor Levi first used the novel to chronicle their daily lives. They described a multicultural society in which Arabs, Berbers, Italians, Maltese, Africans, Muslims, and Jews had lived together easily until the arrival of the colonizers. It was then that racial and religious differences began to matter. Novelists evoked the two worlds of the medina (old Arab city) and the *ville nouvelle* (new city) that accommodated the French and the constant border crossings between them. The *hammam* (Turkish bath) became the emblematic site of local authenticity and segregation.

In 1953, three years before Tunisia was to gain its independence, Albert Memmi (b. 1920) published his semiautobiographical novel. Written two years before *The Colonizer and the Colonized,* his classical study of colonial relations, *Pillar of Salt* provides a case study of the dehumanizing effects of colonial desire both on the subject as well as on the object of domination. The colonizer wants the colonized to forget who he is and to want to become like him. He fosters that desire until it nears fulfillment and then he reveals the hope to have been always empty. Benillouche, the intelligent son of a working-class family granted permission to study at a lycee, swings between his multiple and overlapping identities, at once loving and hating who he is but also the person he is becoming. This is more than self-criticism; it is refusal of self. The hero's highly conflicted relations with his father anticipate the 1960s and 1970s novels of the Moroccans Driss Chraïbi and Tahar Benjelloun, which dwell on the despotic rule of the father, transparent symbol for the patriarchal past, and the need to end it.

During the 1980s, Benjelloun wrote his two-volume novel, *Sand Child* and *Sacred Night,* that won him the Prix Goncourt, the prestigious French literary prize awarded almost exclusively to French writers from France. The novel tells the story of a father's refusal to accept the fact that his eighth child is yet another girl. He must have a son, will have a son. So he turns infant Fatima into Ahmed and produces a freak. This postmodern novel about gender construction in an Islamic patriarchy caused a scandal in Morocco. Benjelloun was accused of pandering to French voyeuristic desire for the exotic and the perverted. Some dismissed the Prix Goncourt as Benjelloun's reward for cultural betrayal.

In Algeria and Egypt, it was women who pioneered the francophone novel.[1] In the 1940s, Assia Debeche wrote about middle-class women's experiences of biculturalism: they were educated to expect opportunities for choice in love and life, but their realities often turned out to be quite different. The francophone Lebanese-Egyptian Andree Chedid explored the same problem two years after the success of the Free Officers' Revolution. Her book *From Sleep Unbound* (1954) was praised, if not warmly, for its bleak depiction of the fate of a woman in a rural Coptic setting where any attempt, however slight, to improve a black destiny was greeted with shock and redoubled rejection. Samya's murder of her foul husband is as much activism as such a woman in such a context could be expected to exercise.

■ THE ARABIC NOVEL

The novel in Arabic developed a little later than the francophone novel. It was too long, too epic a form to suit the purposes of the early arabophone social and cultural reformers. More than the short story, the novel seemed an unfamiliar genre, developed as it had been for the needs and interests of the European bourgeoisie of the eighteenth and nineteenth centuries. Above all, publication was an issue. The new Arabic printing presses were given over primarily to newspapers and journals, which became the most effective outlets for works of fiction. Even today some writers continue to serialize their novels and autobiographies in these publications, which often retain the services of creative writers as though they were journalists.[2] This form of publication lends itself to the cliffhanger style familiar to European readers of nineteenth-century sociorealist fiction.

In Egypt, it was the 1988 Nobel laureate Naguib Mahfouz (b. 1911) who first brought this longer genre to maturity. After publishing a few short stories in the 1930s, he recognized the benefits of a longer literary format for articulating the complexities of contemporary society. His novels from the 1940s until today provide a window on the evolving sociopolitical situation of Egypt and Egyptians in the world system.

In the 1940s, Mahfouz published two novels that revolve around events supposed to have happened during the times of the Pharaohs, focusing on the ancient Egyptians' expulsion of invaders. The allegorical nature of these works is transparent. This was a period of self-searching in Egypt, when local failure to act effectively in an international context was compensated for by recourse to past greatness. This turn to a past antedating the arrival of the Peninsula Arabs became a reflex in other Middle Eastern countries whose intellectuals were struggling with a crisis of identity. In Turkey, for example, just after Atatürk's death in 1938, as his successor was trying to consolidate his power in an atmosphere of uncertainty

© Thomas Hartwell

and growing repression, the novelist Kemal Tahir (1910–1973) wrote *Mother State* about the thirteenth- and fourteenth-century Ottoman Empire when it was at the height of its power and glory.

Along with the Turkish short story writer Sabhattin Ali (1907–1948) and the Turkish novelist Orhan Kemal (1914–1970), Mahfouz pioneered sociorealism in the Middle East. *Midaq Alley* (1947), the first of his novels to be translated into English, reflects the con-

Photo 12.1   Egyptian Nobel laureate Naguib Mahfouz.

cerns of other Middle Eastern writers who turned city neighborhoods into rich microcosms of their countries. The setting here is World War II Cairo, and British global dominion is quickly fading. This intricate novel was followed by his trilogy, comprising *Palace Walk, Palace of Desire,* and *Sugar Street* (1956–1957), that many claim won him the Nobel Prize. Although he wrote the trilogy during the Free Officers' Revolution in 1952, he did not publish it until several years later (see below). The saga of the 'Abd al-Jawads, an upper-middle-class family, it parallels the key events of the first half of the twentieth century. The lives of three generations mirror the crises through which Egyptians were passing from World War I through independence. But once again history provides a disguise for current concerns. Mahfouz draws the reader into the inner sanctum of a traditional home, where women and men interact in a way invisible to the outsider. The reader is privileged to share the first moment of disobedience by a usually submissive wife. There is a penalty to be paid, but the die has been cast. Her children, who witnessed their mother's unwonted daring, become politically engaged. Their different avenues of activism, Muslim Brother as opposed to Communist, often produce internal clashes, but kinship ties do finally survive the stresses.

In 1959, Mahfouz published *Children of Gebelawi,* a novel that tells the story of the Abrahamic faiths and their adherents through the lives of individual members of the Gebelawi family. This book has been banned in several Muslim countries for its negative portrayal of the Prophet of Islam. But Muhammad is not the only one subjected to moral scrutiny. Mahfouz comes down hard on all the great prophets of monotheism, culminating with the prophet of the new age, Arafa the prophet of science, spiritual skepticism, and alienation. It was this book that earned Mahfouz the 1994 knife attack by a zealous Muslim fundamentalist. Mahfouz pursued this existentialist theme throughout the 1960s, depicting hopeless characters in search of some little meaning to give to their lives.

The Six Day War of 1967 produced an intellectual crisis in the Arab world to which Mahfouz reacted very strongly, both in terms of content and of form. Many readers and critics regretted the loss of the linear narrative line of his first novels, as his writing of the 1970s fragmented into the staccato of alarm and surreal confusion. In the 1980s, Mahfouz changed his style and themes again. This time he turned to the classics and wrote modern versions. He produced his own take on *A Thousand and One Nights* and also a travel narrative written in response to the famous travelogue of the fourteenth-century Moroccan traveler Ibn Battutah, which Mahfouz titled in recognition of the influence, *The Journey of Ibn Fattouma* (1983).

The novel has provided many with the frame appropriate to contain nostalgic reflections on a world that has passed. *Fragments of Memory* by

Syrian writer Hanna Mina (b. 1924) tells the tale of a village before the onslaught of foreign values. This village is like the one Muna abandons in *September Birds* (1962) by Lebanese writer Emily Nasrallah. Like many Middle Eastern heroes, Muna is faced with the challenge of modernity, namely that the village cannot provide a sustainable future. Muna leaves for Beirut and does not know who she is now that she is far from home.

Unlike most Arab novelists who place their stories in the city or in the village, the Saudi exile Abd al-Rahman Munif (b. 1933), who now lives in Syria, has situated his novels in the desert. His magnum opus is a five-volume novel entitled *Cities of Salt,* which he published throughout the 1980s. Having begun his career as a petroleum economist, he is intimately familiar with the impact of oil on the economies and lives of people living in oil-rich states. The quintet traces the transformation in the environment as well as in the consciousness of the local, mostly bedouin, inhabitants after the discovery of black gold. The reader witnesses the growing brutalization of the bedouin as they recognize that in this brave new world of competition and profit, there is more to be gained by individual enterprise than by tribal solidarity. This book earned its author the displeasure of his Saudi government, which deprived him of citizenship.

■ THE IRANIAN NOVEL

The Iranian novel appeared before the Arabic novel; the three-volume *Travel Diary of Ebrahim Beg* (1890s) is said to be the first Iranian novel. Iranian writers, more than the Arabs, tended to work in both short story and novel genres. This was true for Hedayat, Chubak, Al-e Ahmad, and Daneshvar.

One of the best-known Iranian novels is Hedayat's *Blind Owl*, which was written by 1930 but not published until 1937 in India and until 1941 in Iran, after Reza Shah abdicated and censorship was lifted. It is a book of highly introspective notes that Hedayat wrote "for my shadow." He describes a husband tortured by his relations with a wife who gives herself easily to her many lovers but not at all to him. He becomes an opium addict, a misfit, a murderer, and a madman. The despair in this novel foreshadowed Hedayat's suicide in 1951.

Chubak wrote several novels that have been praised for their keen attention to detail. In 1963, he published his first novel *Tongsir* to great acclaim. It tells the story of a man from the mountains who takes revenge on those who try to defraud him. At about the same time, both Al-e Ahmad and his wife Daneshvar were actively and publicly engaged in the literary scene, where left-wing intellectuals struggled to resist the shah's attempts to organize and co-opt cultural, but particularly literary, production. Al-e

Ahmad's *The School Principal* (1958), written five years after the end of the Mosaddeq regime, criticizes the current Iranian system of education. Written at a time when commitment was more important than art, its publication was a politico-literary event. The most recent influential novel was *Klidar,* which Mahmud Dowlatabadi (b. 1940) published in 1979. In ten volumes, it is a bildungsroman that tells the story of the nation.

As had been the case with the short story, Daneshvar was the first woman in Iran to write a novel. *A Persian Requiem* (1969) takes place in British-occupied Shiraz toward the end of World War II. Neighbors and kin are at each other's throats, tribal leaders have revolted against the government, and Zari is at home trying to maintain stability and order. She is contrasted to a woman who writes, despite the prohibition on women's literary voices, and who struggles to hold on to her autonomy but is consequently committed to a psychiatric hospital. As can be read in women's writings everywhere, this madness is not a clinical disorder but rather represents a woman's rebellion and society's disciplining of such transgressions. The novel was a bestseller and was translated into several languages (Milani, 1992:59–61, 183).

■ THE TURKISH NOVEL

There are two novelists in Turkey who have earned international acclaim: Yashar Kemal (b. 1922) and Orhan Pamuk (b. 1948). Kemal, who has for decades been a Nobel nominee, pioneered the "village novel." Best known is his quartet entitled *Memed, My Hawk,* translated into almost thirty languages, which revolves around the ultimately unsuccessful resistance of peasants against their landlords. Talat Sait Halman has described his work as "one of the truly stirring achievements in the history of Turkish literature" (Halman, 1982:30).

Orhan Pamuk's first work was a family saga entitled *Cevdet Bey and His Sons* (1979). Much like Mahfouz's trilogy, it followed the fortunes of three generations. This first novel did not enjoy great popularity. In fact, Pamuk did not become famous until the 1990s, when he published his controversial *Black Book* (1990). It is a byzantine mystery about Galip, a lawyer in Istanbul, whose wife, Ruya, and brother-in-law, Jelal, disappear one day. He keeps their disappearance a secret as he tries to follow clues. Jelal is a journalist whose complicated, sardonic articles about Islamic history, literature, and mysticism interwoven with the details of dailiness have earned him a devoted readership. Galip is jealous of Jelal's acclaim but above all of his writing skill. As his search progresses, he steps into Jelal's shoes. He moves into the journalist's abandoned apartment, wears his clothes, reads his personal writings, answers his telephone, and converses with eager fans who call with exciting material. He even imitates Jelal's style and publishes articles in his name. It is his infatuation with this mimicry that costs Jelal his life. Critics, first in Turkey and later abroad, after the book was translated into several languages, were absolutely divided in their reactions. Some hailed this existential mystery novel as extraordinary and tantalizing, whereas others dismissed it. In 1997, the critic Nuket Esen published the second edition of the Turkish and international articles that had appeared on the book. When Pamuk's next book, *A New Life,* was about to be published in 1995, there was so much excitement that by the end of the first day of its sale it had been reprinted several times.

■ **THE ISRAELI NOVEL**

Unlike all other Middle Eastern literatures, with their centuries-old histories of consociations, Israeli literature is just fifty years old. The first Israeli novel, Moshe Shamir's *Beneath the Sun,* appeared two years after the establishment of the state in 1948. It is a highly political work that draws the profile of the new Israeli, the *sabra,* a term used to refer to those who are born on the land of Israel. The *sabra* are entirely enmeshed in the new nation's history and environment but can fall prey to unfriendly neighbors (Yudkin, 1984:42–47). The most frequently translated Israeli novelist is Amos Oz (b. 1939). After beginning his writing career with short stories, he turned to the novel. His work has been described as heavy with threat. This is particularly the case with his best-known novel, *My Michael* (1968). The heroine is obsessed by her paradoxical fear of and desire for the Arab twins she has known since she was a child. Oz's body of work plays on borders, both real and symbolic. This is significant in a country that has from the start been uncertain about and afraid for its geographical limits. Oz has situated many of his writings in the experience of the kibbutz, the communes in which many Israeli socialists lived (Yudkin, 1984:135–143, 168).

Particularly in the post-1967 period, some Palestinians within Israel wrote in Hebrew. Anton Shammas (b. 1941) wrote *Arabesques*, an autobiographical novel that has been hailed by some as a masterpiece of Hebrew prose. Yet despite the critical acclaim, the novel has not yet been accepted as part of the canon of Hebrew literature. Shammas has retrospectively described this work as his challenge to the Israeli claim that the Palestinians could be integrated as Israeli citizens. No matter how assimilated they tried to become in Israeli society, no matter how excellent the Palestinians' command of Hebrew, they could never become Israeli citizens in the full sense of the word.

■ DRAMA: GRAFTING THE NEW ONTO THE OLD

As with the other genres coming in from Europe, Middle Eastern intellectuals sought to find indigenous precedents for the theater. Some Arabs invoked the *maqama,* a tenth-century lyrical art form that told the story of an eloquent rascal who manages to deceive all, particularly a wealthy patron. Others cited the shadow play, which had its origin in the Turkish *karagoz* of the fourteenth century. Like the *maqama,* it is a comedy that revolves around the adventures of the uneducated but smart *karagoz.* Although the *karagoz* does deal with daily life and the struggles of the oppressed, its inherent frivolity and unchanging characters and plots resisted the serious intent of early Middle Eastern dramaturges. According to Halman, other popular performances common in Turkey include "peasant plays, pageants, rites, processions, mock fights, festival acts . . . and *Ortaoyunu* (Turkish *commedia dell'arte*)" (Halman, 1976: 14).

Like the novel and the short story, drama as it is currently construed was introduced into the Middle East through translations. Major plays by William Shakespeare, Molière, and Chekhov were adapted for the Arab stage. Particularly in the torn, nostalgic works of the Russian Chekhov that described the passing of an age and the unknowability of the future, Middle Easterners could recognize the dilemmas through which their own society was passing. The theater appealed to a much wider section of the public because it did not rely on literacy, and it became very popular. It provided a context within which writers could experiment with the introduction of colloquialisms, which were anathema to the writers of prose and poetry who feared the loss of the purity of their languages. With time, successful implementation of the colloquial in conversations between illiterate characters that were often offset by the high classical language of the educated provided models for fiction writers.

In 1873, the Turk Namik Kemal staged his play *Fatherland,* which was enthusiastically greeted by the audiences and censured by the government of Sultan Abdulaziz. Halman claims that this play marked the beginning of "the political significance of literature in Turkish life." Atatürk saw in drama an important aspect of Westernization that he exploited by establishing the City Theater of Istanbul in 1927. Writers in other genres like Yashar Kemal, Nazim Hikmet Ran, Orhan Kemal, and Aziz Nesin experimented in theatrical writing, not always with great success. Much of the dramatic writings of the 1960s are "village dramas," which marked the first significant move away from Western influence (Halman, 1976:13, 37, 41–47).

The name that stands out above all others in the field of Arab drama is that of the Egyptian Tawfiq al-Hakim, who wrote his first plays in the early 1920s. Unlike many of his contemporaries, al-Hakim was not supportive of the burgeoning feminist movement. While others were writing of the injustices women were facing, he criticized the "new woman" who heralded moral chaos. After three years spent studying law in Paris, al-Hakim returned to Cairo in 1928. At this point, he turned to philosophical playwriting and his treatment of women mellowed, as in *Shahrazad* (1934). This change may be due to his experiences with women in Paris, about which he wrote in his autobiography.

In 1960, al-Hakim joined other writers who were criticizing the new regime, brought into power by the Free Officers' Revolution, when he published *The Sultan's Dilemma*. The sultan is a slave whose owner, the previous sultan, had died before manumitting him. He must gain his freedom and can only do so by being bought and then freed by his next owner. He is bought in auction by a woman who has heard of his dictatorial ways but discovers that he is gentle. She gives him his freedom once he has learned its real meaning. In 1964, Yusuf Idris published *Farfoors,* a play that relied on the *karagoz* genre as well as on Sufi dervish dances. He wanted to prove that drama was not new to Arabic literature and that traditional forms could hold the new politically charged content.

In the late 1960s, students throughout the Arab world turned to the theater as a sanctioned space in which to stage their sociopolitical grievances. In Syria, a group of students founded the Thorn Theater Company, which produced skits and plays of surprising daring. The screen of comedy and fiction allowed actors to convey political messages that would elsewhere be deemed sedition. Government officials and censors allowed this dangerous practice to continue, recognizing that the people needed an outlet for their frustration and anger with a repressive regime. Along with other forms of cultural production but more visibly, the theater also helped to fashion a facade of democracy for the Ba'th state.

Writers schooled in the Thorn Theater have continued to write on the razor's edge between dissidence and martyrdom. Some, like Sa'dallah Wannus (1941–1997) and Mamduh 'Adwan (b. 1941), have stayed with the stage. Wannus's first play, *An Evening's Entertainment for the Fifth of June,* came out just a year after the Six Day War in 1967, and it has been described as the richest literary reaction to the terrible defeat. Fearless when it came to open political confrontation, Wannus criticized, even if allegorically, the current Ba'thist regime. First in 1977 with his *The King Is the King* and then fifteen years later with *Historical Miniatures,* he revealed the oppressive strategies of dictatorial rule. In the more recent play, he used the relationship between the fourteenth-century Mongol tyrant Tamerlane and the North African historian Ibn Khaldun to criticize intellectuals for their complicity with a corrupt system. 'Adwan's *The Ghoul* (1996) focuses on the cruelty of the last Ottoman governor to be sent to Syria. The nightmares that torment his sleep might be those of any dictator.

Other graduates of the Thorn Theater like Durayd Lahham have moved from the stage to television or the cinema. Paradoxically, the film industry has become the most radical of all cultural producers: it is exclusively controlled by the Ministry of Culture, yet it is engaged in stringent criticism of the government. What are the political position and ultimate fate of filmmakers like Muhammad Mallas, who are in the pay of the government but whose films, on the rare occasions when they are shown, leave their audiences breathless at their critical audacity? This is what I call commissioned criticism, because it serves to make the government look open-minded and democratic when it so wishes.

■ POETRY AND THE HOLD OF THE DESERT

Of all genres, the most resistant to change was poetry. The new emphasis on personal expression and free style was regarded almost as heresy. Throughout the Middle East, poetry has been and continues to be the most highly prized literary art. In the pre-Islamic period, politics and poetry had been intermeshed, and tribal leaders were expected to be accomplished poets. Islamic rulers generally continued to value the art of poetry and patronized it generously. Wherever it was composed, whether in Arabic, Turkish, or Persian, classical poetry retained elements of its origins in the desert. There were familiar tropes (figurative uses of words), images, meters, and form. Any changes had to be carefully introduced lest the innovation be considered a sign of incompetence. More formulaic even than prose literature, classical poetry did not allow for the expression of individual emotion.

The first attempts to make poetry more responsive to contemporary concerns began modestly in the mid-nineteenth century. Neoclassical poets like the Turkish writer Yahya Kemal Beyatli (1884–1958) and the aristocratic Egyptians Mahmud Sami al-Barudi

43

When you visit me,
Wearing a new dress,
I feel what a gardener feels
When a tree blooms in his garden.

عندما تزورينني
بثوبٍ جديدٍ ..
أشعرُ بما يشعرُ به البُستانيُّ
حينَ تُزهرُ لَديهِ شجرةٌ ..

Photo 12.2 Syrian poet Nizar Kabbani. The poem is "No. 43" from One Hundred Love Letters.

(1839–1904) and Ahmad Shawqi (1868–1932) were to give new life to classical motifs and language, with only slight modification in content. In general, they were formal conservatives (Somekh, 1992:40–41). The first substantive reform of poetry came from such poets as the Turkish writer Ahmet Hasim (1885–1933), the Syrian Khalil Mutran (1872–1949), the Tunisian Abu al-Qasim al-Shabbi (1909–1934), and the Iranian Nima Yushij (1895–1959), who had been inspired by the French and English Symbolists and Romantics like Charles-Pierre Baudelaire and Alphonse-Marie-Louis de Prat Lamartine, William Wordsworth, and Percy Bysshe Shelley. Their experiments with meter, form, and language transformed poetry in the Middle East.

A revolution was in the making, but opposition to free verse remained strong. In Turkey, the Marxist Nazim Hikmet Ran (1902–1963) was the first to be recognized for his free verse. Halman relates how in 1921 Atatürk had urged the already famous poet to "write poems with a purpose" (Halman, 1982:25). He did, but he had to pay for his "obedience." His outright condemnations of social and political injustices as well as his poetic calls for revolution gained such a wide following that he was made to bear responsibility for political unrest. During the late 1930s, just before Atatürk's death, he was imprisoned on the trumped-up charge of conspiracy to overthrow the regime, and his writings were banned. Upon his release, Ran fled to Moscow, where he is buried with great Russian writers like Fyodor Dostoevsky. He is the most widely translated Turkish poet. His poems "Some Advice to Those Who Will Serve Time in Prison" and "Awakening" are written for those who had to undergo what he did but were not as strong:

> I mean it's not that you can't pass
>   10 or 15 years inside,
>   and more even—
> you can,
> as long as the jewel
> in the left side of your chest doesn't lose its luster.

In the Arab world and in Iran, it was women who brought to fruition what male poets had long been trying to achieve. The Iraqi Nazik al-Mala'ika (b. 1923) finally succeeded in introducing free verse into modern Arabic poetry. In 1949, she published her anthology of free verse, *Ashes and Shrapnel*. Although others before her had experimented with this new poetic form, they had had little success; critics accused them of incompetence rather than welcoming the innovation. Her work paved the way for others like the Syrian Nobel nominee Adonis (Ali Ahmad Said, b. 1930) and the Iraqi Badr Shakir al-Sayyab (1926–1964). Both of these writers gained prominence through their adoption of mythic themes of resurrection, particularly in connection with the plight of the Palestinians. In 1968, Adonis published his pathbreaking work, *The Stage and the Mirrors*, which introduces a new poetic lexicon, rhythm, structure, and sensibility. His work is highly philosophical, filled with symbols, allegories, and mythical allusions. He claims that poetry should appeal to the mind, not to the emotions, and because this new poetry is a political weapon, it must be subtly wielded.

The political nature of Arab poetry and the repressiveness of several of the regimes within which these poets function has compelled some to write indirectly, obliquely, surreally, anonymously. Arab women, particularly in more traditional countries like those of the Arabian Peninsula, have often chosen abstract symbolism so as to articulate emotions otherwise considered taboo. This new poetry by women like the Kuwaiti princess Su'ad Mubarak al-Sabah was at first censured, even when not quite understood, because it came from the pen of a woman. In the late 1990s, however, this kind of poetry is finding a new, this time international, audience. In March 1997 and in places as far-flung from the United Arab Emirates as Vietnam and North Carolina, newspapers carried the story of the publication of a new anthology entitled *The Female Poets of the Emirates*.

In Iran, two women, Forugh Farrokhzad (1935–1967) and Simin Behbahani (b. 1927), rebelled against traditional forms and subject matter for poetry. Behbahani's first collection of poetry, *Broken String,* came out as early as 1951. Whereas Behbahani's rebellion took the form of neotraditionalism (Milani, 1992:235–239), Farrokhzad's method involved rejection. In 1955, she published what some considered to be a "scandalously frank" anthology entitled *Captive*. But she is best known for her collection *Another Birth,* which came out in 1964. Like al-Mala'ika, she breaks with formal convention as she describes the oppressive life of a Middle Eastern woman. The personal and the political fuse in a single poetic vision.

■ INDEPENDENCE AND POSTCOLONIAL STRUGGLES

As previous chapters have illustrated, the second half of the twentieth century has witnessed cycles of violence throughout the Middle East. There were liberation struggles followed by socialist activism followed by breakdown of law and order and widespread depression and disappointment. After independence, many wanted to reconstruct their countries and to fashion a local, "authentic" identity. Conflict and violence are so much a part of the history of the Middle East that no consideration of its literature can afford to ignore them.

Writers were concerned to play a role in the new societies that came with independence from colonial rule. Acting as conscience of the people, they set out to "revolutionize the revolution." In 1946, the Iran-Soviet Society sponsored the first congress of Iranian writers, during which the centrality of ideology to literature was announced. Seven years later, in Lebanon, the first editorial of the influential monthly periodical *Al-Adab* declared that all forms of writing must henceforth be politically engaged. The time of art for art's sake had passed, to be replaced by a revolutionary ethic in all creative activities.

□ Paying the Price

This emphasis on political commitment in literature appeared at a time when the Middle East was in the throes of revolutions and wars of liberation. Literature was to make an intervention in the political realm, to praise and promote the social good, and to criticize the retrograde. Wars of liberation from colonial rule were clearly good, but some conflicts were not so easily judged as good or bad. This was the case with the Egyptian Free Officers' Revolution of 1952. It was clearly good in that it brought back Egyptian rule after what some argued was a hiatus of millennia, namely since the Pharaohs. Others soon felt misgivings about the autocratic nature of the *nouveau regime* (new regime).

As mentioned above, Haqqi's 1954 novel *Good Morning!* openly criticized Gamal Abdel Nasser and his new regime. Another lawyer, 'Abd al-Rahman al-Sharqawi (1920–1987), published in that same year *Egyptian Earth*, which the filmmaker Yusuf Shahin turned into a film entitled *The Land*. It examines the impact of the revolution on the lives of the fellahin and shows the oppressiveness of the centralized authority structure that the Free Officers put in place. Again, the plot revolves around the introduction of a symbol of modernization, in this case a road, into a village that has managed to keep itself aloof from the corruption of city life. The fact that the revolution, in which so many had invested great hopes, had brought only misery to the people was difficult for many to accept. The intellectuals were particularly dismayed. There has been speculation that the reason Mahfouz did not publish the trilogy that he had written during the early 1950s until several years later was that the criticism of the new system was too patent; he must have feared punishment.

Many feel ambivalent about this delay, feeling that he should have faced the risk. In the Middle East, writers have a moral authority that is almost unimaginable in the West. They are expected to stand up for their convictions and to lead public opinion. Their boldness may earn them prison sentences, but that is as it should be. The prisoner of conscience, the intellectual who has done time, wears this experience as a badge of honor. Many prisoners of conscience in the Middle East, particularly the Communists, have written of their incarceration.

The Iranian writer Buzurg Alavi (b. 1908), who had become involved in the Marxist Tudeh Party, was imprisoned in 1937. During his four years "inside," he wrote two books: *Scrap Papers from Prison* and *Fifty Three*

Men. These stories about his experiences reveal the intense emotions of the prisoners but also their determination: "I gained in spirits in the prison and became better equipped for the struggle" (quoted in Alvi, 1984:283). Along the same lines, Egyptian writer Sherif Hetata (b. 1923) wrote *The Eye with an Iron Lid* (1982), an intricately told tale of its author's thirteen years behind bars both under the British and then under Nasser. His partner, Nawal El Saadawi (b. 1931), also recorded her months spent in prison under Anwar Sadat in *Memoirs from the Women's Prison* (1983). As mentioned above, Turkey's premier poet Nazim Hikmet Ran wrote extensively about his years "inside." The fact that these intellectuals have had such experiences and that they then publish them gives them a moral authority that others, whose writings may be as "good," may never achieve.

☐ **Algerian War of Independence (1954–1962)**

Tunisia and Morocco gained their independence from the French in 1956, but the Algerians, who had begun their anticolonial war in 1954, did not finally succeed until 1962. The war produced libraries of novels, short stories, and poetry, and even today it haunts the imagination of cultural producers, including filmmakers. Most recently, *Joseph and the Legend of the Seventh Sleeper* (1995) made the rounds of the Arab film festivals. It tells the story of a prisoner of war who escapes to find his companions. He discovers that they, like the quranic sleepers in the cave, perished in a cave with their dog. He buries his erstwhile companions and then is himself killed by traitors. The theme of the betrayal of the revolution has become common as intellectuals watch their country sink into violence, religious extremism, and isolationism.

But in the 1950s and early 1960s, hope was high. Everyone, even the women, were expected to write about the war. Women like Assia Djebar (b. 1936), who wrote *The Thirst* in 1957 about women's doomed thirst for independence, were criticized by the male literary establishment for obsession with individual problems at a time when the nation was in need of all of its citizens to be as united as possible. Later novels by Djebar are careful to place the revolution at the center of the work and to downplay the crises and disappointments in these women's lives. Although she had left the country during the early days of the liberation struggle, she published two novels on women's participation in the war, *Children of the New World* (1962) and *Naive Larks* (1967). Her description of women's mobilization, however, does not indicate any change in their consciousness about what their rights and roles in the postbellum society should be.

In contrast, male writers were writing with dread about women's growing power and influence in a society that was spinning out of control. One of the best-known novels of the war is *Nedjma* (1956) by Kateb

Yacine (1929–1996). The critics have generally interpreted this story of a mysterious beauty, the four suitors to whom she is related, her legendary father, and her French mother to be an allegory for Algeria. I have argued elsewhere that instead it narrates men's growing anxieties as they watch the emergence of the new Algerian woman out of the sea of the war (Cooke, 1997:chap. 3). This thesis is more forcefully brought out in Mohamed Dib's surreal novel, *Who Remembers the Sea* (1962), where the narrator loses his mind as he loses control over his wife, a guerrilla fighter. For those writers like Malek Haddad who left Algeria during the war, the dread of the woman soldier is intense. It is not so surprising, then, that when the war was over, the women were quickly returned to their homes.

The story of women's disempowerment in the aftermath of the war is well known; in fact, Arab women elsewhere often refer to it as the "Algerian lesson." This lesson taught others that they must not allow society to forget women's contributions during a time of crisis and need. In the 1980s, Djebar started to bring out her quartet, which she has described as autobiographical. Each volume presents a radical revision of Algerian colonial history as seen through the eyes of women. In the second volume, *Fantasia: An Algerian Cavalcade* (1985), she links the stories of unknown nineteenth-century women resisters, omitted in the official histories and chronicles, with those of living women who had been active and then silenced during the war, and with her own story.

Djebar's quartet forms part of a national critique on the part of revolutionary women who have recognized, perhaps too late, the dangers of silence. The war of liberation was not a revolution, they claim, because its outcome did not change the material and social conditions for half the population. As long as discrimination against women continues, the expulsion of the French cannot be considered to have been a national success. The recent attacks by Islamic fundamentalists on intellectuals, and particularly women, in the Algerian capital may be seen as the next step in the waging of a war that was not resolved in the early 1960s.

□ The Question of Palestine

Immediately after the departure of the British in 1948, Palestinians wrestled with their new loss of independence. Although most Palestinian intellectuals left in 1948, a few, like the poet Mahmud Darwish (b. 1942), did stay behind what came to be called the Green Line. Darwish's family left in the first exodus and then soon stole back in. They returned after the period for registering Palestinians had passed, and so the poet's writings dwell on the lack of identity papers. His poem "Identity Card" (1965) became emblematic of the Palestinian condition.

After 1967, the Palestinians who found themselves under Israeli rule in the Gaza Strip and the West Bank began to understand why it was that those who had stayed on their land inside the Israeli borders in 1948 were not necessarily complicit, but rather might be regarded as nationalists. The importance of staying, whatever the cost, became a nationalist virtue. Emile Habibi (1921–1996) was a key figure writing inside Israel. He was the founder of the binational Israeli Communist Party and winner of both the Jerusalem Prize for Literature awarded by the Palestinian Liberation Organization and the Israel Prize. In 1974, he published *The Secret Life of Saeed, the Ill-fated Pessoptimist: A Palestinian Who Became a Citizen of Israel*. It tells the picaresque tale of a hapless Palestinian as he stumbles through life and people in Israel.

Two years later, from Nablus inside the Occupied Territories, Sahar Khalifa published the first of her three novels on the experience of occupation by Israeli forces. From *Wild Thorns* (1976) to *Bab al-Saha* (1990), Khalifa paints the canvas of possibilities for resistance. Her heroines demonstrate how some women's ways of fighting are more effective than those of the men. Mothers who give their sons and daughters stones to throw at soldiers confuse the rules of war. Are these women and their offspring civilians or militants? Can they be shot? Or must they be tolerated, their stones deflected? This ambiguity disappeared in the later stage when the women's individual acts of resistance—like the mythical hydra, when one of its heads is cut off, two will appear in its stead—were turned into a unified strategy for revolutionary action. The militarization of local oppositions was named the intifada (uprising). It is arguable that this transformation of individual Palestinian actions into a single movement was disabling for the Israelis (Cooke, 1997:chap. 4).

☐ The War in Lebanon (1975–1992)

Even before the civil war in Lebanon broke out in the spring of 1975, some were sensing its inevitability. This was again true before the Israeli invasion in June 1982. Both al-Samman and Etel Adnan (b. 1925) wrote works that were filled with the dread of anticipation. *Beirut 75* (1974) by al-Samman uncannily predicts the civil war as the novel collapses into a series of nightmares. Five years later at the height of the war, she returned to the nightmare format. Her *Beirut Nightmares* (1979) takes the reader into the horror of the infamous hotels battle, which pitted opposing militias against each other for weeks in the fall of 1976. The heroine, like her author, had been caught in her villa located between the Holiday Inn, the Phoenicia, and the St. Georges hotels, and she strings together the hundreds of gruesome fantasies that haunted her during those bloody days. Many have read in Adnan's *Arab Apocalypse* (1980) a premonition of the Israeli invasion of 1982. The staccato poetry interrupted with symbols and figures lies splattered on the page like shrapnel exploding out of a bomb, like blood spurting out of a wound.

As happened in Iran after the Islamic revolution, chaos in Lebanon produced literature, much of it by women (Lewis and Yazdanfar, 1996: xix–xxi). The Beirut Decentrists, a school of women writing in Beirut during the war, wrote into the space of violence a script for a transformed society that would include all its members and treat them with justice (Cooke, 1988). But during the civil war, they did more than that. These women writers showed how the men were responsible for creating the terrible conditions that threaten to destroy the postindependence country that was so fragile. Hanan al-Shaykh's *The Story of Zahra* (1980) traces the growth in consciousness of a woman who had been a social misfit. As the war rages, she comes to see a role for herself, and she fights in her own limited but intense way to do something to end at least part of the madness.

☐ The Iran–Iraq War

While the war in Lebanon was at its height, further to the east the 1979 Islamic revolution ousted the shah of Iran from the Peacock Throne. Saddam Hussein, the new leader of Iraq, tried to take advantage of what he had mistakenly assumed to be total disarray in neighboring Iran. The war that he launched in late 1980 as a blitzkrieg persisted for eight bloody years. Like many dictators, Hussein had an ambivalent relationship with the intellectual elite of his country. He needed them, and therefore he feared them. Throughout the war, he coerced the writers and artists who could not or did not choose to leave to glorify the war in ink and paint. The Ministry of Culture established literary series and organized festivals designed to serve the purposes of the war. Many did as they were told. Some did not. Under the watchful eye of the censor, some writers even managed to articulate criticism of a war they were being paid to praise. Using allegory and a surreal style, they published writings that vividly evoked the harrowing experiences through which the Iraqi people were forced to pass (Cooke, 1997). Ironically, the Iranian government was doing exactly the same as its enemy, namely, sponsoring books of stories and autobiographies to praise the war.

☐ The Gulf War

The Iraqi invasion of Kuwait on August 2, 1990, and the war that several Western and Arab countries under the leadership of U.S. president George Bush launched against Iraq on January 17, 1991, produced Kuwaiti and Iraqi journals, novels, and short stories that are slowly making their way into print. In *Black Barricades* (1994), Kuwait's leading woman writer Layla al-'Uthman (b. 1951) collects stories she had written during the eight-month occupation of the capital city. The tone is one of confusion, which aptly reflects the mood of the Kuwaitis as well as of the Iraqis. The destitute, illiterate men wreaking havoc in the palaces of the Kuwaiti oil magnates may not know why they are there beyond the looting, but they do know that they do not wish to return to their home country.

Inside Iraq itself, several wrote against the brutality of the allied forces and particularly the U.S. pilots, who seemed to consider their Iraqi targets as no more human than figures in a Nintendo game. The Ministry of Culture has continued its publication of war stories. One of Iraq's leading women poets, Dunya Mikha'il, brought out her *Journal of a Wave Outside the Sea* in 1995. Far from glorifying the war as might have been expected from such a government-sponsored text, this poem depicts extreme alienation in a continuing reign of terror.

■ EMIGRATION AND EXILE

There are many reasons for leaving the country of one's birth. Some, such as education and work opportunities, are voluntary; some, such as political oppression and intolerable violence, are involuntary. The travel of a young man, his head filled with dreams, to Europe; his apprenticeship for a period, usually of seven years; and his disappointed return to his native land for education and the shock of return is a topos informing many Middle Eastern works of fiction during the first part of the twentieth century. The Egyptian writer Haqqi wrote the emblematic text of this "travel and return transformed" genre. His *Saint's Lamp* (1946) follows Isma'il from Cairo to London and then back to Cairo after seven years of training as an eye doctor. The naive young man, initiated into Western life and introduced to a different set of values by a Scottish woman, finds his native country unbearably primitive. He rejects its ways and forces Western medicine and values onto his Egyptian patients. Then he experiences a religious epiphany, which leads him to an understanding that he must resolve the tension between traditional and Western medicine. The novella was hailed as an Islamic model of how to become a Western-style scientist while nonetheless remaining a righteous Muslim.

Twenty years later, the Sudanese al-Tayyib Salih (b. 1929) developed this theme, although without the religious angle, in *Season of Migration to the North* (1966). This novel reverses the nineteenth-century colonialist's move from the metropole to the colony; Mustafa Sa'id goes North (to England) to learn but also to wreak revenge. The story of Mustafa Sa'id has often been compared to that of Othello; it has also been called the answer to Joseph Conrad's *Heart of Darkness* as well as to Frantz Fanon's depiction of the impotence and potential castration of the black man as he confronts the white woman (Fanon, 1967). While studying in London, Sa'id has affairs with three English women. Each ends with the woman's death, the first two in suicide, the third in a suicide-murder. Upon his return to his village in a region remote from the capital, Mustafa Sa'id is himself destroyed by his relationship with a beautiful village girl. The novel bears out Memmi's thesis of the mutually destructive effects of colonialism on both the colonizers and the colonized.

Many Middle Eastern intellectuals have chosen to leave their native lands because they can no longer live there. Sometimes the reasons are economic, sometimes political. For over a century, the Lebanese and Egyptians have left for Europe and the Americas and more recently the Turks for Germany, in search of a prosperity seemingly unavailable in the eastern Mediterranean. Citizens of repressive regimes, like the Iraqi and the Syrian Ba'thist governments and the Islamic Republic of Iran, have fled so as to find a place where they might breathe and speak freely. Many Middle Eastern intellectuals have congregated either in Paris or in London. There they have founded publishing houses and launched newspapers and magazines.

Emily Nasrallah has examined the question of emigration from a Lebanese perspective. *September Birds* (1962), a novel about a village whose vitality was being drained as the young people were lured away to the capital and to the glittering West, was supposed to have a sequel about the return of the migratory birds. The war in Lebanon forced her and others like her to understand that there was to be no return. The war turned the confusion and alienation experienced by those who were left behind into anger, for Nasrallah begins to criticize the émigrés. They should not have gone, not during the war but also not before. Looked at through the prism of war, emigration was tantamount to giving up on one's nation.

Nasrallah goes further in this later period to reveal that emigration was bad for those left behind but also bad for those who undertook it. It transpires that many who left their homes to make fame and fortune had in fact failed. They were not returning because they were ashamed that they had not realized the dream. Throughout the seventeen-year war, Nasrallah remained based in Beirut, leaving only briefly when the conditions deteriorated too greatly. In 1994, she published *Sleeping Embers,* a novel that seemed to bring closure to the question of emigration. Those who left should not come back because when they do, they disturb people's tranquillity by dredging up stories and pains that had been appropriately shelved.

These are difficult issues, for although emigration is chosen and exile forced, there are times when the situation in one's nation is too painful to be borne. How does one draw the line between what can and cannot be borne? After the Israeli invasion of Lebanon, some of the writers who had determined that they would not be driven from their homes started to move out. Ghada al-Samman, for instance, established herself in Paris where she now writes about what it is like to live in a non-Arab country but to retain Arab dreams.

The various political upheavals in the Middle East have caused many to leave their homes without hope of return. We have already discussed the situation of the Palestinians who stayed on their land. There were many, however, who chose or were forced to leave. Many lived and continue to live as refugees in camps around the borders of Israel or in the neighboring countries, waiting for exile to be over and return to their abandoned lands to be possible.

The twentieth century has become the century of mass migration, and so the story of the displaced person has come to symbolize the dilemma of globalization: it is impossible to live at home, impossible to survive outside. Ghassan Kanafani (1936–1972) was one such refugee who went to Beirut. His 1963 *Men in the Sun*, which was turned into a film entitled *The Dupes*, is a visionary text for our times that explores the possible outcome of the choice to leave one's home and to seek refuge in Arab countries. Three men entrust themselves to a Palestinian guide who has promised to drive them across the desert separating Iraq and Kuwait for an exorbitant fee. When they have almost made it, the driver is delayed at a border post. The men, who have temporarily hidden in the empty watertank of the truck, suffocate in the heat. This story tells the story of all hosts of refugees, who soon tire of their increasingly long-term guests and end up abusing them.

Jabra Ibrahim Jabra (1919–1995), who left Palestine for Iraq and later lived throughout the region, has written several novels, all of which delve into the lives of dispersed Palestinians. Perhaps his most important work is *In Search of Walid Mas'ud* (1978), which brings together those who have chosen to write about their situation with others who have decided to fight to change it. They debate the most appropriate means to defend a cause.

After the Islamic revolution and then during the punishing war with Iraq (1980–1988), many Iranians fled the country. They are now scattered all over Europe and North America, where some are writing in the languages of their new countries, but many continue to write in Persian. The latter include Mahshid Amirshahy (b. 1937), with her books *At Home* (1986) and the recently published *Away from Home* (1998), and Goli Taraqqi, who lives in Paris. In 1992, Taraqqi published *Scattered Memories*, a collection of stories about the pains of exile. Like Nasrallah, she reveals the impoverished lives of those who had emigrated and how incapable they are of providing shelter for their stricken relatives. Taraqqi reminds the reader that exile means leaving the physical home where there is privacy and autonomy, but it also entails humiliation since it forces dependence on others. Shahrnush Parsipur, a highly acclaimed feminist writer

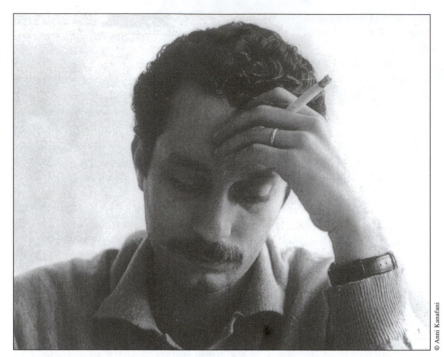

Photo 12.3 Palestinian writer Ghassan Kanafani,
who was murdered in a car-bomb explosion in Beirut in 1972.

whose 1989 book *Women Without Men* was banned by the Islamic Republic, is now in California, where she wrote *Tea Ceremony in the Presence of
the Wolf* (1993). This collection of short stories elaborates on the sense of
terrible loss and the condemnation to perpetual wandering that mark the
experience of exile.

Those who write in exile often feel farther from home than the miles
that mark that distance. Like the Algerians who left during the war of independence, they feel, perhaps, that they should be fighting side-by-side
with those intellectuals who have chosen to stay regardless of the cost. Yet
in a world whose borders are increasingly porous, where migration is a
necessary part of many people's lives, a new kind of cultural nationalism
is emerging that allows those who are living far from their land of birth or
ancestry to retain very real ties of identity. Literary associations in the
Middle East are slowly recognizing that their writers may not live in the
country that they claim as their nation. The Turkish novelist Habib Bektas
(b. 1951) is a good example. Since 1972, he has been living and writing
in Germany. In 1997 his book *The Smell of the Shadow* won the Turkish

Inkilab Kitabevi Press annual prize; it was the first time this coveted prize had been awarded to a nonresident Turk. Bektas justified his Turkishness by claiming that although he may not reside in Turkey, he does live in Turkish. This adoption of the language as the nation is a strategy many writers in exile invoke.

■ THE MUSLIM STATE

The Islamic revolution had been simmering in Iran long before it boiled over. Mention has already been made of Al-e Ahmad and Daneshvar, whose writings during the late 1960s seemed to be calling for reform of a society that was too much given over to the delights of the West. There is a pronounced Islamic tone in what they write. Two years before the revolution, Parsipur wrote *The Heat of the Year Zero*. The heroine's description of suffocation in the overwhelming heat of the summer and her stolen and then censured glances at men anticipated what the new regime had in store for its women.

In the early days of the revolution, the Islamic government of Iran, much like its royal predecessor, concerned itself with cultural production. Whatever was seen to be oppositional to its specifically Islamic interests was carefully censured. The case of Salman Rushdie has entered the annals of world history. Some writers complied with the government's will and wrote piously about the virtues of the revolution. Others, many of them women, protested the new restrictions, for example, A. Rahmani's "Short Hike," which acts out a tense moment of defiance between an Islamic guard and the woman he has just reprimanded for revealing a strand of hair. Milani has noted that in the short two-year period between 1983, when compulsory veiling was generally enforced, and 1985, "126 books by or about women were published in Iran." Restrictions had forced women to speak out (Milani, 1992:231).

As previous chapters have explored, it is not only in Iran that Muslims have called for the establishment of an Islamic state. After the abolition of the Ottoman caliphate in 1924 and the consequent secularization of Turkey, Muslims elsewhere in the Middle East became nervous. This was particularly true in Egypt, where the first formal association of Muslim revolutionaries was established in 1929. Other such groups formed, and many remain active today in many countries of the Middle East. Their increasing prominence in public life became a theme in literature from the 1970s on. In 1977 during a period spent in exile in Germany, the Egyptian 'Abd al-Hakim Qasim (1935–1990) wrote a story about the attempted conversion to Islam of a poor Coptic umbrella maker. "Al-mahdi" explores the new animosities arising between Christians and Muslims, who had always lived together peacefully. The story also reveals the growing chasm between young Islamists and more traditional Muslims in rural Egypt.

The Islamists have played contradictory roles in the history and politics of their countries. In Egypt, for instance, they helped leaders like Nasser come to power, but they have also sought to remove such leaders. During the mid-1960s, Nasser arrested several Muslim leaders. Their years in prison produced several memoirs, of which arguably the most interesting is that of Zaynab al-Ghazali (b. 1912). Since 1935, she has been the leader of the Muslim Ladies' Association, and during her tenure it has been closely associated with the Muslim Brotherhood. In 1965, she was imprisoned for a year in the War Prison with her male colleagues. That experience inspired her book *Days from My Life* (1977). Less memoir than inspirational literature, this text recounts the tortures and miracles that mark their subject as especially blessed. This autobiography could also be read as a model for young women seeking guidance as they try to combine their scripturally defined roles as servants of God with those as wives and mothers.

In 1981, a group of Islamists assassinated President Anwar Sadat. They charged him with making an unpardonable compromise in promoting the Camp David Accords with Israel. The Islamists' do not confine their targets to political leaders, however. As seen in Algeria in the 1990s, Islamists are increasingly focusing their attention on intellectuals who are charged with secularism and perversion of the people's morals. In 1992, Egyptian fundamentalists assassinated journalist Farag Foda for his critique of their discourse. Most annoying to them had been his book *Before the Fall* (1992). That summer, they published in paperback format the proceedings of a trial they had conducted, entitled *Nawal El Saadawi in the Witness Stand*. With its cover picture of a wild white-haired woman staring out from behind bars, the book was so widely distributed that it could be found in the streets of Cairo on the blankets of sidewalk book vendors, selling for a few piasters. These echoes of the fatwa (death sentence) Ayatollah Khomeini had pronounced on February 14, 1989, against Rushdie for his *Satanic Verses* were too loud to be ignored. Moral censure of literature had escalated to sanction of deadly assaults on the authors. El Saadawi, who is used to threats from governments and Islamists, did not shake this threat off as idle. When the government, which had itself imprisoned her for a few months during Sadat's regime, sent guards to keep watch on her apartment, she realized that she had to leave. She went to Duke University in North Carolina in the United States, where she spent most of the following four years writing her autobiography.

Nawal El Saadawi was condemned to death because of two books. *The Fall of the Imam* (1987) is the lyrically told tale of the assassination of the highest authority in the land, a transparent reference to Sadat's assassination, and of the pursuit and execution of his assassin, who is also his illegitimate

Photo 12.4 Mourners at funeral for Egyptian author Farag Foda, who was assassinated in 1992.

daughter, Bint Allah. *Innocence of the Devil* (1992) takes place in a psychiatric hospital where one of the patients imagines himself to be God, and another is called Eblis, the Arabic word for Satan. In each novel, God is the main character, yet he is constantly merging into the personas of other tyrannical male authority figures.

Unlike El Saadawi's earlier fiction, in which women are confined to the role of victim, these two most recent novels explore the ways in which women brought up in monotheistic religions resist the tyranny of God. It is not so much patriarchy that is the central concern, but rather monotheism, particularly when it is pushed to its extreme as in the current fundamentalist phase, that exonerates men from responsibility when they brutalize women. El Saadawi depicts these men as fearing women, whom they link with the devil. It is this fear of women-devils that El Saadawi provides as key to understanding why it is that men perpetrate violence against women and then justify their actions in religious terms. The devil, a character called Eblis, is a great friend of women, empowering them when they face injustice. He possesses their bodies so that they may have the strength to fight. Unlike God, who is constantly disguising himself, slipping into other forms, Eblis remains the same and easily recognizable. At the end, "God" proclaims Eblis innocent and thus destroys him and hence himself. The collapse of the God-Satan tension reveals the vanity of trying to know God through his opposite. The God who is paired with the devil is the God of organized monotheistic religions. This sacred-profane binary is only one aspect of the true God. The God who is knowable through his opposite is a tyrant who must be resisted. These two novels are open attacks on the hypocrisy and emptiness of religions when they are diverted to promoting human interests and away from meeting human needs.

■ TRANSLATION AND RECOGNITION

In conclusion, it is important to note that Middle Eastern literature is now entering the mainstream of world literature. The 1980s was the decade of translation and of international recognition for the literature of the Middle East. In 1988, Mahfouz became the second Middle Eastern writer to win the Nobel Prize in Literature, having been preceded by the Israeli Shmuel Yosef Agnon (1888–1970) in 1966. In 1989, the Moroccan Tahar Benjelloun won the Prix Goncourt, the first Arab to be awarded this coveted French prize. In 1997, the Turk Yashar Kemal was awarded Italy's most prestigious prize, the Nonino Literary Award.

At the same time, Arabic, Hebrew, Persian, and Turkish fiction and poetry were being translated into European languages. Previously the translation process had been idiosyncratic; random works appeared according to individual tastes of translators. By the mid-1980s, however, the translation process became more systematic, particularly with respect to Arabic works. In 1981, the Palestinian poet and literary critic Salma al-Khadra' al-Jayyusi founded her Project for Translation from Arabic (PROTA) in the United States. At first, these translations found homes in marginal presses dedicated to publishing works by writers from the global South. By the late 1980s, however, major European and U.S. and even Japanese publishing houses, including some university presses that are coming to consider Middle Eastern literature as potential textbooks, started adopting Middle Eastern literary series as well as individual authors.

The growth of the translation industry is significant for readers, who now have unprecedented access to the cultural imaginary of people they had previously known through the stories of scholars and travelers only. It is important, above all, for the writers and particularly for those who have already gained a share of recognition abroad. They are writing with the awareness that their works will be translated, that what they say about their culture is being consumed far from the local readership they had originally targeted. Writing thus entails consequences that must be anticipated. Self-criticism must become what the Moroccan cultural critic 'Abdelkebir Khatibi has called "double critique." The eye turned in on the injustices of a society must simultaneously look out to discern the contours of the enemy without. Local tyrannies must be held in balance with the dangers of global hegemony, with the understanding that the one interacts with the other. This double critique changes the way people think and write, and this changed writing is cultivating new tastes and creating new markets. Middle Eastern writers looking toward the twenty-first century are seeing their work becoming part of a global project in which they will play an increasingly visible role.

■ NOTES

I am indebted to Guven Guzeldere for information, invaluable advice, and stimulating conversations about Turkish literature. Warm thanks to Mohamad Tavakoli-Targhi for a careful reading of the penultimate version of the chapter and for wonderful suggestions.

1. Memmi notes that between 1947 and 1986, Algerian women had published thirty-seven novels and short story collections (Memmi, 1987:6).
2. For example, Nawal El Saadawi first published her autobiography, *My Papers My Life,* in 1995 in *Al-Musawwar,* a magazine that is distributed throughout the Arab world.

■ BIBLIOGRAPHY

Alvi, Sajida. 1984. "Buzurg Alavi's Writings from Prison (1940s)." Pp. 274–291 in Thomas M. Ricks (ed.), *Critical Perspectives on Modern Persian Literature.* Washington, D.C.: Three Continents Press.
Badawi, Mustafa M. (ed.). 1992. *Modern Arabic Literature.* Cambridge: Cambridge University Press.
Cooke, Miriam. 1988. *War's Other Voices: Women Writers on the Lebanese Civil War.* Cambridge: Cambridge University Press.
———. 1997. *Women and the War Story.* Berkeley: University of California Press.
Daragahi, Haideh. 1984. "The Shaping of the Modern Persian Short Story." Pp. 104–123 in Thomas M. Ricks (ed.), *Critical Perspectives on Modern Persian Literature.* Washington, D.C.: Three Continents Press.
Fanon, Frantz. 1967. *Black Skin, White Masks.* New York: Grove Press.
Hafez, Sabry. 1992. "The Modern Arabic Short Story." Pp. 270–328 in Mustafa M. Badawi (ed.), *Modern Arabic Literature.* Cambridge: Cambridge University Press.
Halman, Talat Sait (ed.). 1976. *Modern Turkish Drama. An Anthology of Plays in Translation.* Minneapolis: Bibliotheca Islamica.
———. 1982. *Contemporary Turkish Literature.* Rutherford, N.J.: Fairleigh Dickinson University Press.
Hillman, Michael. 1984. "Al-e Ahmad's Fictional Legacy." Pp. 331–342 in Thomas M. Ricks (ed.), *Critical Perspectives on Modern Persian Literature.* Washington, D.C.: Three Continents Press.
Jayyusi, Salma Khadra. 1992. "Modernist Poetry in Arabic." Pp. 132–179 in Mustafa M. Badawi (ed.), *Modern Arabic Literature.* Cambridge: Cambridge University Press.
Lewis, Franklin, and Farzin Yazdanfar. 1996. *In a Voice of Their Own: A Collection of Stories by Iranian Women Written Since the Revolution of 1979.* Costa Mesa, Calif.: Mazda.
Memmi, Albert. 1987. Introduction to *Anthologie du Roman Maghrebin.* Paris: Nathan.
Milani, Farzaneh. 1992. *Veils and Words: The Emerging Voices of Iranian Women Writers.* Syracuse: Syracuse University Press.
Moayyad, Heshmat (ed.). 1991. *Stories from Iran: A Chicago Anthology 1921–1991.* Washington, D.C.: Mage.
Najmabadi, Afsaneh. 1998. "Crafting an Educated Housewife in Iran." Pp. 91–125 in Lila Abu-Lughod (ed.), *Remaking Women: Feminism and Modernity in the Middle East.* Princeton: Princeton University Press.
Ricks, Thomas M. (ed.). 1984. *Critical Perspectives on Modern Persian Literature.* Washington, D.C.: Three Continents Press.
Somekh, Sasson. 1992. "The Neo-Classical Arabic Poets." Pp. 36–81 in Mustafa M. Badawi (ed.), *Modern Arabic Literature.* Cambridge: Cambridge University Press.

Tavakoli-Targhi, Mohamad. 1990. "Refashioning Iran: Language and Culture During the Constitutional Revolution." *Iranian Studies* 23:77–101.
———. 1999. Interview by author, South Bend, Indiana, February.
Yudkin, Leon I. 1984. *1948 and After: Aspects of Israeli Literature*. Manchester: University of Manchester Press.

■ 13 ■

Trends and Prospects

Deborah J. Gerner

As the previous chapters have illustrated, the Middle East is a diverse area with significant strengths and achievements, as well as complex and difficult challenges. Its long history as the crossroads for numerous ethnic and linguistic groups, the presence of oil under its desert sands, the significance of the land for the three major monotheistic religions, the diverse forms of political structure, and the complicated foreign policy relationships within the Middle East and between the region and the rest of the international community are among the factors that make the Middle East endlessly fascinating to students and scholars in a variety of disciplines.

Much of what we have discussed in this volume has looked backward, as we traced the imprint of the Middle East upon the world and of the world on these twenty-plus countries. In this final chapter, we look to the future and consider several acute challenges facing Israel, Iran, Turkey, and the Arab world in the twenty-first century and beyond. Among the most notable issues are those related to the role of culture and religion in shaping society, the urgency of economic development, the legacy of European colonialism, and the desire for increased accountability of Middle Eastern governments.

■ UNDERSTANDING THE CONTEMPORARY MIDDLE EAST

In introducing the region in Chapter 2, geographers Ian R. Manners and Barbara McKean Parmenter describe

the ways in which water links politics, economy, and religion; the ways in which cities are shaped both by global (trading connections, colonial experiences, labor migration, flows of capital) and local practices and imaginings; and the ways in which species, water, people, goods, capital, and ideas move across political boundaries . . . [and] the ways in which the past may be present in the memories of people and in the conscious and unconscious constructions of the histories of places.

Their discussion illustrates that there are a myriad of different mental maps of the Middle East, defined not only by state boundaries but by history, economic interactions, cultural patterns, and natural resources, among other attributes. All are important if we want to understand this region.

In contrast to the rich description that has been presented by authors in this book, many Europeans and North Americans still view the Middle East as "the exotic Orient" referred to in Edward Said's famous 1979 book, *Orientalism:* culturally undeveloped and unsophisticated when compared to Europe, with anachronistic and undemocratic political institutions that are inferior to those of "the West" and an incomprehensible dominant religion—Islam—along with small Christian and Jewish communities that are seen as quite dissimilar to the Christians and Jews of Europe.[1] This unfortunate attitude is heavily biased by what the Middle East is *not:* it is not Europe or the United States or Canada.

Once we stop analyzing the Middle East in terms of what it is not and look at what it *is,* we can recognize that these are ancient lands, full of great achievements and of severe difficulties; in these aspects, the Middle East is not unlike other parts of the world. It is also a region with a rich cultural heritage, one aspect of which miriam cooke explores in her discussion of Arabic, Turkish, Persian, and Hebrew literatures. In Chapter 12, Cooke illustrates the myriad ways that "Middle Eastern literatures have become privileged sites for recording and engaging with sociopolitical tensions and conflicts," particularly those related to independence and postcolonial struggles.

Because of its colonial involvement and geographical proximity, the European view of the Middle East's literature, art, and philosophy had a substantial influence on the self-perception of Middle Eastern elites. Until relatively recently, most Middle Eastern intellectuals—and most of the sons of political leaders—were educated in Europe or North America. Even within the region, Western-oriented institutions such as the American University in Cairo and the American University in Beirut educated a disproportionate number of professionals and government officials. For individuals who were not part of this privileged strata, education was predominantly traditional, focusing on quranic learning.

In the last decades of the twentieth century, this situation began to change. Modern communication systems were installed in all but the most remote villages, modernizing governments instituted comprehensive literacy programs, and, aided by the availability of revenues from petroleum, distinctly Middle Eastern secular universities, with large student bodies drawn from both the middle and working classes, began to thrive. As seemingly mundane items such as transistor radios, cassette players, videocassette recorders, and photocopiers became more common, the various cultures of the Middle East could begin to define themselves for themselves without the intermediation of European interpreters.

But at the turn of the millennium, it is still unclear exactly what this voyage of cultural discovery will uncover. For instance, setting stereotypes aside, does the Middle East represent a single, distinct culture? This is a more difficult question to answer, even within the Arab world (let alone the entire region), than it might at first appear.

There is arguably a pivotal region of the Middle East where a shared dominant cultural identity exists, coinciding with the centers of classical Muslim and Arab power: Cairo, Damascus, and Baghdad. It is not surprising that the two major pan-Arab political movements, Ba'thism and Nasserism, came out of this core region. Indeed, the area still exercises a profound influence on Arab culture as a whole, although in the 1990s this has come more from the soap operas of Cairo's television studios and the lyrics of popular music than from the writings of intellectuals or the speeches of charismatic political leaders. In addition, as Laurie King-Irani points out in Chapter 9, the legacy of Arab "nomadic peoples and their traditions have left a deep imprint on Middle Eastern culture, society, and politics" in ways that may transcend state borders.

Nonetheless, it is problematic to suggest that the entire Middle East is part of a single cultural unit. Lisa Taraki's comment in Chapter 10 regarding the "multiplicity of social, economic, political, and cultural forces and factors [that] have shaped the statuses, experiences, and living conditions of Middle Eastern women" applies equally to Middle Eastern men. For instance, despite sharing the Arabic language and Muslim religion with the "Arab core," the Gulf region is distinct. The states that arose in the shadow of Ibn Saud and the stark fundamentalism of the Wahabi movement have relatively little in common with the more cosmopolitan, urbanized populations of the eastern Mediterranean.

Across the Gulf, Shi'a Iran stands culturally separate—as it has for three millennia—and could logically be considered the southernmost country of Islamic Central Asia rather than the eastern boundary of the "Middle East." To the west and south of Egypt, the Arab identity of the Maghreb is similarly in question. Sunni Islam and the Arabic language are firmly in place, but the Maghreb is buffeted by conflicting cultural pressures: from nearby Europe, from indigenous Berber communities, and from sub-Saharan Africa, whose influence, particularly on the border states of Comoros, Djibouti, Mauritania, Somalia, and Sudan, has been profound. As a nation-state established primarily by twentieth-century immigrants from Europe and their descendants, Israel is a cultural anomaly within the Levant.

Finally, Turkey faces a particularly difficult situation. Since the end of the Ottoman Empire, when the new Turkish republic adopted many European political and economic institutions, Turkey has tried without success to gain acceptance by Europe. Even Turkey's membership in the North Atlantic Treaty Organization (NATO) has not been sufficient to overcome European reluctance to view Turkey as an equal partner. The Ottoman legacy complicates Turkey's relationship with the Arab states, many of which are hesitant to grant Turkey a position of influence in the region. The "Kurdish situation," discussed by Mary Ann Tétreault in Chapter 5, creates additional difficulties with neighboring Iraq and Iran. With the decline of Communist power in the Balkans and in central Asia, Turkey now has the opportunity to provide economic leadership to weaker states that were once part of the Ottoman Empire, much as Japan has done in its economic interactions with areas that it once controlled militarily. However, such a strategy will pull Turkey even further from the Arab world.

The issue of culture is related to one of the region's major quandaries: What role should religion, ideology, and "cultural morality" play in the determination of political and social policies? What is the appropriate relationship between governmental leaders and religious figures? What forms of political leadership are available to women? In many countries, the answer is clear: Islam, politics, and society have again become inextricably linked and now dominate nearly all discourse regarding such basic cultural values.

John Esposito and Mohammed Muqtedar Khan explain in Chapter 11 that this widespread Islamic resurgence is a "grassroots response to multiple crises . . . [in] a struggle for both cultural authenticity and self-determination." It cannot be dismissed as epiphenomenal, as many believed immediately after the Islamic revolution in Iran, nor can it be pigeonholed as simply part of the "clash of civilizations," as some commentators would like (Huntington, 1993). While the Islamic resurgence is the dominant response within the Middle East to questions of morality and government, it is important to remember that Christian and Jewish believers also have religiously based answers to these fundamental political and lifestyle concerns.

■ **ECONOMIC DEVELOPMENT**

A second crucial task facing the countries of the Middle East is economic development. Extremes of poverty and wealth exist in the region—Mauritania is one of the poorest countries in the world, Kuwait one of the wealthiest—but neither extreme is typical of the area as a whole. The great majority of the population live in countries such as Egypt, Turkey, and Iran that have a level of development similar to that found in much of Asia and Latin America.[2] These countries struggle to create a basic industrialized infrastructure (roads, bridges, airports, electrical and communications grids) while simultaneously wondering how to position themselves within a global system that has, at least for the world's wealthiest states, become postindustrial.

As in most of the developing world, such efforts are frequently complicated by accumulated debt from prior failed projects, outmoded governmental institutions, and the social stress involved in adjusting to a society that is halfway between farm and factory, between the ancestral village and the "global village." The economic and political legacies of European imperialism in the Middle East have also hindered the creation of autonomous industrial programs independent of foreign assistance, external borrowing, or intervention by international organizations, a pattern that is characteristic of historically colonized states throughout the world.

In addition, as economist Elias Tuma and sociologist Valentine Moghadam discuss in Chapters 7 and 8, domestic obstacles such as burgeoning urbanization and the environmental problems that this often creates, rapid population growth relative to available resources, rising unemployment, and restrictions on economic opportunities for women have also contributed to economic stagnation and have made autonomous development an elusive goal. Finally, since independence, numerous Middle Eastern countries have had their economic development disrupted by internal civil war (e.g., Algeria, Lebanon, Somalia, Sudan, Turkey), international war (e.g., Kuwait), or both (e.g., Egypt, Iran, Iraq, Israel, Syria).

For all of these reasons, economic development in most of the region has proceeded in a two-steps-forward, one-step-back manner, rather than showing either the exceptional expansion of the "Asian tigers" or the near absence of growth found in parts of Africa. There are few signs that this will change, yet addressing these development problems is key to bettering the lives of Middle Easterners. It is also essential to reduce the sense of frustration that many young people now feel when they compare their circumstances with the images of life in Los Angeles, London, and Paris that they observe every time they turn on a television set. Without an improvement in economic conditions, support for political and religious fundamentalism is likely to continue.

One characteristic of some Middle Eastern economies makes them different from most other countries: the role of oil extraction. From Algeria to Yemen, petroleum has paid for many development projects. Indeed, during the 1970s and early 1980s oil wealth was a major distinguishing feature of the region. Yet by the end of the 1990s, the price of oil had fallen to levels more or less comparable to those prior to the price increases of the 1970s. The return of oil prices to lower levels has forced retrenchment in the oil-based economies. This may not be all bad: Extravagant showcase projects have been terminated and massive weapons acquisition programs have been curtailed, for instance. And countries without large oil reserves—for instance, Egypt, Turkey, and Morocco—have benefited from lower energy costs.

Furthermore, the "oil decade" of 1973 to 1983 left two positive legacies. First, it led to the establishment of a large, indigenous professional class of engineers, bankers, doctors, and educators. (Ironically, because of the wide use of expatriates, these professionals are often from countries without oil wealth, notably Egypt, Jordan, and Palestine.) Second, even after taking into account failed and inappropriate projects, worthless boondoggles, and greed and corruption, oil revenues did pay for considerable basic infrastructure in much of the region. Both of these factors should facilitate further economic growth and development.

The future role of oil in the economies of the Middle East is anything but clear. For at least a decade, analysts have been predicting that the rise of an industrialized consumer culture in Asia would accelerate the demand for oil and push petroleum prices to new heights, once again providing oil-based economies (whether in the Middle East or elsewhere) with the economic power they had in the 1970s. But to date this increased demand has not materialized; in fact, petroleum prices fell dramatically in the late 1990s in response to the economic recession in Asia. Even if demand for oil does pick up, sharp price increases may be constrained by the availability of new supplies from various parts of the former Soviet Union.

■ **ETHNONATIONALIST CONFLICTS**

A third set of issues is also related to the historical legacy of colonialism: the ethnic, religious, and territorial conflicts that occur as Middle Eastern peoples respond to situations created nearly one hundred years ago and attempt to gain increased control over their political lives (Humphreys, 1999:261). In Chapter 3, historian Arthur Goldschmidt Jr. analyzes the interaction of foreign and indigenous political entities that led to the creation of states whose boundaries rarely reflect the distribution of the region's nationalities. The results have been problematic for decades.

The current circumstances of the Kurds is a key example both of this lack of correspondence between state boundaries and national groups and of the role that outside powers have played in the region. British interest in the petroleum resources of Kurdistan led to the division of the Kurdish nation among Iran, Iraq, Turkey, and Syria rather than its unification into an independent Kurdish state. The continuing tension between Palestinians and Israeli Jews over what was once the British mandate of Palestine is another example of this phenomenon. Peace studies scholar-activists Simona Sharoni and Mohammed Abu-Nimer (Chapter 6) provide a framework for understanding this long-standing conflict and reflect on the prospects for its resolution on terms that are both just and enduring. Unfortunately, both these and other ethnonationalist conflicts in the Middle East have persisted since the end of World War I and by now defy easy solutions.

■ POLITICAL ACCOUNTABILITY

A final task facing the Middle East is the necessity to develop political systems that are supported by and accountable to the people over which they exercise governance. The wave of transitions to more democratic governance that swept across much of the world in the 1980s and 1990s has not entirely bypassed the region, but neither have we seen the large-scale reforms that have been observed in parts of Africa and Latin America. Unless the Middle East is atypical in its political evolution, we would expect to see democratic pressures play a more prominent role in the near future.

There are several significant dimensions to the challenge of increasing political accountability. First, like governments everywhere, Middle Eastern states must find a way to accommodate the demands of the expanding professional and middle classes for increased influence and control over material and symbolic resources. One of the likely demands raised by these groups will be a substantial reduction in military expenditures. Military spending is an attractive target: the sheer amount of money involved is very large and there is widespread sentiment that those funds could perhaps be better spent on socioeconomic programs that provide greater good for society. Furthermore, because military spending occurs secretly under the guise of "national security," it is prone to both waste and corruption, neither of which has wide acceptability in the eyes of the new professional and middle classes. Finally, with the collapse of the Soviet Union, the moderating of the Iranian government's foreign policies, and the ongoing Arab-Israeli peace process, it is not clear who the enemy is.

At the same time, as political scientists Deborah Gerner and Philip Schrodt discuss in Chapter 4, the military remains a formidable force in Middle Eastern politics. Many governments have used military perks to co-opt potential opponents and secure the loyalty of ethnic minorities. The military also tends to be closely associated with internal security services, which can enable it to be tremendously disruptive in an unstable situation (as Algeria has demonstrated in the 1990s). The close association of the military with an established regime—as found in Jordan, Libya, and Iraq, among others—further complicates any serious attempt to reduce military influence.

The Middle East is currently in the midst of a tremendous transformation as the aging post–World War II generation of leaders is replaced by significantly younger rulers. This, too, has implications for how the issues of leadership and political accountability might play out. In some instances, particularly simple dynastic progressions, the transitions may well be routine; thus far, the new monarchs have shown significantly more interest in—even enthusiasm for—political reform than their predecessors. In contrast, replacing personalistic leaders who have governed for decades, such as Syria's Hafez al-Assad, Palestinian Yasser Arafat, Saddam Hussein of Iraq, and Libya's Muammar Qaddafi, is likely to be messy, notwithstanding the existence of formal institutions intended to address this situation.

The generational issue may also resolve itself relatively easily in those states that have strongly bureaucratized state structures, such as Egypt and Tunisia, and could be less pronounced in parliamentary states such as Turkey. However, it is interesting to note that generational change has had a major impact even in the most stable republic of the region, Israel. While Israel's formal institutions of governance have remained more or less intact,[3] the character of Israeli political parties has changed profoundly. Over the past decade, Israel has been transformed from a European-style system of two major parties differentiated on ideology to a situation in which the Likud and Labor Parties together control fewer than half of the seats in the Knesset and many of the successful new parties are based at least in part on ethnicity.

A third aspect of political accountability has already been alluded to: the need for governments to determine how best to deal with the existence of political Islam. For secular elites faced with a strong Islamic challenge, options include co-optation, combat, cooperation, and coping. One of the unknown variables is whether Islam is appealing to a given population on its own merits or if its current popularity rests primarily on its status as the most effective source of opposition to the state (given that other alternatives have been cut off).

Many analysts believe that Iran represents the latter scenario: what Khomeini offered was a way to get rid of the shah. Turkey, in contrast, had ample opportunities for secular (and military) opposition; nevertheless, a strong traditionalist Islamic movement has arisen there. In this case, the impetus may be similar to what is driving Christian fundamentalism in the United States or the Orthodox Jewish political parties in Israel: the willingness of the Islamic movement to advocate on behalf of a social agenda that the established political parties are not eager to embrace. Unfortunately, neither Turkey nor Iran necessarily tell us much about what would happen in the Arab states. The cases of Syria in the early 1980s and Algeria (and, more mildly, Egypt) today suggest that the clash of state and mosque could be socially disruptive and potentially violent.

At the same time, it is important to keep in mind that the emergence of reform movements grounded in religion is a common response to modernization, not a characteristic unique to Islam or to the Middle East. Hindu fundamentalism is a similarly powerful force in contemporary India, for instance. While religious movements have at times totally transformed their societies—the Protestant Reformation in Europe is a prime example—the far more common pattern is for a religious movement to induce a series of changes, then fade in influence. Previous Islamic political waves in the Middle East often followed this evolutionary process and it is quite possible that the current period may repeat this historical pattern.

■ CONCLUSION

The twenty-first century opens with the Middle East oscillating between modernity and traditionalism, secularism and religious resurgence, economic growth and stagnation, peace and war. The tasks facing the peoples and governments of the region are compelling: it will not be easy to break free of the legacy of colonialism, address long-standing domestic and international conflicts, pursue economic and political development, and (re)create an identity (or identities) that can bring people together rather than split them into ever-more-narrowly defined groups. Fortunately, the people of the Middle East—Arabs, Persians, Israelis, Turks, and others—bring a diverse array of skills, aspirations, and resources that will aid them in this endeavor.

■ NOTES

1. In a recent book, historian R. Stephen Humphreys provides an astute description of one of the strongest stereotypes held by some in the United States:

> No creature in the American political bestiary is more enduring than the Middle East Madman. This creature takes varying forms—the ranking dictator in khaki uniform; the bearded terrorist, head wrapped in the ever-present checked kaffiyeh, bearing a thin smile and a ghostly light in his eyes; the dour yet fiery fundamentalist cleric, likewise bearded and eyes aglow, but wearing a turban and gown. But at bottom they are all alike. . . . They fill the air with terrifying threats, grotesque fabrications, and grandiose dreams of revenge and glory. Most of all they are simply out of touch with reality. They are madmen, impervious to reason and logic, utterly beyond the understanding of rational Westerns.
>
> The Middle East certainly has its full share of extravagant rhetoric and preposterous claims—though some might say the same thing about the United States—but the Middle East Madman is a mythological beast,

or nearly so. When we look beyond the facade of theater and posturing, we will almost always discern a hard-headed politician who knows perfectly well how to set his goals and to craft strategies for achieving them. (Humphreys 1999:83)

2. A small number of countries in the region—Israel, Bahrain, and the United Arab Emirates most conspicuously—have embarked on policies designed to strategically situate themselves in a computerized, global economy. But these states have small populations and are, arguably, more akin to Singapore or the Bahamas than to Taiwan or Mexico.

3. Israel made an institutional change in the method of electing its prime minister that has coincided with the weakening of control of the major parties in the Knesset. However, decreasing the power of the Labor and Likud Parties was not the intended effect of the modification of the electoral laws and generational politics played little role in their passage.

■ BIBLIOGRAPHY

Ayubi, Nazih N. 1995. *Over-Stating the Arab State: Politics and Society in the Middle East.* London: I. B. Tauris.

Baaklini, Abdo, Guilain Denoeux, and Robert Springborg. 1999. *Legislative Politics in the Arab World: The Resurgence of Democratic Institutions.* Boulder, Colo.: Lynne Rienner.

Cleveland, William L. 1994. *A History of the Modern Middle East.* Boulder, Colo.: Westview Press.

Humphreys, R. Stephen. 1999. *Between Memory and Desire: The Middle East in a Troubled Age.* Berkeley: University of California Press.

Huntington, Samuel. 1993. "The Clash of Civilizations," *Foreign Affairs* 72: 22–49.

Lesch, Ann M., and Dan Tschirgi. 1998. *Origins and Development of the Arab-Israeli Conflict.* Westport, Conn.: Greenwood Press.

Mallat, Chibli. 1996. *The Middle East into the 21st Century: Studies on the Arab-Israeli Conflict, the Gulf Crisis and Political Islam.* Reading, UK: Ithaca/Garnet Publishing.

Roded, Ruth, ed. 1999. *Women in Islam and the Middle East: A Reader.* London: I. B. Tauris.

Said, Edward W. 1979. *Orientalism.* New York: Vintage.

▪ Appendix 1 ▪
Acronyms

AHC	Arab Higher Committee for Palestine
AMU	Arab Maghreb Union
ARAMCO	Arabian American Oil Company
B.C.E.	Before the Common Era
C.E.	Common Era
CIA	Central Intelligence Agency
CMRN	Comiteí Militaire de Redressement National
DFLP	Democratic Front for the Liberation of Palestine
DHS	Demographic and Health Surveys
DNA	deoxyribonucleic acid
ESCWA	Economic and Social Commission for West Asia
FBD	father's brother's daughter
FIS	Islamic Salvation Front
FLN	National Liberation Front
GAP	Güneydocu Anadolu Projesi
GCC	Gulf Cooperation Council
GDP	gross domestic product
GNP	gross national product
ha	hectares
HDI	Human Development Index
ILO	International Labor Organization
IMF	International Monetary Fund
IPC	Iraq Petroleum Company
ISI	import substitution industrialization
KDP	Kurdistan Democratic Party
MENA	Middle East–North Africa
MTI	Islamic Tendency Movement
NATO	North Atlantic Treaty Organization
NDP	National Democratic Party
NGO	nongovernmental organization
OAPEC	Organization of Arab Petroleum Exporting Countries

OECD	Organization for Economic Cooperation and Development
OPEC	Organization of Petroleum Exporting Countries
PCP	Palestine Communist Party
PDR Yemen	People's Democratic Republic of Yemen
PFLP	Popular Front for the Liberation of Palestine
PKK	Kurdistan Workers Party
PLO	Palestine Liberation Organization
PNA	Palestinian National Authority
PROTA	Project for Translation from Arabic
PUK	Patriotic Union of Kurdistan
SAVAK	Sazman-e Ettelaatva Amniyat-e Keshvar
UAE	United Arab Emirates
UAR	United Arab Republic
UN	United Nations
UNDP	United Nations Development Programme
UNESCO	United Nations Educational, Scientific, and Cultural Organization
USFP	Socialist Union of Popular Forces
USSR	Union of Soviet Socialist Republics, the Soviet Union

▪ Appendix 2 ▪

Basic Political Data

The Basic Political Data appendix was compiled by David Dolson and Deborah J. Gerner based on information from a variety of sources. Accurate data on Middle Eastern political events are often difficult to obtain, and conflicting accounts and dates are common. Although we have used at least three different sources to corroborate each datum, readers may nonetheless find discrepancies in other sources.

The United Nations Development Programme's Human Development Index (HDI) is a composite measure based on life expectancy; adult literacy; combined primary, secondary, and tertiary enrollment in school; and adjusted per capita income in each country. The *Score* can range from 0.0 to 1.0, with higher numbers reflecting greater development in terms of longevity, knowledge, and a decent standard of living.

Democratic and Popular Republic of Algeria
Capital City Algiers
Date of Independence from France July 3, 1962
Population 30,480,793 (1998 estimate)
HDI Score 0.746
Rulers Since Independence
   1. President Ahmed Ben Bella, 1962–June 1965
   2. President Houari Boumedienne, June 1965–December 1978
   3. President Benjedid Chadli, February 1979–1992
   4. Five-member High Council of State (HCS), headed by Muhammed Boudiaf, fulfills the function of the head of state until January 1994
   5. President Liamine Zeroual, appointed January 30, 1994
   6. President Liamine Zeroual, November 16, 1995–April 25, 1999
   7. President Abdelaziz Bouteflika, elected on April 15, 1999, after all six rivals withdrew, charging electoral fraud

State of Bahrain
Capital City Manama
Date of Independence from Great Britain August 15, 1971
Population 616,000 (1998 estimate)
HDI Score 0.872
Rulers Since Independence
 1. Emir Isa ibn Salman al-Khalifa, 1961–March 6, 1999
 2. Emir Hamad ibn Isa al-Khalifa, March 6, 1999–

Federal Islamic Republic of the Comoros
Capital City Moroni
Date of Independence from France July 6, 1975
Population 546,000 (1998 estimate)
HDI Score 0.411
Rulers Since Independence
 1. President Ahmed Abdallah, July 1975–August 1975
 2. Coup led by Ali Soilih, August 1975; president, 1976–1978 (assassinated)
 3. President Ahmed Abdallah, reinstated in coup by mercenaries under Robert Denard, 1978–November 27, 1989 (assassinated)
 4. Robert Denard, November 27, 1989–December 15, 1989 (removed by French government)
 5. Said Djohar, December 16, 1989–March 1996
 6. President Mohammad Taki Abdoulkarim, March 1996–April 30, 1999
 7. Coup led by Col. Assoumani Azali, April 30, 1999–

Republic of Djibouti
Capital City Djibouti
Date of Independence from France June 26, 1977
Population 441,000 (1998 estimate)
HDI Score 0.324
Rulers Since Independence
 1. President Hassan Gouled Aptidon, June 24, 1977; reelected June 1981, April 1987, and May 1993
 2. President Ismail Omar Guelleh, elected April 1999

Arab Republic of Egypt
Capital City Cairo
Date of Independence from Great Britain February 28, 1922
Population 66,050,000 (1998 estimate)
HDI Score 0.612
Rulers Since Independence
 1. King Fu'ad I, 1917–1936
 2. King Farouk, 1936–1952 (overthrown in coup led by Col. Gamal

Abdel Nasser and Abdul-al Hakim)
3. President Mohammed Neguib, June 1953–November 1954
4. Prime Minister Gamal Abdel Nasser, 1954–1956; president, 1956–1970
5. President Anwar Sadat, 1970–October 1981 (assassinated)
6. President Hosni Mubarak, October 14, 1981– ; reelected 1987, 1993, 1999

Islamic Republic of Iran
Capital City Tehran
Date of Independence Not colonized
Population 68,960,000 (1998 estimate)
HDI Score 0.758
Twentieth-Century Rulers
1. Qajar dynasty: Muzaffar al-Din, 1896–1907; Muhammad Ali, 1907–1909; Ahmad, 1909–1924
2. Pahlavi dynasty: Reza Shah, 1925–1941; Mohammad Reza Shah, 1941–1979
3. Religious leaders: Ayatollah Ruhollah Khomeini, 1979–1989; Hojatolislam Sayyed Ali Khamenei, 1989–
4. Presidents: Mehdi Bazargan, 1979–1980; Abolhassan Bani-Sadr, 1980–1981; Muhammad Ali Raja'i, 1981; Sayyed Ali Khamenei, October 1981–July 1989; Hojatolislam Ali Akbar Hashemi Rafsanjani, July 1989–1997; Mohammad Khatami, 1997–

Republic of Iraq
Capital City Baghdad
Date of Independence from Great Britain October 13, 1932
Population 21,722,000 (1998 estimate)
HDI Score 0.538
Rulers Since Independence
1. King Faisal I, 1921–1933
2. King Ghazi ibn Faisal, 1933–1939
3. King Faisal II, 1939–July 14, 1958 (overthrown in coup)
4. Brig. Gen. Abdel Karim Qasem, July 14, 1958–February 1963 (overthrown)
5. National Council of Revolutionary Command led by Prime Minister Ahmad Hasan al-Bakr and President Abd al-Salaam Arif, February 1963–November 18, 1963 (overthrown)
6. President Abd al-Salaam Arif, November 1963–April 1966 (died in accident)
7. President Abd al-Rahman Arif, April 1966–July 17, 1968 (overthrown)
8. Revolutionary Command Council led by President Ahmad Hasan al-Bakr, July 17, 1968–July 16, 1979
9. President Saddam Hussein, July 16, 1979–

State of Israel

Capital City Tel Aviv or Jerusalem; contested internationally
Date of Independence from Great Britain May 15, 1948
Population 5,644,000 (1998 estimate)
HDI Score 0.913
Rulers Since Independence
1. Prime Minister David Ben-Gurion, 1948–1953
2. Prime Minister Moshe Sharett, 1953–1955
3. Prime Minister David Ben-Gurion, 1955–1963
4. Prime Minister Levi Eshkol, 1963–1969
5. Prime Minister Yigal Allon (acting), 1969
6. Prime Minister Golda Meir, 1969–1974
7. Prime Minister Yitzhak Rabin, 1974–1977
8. Prime Minister Shimon Peres (acting), 1977
9. Prime Minister Menachem Begin, 1977–1983
10. Prime Minister Yitzhak Shamir, 1983–1984
11. Prime Minister Shimon Peres, 1984–1986
12. Prime Minister Yitzhak Shamir, 1986–1992
13. Prime Minister Yitzhak Rabin, 1992–1995 (assassinated)
14. Prime Minister Shimon Peres, 1995–1996
15. Prime Minister Benjamin Netanyahu, 1996–1999
16. Prime Minister Ehud Barak, May 1999–

Hashemite Kingdom of Jordan

Capital City Amman
Date of Independence from Great Britain May 25, 1946
Population 4,435,000 (1998 estimate)
HDI Score 0.729
Rulers Since Independence
1. Emir, then King Abdullah, 1921–July 1951 (assassinated)
2. King Talal, 1951–1953 (abdicated)
3. King Hussein I, 1953–February 7, 1999
4. King Abdullah II, February 7, 1999–

State of Kuwait

Capital City Kuwait City
Date of Independence from Great Britain June 19, 1961
Population 1,913,000 (1998 estimate)
HDI Score 0.848
Rulers Since Independence
1. Shaikh Abdullah III al-Sabah, 1950–1965
2. Shaikh Sabah al Salim al-Sabah, 1965–1977
3. Shaikh Jabir al-Ahmad al-Jabir al-Sabah, December 31, 1977–

Republic of Lebanon
Capital City Beirut
Date of Independence from France November 22, 1943
Population 3,506,000 (1998 estimate)
HDI Score 0.796
Rulers Since Independence
1. President Bishara al Khuri, 1943–1952 (prime ministers: Riyad al-Solh, Sami al-Solh)
2. President Camille Chamoun, 1952–1958 (prime ministers: Abdallah al-Yafi, Sami al-Solh, Rashid Karami)
3. President Fu'ad Chehab, 1958–1964 (prime minister: Rashid Karami)
4. President Charles Hilu, 1964–1970 (prime minister: Rashid Karami)
5. President Sulayman Franjiyya, 1970–1976 (prime ministers: Rachid Anis al-Solh, Rashid Karami, Saeb Salaam)
6. President Elias Sarkis, 1976–1982 (prime minister: Salim al-Hoss)
7. President Beshir Gemayel, 1982 (assassinated)
8. President Amin Gemayel, 1982–1988 (prime ministers: Shafiq al-Wazzan, Rashid Karami, Salim al-Hoss)
9. Gen. Michel Aoun, 1988–1990 (prime minister Salim al-Hoss)
10. President Elias Hrawi, 1990–1998 (prime ministers Salim al-Hoss, Umar Karami, Rafiq al-Hariri)
11. President Emile Lahoud, 1998– (prime minister Salim al-Hoss)

Socialist People's Libyan Arab Jamahiriyah (Republic)
Capital City Tripoli
Date of Independence from Italy December 24, 1951
Population 5,691,000 (1998 estimate)
HDI Score 0.806
Rulers Since Independence
1. King Idris, 1951–1969
2. Col. Muammar Mohammed Qaddafi, leader of the revolution, September 1969–

Islamic Republic of Mauritania
Capital City Nouakchott
Date of Independence from France November 28, 1960
Population 2,511,000 (1998 estimate)
HDI Score 0.361
Rulers Since Independence
1. President Mokhtar Ould Daddah, 1961–July 10, 1978 (overthrown in military coup)
2. Lt. Col. Mustapha Ould Mohammed Salek, July 10, 1978–June 1979 (forced to resign)

3. Lt. Col. Mohammed Mahmoud Ould Louly, June 1979–January 4, 1980 (overthrown)
4. Lt. Col. Mohamed Khouna Ould Haidalla, January 4, 1980–December 1984 (overthrown)
5. Col. Maaouya Ould Sidi Ahmed Taya, December 1984; elected president in first multiparty elections, January 24, 1992

Kingdom of Morocco

Capital City Rabat
Date of Independence from France March 2, 1956
Population 2,446,645 (1999 estimate)
HDI Score 0.557
Rulers Since Independence
   1. King Mohammed V, March 2, 1956–1961
   2. King Hassan II, March 3, 1961–July 23, 1999
   3. King Mohammed VI, July 23, 1999–

Sultanate of Oman

Capital City Muscat
Date of Independence Never officially a colony, but strong British influence
Population 12,364,000 (1998 estimate)
HDI Score 0.771
Twentieth-Century Rulers
   1. Sultan Faisal ibn Turki al-Said, 1888–1913
   2. Sultan Tamir ibn Faisal al-Said, 1913–1932
   3. Sultan Said ibn Tamir al-Said, 1932–1970
   4. Sultan Qabus ibn Said al-Said, 1970–

Palestinian Territories: West Bank and Gaza Strip

Capital City Contested internationally
Date of Independence The PNA gained control from Israel of most of the Gaza Strip and Jericho areas in May 1994. Subsequent agreements have increased the land under Palestinian or joint Israeli-Palestinian jurisdiction.
Population
   Gaza Strip: 1,020,813 (1997 estimate)
   West Bank: 1,869,818 (1997 estimate)
HDI Score n/a
Rulers Since Gaza-Jericho Agreement
   1. Yasser Arafat, elected president, January 1996

State of Qatar
Capital City Doha
Date of Independence from Great Britain September 3, 1971
Population 697,000 (1998 estimate)
HDI Score 0.84
Rulers Since Independence
1. Emir Ahmad ibn Ali, 1971–1972
2. Emir Khalifa ibn Hamad al-Thani, 1972–June 27, 1995
3. Emir Hamad ibn Khalifa al-Thani, June 27, 1995–

Kingdom of Saudi Arabia
Capital City Riyadh
Declaration of United State September 1932
Population 20,088,000 (1998 estimate)
HDI Score 0.778
Rulers Since Independence
1. King Abdul Aziz ibn Saud, 1932–1953
2. King Saud, 1953–1964
3. King Faisal, 1964–1975
4. King Khalid, 1975–1982
5. King Fahd, 1982–

Somali Democratic Republic
Capital City Mogadishu
Date of Independence from Italy and Great Britain July 1, 1960
Population 6,842,000 (1998 estimate)
HDI Score 0.200
Rulers Since Independence
1. President Aden Abdulla Osman, 1960–1967
2. President Abdirashid Ali Shirmarke, 1967–1969 (assassinated)
3. Maj. Gen. Mohammed Siad Barre, 1969–January 27, 1991
4. No functional government, 1991–

Democratic Republic of Sudan
Capital City Khartoum
Date of Independence from Great Britain January 1, 1956
Population 33,551,000 (1998 estimate)
HDI Score 0.343
Rulers Since Independence
1. Prime Minister Ismail al-Azhari, 1956
2. Prime Minister Abdulla Khalil, 1956–1958
3. Prime Minister Ibrahim Abboud, 1958–1964
4. Prime Minister Sir el-Khatim el-Khalifah, 1964–1965

5. Prime Minister Muhammed Ahmad Mahgoub, 1965–1966
6. Prime Minister Sayed Sadiq el-Mahdi, 1966–1967
7. Prime Minister Muhammed Ahmad Mahgoub, 1967–1969
8. Prime Minister Abubakr Awadallah, 1969
9. President Jaafar Mohammed Nimeiri, May 1969–April 1985 (overthrown)
10. Lt. Gen. Abdel Rahman Swareddahab, chairman, Transitional Military Council, April 6, 1985–1986
11. President Ahmed Ali al-Mirghani and Prime Minister Sadia al-Mahdi, 1986–June 30, 1989 (overthrown by military coup)
12. Prime Minister Omar Hassan Ahmed al-Bashir, June 30, 1989– ; appointed president October 16, 1993

Syrian Arab Republic
Capital City Damascus
Date of Independence from France April 17, 1946
Population 16,673,000 (1998 estimate)
HDI Score 0.749
Rulers Since Independence
1. President Shukri al Quwatly, 1946–1949 (overthrown in bloodless coup)
2. Gen. Husni al Zaim, March 1949–August 1949
3. Gen. Sami al Hinnawi, August 1949–December 1949
4. Col. Adib Shishakli, December 1949–February 1954 (overthrown)
5. President Sabri al Asali, 1956–1958
6. Gamal Abdel Nasser, president of United Arab Republic (Egypt and Syria), 1958–1961 (Abdul-Hakim was the Syrian supervisor during this time)
7. President Nazim al Qudsi, 1961–1963
8. Gen. Amin al Hafiz, 1963–1966
9. President Salah al Jadid, 1966–1970 (overthrown in bloodless coup)
10. President Hafez al-Assad, 1970–

Republic of Tunisia
Capital City Tunis
Date of Independence from France March 20, 1956
Population 9,380,000 (1998 estimate)
HDI Score 0.744
Rulers Since Independence
1. Prime Minister Habib Bourguiba, 1956–July 1957 (becomes republic)
2. President Habib Bourguiba, July 1957–November 1987 (removed in bloodless coup)

3. President Zine El-Abidine Ben Ali accedes to the presidency, November 1987; elected in multiparty elections October 1999

Republic of Turkey
Capital City Ankara
Date of Independence from Ottoman Empire October 29, 1923
Population 64,557,000 (1998 estimate)
HDI Score 0.796
Rulers Since Independence
1. President Mustafa Kemal (Kemal Atatürk after 1933), 1923–1938
2. President Ismet Inönü, 1938–1950
3. President Mahmud Celal Bayar, 1950–May 27, 1960 (overthrown by military coup)
4. General Cemal Gürsel, May 27, 1960–October 1961
5. President Cemal Gürsel, October 1961–1966
6. President Cevdet Sunay, 1966–1973
7. President Fahri Korutürk, 1973–September 12, 1980 (overthrown by military coup)
8. General Kenan Evren, September 12, 1980–1982
9. President Kenan Evren, 1982–October 1989
10. President Turgut Ozal, October 1989–April 1993
11. President Suleyman Demirel, April 1993–

United Arab Emirates
Capital City Abu Dhabi
Date of Independence from Great Britain December 2, 1971
Population 2,303,000 (1998 estimate)
HDI Score 0.855
Rulers Since Independence
Shaikh Zayid ibn Sultan al Nuhayyan, 1971–

Yemen Arab Republic (North Yemen), independent from Ottoman Empire in 1918
1. Imam Yahya, 1918–1948 (murdered in an attempted coup)
2. Imam Ahmad ibn Yahya, 1948–1962
3. Muhammad al-Badr, 1962 (overthrown after one week)
4. Brig. Gen. Abdullah Sallal, 1962–1967
5. President Abdul Rahman al Iryani, 1967–1974
6. President Ibrahim Hamdi, 1974–1977
7. President Ahmad Hussein Ghashmi, 1977–1978 (overthrown in coup)
8. President Ali Abdullah Salih, 1978–1990

People's Democratic Republic of Yemen (South Yemen), independent from Great Britain in 1967
1. President Qahtan al Sha'bi, 1967–1969 (overthrown)
2. President Salim Rubayyi'ali, 1969–1978 (executed)
3. President Abd al Fattah Ismaíil, 1978–1980 (resigned)
4. President Ali Nasser Muhammad, 1980–1986
5. President Haider Abu Bakr al Attas, 1986–1990

Republic of Yemen
Capital City San'a
Date of Unification May 22, 1990
Population 16,388,000 (1998 estimate)
HDI Score 0.356
Rulers Since Independence
1. President Ali Abdullah Salih, 1990–

■ BIBLIOGRAPHY

Agonafer, Fantu. 1979. "Djibouti's Three-Front Struggle for Independence: 1967–1977." Ph.D. diss., University of Denver.

Anderson, Ray R., Robert F. Siebert, and John G. Wagner. 1998. *Politics and Change in the Middle East*. Englewood Cliffs, N.J.: Prentice-Hall.

Bosworth, C. E., E. Van Donzel, B. Lewis, and Ch. Pellat (eds.). 1983. *Encyclopedia of Islam*. Vol. 5. Leiden, Netherlands: E. J. Brill.

Burr, J. Millard, and Robert O. Collins. 1995. *Requiem for the Sudan War, Drought, and Disaster Relief on the Nile*. Boulder, Colo.: Westview Press.

Collelo, Thomas (ed.). 1988. *Syria: A Country Study*. Area Handbook Series. Washington, D.C.: Government Printing Office.

———. 1989. *Lebanon: A Country Study*. Area Handbook Series. Washington, D.C.: Government Printing Office.

Congressional Quarterly. 1995. *The Middle East*. 8th ed. Washington, D.C.: Congressional Quarterly.

Europa Publications. 1995. *The Middle East and North Africa*. 41st ed. Rochester, Kent, UK: Staples Printers Rochester Limited.

Gordon, April A., and Donald L. Gordon (eds.). 1996. *Understanding Contemporary Africa*. 2d ed. Boulder, Colo.: Lynne Rienner.

Handloff, Robert E. (ed.). 1990. *Mauritania: A Country Study*. Area Handbook Series. Washington, D.C.: Government Printing Office.

Hiro, Dilip. 1996. *Dictionary of the Middle East*. New York: St. Martin's Press.

Korbani, Agnes. 1995. *The Political Dictionary of Modern Middle East*. Lanham, Md.: University Press of America.

Legum, Colin (ed.). 1976–1993. *Middle East Contemporary Survey*. The Shiloah Center for Middle Eastern and African Studies, Tel Aviv University. Vols. 1–12. New York: Holmes and Meir.

Lewis, I. M. 1988. *A Modern History of Somalia: Nation and State in the Horn of Africa*. Boulder, Colo.: Westview Press.

Makinda, Samuel M. 1993. *Seeking Peace from Chaos: Humanitarian Intervention in Somalia*. Boulder, Colo.: Lynne Rienner.

Metz, Helen Chapin (ed.). 1989. *Libya: A Country Study*. Area Handbook Series. Washington, D.C.: Government Printing Office.

———. 1990. *Iraq: A Country Study*. Area Handbook Series. Washington, D.C.: Government Printing Office.

———. 1991. *Egypt: A Country Study*. Area Handbook Series. Washington, D.C.: Government Printing Office.

———. 1991. *Jordan: A Country Study*. Area Handbook Series. Washington, D.C.: Government Printing Office.

——— 1992. *Sudan: A Country Study*. Area Handbook Series. Washington, D.C.: Government Printing Office.

———. 1993. *Saudi: Arabia A Country Study*. Area Handbook Series. Washington, D.C.: Government Printing Office.

———. 1993. *Somalia: A Country Study*. Area Handbook Series. Washington, D.C.: Government Printing Office.

———. 1994. *Algeria: A Country Study*. Area Handbook Series. Washington, D.C.: Government Printing Office.

———. 1994. *Persian Gulf States:Country Studies*. Area Handbook Series. Washington, D.C.: Government Printing Office.

———. 1995. *Indian Ocean: Five Island Countries*. Area Handbook Series. Washington, D.C.: Government Printing Office.

Nelson, Harold D. (ed.). 1986. *Morocco: A Country Study*. Area Handbook Series. Washington, D.C.: Government Printing Office.

———. 1987. *Tunisia: A Country Study. Area Handbook Series*. Washington, D.C.: Government Printing Office.

Newitt, Malyn. 1984. *The Comoro Islands: Struggle Against Dependency in the Indian Ocean*. Boulder, Colo.: Westview Press.

Ottenheimer, Harriet, and Martin Ottenheimer. 1994. *Historical Dictionary of the Comoro Islands*. African Historical Dictionaries, no. 59. Meutchen, N.J.: Scarecrow Press.

Simon, Reeva S., Philip Mattar, and Richard W. Bulliet (eds.). 1996. *Encyclopedia of the Modern Middle East*. 5 Vols. New York: Simon and Schuster.

Sluglett, Peter, and Marion Farouk-Sluglett (eds.). 1996. *The Times Guide to the Middle East*. London: Times Books.

United Nations Development Programme. 1998. *Human Development Report 1998*. New York: Oxford University Press.

Wright, John W. (ed.). 1998. *The New York Times Almanac 1999*. New York: Penguin Books.

▪ The Contributors ▪

Mohammed Abu-Nimer is assistant professor of political science at American University in Washington, D.C.

miriam cooke is professor of Asian and African languages and literature at Duke University in North Carolina.

John L. Esposito is professor of religion and international affairs and director of the Center for Muslim-Christian Understanding at Georgetown University in Washington, D.C.

Deborah J. Gerner is associate professor of political science at the University of Kansas in Lawrence.

Arthur Goldschmidt Jr. is professor of history at Pennsylvania State University in University Park.

Donald L. Gordon is professor and chair of political science and director of the African-Asian program at Furman University in South Carolina.

Mohammed A. Muqtedar Khan is a Ph.D. candidate in international relations at Georgetown University in Washington, D.C., and visiting professor of political science at Washington College, in Maryland.

Laurie King-Irani is the editor of *Middle East Report* in Washington, D.C.

Ian R. Manners is professor of geography at the University of Texas at Austin.

Valentine M. Moghadam is director of women's studies and associate professor of sociology at Illinois State University in Normal.

Barbara McKean Parmenter is lecturer in the School of Architecture at the University of Texas at Austin.

Philip A. Schrodt is professor of political science at the University of Kansas in Lawrence.

Simona Sharoni is a member of the faculty at Evergreen State College in Olympia and research fellow at the Jackson School of International Studies at the University of Washington in Seattle.

Lisa Taraki is associate professor of sociology at Birzeit University in Palestine.

Mary Ann Tétreault is professor of political science at Iowa State University in Ames.

Elias H. Tuma is emeritus professor of economics at the University of California at Davis.

▪ Index ▪

Abasiyanik, Sait Faik Aziz, 354
Abbasid caliphate, 43–45, 46
Abu-Nimer, Mohammed, 161
Adivar, Halide Edip, 351
Adonis (Ali Ahmad Said), 366–367
Agnon, Shmuel Yosef, 380
Agrarian reform, post–World War II, 222–223
Agriculture: arable land and, 202, 221, 223; cooperatives, 222–223; duality in, 223; gross national product and, 221; labor force in, 246–247, 248; post–World War II period, 220–223; rain-fed, 15; resources, comparative, 202; tractor use in, 223. *See also* Water resources
Alavi, Buzurg, 368–369
Alexander the Great, 36
Algeria, 389; French imperialism in, 61; women's activism in, 308, 309
Amin, Qasim, 350
al-Amir, Daisy, 356
Anglo-Egyptian Treaty, 210
Ankara, 22
Arab, use of term, 2
Arab Apocalypse (Adnan), 371
Arab Empire, 43–45
Arab Higher Committee for Palestine (AHC), 170
Arab Jews (Mizrachim), 166–167
Arab League, 9, 141, 151–152, 205
Arab nationalism: defined, 63; political Zionism and, 65–66
Arab Revolt, 55, 56, 132, 169–170
Arab socialism, 67–68; and Nasserism, 105
Arab Socialist Union (ASU), 105, 106
Arabic language, 8
Arab-Islamic civilization: Arab conquests/empire in, 42–45; Muhammad and rise of Islam in, 40–42; nomadic life in, 39–40;

Turkish and Mongol invasions and, 45–46. *See also* Ottoman Empire
Arab-Israeli conflict, 69–73; Camp David Accords, 73, 167, 175–176, 188; Cold War politics and, 141–142; domestic politics and, 85–86; Egyptian-Israeli war, 147, 328; external dimensions of, 141–142; Gulf War, 77–78, 139–140, 180–181; Lebanon and, 85; peace negotiations/treaties, 78–79; regional domestic politics and, 85–86; Six Day War (June 1967), 70, 172; Soviet involvement in, 72; UN Resolution 242, 70–71; United States' involvement in, 72–73; War of Attrition (1969), 71; war of October 1973, 142, 174. *See also* Israeli-Palestinian conflict
Arafat, Yasser, 70, 71, 144, 182
Ashkenazi Jews, 166, 277
al-Assad, Hafez, 108, 109
Assyria, 35–36
Aswan Dam, 16, 17, 67, 137
Autocracy, 49
Aziz ibn Saud, Abdul, 134

Baalbaki, Layla, 355–356
Ba'thism, 69, 97, 104–105, 108, 385
Babylonia, 34
Bahrain: political system of, 110, 115
Baker, James, 181
Balfour Declaration, 13, 57, 58, 83, 169, 211, 322
Barak, Ehud, 79, 85, 168
Barzani, Mullah Mustafa, 144, 145
Bashu (Iranian film), 6
Basra, 20
Begin, Menachem, 72, 73, 176
Behbahani, Simin, 367
Beirut Nightmares (al-Samman), 371
Bektas, Habib, 376–377

409

▪ About the Book ▪

Understanding the Contemporary Middle East is an interdisciplinary book designed for use both as a core text for "Introduction to the Middle East" courses and as a supplement in a variety of discipline-oriented curriculums. The geographical domain of the volume is the Arab world (the Levant, the Arabian Peninsula, and North Africa), Iran, Israel, and Turkey; its temporal focus is post–World War II, with a particular emphasis on the 1990s.

There are very few books for classroom use that introduce students to the Middle East as a whole rather than focusing on a specific discipline. *Understanding the Contemporary Middle East* fills this gap. The fifteen authors, writing with clarity and precision, address a range of crucial issues facing the region in the twenty-first century: there are chapters addressing geography, history, politics, economics, international relations, the Israeli-Palestinian conflict, the status of women, religion, class and ethnicity, patterns of population growth, and the literature of the region. Each chapter provides up-to-date—and engaging—description and analysis, along with suggestions for further reading. Numerous maps and photographs help the reader gain a feel for the region.

Deborah J. Gerner is associate professor of political science at the University of Kansas. She is author of *One Land, Two Peoples: The Conflict over Palestine,* as well as numerous articles dealing with the international relations and domestic politics of the Middle East.